THE AMERICAN FAMILY
AND THE STATE

THE AMERICAN FAMILY AND THE STATE

Edited by
JOSEPH R. PEDEN and FRED R. GLAHE

Foreword by
Robert Nisbet

Pacific Studies in Public Policy

PACIFIC RESEARCH INSTITUTE FOR PUBLIC POLICY
San Francisco, California

ISBN 0-936488-05-0 (paper)
    0-936488-12-3 (cloth)

Library of Congress Catalog Card Number 85-63547

Printed in the United States of America

Pacific Research Institute for Public Policy
177 Post Street
San Francisco, California 94108
(415) 989-0833

Library of Congress Cataloging in Publication Data

American family and the state
    (Pacific studies in public policy)
    Bibliography: p.
    Includes index.
    1. Family policy—United States. 2. Family—United
States. 3. United States—Social policy. I. Peden,
Joseph R. II. Glahe, Fred R. III. Pacific Research
Institute for Public Policy.
HQ536.A546 1986   306.8'5'0973   86-63547
ISBN 0-936488-12-3
ISBN 0-936488-05-0 (pbk.)

The Pacific Research Institute for Public Policy is an independent, tax-exempt research and educational organization. The Institute's program is designed to broaden public understanding of the nature and effects of market processes and government policy.

With the bureaucratization and politicization of modern society, scholars, business and civic leaders, the media, policymakers, and the general public have too often been isolated from meaningful solutions to critical public issues. To facilitate a more active and enlightened discussion of such issues, the Pacific Research Institute sponsors in-depth studies into the nature of and possible solutions to major social, economic, and environmental problems. Undertaken regardless of the sanctity of any particular government program, or the customs, prejudices, or temper of the times, the Institute's studies aim to ensure that alternative approaches to currently problematic policy areas are fully evaluated, the best remedies discovered, and these findings made widely available. The results of this work are published as books and monographs, and form the basis for numerous conference and media programs.

Through this program of research and commentary, the Institute seeks to evaluate the premises and consequences of government policy, and provide the foundations necessary for constructive policy reform.

V

CONTENTS

PART IV   THE IMPACT OF ECONOMIC AND SOCIAL POLICY ON FAMILY LIFE

10

Inflation, Migration, and Divorce in Contemporary America
—Lowell Gallaway and Richard Vedder

11

Government Policy and the Distortions in Family Housing
—Dwight R. Lee

LIST OF FIGURES

LIST OF TABLES

FOREWORD

The American Family and the State is an important work of scholarship in its own right. Its value, however, is considerably enhanced by its publication at this particular time, when a kind of renascence is taking place in studies of the position of the family in the modern welfare state. American scholarly interest in the family was for too many years confined largely to the internal, the interpersonal, and psychological aspects of the family; the structural relation between family and other institutions, including the state, tended to be ignored or else swept under the ever spreading welfare carpet.

The great virtue of this book is its structural approach to both family and state, and its frank, extremely perceptive, and wide-ranging observations of the conflicts, potential and actual, that so often threaten any harmonious institutional relation between state and family. Under the intent and rhetoric of ministering to the family, of reinforcing it in society, the state often winds up actually damaging the family as a repository of vital authorities and functions. As this book makes very clear, there is conflict rather than consensus of purpose in many of the state's ostensibly compassionate ventures (and their immediately supporting agencies) in the realm of kinship.

There is a long history behind current tensions and conflicts between family and state. The family is much the older of the two institutions. Kinship was for a very long time man's only form of social organization. Everything important in society flowed directly from one or other of the statuses of sex, age, and genealogy. Family—in the wide sense of the word—was the sole nexus between the individual and nature, world, and cosmos. It and its folkways were the indispensable protection against the uncertainties of life. It was the family that made possible the individual's entry into the world, that controlled every phase of his life thereafter, and that committed him at death to his ancestors.

The first great crisis in the kinship order was not—with all due respect to the Freudians—the uprising of the sons against the fathers out of lust for the mothers. It was, as nearly as we can deduce it from such evidence as there is, rather the revolt of the sons against the fathers over the issue of war, more specifically, over the kind of organization and power necessary for the sons to fight efficiently against external enemies. Kinship society, by structure and stratification, can be admirable in meeting the problems of life in peacetime. It is far from adequate, however, when it must confront the needs of defense and attack in war.

Of all who have written on this important point, the learned English jurist Edward Jenks, writing at the turn of the century, has shed the most light. The family, Jenks observed, is constructed of principles diametrically opposite to those inherent in the state. The family originated as regulator of procreation and of all the consequences, social, economic, religious, of the assimilation of the young into the social order. The state, on the other hand, originated in war, more specifically, in the warrior chief and the war band that was mobilized whenever external attack threatened. Kinship society tends everywhere to be cellular, with the group instead of the individual the irreducible unit of society. Caste, flowing from genealogy and age, is dominant over the more contractual forms of relationship. Law is little more than custom and tradition as interpreted by the old and wise in the community. Finally, kinship society is exclusive by nature; there is no lust for numbers; suspicion and apprehension face every stranger, and indeed every newcomer beginning with the newly born.

Military organization, Jenks pointed out, is, and must be if it is to be successful, founded on contrary principles. Youth, not age, is requisite for effectiveness in war; the relation between the warrior and the war chief is inherently contractual—even if the warrior has been conscripted—in the sense that it is limited to the duration of the war and is explicit in matters of booty and other types of reward. Not tradition but *command,* reaching from the top directly down to each warrior, is the heart of the military system of control. Any intermediate groups are strictly tactical, without legitimacy of their own. Far from being cellular, military organization can be said to be individualistic in that each soldier is by design a replaceable part. There is an inherent secularizing proclivity to the war band through its wresting of its individual members, however briefly and infrequently, from their sacred kinship and religious ties.

The war band is the seed of the political state. Everywhere the state, as we first encounter it in history, is simply the institutionalization, and projection to wider areas of function and authority, of the command-tie that in the beginning binds only the warrior-leader and his men. To be sure, states from the beginning have taken on the trappings and nomenclature of family and of religion—a tribute to the lingering loyalties of subjects to family and cult. But the trappings notwithstanding, the essential core of the state is the military bond.

"The war chief and his band," writes Jenks, "are the earliest form of the state. At first, no doubt, they are considered as temporary institutions; but successful institutions have a tendency to become permanent. . . .

"The two institutions, the Clan and the State, stand thus face to face with each other. Linked together against external attack, they are pledged to the deadliest internal warfare. . . . The leading characteristics of the Clan are a caste organization, a respect for the autonomy of its constituent groups, and exclusiveness. The principles of the State are precisely the opposite—encouragement of individual ability by the offer of splendid rewards, an insistence on absolute and direct obedience by every one of its members to its acknowledged head, and willingness to purchase ability wherever it can get it."[1]

The kind of conflict described by Jenks is a vivid aspect of the history of each of the great civilizations that appeared on the world scene about 5,000 years ago—China, India, Sumer, Egypt, and somewhat later Greece and Rome. The sagas, epics, and legends are almost entirely recordings, celebrations actually, of great deeds done by the heads of great families, by military commanders, and by individual soldier-heroes. Homer offers us the picture in his *Iliad* and *Odyssey* of a Greek society just beginning to face the pangs of conflict between

---

1. Edward Jenks, *Law and Politics in the Middle Ages* (New York: Henry Holt, 1898), pp. 308–9.

its age-old kinship structure and the pressing needs of war. Eventually the political state won out. In Athens this victory was dramatized by the famous Cleisthenean Reforms, which abolished the ancient kinship structure and brought in the city-state built from the start on sovereignty, individualism, and a preponderance of contractual ties. Kinship status withered.

Roman society—on which we have such an abundance of exact and careful records—is one long saga of conflict between the immemorially established *patria potestas,* the sacred and imprescriptible sovereignty of the family in its own affairs, and the *imperium militiae,* the power vested in military leaders over their troops. Under the Republic, at least down to its final couple of centuries, a strict rule, imposed by the senate, required all returning soldiers to halt outside the city's walls, disband, and change into civil dress before entering the city. There was, obviously, no disposition on the part of the senate—its true name the Conscript Fathers, each of whom was the sovereign of his own family—to allow any of the strength and aggressiveness native to the army to spill over into civil society.

But the tragedy of Rome lay precisely in this spilling over of the *imperium* onto the sacred *patria potestas* of civil, kinship society. As many historians of Roman law have pointed out, the history of that law is one of successive recoils of the *patria potestas* before the advancing might and popularity of Rome's legions, cemented together by the *imperium.* When Empire replaced Republic toward the end of the first century B.C. and when Augustus Caesar became the first emperor, the *imperium* became triumphant for good over the *patria potestas.* The next two centuries of Roman social history are dominated by the successive invasions of the state bureaucracy into traditional kinship society—specifically into the realms of social control, education, social welfare, religion, marriage, even birth and death. By the fourth century, Rome had become the first all-out totalitarian society in world history, its sole foundation the army, its sovereignty no more than the relentless expansion of the military *imperium* over all elements of Roman society, its population now a vast aggregate of legally free, socially separated individuals instead of the "little republics" and the "smaller patriotisms" that the famed Roman family system had once projected.

The eventual fall of the Roman Empire in the West was preceded, as historians beginning with Gibbon and Montesquieu have continually stressed, by several centuries of manifest decline. Rome's steady centralization of power, collectivization of social functions, ubiquitous bureaucracy, and militarization of more and more centers of Roman life—all inevitably resulted in a population that would increasingly become a vast mass characterized, as a great deal of the literature of the time attests, by epidemic rootlessness, fragility of community, and alienation. By the fifth century, the once-proud Roman family had been ground down by the twin forces of centralization and atomization into the kind of frail, functionally depleted, and impotent group that we are coming to know only too well in widening parts of the United States today. By the time the Justinian Code was compiled in the sixth century in the West, the Roman family's once large place in law had dwindled to but a shadow of its former glory.

But history is a panorama of pendular swings and cyclical rises and falls. The disappearance in the West of nearly all the powers, authorities, functions, and trappings of the Empire did not for long leave anything like a vacuum. A totally new form of society developed, one that was formed in almost equal measure of survivals of Roman polity and of the kinship-based institutions of the Germanic peoples who so thoroughly inundated all of Western Europe. Where the Roman Empire had luxuriated in, and eventually been corrupted by, centralization of power, the European society that stretches from about the seventh century down to the fifteenth is notable—or notorious, depending on viewpoint—for its decentralization, its localism, its divisions of authority, and its profusion of groups and associations enjoying a wide measure of autonomy (at least by the standards of imperial Rome and of the later modern European states).

Family and state wax and wane inversely to each other, as I have stressed, and there is no mystery in the fact that the family—all the way from household group through the clan, the kindred, and even wider kinship groupings—prospered in terms of assertion of its natural authorities and functions, not to overlook social cohesion. The idea of the state is a weak and wavering idea throughout the Middle Ages. The so-called Holy Roman Empire was, as someone observed long ago, neither holy, Roman, nor an empire. Roman political concepts were periodically drawn from the texts to emblazon some feudal government, but the contrast between rhetoric and reality was very broad.

From the weakness of the state, and of principles of centralization in church as well as polity, it followed that group and associational life would flourish. By the twelfth century a whole profusion of novel groups was evident: guilds, village communities, monasteries, universities, fiefs of every kind and description. The principle of representation is essentially a medieval invention; so is parliamentarism, and so also is trial by juries of peers. Inevitably the kinship tie would flourish in this general atmosphere of localism, intermediation, decentralization, and absence of a strong and bureaucratic state.

Lord Acton wrote: "Modern history tells how the last four hundred years have modified the medieval conditions of life and thought." Or, in other words, the pendulum of history swings. From approximately 1500 down to 1800 in the West, the historical record is one of a waning of medieval decentralization and pluralism and a regeneration of the Roman imperial idea of the state, adapted of course to postmedieval political and social realities. By the seventeenth century the dominant position of the state in Europe was once again assured; systems of national law, national economy, national religion, and national culture were firmly emplaced. The historic rights of village communities and towns, of monasteries and guilds, of the old aristocracy, and inevitably of the kinship sphere—given all the other curtailments—perceptibly lessened in number and power.

The history of political theory between 1500 and 1800 offers us an almost perfect mirror of what was going on institutionally in Western Europe. Jean Bodin, commonly credited with the earliest utterance of the doctrine of national political sovereignty, writing in the sixteenth century (with one foot in the medieval past, the other in the future), took care to give maximum rights to family and other surviving medieval groups. There is little trace of either Roman law or an atomistic version of natural law individualism in his *Commonwealth*. When we come to Hobbes in the next century, a major change is evident. For Hobbes there is little room left in his *Leviathan* for social groups, which he likens to "worms in the entrails of natural man." Natural law, Hobbes declares, has in it no place for groups other than the state itself and for component elements other than the natural individual. Relax the absolute power of the state and human beings are threatened instantly by return to the dread, fearsome state of nature. Even the family is given but a precarious status by Hobbes; its authority is no more than that conferred by a "tacit contract" between parents and children, one subject to the overweening power of the state. Large families are frowned on by Hobbes because of their notable proneness to subversion and civil discord. Hobbes's *Leviathan* is a masterpiece of desocialization.

It was Rousseau, however, who carried political absolutism to its greatest lengths and who also founded, willy-nilly, the totalitarian mystique of politics. Legitimacy is given the state by what Rousseau called the *General Will,* the kind of collective will that is possible once the people conceive themselves as first and foremost *citizens* and thereby freed of traditional identities, constraints, traditions, and non-political values. The General Will is, Rousseau insists, absolute, imprescriptible, and capable of penetrating the deepest recesses of each individual citizen. Around it will be formed a "civil religion." Citizens whose behavior violates the tenets of the civil religion are subject to banishment or even the death penalty. The prime objective of the General Will is that of remaking not only social organization but human nature itself; this can be done, Rousseau assures us, only by the individual's abdicating, or being forced to abdicate, all of his traditional social roles, thus leaving his inner being "free" to belong completely and irrevocably to the sacred General Will. Individuals are thus "forced to be free."

Even the family must be destroyed, for it is, of all groups lying between man and state, the most recalcitrant when the state seeks to fuse itself directly with the individual consciousness. It is, Rousseau writes, the family preeminently that instills in us love of property and possessions, and pride that becomes the window to inequality; it is the family that prevents our easy acceptance of unity and uniformity over diversity.

"Should the public authority, by taking the place of the father, and charging itself with that important function, acquire his rights by discharging his duties, he would have the less cause to complain, as he would only be changing his title, and would have in common under the name of *citizen* the same authority over his children as he was exercising separately under the name of *father.*"[2]

In that paradigm for totalitarianism, social man is subsumed forever by political man. The most ancient form of the social bond is negated in behalf of the political state, itself as we have seen the child of war and of military command. Both Leninism and Hitlerism aimed essentially at fulfillment of Rousseau's ideal of an order freed forever of all influences, beginning with the family, that would by their pres-

2. Jean-Jacques Rousseau, "Discourse on Political Economy," in *The Social Contract and Discourses,* ed. and trans. G. D. H. Cole (New York: E. P. Dutton, Everyman's Library, 1950), p. 309.

ence militate permanently against the total state. Hence the stripping of the family of as many of its natural functions and authorities as possible, in order to demean it, and the incessant movement by the state to push into every household reminders of the supreme power of the state.

We do not, fortunately, face that kind of war against the family in the United States and the West generally. The war we do face is not, however, free of a certain degree of hostility to the family, hostility that stems from the well-founded belief among certain zealous political reformers that the strong family, by its very existence, is the natural ally of the social differences and economic inequalities which the modern reformer so often abominates. Because of that hostility and because, too, of sheer ignorance among bureaucrats and other political power-holders of the functional and structural requirements of the stable family, a very considerable amount of ostensibly democratic and liberal legislation, in areas of taxation, protection of individual rights, responsibility for the child, and, not least, the administration of welfare for the indigent and socially deprived has had the effect of actually weakening the already beset and beleaguered kinship community. In short, the oldest and most universal of institutional conflicts, that between state and family, continues in even the most democratic societies on earth in this century.

I am confident that the attentive reading of this fine and salutary study of state and family will carry us, administrators, politicians, and ordinary citizens alike, a long step forward in understanding the indispensability of the family to democracy and also the complexities that attend the family's relationship to democracy.

Robert Nisbet
Albert Schweitzer Professor Emeritus,
Columbia University
Adjunct Scholar,
American Enterprise Institute

INTRODUCTION: THE AMERICAN FAMILY IN A FREE SOCIETY

Joseph R. Peden and Fred R. Glahe

The *raison d'être* of this book is best stated by William Baumgarth in the first chapter: "The first thing to be observed about contemporary political-philosophical reflection upon the family is that there is very little of it." Compared to classical or early modern thinkers, political theorists of the twentieth century have largely ignored the family as a central concern. As a result, the subject has tended to become the province of psychologists, who generally ignore the family's relationship with the state, or sociologists, who often assume the propriety of its subordination to the organized will of the political authorities. This book is an attempt to open a wider dialogue on the family, with a focus on its dynamics and interaction with the state in American society.

Baumgarth suggests that the tendency to ignore or denigrate the family in modern political thought is due to a rejection of the concept of the primacy of natural order in human affairs, a rejection that is necessary whenever the principle of equality is held as an absolute value. He traces the problem to Rousseau, who considered all social institutions to be artifacts—a result of human will. Thus the family, like all other social entities, is a transitory, historically conditioned, and malleable institution that can be bent or shaped to human sovereign will, especially as embodied in the state.

To political philosophers like Mark Poster, family structure is to-

1

tally open to change because all traditional norms are ahistorical and "ideological" in character, hence disposable at will. The contemporary family is but a reflection of bourgeois, individualistic, capitalist society.

Baumgarth finds that for John Rawls "not only is the family not essential for the just society" but it actually impedes the application of his second principle, which holds that social and economic inequalities are tolerable "only insofar as they benefit the least advantaged social group." The Rawlsian family, says Baumgarth, remains "as an accident of history: at best, tolerable; at worst, the subject of interventionist educational and redistributional projects of a theoretically punitive kind."

Baumgarth's study of F. A. Hayek's political thought shows that, insofar as he has taken any interest in the family, Hayek shares the general modern avoidance of the family as a society grounded in nature. But Hayek, unlike Poster and Rawls, sees no inherent disadvantage in inequalities. Instead, he views them as positive forces in the evolution of societies. Egalitarianism impedes the necessary experimentation that societies need to respond creatively to new situations.

Hayek's evolutionary vision of society is that it should be a spontaneous order in which humans possess maximum freedom to experiment, in order to find the social forms or instruments that will lead to a more humane environment. As an economist, Hayek has used this social theory to support his defense of the free market. As a political philosopher he has used it to denounce the enacting of legislation, what he calls "rationalistic constructivism," rather than depending on the emergence of legal rules from individual case law, as in the English common law or law merchant.

The question of whether or not the family is grounded in nature is crucial for any effective defense of its autonomy against the state, for the state itself is clearly an artifact of human creation. Historians and anthropologists would agree that the state is a creation of man, coming into being at specific times and places as societies reach certain levels of organizational complexity. But the family, in its minimal nexus of parent and child, must be co-temporal with the origin of the human race and natural in its grounding in the biological relationship of parent and child arising from procreation and nurturing. It is biologically necessary that an infant be nurtured by some adult for several years before it can fend for itself. While the essence of the familial entity is not necessarily procreative, it certainly centers on the responsibility for nurturing children until they reach self-sustaining autonomy.

The state, however, is not biologically necessary. Men and women have survived and even flourished outside its purview or power. Thus, in the hierarchy of ontological orders, the family precedes the state in origin and in natural grounding, with the state secondary to the family. In the same sense, the sovereignty of individuals precedes that of both the state and the family, because both are subordinate ontologically to the individual beings who initiate and participate in them.

Yet, when the state appears in human societies, it is remarkable how often it seeks to ape the family in its structure, authority, and symbolism. Historians report that monarchy is the most common kind of state structure, and everywhere its priestly and hereditary character and limited powers are reminiscent of those found in the patriarchial family. The loyalty and deference shown to kings by their subjects rest on their perception of paternal concern, respect for individual dignity, and mutual advantage.

A king or a father who plays the tyrant ends by destroying the solidarity of his society, state, or family. The more abstract and rationalistic a state's ideology and structure, and the less familial it shows itself, the more difficulty it has in holding the affection, loyalty, and confidence of its subjects. Its authority must be exercised increasingly by force rather than love. The affective links between rulers and ruled become attenuated, or disappear entirely. Mutual advantage is less obvious and plays a less significant role. The personal gives place to the bureaucratic, and the human affective relationships are reduced to abstractions and are seen as exploitive.

The deliberate invocation of familial symbols and values in the modern rationalist state is understandable. The "Big Brother" of Orwell, the Führer of Hitler, and the fatherly and motherly politicians of certain democracies all bolster the artificial and abstract authority of the modern head of state with the dignity, authority, and natural parental caring associated with leadership in families. That we should increasingly find political leaders wishing to characterize the state as a family is understandable. In fact, it may be an intelligent response to an instinctive fear that the populace has become alienated from traditional political institutions.

Yet the modern state is almost bound to be hostile to the family itself. It cannot tolerate any rival to itself for the loyalty and obedience of its subjects. Like the church, the family's sovereignty rises from an order of reality that the state cannot share. For, just as the church takes its authority from the supernatural order, the family derives its autonomy from the natural order and voluntary contract. In contrast, the state can claim only divine will, social contract, conquest, or coercion as the basis for its authority.

The French philosopher Gabriel Marcel, in his book *Homo Viator,* argued that the "modern state will tend finally to kill everything which it claims to sanction or foster in human beings, for it is beyond its power either to give life or to reveal and recognize it." Marcel insists that the family is by nature more than a legal entity. It exists only on condition that it is perceived not only "as a value but as a living presence." As a "presence," the family is experienced at specific moments as a kind of "protective skin" placed between the self and the external world, which is seen as foreign and threatening. The family is the "matrix of individuality," the meeting place of the physical life force and the spiritual. It is a recognized hierarchy in which one is caught up from the beginning of one's existence. One's being is rooted in it. One enjoys through it a kind of consubstantiality with a lineage that stretches back in time, eventually encompassing the whole antecedent human race. If this lineage is destroyed, if this hierarchy is abolished, the family itself loses its status as a value. It becomes instead a net which holds one captive and from which one must seek escape.

To Marcel, the family belongs to an order of reality or presence that he conceptualizes as a mystery, an entity in which the observer is himself vitally and effectively a part of the reality observed. In essence, it is not a legal contractual association of interests—procreative, romantic, economic, or social. A family that views itself solely as an association of common interests, a corporation for organizing production or maximizing wealth or pleasures, is setting itself up for bankruptcy and dissolution. It is a multifaceted relationship—ineffable, creative, sacral, and empowering. It is our most human experience.

To move from this notion of family as mystery to examining the economics of families may seem a strange and sharp disjunction. Yet, it is not. Rather, such an examination is essential for a fuller view of the family in a free society, and thus it is that half the contributors to this collection of essays are economists or economic historians. Indeed, economic analysis and theory, building on the work of Gary Becker and others, may provide us with a significant insight into the more general dilemmas of the relationship between the family and the state.

The basic principle of the free market approach to economic theory is that the market process works best when free of arbitrary intervention in economic decision-making by government authorities. Apart from general laws governing the enforcement of contracts and prohibition of theft and fraud, the use of the coercive power of the state to regulate, subsidize, and command market operations tends to misallocate resources and creates privilege for some at the expense of others. Allowing the market process to proceed, without noneconomic barriers or legislatively created one-sided advantages, generally produces efficient satisfaction of the needs of consumers and equal freedom to engage in market exchanges.

But how does the market know what is needed, or what is the most efficient use of resources? The mechanism was described by Adam Smith somewhat inadequately as "an invisible hand," which directed the individual actors to adjust their decisions constantly toward the goal of optimal efficiency based on calculation of their individual self-interests. Errors were swiftly punished by the reaction of the market itself, which signaled its judgment by losses of profit and failure of enterprises.

More recent economic theorists, such as Carl Menger and F. A. Hayek, offer a more sophisticated explanation of the process by which an economic order can be created by the spontaneous decisions of an unrelated series of actors, each with imperfect knowledge and each following his quite diverse self-interests. These acts are not undertaken at the command of any single overriding authority; rather, they are the product of the individual wills of the discrete actors and the general and impersonal laws of the marketplace, i.e., the laws of supply and demand, marginal utility, etc. The flow of information through the marketplace allows a constant reevaluation of decisions and correction of errors, and maximizes efficient production of societal needs for a given cost.

This theory of a spontaneous order created by the dynamics of the market economy has also been used to analyze the workings of other societal organizations. The distinguished physicist Michael Polanyi defended the concept of freedom in the scientific community by showing how, when unrestrained by monopolization of resources or restrictions on flow of information, the scientific community represents a well-functioning spontaneously ordered society. Hayek has also tried to apply the theory to explain the evolution of law, particularly common law, which he contrasts with the less "tested" method of law enacted by statute.

Why then can we not apply the model of a spontaneous order to understand optimal functioning of the family? Cannot the family rightly be viewed as a spontaneously ordered society? Does it not wax and wane in size through marriage, births, deaths, divorces, or adoptions? Does it not fluctuate in the scope of its operations, its geographic locale, its emotional intensity, its set goals, and the kinds and values of its resources? Do not both formal and informal authority shift among individual members according to changing circumstances? Does not its psychological intimacy heighten the level of knowledge and predictability among its members? Is it not more likely to generate self-discipline, commitment, and enthusiasm for its common goals than less emotionally intense and less interdependent social entities? These questions suggest that, indeed, the model of a spontaneous order may be a useful analytic tool to develop a theory of the family in relation to the state.

The family's structural modes may vary from culture to culture: Some are based on monogamy, others on polygamy or, more rarely, polyandry; most are patriarchal, at least formally, but matriarchy not infrequently exists informally. Methods of child rearing vary widely, as does the division of responsibilities among age-sets and sexes. Many other characteristics of families also vary widely.

Yet, this very diversity points to spontaneous order! Whatever the culture, the family is a voluntary society. It begins in contract and, formally and informally, continues to be contractual, not coercive. (Even the child, though thrust into its midst by nature rather than its own will, gradually emancipates itself, and the child's continued membership becomes voluntary as soon as it is able to make such a choice.) The family is a dynamic social entity; diversity and change are characteristic; day by day, hour by hour, the family reveals itself in a voluntary, spontaneous ordering.

What kinds of problems does state intervention in this order—the life of the family—generate? Some of these problems are explored in papers in this volume. Historian Murray Rothbard (chapter 4) describes how ideological progressives attempted to use state power to impose their moral values on American families whose religious and marital values and family life-styles they deplored. Barry Poulson (chapter 5) shows how the public system of education was designed to impose a specific set of values on the children of the masses, particularly those children of immigrant working-class families. Jacqueline Kasun (chapter 12) documents a similar phenomenon in contemporary society, in which an ideological interest group of professional sex-education specialists and population-control advocates have captured, through the manipulation of state organs, a vast audience for its intensive ideological objectives. Brigitte Berger (chapter 13) describes the scandal that government regulation of foster care has generated.

Why is state intervention in family life so counterproductive to the best interests of family welfare? For much the same reasons that its intervention in the marketplace is generally so damaging to the latter's efficiency.

First, the state, like individual actors, always has imperfect knowledge. But the more complex the problem, the more numerous its individual participants, the more difficult it is to calculate the consequences of any action or to coordinate its operations. And the larger the numbers affected by the decisions, the larger the potential damage. Moreover, the state, unlike firms in a competitive market, is not subject to a truly effective feedback mechanism such as a profit-and-loss statement.

Secondly, to the state, a family is a statistically delineated abstract object of state-directed action. It cannot be otherwise, given the bureaucratic command structure of the modern state. Yet the family in reality is always a discrete, unique entity. Stripped of its individuality and made the object of the blunt instrument of state intervention, the family is almost certainly likely to suffer some damage.

Thirdly, even when its intentions are good, the state's attempts to address the needs of a family will have consequences unforeseen and unintended. Dwight Lee (chapter 11) demonstrates this phenomenon in his discussion of how the federal government's housing policy resulted in a significant misallocation of investment funds—the unintended and unforeseen consequence of which will be to diminish the amount of capital investment available to sustain continuing economic growth. The acknowledged good of better housing in the short term may have undermined the potential for long-term growth and improvement of the economic welfare of all. Similarly, government fiscal and monetary policies have contributed to inflation, which, as the paper by Lowell Gallaway and Richard Vedder (chapter 10) argues, may bear some relationship to divorce rates. Inflation, it is argued, may effect a fall in real income, thus causing financial problems and interpersonal tensions in the family. Even when inflation is anticipated, Gallaway and Vedder argue that induced changes in nominal interest rates (for home mortgages and other loans) serve to reduce family mobility, removing an important "safety valve" that can alleviate family tensions associated with location.

A fourth reason why government intervention is inimical to the welfare of the family lies in the nature of American society itself. In a relatively homogeneous culture, some reasonably typical pattern of family structure and values might be used to "predict" and plan state policies regarding families. The damage might be contained and affordable. But in the United States, the multiethnic, multireligious, pluralistic character of the population, spread out over vast geographic space with diverse climates, topographies and natural resources, with its wide variations in incomes, jobs, and life styles, renders any general plan of intervention on a national scale both crude and unpredictable in its consequences.

Even if a sociologist or statistician could delineate a "typical" working-class, white, Catholic, Irish-American, urban, New England family of four—father, mother, and two children of school age—with an identifiable special need, the existential reality of a single such family could not be captured. No government agency could determine the impact of its intervention on the internal power relationships between husband and wife, the loss of parental authority that dependence on an outside benefactor creates, the misallocation of family resources that may result from too easy access to a specific incentive spurred by government subsidy or privilege. The unintended effects on the integrity or autonomy of the family are incalculable.

The state, at least in a democracy, uses its legislative and administrative powers to create general laws or procedures under which all must live and to which all must conform their own activities. Such instruments of coercion necessarily restrict the spontaneous ordering of the society. The greater the amount of such coercive interventions and the wider the scope of their application, the smaller the area for spontaneity, creativity, experimentation, and personal achievement. In economic theory, the need for freedom in the market is justified, not only by its demonstrated capacity for static efficiency, but also by its promotion of technological progress and the betterment of human society as a whole. The same argument holds for the market that is the family. Its efficiency as a human entity, its social and psychological betterment, seem best achieved through freedom, not the indiscriminate instrument of state interventionist control.

Although Marcel warns us that to treat the family as merely a contractual association of interests is to rob it of its essential nature, historically families *do* function as economic units. The domestic household is itself a minieconomy, as Poulson (chapter 2) demonstrates in his description of the family as an economic organization. It functions as a voluntary exchange and transactional entity analogous to the business firm. Subtle mechanisms for economizing on transactions costs are developed as members pursue their objectives. In addition, the family frequently operates as a producer of goods and services for an external market. Though Poulson believes that this role of the family has declined as alternative modes of organization such as the corporation have expanded, the family business remains a predominant form of business organization in the United States. Professor Peter Davis, director of Executive Education at The Wharton School of the University of Pennsylvania, estimates that at least 60 percent of the gross national product is generated by family firms, and that more than 75 percent of private corporations, partnerships, and proprietorships are family dominated. Even among the largest corporations, the Fortune 500, some 30 percent are controlled by a family.

It seems clear that the family retains enormous influence in the functioning of the economy at large. The spontaneous, voluntary character of the family must contribute significantly to the dynamic quality of the larger economy to which it contributes so much of its own energy, commitment, and talent. As Poulson suggests, economists have a well-developed theoretical analysis of the optimal relationship between the state and the market. But what has been lacking is a broad theoretical framework for the analysis of the optimal relationship of the family and the state. Such an analysis can come none too soon, in view of the crisis in family life that has been developing in recent years.

Much of the crisis in family-state relations arises from the notion that the family and the individual are at odds. The state, in its role as defender of individual rights, inevitably finds itself at odds with the collectivity we call family. Just as the citizen is expected to accept the curbing of certain of his rights as the price of membership in the political community of the state, so the individual who enters a family must expect to tailor his individual autonomy to fit the requirements and to enjoy the benefits of the familial community. Problems arise either when the family seeks to use state coercive power to maintain its integrity and its structure, or when the state uses its own power to disrupt the discipline and solidarity of the family. For example, the rights of children, and the rights of parents in raising children, are a fertile field for bitter disputes between the family and the state.

The use of political power to intervene in the lives of families, described so vividly in Rothbard's historical account of the policies of the early twentieth-century Progressive movement, is further documented in Henry Holzer's survey (chapter 6) of the prevailing judicial philosophy of the United States Supreme Court. Reviewing only three categories of cases involving family rights—those regulating marriage, the definition of family membership, and facets of procreational rights—Holzer characterizes the general principle of the Court's judicial philosophy as "traditional collectivist statism." Time after time, he documents that the Court majority and minority joined in asserting the right of "society" to regulate the practices of individuals and familial groups in their sexual, procreative, and marital relationships. Nothing is beyond the purview of the state if a "compelling state interest" can be shown.

The state-enforced "societal norms," which limit the autonomy of the family, leave the state's agenda for intervention open-ended. Historically, governments of the individual American states have banned interracial marriages, prohibited religiously permitted polygamy, compelled sterilization of persons they declared to be mentally incompetent or habitually criminal. They have allowed abortion, and banned it; they have forbidden divorce except in cases of adultery, and have allowed it by mutual consent; adultery is a crime in some states, not in others. The law is what the law says it is; and the rights of individuals and families to autonomy, self-definition and voluntarism in their sexual and procreative practices must bend to the latest decisions of courts and legislatures, acting upon the "compelling state interest" of the moment.

Is there any alternative to such legal despotism? Is there any way in which the liberty of individuals in a familial relationship can be protected? The papers in this volume by Roger Arnold (chapter 7) and by Paul Horton and Lawrence Alexander (chapter 8) take up one alternative possibility: to deregulate the family by allowing it to regulate itself through freedom of contract. In effect, they examine the possibility of taking the principles of laissez faire, or the spontaneous ordering of the free market through freedom to contract, and applying them to family affairs. Arnold probes the question of what the appropriate structure for property rights in divorce cases would be if a Lockean view of freedom of contract and "natural rights" were consistently followed.

Horton and Alexander find that many critics believe a trend toward free contracting in family matters is already in progress, as the state has withdrawn many of its older regulatory restrictions on divorce, extramarital sex, the rights of married women, contraception, and abortion. Yet, they question whether these trends signal the advance of the right of contract within family relationships. Just because the state withdraws its prohibition in a specific case, it does not necessarily permit freedom of contract to govern the field. For instance, although the state now permits abortion, it continues to hedge such a "right" by restrictions on the timing of the abortion, who must be notified, and other bureaucratic procedures. In effect, decriminalization is not the equivalent of freedom to contract. As these authors conclude, "only time will tell" if the state is trying to yield to the principle of freedom of contract, or is simply redrafting regulations partially in response to some newly identified compelling state interest.

Another argument discussed by Horton and Alexander asserts that one cannot have self-regulation by contract without infringing on the very spontaneous nature of marital and familial relationships through the need for state enforcement of the contract. To some critics, contract is unintelligible without enforceability. Horton and Alexander reject this alleged identity of true contract with enforceability. They argue that contract without enforceability is compatible with both family and other relationships, such as partnerships, clubs, and relations between employers and employees. In such relationships, considerations of legal enforceability are of secondary importance and are rarely envisioned or asserted. In their judgment, the recognition of contract as a valid concept, even if nonenforceable, would "create the perception of an intermediate ground—and a wide and healthy range of strategies —between two largely undesirable alternatives," that is, state regulation or the notion of contract as equated with "legal enforceability of bargained-for exchange." Clearly, this kind of conceptualization of contract as it functions in familial relationships is most compatible with the idea of the family itself as a spontaneous social order.

There is one area of familial relationship in which freedom of contract as a solution excluding state intervention does not readily apply: parental authority over children. Law and custom too often treat children as second-class persons whose social and legal standing is inferior to that of adults. Children are considered subject to the authority of adults in ways that adults may not be. They are subject to laws that do not apply to adults. They are deprived of equal protection of law simply because they are defined as "minors." These "arrangements of unequal liberty," as Lyla O'Driscoll (chapter 3) characterizes them, strain the notion of contract as the basis of parent-child or adult-child relationship because contract implies equal status for all parties to the contract. Clearly children do not enjoy such equal status or freedom of choice in contracting with adults. This inequality is sustained, and even fostered, by the state. It constitutes a significant opening for state intrusion into, and overview of, almost every aspect of parent-child relationships.

O'Driscoll believes that the absence in American law and social practices of a coherent theory of the nature of the family allows abrupt shifts in rationales for intervention by the state as one moves from one set of problems to another. Briefly, she describes four theories of the family: the authoritarian, which emphasizes the parents' right to command and the child's duty to obey; the sentimental, which focuses on the psychological and emotional basis for parent-child relationships; the paternalistic, which stresses the role of the parent as limiting the child's freedom for its own good; and the economic, which bases family relationships on exchange and supply of needs.

Paradoxically, each of these is invoked both by those supporting state intervention and by those opposing it. Their respective positions vary with the circumstance and issue. Looking more closely at the sentimentalist and authoritarian theories, O'Driscoll insists that neither is necessarily incompatible with the other, or with the recognition of the moral equality of all persons regardless of age. But she also warns against an "*excessive* focus on rights, duties, and the like— and *inordinate* appeal to these grounds in matters large and small." She concludes by asserting that the idea of the family as "a social structure governed by justice, defined by rights and duties, and animated by love" is intelligible and workable.

However, where to draw the line upon state intervention and supervision of the family remains problematic. This is most graphically illustrated by John Johnson's paper (chapter 9) on the changing concept of what constitutes child abuse. Few states even have clear definitions of what constitutes child abuse. As recently as ten years ago, only eight states defined "neglect," only twenty-two even used the term "neglected child," while twenty-three others spoke of the "deprived child," "dependent child," or "dependent and neglected." But by the 1980s almost every jurisdiction had changed its child neglect laws, sometimes two or three times. While the concept of physical battery is grounded in a long tradition of legal precedent and definition, neglect continues to be open-ended in specificity, especially as it seeks to encompass educational, emotional, psychological, and sociological deprivations, as well as the more easily defined physical or safety endangerments.

To compound the problem of lack of agreement in definitions of neglect or abuse, the new laws greatly expand the numbers and kinds of persons who are mandated by law to report suspicious incidents of alleged child abuse or neglect. The numbers of mandated "informers" have become so great that legislators have had to grant immunity from civil or criminal liability for false charges and invasion of privacy for such "guardians" of youth.

Under these circumstances, one should not be surprised that an explosion of reported cases of child abuse soon outstripped the ability of social services and judicial agencies to respond appropriately in upholding the new standards. It is also not surprising that new state enforcement systems seem to focus on the less politically influential minority families. Johnson concludes: "Never before have so many families been caught up in the net of official investigation and case processing; our best estimates today tell us that about 1 million U.S. families receive an official investigation that results in a *substantiated* claim of abuse or neglect *each year*. Several million others are investigated by official agents, which is in and of itself a great source of anxiety, stress, conflict, and stigma."

Has all this governmental intervention improved the lot of American children? Johnson reports that "recent empirical evidence leads us to see that governmental efforts may serve to create and sustain some kinds of problems, and specifically in the case of official interventions into family life, they may make problems worse for the individuals involved. This realization produces a new circumspection and caution about the rule of governmental action in resolving family problems, and paves the way for more informed political action." Withdrawal of the state from some areas of family life, or at least a narrowing of its legitimate point of intrusion, might allow spontaneous social and cultural forces to respond more effectively to changing standards of what is morally permissible or adequate in intrafamily relationships.

Another major point of intrusion by the state into family life is justified by the state's assumption of the task of redistributing wealth. Our contributors offer several possible alternatives to the present system, which despite ever growing expense, nevertheless seems to have contributed to even further dysfunctioning of the family, including increased rates of divorce and illegitimacy.

The paper by Gregory Christainsen and Walter Williams (chapter 14) argues that the observed patterns of wealth redistribution and their consequences are the predictable result of institutional arrangements that permit modern democracies to operate in a relatively unconstrained manner. The very existence of a federal income tax, for example, was deemed unconstitutional until the twentieth century. Now, however, the state is empowered to confiscate income for almost any purpose deemed "in the public interest." But in a modern unconstrained democracy, the state is governed primarily by coalitions of special interest groups, not necessarily by the majority sentiment of its citizens. Because of special interest pressures, income redistributions include benefits to middle- and upper-class families as well as to the poor, and the various interventions entail dysfunctions that impair almost everyone's long-run welfare. The authors urge a critical appraisal of alternatives to existing political institutions.

J. Craig Peery concludes the volume (chapter 15) by examining some of the private alternatives that currently exist with respect to family concerns. Peery reports that a recent survey of some 300 corporations revealed that they are already actively engaged in a myriad of programs that are immediately directed toward the improvement of familial solidarity, health, education, and financial security—all this apart from payment of wages or salaries. The motives for business involvement are not paternalistic or philanthropic; they are always justified by an economic analysis of what factors contribute to more efficient production and profits. Happy, healthy, well-educated, and anxiety-free employees and their families are necessary for the long-term success of any business. However, as Peery points out, the role of business corporations in sustaining the integrity and health of the family has been largely ignored by federal social welfare officials and politicians. As Peery notes: "Sometimes intentionally, sometimes inadvertently, America's corporations are developing programs that have a positive influence on family life." Why have these not been more extensively explored by both government and social scientists?

The nature of the relationship between the modern state and the family is such that it requires the efforts of scholars from many different disciplines to depict its true character in its multidimensional complexity. It was the intention of the sponsors and editors of this volume to espouse a multi-disciplinary approach by commissioning fifteen papers, which represent the efforts of seventeen scholars from a wide variety of disciplines: economics, sociology, history, law, philosophy, and political theory.

While it was expected that all the contributors would be critical in some way of the present state of affairs—because that is one major function of scholarship—it was surprising to find in all the papers, implicitly or explicitly, a sense of something missing. Poulson came closest to expressing it in his appeal for a new theoretical framework that would do for critics of family-state relationships what the theory of the free market does for critics of economy-state relations. The interventionist model of the state as it relates to the family is more and more seen as dysfunctional, even counterproductive, in its attempt to "do good" for families, which are themselves depicted as dysfunctional in some respect. But if the interventions fail to achieve their goals, or if they create new problems through their unintended and unforeseen consequences, what must be done?

It is fair to say that the overwhelming response of our contributing scholars has been to recommend less and less state intrusion into the affairs and decisions of families. What is missing is a coherent theoretical framework for separation of family and state that will protect the rights of individuals and yet not destroy the "mystery" that is the family.

The best contribution this collection of essays may make is to focus attention on this critical problem and to hint at the locus of a possible solution. The economists who have contributed to this work have used free market theory as their critical framework in studying the impact of government policies on families. Those familiar with the work of F. A. Hayek know that he believes the free market system is intimately linked to the social theory of spontaneous order. What we may be looking for in this volume is a social theory that will treat the family as a kind of spontaneous order in which individuals and groups make rational decisions based on their own estimation of their self-interest, decisions which in the larger arena of society work to the welfare of the whole. Such a social theory of the dynamics of free families in a free society, one implying that state intrusion be strictly limited to defending individual liberties, might become a mighty intellectual weapon in warding off the destructive forces of modern government.

This introduction can only highlight some of the many questions and hypotheses presented by this dilemma. Yet it is hoped that it provides the reader with a framework for understanding and a place to begin, just as this book itself may serve as an opening wedge for a new view of the family in its relationship with the state in a truly free society.

PART I

THINKING ABOUT THE FAMILY

1

THE FAMILY AND THE STATE IN MODERN POLITICAL THEORY

William Baumgarth

THE FAMILY IN EARLY MODERN THOUGHT

The first thing to be observed about contemporary political-philosophical reflection upon the family is that there is very little of it. In the history of political thought, the family has, in the classical works, occupied an important, albeit secondary place. Can we think of Plato's *Republic* without remembering Socrates' abolition of the private family? Can we appreciate Aristotle's criticism of Plato without realizing the importance the *Politics* gives to the family as a material cause of the *polis*? Substantial portions of Hobbes's writings on politics and of Locke's *Treatise on Civil Government* are given over to reflections upon the family. As late as the nineteenth century, discussions of the family have a notable place in political theory, as a reading, say, of the *Communist Manifesto* or other of Marx's writings would show. And, of course, Marx's great mentor Hegel devotes much attention to the place of the family within civil society and in relationship to the state.

Why, then, the relative silence of our contemporaries on this question? I hazard the following suggestion: The disregard for the family is a function of a turning away from the concept of nature in modern political thought and a focusing on the concept of equality in its stead. For the early modern thinkers, nature is viewed as something negative—something to oppose to the strictly human, something to escape from. Hence the state of nature in the early modern period is either one of gross difficulties, as in Hobbes or in Spinoza, or one of annoying inconveniences, as in Locke.[1] With Rousseau's criticism of the early moderns there begins a more radical depiction of the dichotomy between human phenomena and nature. The early moderns had viewed man as a creature of passion, reason being a mere instrument for satisfying the desires in a harmonious fashion. Will becomes the central theoretical preoccupying faculty for the early moderns. Unlike reason, which clearly differentiates men, since it is clearly unequally distributed, will appears to be more or less equally possessed by all. Society appears as an artifact of will, as a derivation from a contract.[2] The notion of the social contract is the heart of Rousseau's political teaching.

Rousseau's writings link him to his predecessors but also, and more important, issue in a break with them. If society is an artifact, a result of will, then so are all social institutions—the political community as well as intermediary associations including, ambiguously, the family.[3] As we will see in our discusson of Robert Nisbet's analysis, the important theme of political philosophy for Rousseau is will: the individual will and the collective will, the citizen and the sovereign.[4] The radical departure of Rousseau from previous modern thinkers resides in his opposition of nature to history. That is, the post-Rousseauian political thinker is not concerned with will alone but with the historical context within which that will operates, that context being both a product of will as well as an informing force upon its subsequent workings.[5]

Briefly, then, Rousseau's influence can be seen in two ways affecting subsequent discussions of the family. In the writings of liberal thinkers like Kant, the Rousseauian emphasis upon will translates into an overriding concern with moral autonomy. All rational beings are equal in their capacity for moral intention, and such intention is the essence of the moral phenomenon. That is to say, all men are equal

---

1. Leo Strauss, *Natural Right and History* (Chicago: University of Chicago Press, 1971), pp. 184, 228.
2. Ibid., p. 119.
3. Ibid., pp. 277–78.
4. Robert Nisbet, "Rousseau and the Political Community," in *Tradition and Revolt* (New York: Random House, 1968), p. 17.
5. Strauss, *n*. 1, p. 271.

in this most important respect, and the aim of philosophy is to discuss such equality as it exists in the individual as well as in the "kingdom of ends," the ideal, though perhaps unrealizable, community.[6] The family, then, has no special place for philosophers, but can perhaps be relegated to those who study nature: scientists. Such is the case today, when it is obvious that the vast bulk of writing on the family is found in disciplines like sociology: empirical investigations aspiring to descriptive richness but eschewing prescriptive theorizing.

From the point of view of Kantian moral theory, the family merits little philosophical attention. The same conclusion is arrived at by those students of society who have been influenced by Rousseau's historicism. If the human will develops not only in the individual but in the race, then such development might display a logic. We will call that logic "history" and define it, in the modern sense, as the chronicle of man's making of his own nature through the exercise of his freedom within a given, but changing, context. A belief in the self-making of man by man we will term *historicism*. Historicism includes a belief that all thinking is thinking with a horizon.[7] No thought, that is, can transcend the historical parameters of an individual's epoch. The most acute of thinkers merely articulates more consistently what is already in the air intellectually. Times and their beliefs change, but such change is the result of will (of action, of historically contexted freedom) concretized, say, in labor. Philosophy, thus, loses its significance since it, like all thinking, is provincial, despite its universalistic pretenses.[8] Of course if thinking even at its highest is unable to attain immortality, the same is true for institutions. Thus the family becomes one more transitory human phenomenon. It is perceived as timeless only by those blinded by the ambition and provinciality of their times. The family is a product, and a producer, of history whose form is a matter of historical note. As such, we have no guarantees about its future either with regard to its form or its mere existence. Certainly the family can, then, not be the proper object of normative theorizing since the values it embodies are specific to a historical setting and may be dysfunctional elsewhere. The proper study of the

6. Immanuel Kant, *Fundamental Principles of the Metaphysic of Morals*, in *Kant Selections*, ed. Theodore Meyer Greene and trans. T. K. Abbott (New York: Charles Scribner's Sons, 1957), pp. 313–14.

7. Strauss, *n*. 1, pp. 16–17, 27.

8. Karl Marx, *The German Ideology*, Robert Tucker, ed. in *The Marx-Engels Reader*, (New York: W. W. Norton and Co., 1978), pp. 154–55, 165.

family is, then, not the task of the ahistorical sociologist or economist but rather of the theoretically informed historian.

Such a view of the family is easily illustrated by way of the writings of Marx or those of his followers. That is to say, all family structures must be theoretically located within a given economic context that embraces both man's technological relationship to nature and man's social setting. That context Marx terms a *mode of production*. History is the saga of the logic presented by the various ascents and declines of these modes of production.[9]

Let us sum up our suggestion. Political philosophy cannot be detached theoretically in a radical fashion from moral philosophy. For the classical thinkers, nature is the foundation of all philosophizing, including ethical theorizing.[10] The family, then, merits political philosophical attention insofar as (and for the ancients it is a matter of affirmation) the family is natural. The mainstream of modern philosophy views nature as either a matter of indifference to the ethical theorists (Kant, Marx) or as something to be overcome (Hobbes). What replaces nature thematically is either what we have described above as the modern sense of "history" or an occupation with equality. Discussions of the family, as we shall illustrate, are usually, then, either subordinated to matters of historical note or else they occur in the context of theories about equality. The main question of the contemporary political theorists regard either the outliving by the family of its once functional historical role or the extent to which the family assists or impedes efforts in the direction of moral autonomy or equality, particularly equality of opportunity.

FIVE CONTEMPORARY VIEWS

We will begin with an examination of five contemporary social theorists on the question of the family. Although only two can be described as professional philosophers, all of the theorists to be discussed are interested in wide, interdisciplinary themes and all are informed more or less explicitly by philosophical traditions. The authors chosen, then, are by no means the only ones to discuss the family. Their importance rests upon the kind of arguments they make either in defense of or against that institution. We begin with two philosophical

9. Ibid.
10. Strauss, *n*. 1, p. 81.

theorists whose positions on the family are either hostile or lukewarm. Mark Poster will serve to exemplify the radical or historicist stance toward the family, while John Rawls is recognizable as a present-day American liberal, or progressive, regarding family policy proposals. We will then treat a variant of Catholic social thought (at least as it was in the philosophically interesting pre-Vatican II tradition) contained in the Thomism of Yves Simon. The secular traditionalist view will be studied in the work of Robert Nisbet. Finally, we will examine F. A. Hayek's consideration of the family in the context of his discussion of equality as an illustration of a relevant classical-liberal defense of the family. In the light of Hayek's broader argument, we will go beyond his explicit treatment of the family and, assisted by some other sympathetic sources, attempt to show the common-sensical soundness of much of Hayek's observations as a basis for public policy. Since, in all but one instance, the family is not the central concern of the theorist, it will be necessary for us to include in our analysis abridgement of other aspects of the author's overall theory.

Mark Poster

Mark Poster attempts to offer a *Critical Theory of the Family.*[11] The notion of "critical" here is a technical one. With regard to social theory, according to Poster, theories are either critical or ideological. Ideological theories are those that suppose any constants in human nature.[12] Needless to say, the term "ideological" is not an honorific one. This is because all ideology is a defense of the status quo. Since theories that suppose constants in human nature lower our expectations regarding what is politically possible, all such accounts are ideological. It would seem, therefore, that the vast bulk of the tradition of western political thought (at least up until Rousseau and, of course, including Hegel) is "ideological." According to Poster, we cannot tell what is possible and what is not politically until we have acted ourselves. To listen to others would simply be an inauthentic capitulation to ideology. Nothing ventured, nothing gained.

Critical theory, on the contrary, is always overtly political: It espouses change. Such change will not be willy-nilly but rather in the direction of radical egalitarianism. As critical, "a theory must account

11. Mark Poster, *Critical Theory of the Family* (New York: Seabury Press, 1978).
12. Ibid., p. xix.

for its object as historical in nature and must fix the location of its object socially, defining the limits of the structure in terms of the freedom of people to regulate their lives collectively and democratically."[13] Critical theory is critical in a related sense: Most of Poster's analysis consists in a qualified dismissal of the theories of the family developed by noncritical theorists. Unfortunately, this lack of emphasis upon positive norms makes for a confusing standard by which to judge or to recommend public policy. Since the only clarity we have is the perception of the oppressiveness of current practice, then we might be permitted a bit of uncertainty with our prescriptions for the future. Even then, though, we must say something about our destination. Poster sometimes suggests that a radical democracy is the desired end, as we have quoted above. Yet such democracy appears to be a mere preface: "If every human being had the right and the capacity to participate equally in determining the nature of the social system, then perhaps the problem of ideology would be reduced considerably."[14] It is difficult, in discussing such critical theory, not to be as negative toward it as it is toward the established values and institutions.

Returning to the precise sense of "critical": Such theories have their proximate source in the Frankfurt school. The Frankfurt school is first of all Marxist in its lineage. The departure from Marx is due to a rejection of Marx's optimism about the revolutionary potential of the working class. For adherents of this school, the capitalist order has imposed a global universe of discourse that makes even the contemplation of a radical alternative to capitalism impossible. Positivism in philosophy and behaviorialism in social science represent the triumph of ideological suppression of dissent. The Frankfurt school attempts to supplement Marxist economic analysis of capitalism with material from Freud. That is to say, the economic exploitation of the working classes is assisted by or exacerbated by the extraction of a "sexual surplus" no longer necessitated by conditions of natural scarcity. The impetus for revolution must come from the unconscious resources of the psyche as well as from economic discontent.[15] The taboos placed by class society upon sexual fantasies, the prohibitions upon all but heterosexual, monogamous married love, testify to the revolutionary

13. Ibid., p. xix.
14. Ibid., p. xix.
15. Ibid., pp. 53, 62–63.

potential of the sexually "polymorphously perverse," who thus replace the working class as the instrument of revolution.

Mark Poster's dismissal of alternative theories about the family is rooted in the related charges that such theories are individualistic or ahistorical. Since the individual does not have the ability to transcend his social setting, all theories advocating individualism are but reflections of the class order or their historical setting. Freud's theory of neurosis is a brilliant revelation of the capitalist psyche, but what Freud describes as a universal crisis of the individual soul, the Oedipus complex, is but a symptom of bourgeois maladies.[16] More sophisticated patrons of depth psychology, like Jacques Lacan, fail to see the historically limited horizons of their analytic tools.[17] The same is true, of course, of more empiricist investigators (like Talcott Parsons), who erect the model of the bourgeois family into a universal norm for the rest of developing mankind.[18] Marx, of course, failed to see the vested interest of the working-class male in the domination of his wife and children.[19] And, despite their rejection of Marx's uncritical optimism, even the adherents of the Frankfurt school evince a male supremicist lingering for the patriarchal family, substituting, in Poster's phrase, "cosmic cop-outs" for concrete historical analysis. Although Marx may have erred in linking the family structure too mechanistically with given modes of production, a Frankfurt theorist like Marcuse is guilty of a more reactionary sin: He "celebrated the very individual autonomy which he sharply rejects elsewhere in the text as a liberal illusion bound to the performance principle," that is, roughly, The Work Ethic.[20]

For Poster, the contemporary "family" is but one model of what historically families have been and what possibly they might be. Poster, despite his commendations of the bourgeoisie for refraining from medieval child-beating, favorably contrasts both the aristocratic and the peasant family of the feudal period with the dominant capitalist forms. The aristocratic and the peasant household eschewed the capitalist obsession with cleanliness, concretized in bowel training and in the curbing of childhood sex-play.[21] Although enlightened thinking has curbed

16. Ibid., p. 40.
17. Ibid., p. 96.
18. Ibid., p. 83.
19. Ibid., p. xviii.
20. Ibid., p. 62.
21. Ibid., p. 187.

"castration threats and rigid anal discipline," Poster bemoans that "toilet training is still atttempted early and is done with scrupulous attention to remove wastes from the child's body."[22] The attention to such discipline is undoubtedly related to punctuality, self-discipline, and other bourgeois perversions. In feudal times, "beatings on the backside contributed not to a secret sense of guilt, not to traits of cleanliness, order and punctuality."[23]

The bourgeois family, which by dint of emulation has replaced the less inhibited working-class family, has substituted for overt forms of discipline the more insidious threat of withdrawal of love. This results in (1) the child giving up sensual gratification in exchange for parent love and (2) the subsequent identification of the child with the parent of the same sex. In turn, as patterns of male dominance and age difference emerge, "the bourgeois family structure is suited preeminently to generate people with ego structures that foster the illusion that they are autonomous beings."[24]

The evils of the bourgeois family are legion: male and age-oriented domination, the restriction of role models for children to their parents, limitations on sexually accessible objects for all family members and the sole sexual legitimacy of the heterosexual couple, the totality of parental authority over the children based upon the withdrawal of love, and the absence of wider community dependence.[25] This bourgeois family structure has of late experienced a crisis, as a result (according to Poster) of increased permissiveness, increased toleration of divorce, feminist demands, the persistence of the idea of romantic love as a basis of a marriage, the persistence of the stereotype on which the narrow nuclear family is based. All in all, Poster presages a dim future for the bourgeois family.[26]

Poster demands in his vision of the future a cessation of the attraction of the "ideologies" of romantic love and maternal care, the democratization of relationships between husband and wife and between parents and children within the family, the integration of the family into a wider democratic community, and the disappearance of sex, age, and class as sources of social status. "Multiple patterns of

22. Ibid., p. 201.
23. Ibid., p. 182.
24. Ibid., p. 178.
25. Ibid., p. 202.
26. Ibid., p. 200.

marital relations must be recognized, so that feelings of affection can expand throughout the community."[27] The problems diagnosed by Freud in the form of the Oedipus complex are related to class society. If children were raised in a kibbutz-type setting, these difficulties would not appear. Children would not be closely tied to any particular parental authority figures but, rather, would be tied in to a larger community for both work and identification purposes.[28] If such communal arrangements seem not very helpful with regard to immediate public policy issues, Poster discerns some hope in even more pedestrian efforts at change: "Current efforts to politicize issues of family structure, such as the rights of gays to marry, the rights of women to control their reproductive capabilities, and so forth, open up for the first time new levels of social reform."[29] Although Poster talks about the relative autonomy of the family vis-à-vis the mode of production, it seems hard to credit his materialist argument at all if such experiments were possible in what he believes to be a repressive bourgeois society.

John Rawls

Ending the prolonged period of less-than-benign neglect for ethical theory endemic to academic positivism, John Rawls's *A Theory of Justice* appeared as a Godsend to philosophers paralyzed by the fact-value dichotomy or bored by analytic word-chopping. Rawls attempted to resurrect what the original liberal thinkers had sought to accomplish in their state-of-nature theories: an account of justice that the reader would find conformable with his or her considered judgments about that phenomenon when he or she would be in a state of "reflective equilibrium." In short, just as we might revise our judgment about events in the light of an attractive theory explaining those events, so, when presented with a set of theoretical explanations of the nature of justice (constructed originally from "considered judgments"), we might in the light of the best such construction amend our ethical intuitions.[30]

Rawls's theory involves two principles: (1) each person's right to

---

27. Ibid., p. 204.
28. Ibid., pp. 204–5.
29. Ibid., p. 203.
30. John Rawls, *A Theory of Justice* (Cambridge: Harvard University Press, 1981), pp. 49–51.

the most extensive system of liberty for each compatible with a similar system of liberty for all, and (2) an arrangement of social and economic inequality that will be of the greatest benefit to representative members of the least advantaged social group, such inequality to be connected to positions available under the rubric of "fair equality of opportunity." The principle of liberty has priority over the second principle, and within the latter, the provision of fair equality of opportunity has precedence over what Rawls calls the "difference principle" ("greatest benefit of the least advantaged"). The summary of Rawlsian justice is that "all social primary goods—liberty and opportunity, income and wealth, and the bases of self-respect—are to be distributed equally unless an unequal distribution of any or all of these goods is to the advantage of the least favored."

This definition of justice is a more precise interpretation of the second principle, which permits inequalities provided that such are "equally open" and "for the advantage of all." "Equally open" might mean equality regarding careers open to talents: a system of natural liberty. Now such a system will contain many factors of an arbitrary kind influencing such inequality. More to our point, besides intelligence and other natural assets, the family operating through inheritance, reputation, environment, and other less tangible channels, may be a source for the advantages of some and the disadvantages of others. The liberal construction of the second principle corrects this condition by demanding "fair equality of opportunity": those with similar skills should have similar opportunities. Specifically, "It may be worthwhile to recall the importance of preventing excessive accumulations of property and wealth and of maintaining equal opportunities of education for all."[32]

The problem of the liberal construction is that, although it abstracts from the morally arbitrary elements connected with the historical accidents of family, it permits too much in the way of influence due to another morally arbitrary source: the natural lottery.[33] From Rawls's moral point of view, no merit comes from accidents of birth per se. Intelligence per se, then, ought to be no more a source of merit, or of advantage, than family name. What, though, of merit arising from a proper management of circumstances? Such a proper use may itself

31. Ibid., p. 303.
32. Ibid., pp. 72–73.
33. Ibid., p. 74.

be the result of either (1) accident, in which case it cannot be a source of merit, or (2) a natural gift, itself the result of the "natural lottery" and therefore in itself not properly in the moral sense a title to advantage. For Rawls, then, just as we do not bow to nature in the form of natural disasters of a physical type, neither should we bow to it in terms of natural disadvantages of a personal kind, since these are not personally merited. Nor, as we have seen, are natural advantages merited. The latter must, in Rawls's mind, be made to serve the former.

How, though, does Rawls hope to convince those of us who might be so advantaged to bow to the demands of justice? We will all admit that nobody is a good judge when it comes to evaluating his own case. Justice must mean impartiality, fairness. To see the reasonableness of the two principles we must go back to an "original position." This, as I have suggested, is a concept borrowed from the state-of-nature theorists. It is a state of affairs that antedates political convention. But for Rawls one does not (as one might for Hobbes) need a time machine to get to the original position. Nor will one (as one might for Locke) require fare for passage to exotic, primitive backwaters. Anytime one wishes one can visit the original position at will, as a "thought experiment," by stepping behind the "veil of ignorance," where the conditions of impartiality are guaranteed by the epistemologically amnesic conditions of the transitory inhabitants of that zone.[34]

Although I am equipped with all the latest findings of psychological, economic, and sociological science, although I am rational enough to find the proper means to pursue whatever ends I have in mind, I, in that state, do not know who I am. That is, I do not know what social status I occupy, how wealthy I am, what ethnic stock I derive from, what occupations or family position I might have: All relevant personal information is not accessible to me.[35] So, since I want to minimize my risks when society is finally (hypothetically) called into existence, I minimize my chances. I want equal liberty because I do not know what kinds of opinions I might have politically or religiously—they might be very unpopular. I want fair equality of opportunity because I might not come from a family of wealth. And *if* inequalities are permitted, I want them to redound to the least ad-

34. Ibid., p. 136.
35. Ibid., pp. 137, 142.

vantaged because when I emerge from the original position, I might be one of those least advantaged.[36]

Whereas the early liberal theorists had advocated a form of government in which legislation would be legitimate only through the consent of the governed, under Rawls's conception, since we already know what people ought to consent to, then it seems that it would be morally permissible, if the power were given, to impose a Rawlsian constitution upon the citizenry. At any rate, there is nothing in Rawls's "moral intuitions" that cannot be found in the editorial pages of any liberal newspaper. If the "least advantaged" are unable to articulate their own needs, much less able to generate a philosophical structure like *A Theory of Justice*, there will always be room for an enlightened elite that is ready, through force of guilt or cunning, to step in as full-time social guardians of the disadvantaged. The present orientation of higher education makes possible an increasing stock of such socially minded planners.

The family's place in such a conception is not an entirely hospitable one.[37] On the positive side, the fact that each individual in the original position may be a parent motivates planning for the well-being of future generations in the construction of a just society.[38] Then, the family inculcates in the child a necessary prologue to the morality of principles upon which justice is based. This is the obedience-oriented, love-rewarded morality of adult authority, based upon precepts not fully grasped in their rational dimension by the child.[39] Transitional to the stage of principle is the morality of associations: school, club, neighborhood, and other more or less transitory positions. The family, thus, is a setting wherein morality is inculcated in its most rudimentary and temporary modes. Yet the family is not necessary for progress to higher modes: "In a broader inquiry the institutions of the family might be questioned, and other arrangements might indeed prove to be preferable. But presumably the account of the morality of authority could, if necessary, be adjusted to fit these different schemes."[40] Without the institution of the family we could still move toward a Kantian kingdom of morally autonomous ends divorced from nature.

36. Ibid., p. 176.
37. For a complementary remark, Ibid., p. 105.
38. Ibid., pp. 128–29.
39. Ibid., pp. 466–67.
40. Ibid., pp. 462–63.

"Once a morality of principle is accepted, however, moral attitudes are no longer connected solely with the well-being and approval of particular individuals and groups, but are shaped by a conception of right chosen irrespective of these contingencies. Our moral sentiments display an independence from the accidental circumstances of our world. . . ."[41]

How necessary is the family? For Rawls, not only is the family not essential for the just society, it actually impedes the application of the second principle. Abolish inheritance and you still cannot achieve a strict "fair equality of opportunity": "Even the willingness to make an effort, to try, and so to be deserving in the ordinary sense is itself dependent upon happy family and social circumstances."[42] As long as the family persists, there will be inequality between individuals, since, "if there are variations among families in the same sector in how they shape the child's aspirations, then while fair equality of opportunity may obtain between sectors, equal chances between individuals will not."[43] Should we then abolish the family in order to usher in undiluted justice (say, as Plato does)? While theoretically unobjectionable, such a project for Rawls is both impractical and unnecessary. "Taken by itself and given a certain primacy, the idea of equality of opportunity inclines in this direction. But within the context of the theory of justice as a whole, there is much less urgency to take this course."[44] The "difference principle" so defines the basis of social and economic inequalities as to make those that still exist easily tolerable, since they are now made to work in behalf of the least advantaged.[45] The family, then, remains as an accident of history: at best, tolerable; at worst, the subject of interventionist educational and redistributional projects of a theoretically punitive kind.

Yves Simon

Unlike liberal theorists, Yves Simon believed government to be not a necessary evil but a genuine good.[46] The study of politics involves

---

41. Ibid., p. 475.
42. Ibid., p. 74.
43. Ibid., p. 301.
44. Ibid., p. 511.
45. Ibid., p. 512.
46. Yves R. Simon, *Philosophy of Democratic Government* (Chicago: University of Chicago Press, 1958), p. 59.

two principles: that of authority and that of autonomy. For Simon, the least interesting, the most accidental feature of authority involves its character as substitutional. The guidance a parent offers a child illustrates this character, as does the guidance that the mentally competent offer the retarded. Whenever adults themselves lack the capacity to be prudent, those who maintain such virtue exercise such substitutional authority over them. This form of authority is legitimate only insofar as it is genuinely necessary: In normal cases its exercise is transitory.[47]

Human goods are such that even if there is unanimous consent about a given end, the choice of means to pursue that end may be a matter of debate. A prudent choice of means, that is, is never so fully determined by the end to be achieved as to render that choice totally intelligible, totally explainable in a fashion amenable to rule-bound reference. *If* a collective action by a community is required, even if the community is composed of virtuous citizens, disagreement about means will impede such action unless there exists a source of authoritative judgment.[48]

Within a given community, individuals and families *rightly* pursue particular goods. In fact, if everyone in a community were forced to pursue the common good materially, that community would be a dead one.[49] To an extent the common good *requires* individuals to pursue their particular good. Simon's classic example is the wife's desire to defend her guilty husband, a legitimate and necessary obligation counterpoised to the court's obligation to pursue impartial justice.[50] Even in the realm of genuine public goods, each proponent (doctors, generals, teachers) views one public function the sole public function.[51] Public goods, theorizes Simon, require the organization and setting of priorities, a matter that their various practitioners would be prone to overlook, given their dedication to a *partial* but common service. In Aristotelian terms, Simon is here referring to politics as the architectonic science.

Thus, rightfully, individuals may hold views, in a formal fashion, of the common good that really impede communal action. The com-

47. Ibid., pp. 8–9, 37.
48. Ibid., pp. 27–28, 32–33.
49. Ibid., p. 55.
50. Ibid., p. 41.
51. Ibid., pp. 55–56.

mon good must be viewed, however, in a material—that is, a concrete—mode.[52] The most essential function of authority for Simon involves the *conscious* pursuit of the common good. To repeat, this places him at odds with the bulk of the classical liberal tradition. Some of this disagreement involves the question of government as an evil, which Simon denies. More important, we believe, is the classical liberal belief in the power of the "invisible hand." In its most articulate form, that of Hayek's "spontaneous order," the liberal theorist denigrates the kind of simple order generated by limited mortals, usually in the form of commands, preferring the more complicated order generated from human needs by a multitude of actors seeking no other good but self-interest: as Hayek puts it, of human acting, but not of human design; as earlier theorists conceptualized it, the creation of public benefits from private vices.[53]

Unlike the proponents of classical liberalism, Simon believes individual reason to have an architectonic role in the production of order within society. Like the liberal, though, Simon is not romantic about the sheer goodness of governmental power. It can, of course, be invasive of values rightfuly esteemed in a decent community. Hence Simon distinguishes between democratic government, which is but a specification of the personnel, and "political" goverment, which provides bulwarks between the citizen and state power.[54] "Political" governments need not be democratic. Aristocracy in circumstances has checked despotic monarchical power. Nor need democracy be necessarily "political," since the masses can themselves be despotic. The family can, of course, be one such bulwark or protective sphere. Furthermore, as we shall comment upon below, the best sort of government skillfully delegates responsibilities to infragovernmental organizations.[55] Such delegation or, better, recognition and protection of local or familial prerogative is for Simon not merely prudent but eminently just. It illustrates what Simon terms the principle of autonomy.

In the political community, as we have seen, there are two major orders. The one pursues the particular good: the household or the

---

52. Ibid., p. 48.
53. F. A. von Hayek, *The Constitution of Liberty* (Chicago: University of Chicago Press, 1960), pp. 160–61.
54. Simon, *n*. 46, p. 72.
55. Ibid., p. 131.

family. The other, at least in a formal sense, pursues the common good: the order of function (public health, police power, etc.). "The metaphysical law which demands such diversity demands also that no task which can be satisfactorily fulfilled by the smaller unit should ever be assumed by the larger unit.[56] What Simon terms the principle of autonomy enunciated above requires that "satisfactorily" mean more than simple efficiency. Whenever a larger unit does the task of a smaller, the latter unit does not have the opportunity to fulfill itself through work (smaller units here can be either smaller jurisdictions of government or the household or the individual). Whatever need *not* be done by government at any level *must* not be done. If it were done, that would constitute paternalism: unnecessary substitutional authority. Simon is willing here to trade off efficiency against the gain in autonomy, in self-governance, and self-actualization.[57] Needless to say, then, where a task can be done better by the family, or where it can be done despite some loss of efficiency, it is desirable and just that the family, not the state, attempt that task. The task of education immediately comes to mind here.

According to Simon, two principle threats assault the family. The first involves a preoccupation with equality of opportunity. Assaults on inheritance, as we have seen, illustrate this danger. "But if the right of inheritance is suppressed, all are deprived of the advantages procured by a system of economic circumstances favorable to conjugal faithfulness and paternal devotion, favorable to the stability of the home, and capable of giving man great comfort in his unequal struggle with time and death."[58] In the area of education, the unequal conditions of families with regard to the generation of atmosphere and traits conducive to learning make some advocates of equality of opportunity appear as radical in their demands for the abolition of the family as does Plato's *Republic*. Simon counters, "A policy of equal opportunity begins to be harmful when it threatens to dissolve the small communities from which men derive their best energies in the hard accomplishments of daily life."[59] The fulfillment of a potential skill and its contribution to the life of a community may be a good thing, but it is only one good among many. The proponents of equal-

56. Ibid., p. 129.
57. Ibid., p. 130.
58. Ibid., p. 228.
59. Ibid., pp. 228–29.

ity of opportunity wear ideological blinders with regard to other values. "By mistake the great goods connected with integration in a stable home were not counted among the goods for the possession of which there is a question of giving individuals opportunity and equal opportunity."[60]

The second danger to the family comes from technological advance and subsequent urbanization. The family has its most conclusive setting in the countryside, namely, in the farm-situated economy, with its simple tasks capable of fulfillment by all, conducive to democratic rotation of power, where smallness gives each individual a better chance of recognition.[61] The city, on the other hand, as a quickly changing environment, endangers stability in familial relations: "Insofar as men deprived of community life and delivered to loneliness are ready material for antidemocratic movements, it must be confessed that technology, by creating circumstances unfavorable to the family community, prepared material for government by the leaders of the mob."[62]

On the other hand, the rural setting goes hand in hand with paternalism: There is a chance to be recognized, but recognized as a child. True justice cannot occur within the family, which is based upon love, not ethical reflection.[63] Then again, the rural family is insular, possessed of a fear of, or hostility to, strangers. The city, on the other hand, through its anonymity offers a wider possibility for individual autonomy. And of course, it may be a better setting for the development of toleration or cosmopolitan sentiments.[64] At any rate, Simon is not an enemy of technological growth and wishes for some balance to be struck between the ascending town and the declining countryside.[65]

Robert Nisbet

For Robert Nisbet also, the direction of modern society is not conducive to the preservation of the family. Although the decline of the church is widely bemoaned, the continued transfer of functions once performed by the family to other institutions, especially the state, makes such regret mere handwringing. If professional child-care centers re-

60. Ibid., p. 228.
61. Ibid., p. 306.
62. Ibid., p. 316.
63. Ibid., p. 303.
64. Ibid., pp. 317, 303.
65. Ibid., pp. 320–21.

place parental day care, then all the governmental subsidies and all the national conferences on family life will fail to restore the imperiled family institution. The rub is, therefore, that the more that is done by government to "save the family," the more the family becomes imperiled.[66]

Why is the family worth saving? First, according to Nisbet, because, unlike the anonymity the citizen shares in the state, within the family (and other "intermediate institutions") there is genuine community. The "anomie," "alienation," and boredom of contemporary society are signs of a decline of community.[67] What emerges to replace such communities as once did exist is the illusory community of the state.[68] We feel attachment to the families, the seen, the tangible. Modern government, to a preeminent degree, and modern large organizations cannot give us that tangibility and hence cannot generate that affection. That man is a social being means, for Nisbet, that the "atomistic individual" is an abstraction: Man always exists within social contexts. And the social context most conducive to concrete perception of participation and freedom are the intermediary associations, above all else the family.[69]

In the second place, the family provides the individual with genuine protection of his rights and happiness, the main danger to which is the growth of the state. As we shall see, the main tendency is for a continually fragmented citizen body to confront a continually growing state power. There must be effective buffers between the citizen and the state. These buffers must not be mere paper constitutional provisions but rather they must be pluralistic social forces. Among these genuine checks upon state power is the family.[70]

For Nisbet, the spirit of étatism constitutes the single most dangerous threat to liberty in the modern age. That spirit is to be found in early modern thinkers like Hobbes, but more especially in Rousseau. As we have noted above, Rousseau's writings seem ambivalent toward the family. In the *Discourse on Inequality* he treats the family as a natural institution (we must bear in mind, though, that the *most*

---

66. Robert A. Nisbet, *The Quest for Community* (New York: Oxford University Press, 1953), pp. 57, 61.
67. Ibid., p. 17.
68. Ibid., p. 33.
69. Ibid., p. 50.
70. Ibid., p. 271.

natural state for man is one of sheer asociality).[71] In the writings that Nisbet stresses, especially the *Social Contract*, Rousseau displays a hostility for all intermediary associations: the state, representing the General Will, is congruent with the will toward equality present in each citizen but opposed to wills oriented toward particular goods. Intermediary associations, like the family, are the breeding ground of those divisive wills. The society of the *Social Contract* thus presents us with the citizen as subject and the citizen as legislator.[72] It is a triumph of morality over nature, of willed equality over natural inequality. To the extent to which the family exists, to that extent the triumph would seem regrettably incomplete.

The isolated citizen and the sovereign community are characteristic of all modern political life subsequent to Rousseau. In totalitarian regimes, "What works toward the creation of the masses works also toward the establishment of the absolute state. And everything that augments the power and influence of the state in its relation to the individual serves also to increase the scope of the masses."[73] But even liberal capitalist democracy manifests a similar, but controlled tendency: "Society was envisaged by the classical economist as being, naturally, an aggregate of socially and culturally emancipated individuals, each free to respond to the drives that lay buried in his nature."[74] The model of economic man so envisioned, according to Nisbet, is an abstraction from the orderly stability of the intermediary associations that survived the atomistic divisions sponsored by the modern state: "Most of the relative stability of nineteenth century capitalism arose from the fact of the very *incompleteness* of the capitalist revolution."[75] That revolution, which is in fact not a revolution of capitalism but, as Nisbet concedes, one of the modern state, is the cause of what politically is perceived as powerlessness and what psychologically passes as alienation. "To compare the position of the political power of the State in the thirteenth century with that power today is to realize that fundamental among all the 'emancipation' of modern history has been the emancipation of the State from the restrictive

---

71. Strauss, *n*. 1, p. 291.
72. Nisbet, *n*. 66, pp. 146, 150–51.
73. Ibid., p. 198.
74. Ibid., pp. 236–37.
75. Ibid., p. 237, emphasis in the original.

network of religious, economic and moral authorities that bound it at an earlier time."[76]

Nisbet would wish for the revival of a liberalism akin to that of Félicité Robert de Lamennais: "It is neither the individual nor the state that forms the basis of Lamennais's philosophy of freedom. It is the intermediate association. Not natural man but social man is the unit of society, and man is made social only by his membership in the smaller associations of family, church, community, and guild."[77] Property for Lamennais is important because only in it resides the family's security. And the family is the only source through which the individual gains conscious membership into the wider society of the living and the dead.[78] Lamennais is opposed to centralization of any kind: The proper political relationship is not that between the sovereign community and the naked citizen but that between the central government and living, local communes.[79]

There need not be an essential tension between capitalism and the family, Nisbet concludes. The family, after all, supplied for earlier capitalism its stability by giving material inducement to its members to improve their households. "Had it not been for the profound incentives supplied by the family and, equally important, the capacity of the extended family to supply a degree, however minimal, of mutual aid in time of distress, it is a fair guess that capitalism would have failed before it was well underway."[80] A capitalism based upon intermediary institutions is the best obstacle to the growth of the state, whereas without such institutions, with people a pile of disconnected, individualistic atoms, capitalism only invites such a statist political order.[81] Nisbet then calls for a new policy of laissez-faire: "To create conditions within which autonomous individuals could prosper, could be emancipated from the binding ties of kinship, class, and community, was the objective of the older *laissez-faire*. To create conditions within which *autonomous groups* may prosper must be, I believe, the prime objective of the new *laissez-faire*.[82]

76. Ibid., p. 109.
77. Nisbet, "The Politics of Pluralism: Lamennais," *n.* 4, p. 39.
78. Ibid., p. 42.
79. Ibid., pp. 42–43.
80. Nisbet, *n.* 66, p. 68.
81. Ibid., p. 241.
82. Ibid., p. 278.

F. A. Hayek

F. A. Hayek's liberalism has been conceived of as a conscious attempt to break theoretically from what he perceives to be the rationalist, or pseudoindividualistic, assumptions of the continental liberal tradition. The virtue of a free society, according to Hayek, rests upon its ability to use successfully the information a multitude of social actors possess *qua* individuals but which no one of them commands as a whole. Centralized planning, the command economy, subordinates the variety of human knowledge to the beliefs and desires of the planner. It must also be emphasized that even the individual actor behaves in a fashion that he cannot fully explain in terms of rules he can fully articulate. The progress of civilization depends upon the growth of spontaneous order—the result of human action but not of deliberate human design.[83] Just as language is the product of no one speaker, but enables many speakers to pursue varied, unique projects, so also do custom and the market manifest a complex order that is truly social: not reducible to individual intent, though of inestimable importance in assisting individual plans. Rationalistic liberalism extolls the virtue of reason; Hayekian liberalism attempts a critique of reason's pretenses.

Hayek does not spend much time discussing the family in his *magnum opus* of political theory, *The Constitution of Liberty*. When he does, however, his remarks are centered upon a discussion of equality of opportunity. Strict proponents of equality of opportunity oppose themselves to the family with regard to inheritance and educational advantages (familiar from our reading of Simon and Rawls). In short, these egalitarians wish to remove what they view as the harmful obstacle nurture places upon nature. But, Hayek objects, if a characteristic possessed by an individual is of value to society, what differences does it make if that trait is the result of convention or accident, such as family setting, or a result of natural gift? If equality of opportunity demands meritocracy, then are the biological traits inherited from our parents any more merited than, say, inheritance of money or of a good name?[84]

Note here the similarity of argumentation in Hayek and Rawls: For

83. Hayek, *n*. 53, pp. 62–63.
84. Ibid., p. 90.

both, the notion of merit is highly problematic.[85] Ultimate for both theorists, merit is a Kantian phenomenon: entirely unseen by observers, tied to effort or good will rather than to result. Since results are tied to morally arbitrary factors, Rawls and Hayek view our evaluations of results as a matter of convention, of appearance, not connected with nature. For Rawls, the fact that intelligence is as unearned an asset as inheritance entails that both be subject to egalitarian legislation; for Hayek, since both assets are equally unsupported by merit, neither ought to be expropriated or manipulated coercively by the government.

Further features of Hayek's defense of the family connect it with the notion of the spontaneous order. Few would deny that there are certain socially valuable traits the development of which may require more than one generation. Disciplined habits, manners, long-run perspectives are in many cases the result in children of certain established family backgrounds. While such traits are usually valued, others may be of service when societal changes ensue. What these others may be is to some extent at present unkown. Inherited wealth is the concrete instrument by which the near necessary conditions for those traits are transmitted to the next generation: "The fact is that it is no less of an advantage to the community if at least some children can start with the advantage which at any given time only wealthy homes can offer than if some children inherit great intelligence or are taught better morals at home."[86]

In a progressive society, what is a luxury one year becomes a "necessity" for many in the next. It is of value to a community, therefore, that varying life-styles be experimented with to reveal their virtues and shortcomings. In a planned society, such a function would have to be assigned arbitrarily by authority. In a free society, the accident of inherited wealth plays the same role.[87] The burden of such experimentation in the planned society would be borne by almost everybody in that society through taxation; failure would be costly. In a society characterized by spontaneous order, such failures in "life styles" would affect usually only those rich enough to indulge; successes, of course, could gradually be imitated by all, in the way in which fads

85. Ibid., pp. 94–95.
86. Ibid., p. 90.
87. Ibid., pp. 44–45.

in language catch on and Edsels meet their demise. Accumulated capital in the form of inheritance plays here for Hayek a productive social role.

Besides the danger of impeding spontaneous order inherent in a unified state educational system, particularly one with radical egalitarian premises, Hayek has a positive argument in favor of the family's role in education. "A passionate desire for knowledge or an unusual combination of interests may be more important than the more visible gifts of any testable capacities; and a background of general knowledge produced by family environment often contributes more to achievement than natural capacity."[88]

HAYEKIAN THEMES

Allan Carlson's writings on the family are an unusual blend of Nisbetian and Hayekian themes. For Carlson, the modern family and capitalism are interdependent. The prosperity brought about by the market has eliminated the cruel treatment, sexual harassment and amoral neglect of the child in precapitalist Europe.[89] In turn, the family has given the economy a highly mobile community, responsive to market factors. If, as in the view of the classical economists, man is by nature indolent, then the family provides a powerful incentive for productivity: the improvement of the material estate of our loved ones.[90] In explicitly Hayekian terms, Carlson attributes the successes of capitalism to a continuing precapitalist moral tradition. Such a tradition, the result of nobody's planning, which reason is made to serve rather than to construct, prevented the capitalist order from succumbing to nihilistic individualism.[91] It is no mistake that Marxists attack the family; for Carlson, the family provides a context for the development of discipline, promptness, future-orientation—all the traits required by progressive capitalism.[92] Carlson has noted that positive state intervention to assist the family has in fact led to further atrophy of the

---

88. Ibid., p. 386.
89. Allan Carlson, "The Family and Liberal Capitalism," *Modern Age* 26 (nos. 3–4, Summer–Fall 1982): 367–68.
90. Ibid., p. 368–69.
91. Ibid., p. 369.
92. Ibid., pp. 366, 371.

family's role.[93] Carlson's general advice for public policy is for non-discrimination against the family, particularly in areas of taxation.[94]

Paul Schrecker's description of the functions of the family is reminiscent of a Hayekian theme. Schrecker illustrates his thesis about the family's role as the main conveyor of tradition by attention to language. There are many aspects to language that can be taught by rules, but what Schrecker calls the "inner form" of the language cannot be taught without apprenticeship, without imitation. "The highest norm, the 'inner form' of a language, is refractory to rational apprehension; accent, intonation, and similar phonetic factors resist rational definition—let alone systematic acquisition by any means other than imitation—quite as stubbornly as any sensorial quality."[95] The setting for imitation is what the family provides.

Why not, though, admit that not all families succeed at such apprenticeship? Why not relegate such responsibility to the experts via a state-imposed system? We note that such a system would imitate the most radical proposals of Plato's *Republic*: The child must be removed from the parents before the near-irreversible effects of a bad imitative model have set in.[96]

Schrecker's response is that language is more than a vehicle for the communication of facts.[97] To have such an expert-dominated system might purge language of otherwise desirable facets, like its use in storytelling. Mistakes, to be sure, are made in the family. But these do not spread far, whereas the mistakes made and the idiosyncrasies generated by centralized language-teaching at the infantile stage may become irreversible and universal.[98] And who, by the way, is to judge what is to be so taught?[99] Would that not be to subordinate language, which is so rich (as a "spontaneous order" ought to be), to the limited judgment of the linguistic "experts"? Even highly technical languages, like mathematics, require some plasticity, and given the "tacit

93. Allan Carlson, "Families, Sex, and the Liberal Agenda," *The Human Life Review* 6 (no. 3, Summer 1980): 31.

94. Allan Carlson, "Taxes and Families," *The Human Life Review* 9 (no. 1 Winter 1983) 38–45.

95. Paul Schrecker, "The Family: Conveyance of Tradition," in R. Anshen, ed., *The Family: Its Function and Destiny* (New York: Harper and Brothers, 1959), pp. 495–96.

96. Ibid., p. 501.

97. Ibid., p. 500.

98. Ibid., p. 502.

99. Ibid., p. 501.

dimensions" of language, its refusal to be fully comprehended save in imitation, how much of that "expert knowledge" would be effective anyhow in getting children to speak? "A frozen correctness of language conveyed to and enforced upon the children by the most rational means and suppressing their linguistic spontaneity might actually not only reduce language to the function of a mere mechanical instrument of communication—and thus render true an otherwise unwarranted philosophy of language—but in addition eventually destroy creative thought by depriving it of the supple and responsive means of expression on which it depends."[100]

For Schrecker, language is but a single instance of the way in which the family transmits tradition. "Tradition" here means, in part, those rules we operate under but which we can never fully articulate.[101] Tradition seems to have a form or logic to it, as it does in Hayek's spontaneous order. Schrecker's view is close to that of Michael Oakeshott, who posits a real difference between knowledge summed up in formulas and practical knowledge, learned only through imitation and always within a given practice (like language, morality, science). Practical knowledge involves a discernment of a logic in such a practice; Oakeshott calls it the pursuit of an intimation. In speaking, for example, no set of grammatical rules can tell me what to say: that will depend upon by discernment of what my context entails as appropriate. My judgments about appropriateness are themselves the result of my initiation into some such activity as speaking by way of apprenticeship, imitation of speakers.[102]

At any rate, for Schrecker radical change in mores requires political suppression or manipulation of the family. The family as such, though, never itself disappears. After the new regime is set in place, it also requires an effective way of transmitting its norms. The family then is made to convey new content. The experience of the family in the USSR illustrates Schrecker's point.[103]

Let us summarize the virtues and defects of Hayek's argument as well as the arguments of the two other theorists influenced by Hayek's viewpoints. One basic weakness is the notion of merit in Hayek. It

---

100. Ibid., p. 503.
101. Ibid., p. 500.
102. Michael Oakeshott, "Rationalism in Politics," "Rational Conduct" and "Political Education" in *Rationalism in Politics* (New York: Methuen Co., 1981), pp. 32–34, 97–100, 134–36.
103. Ibid., pp. 508–09.

suffers from its Kantian connection with intention, with unseen effort. Its abstraction from nature and its grounding in will detach justice from any connection with excellence, with accomplishment. On this basis, the choice between Rawls and Hayek appears settled by an arbitrary choice, there being no objective standard, like nature, to which to appeal. Again, although there is much to be said about the role of tradition in society, if we reduce ethics to mere tradition, we arrive at a form of historicist relativism. Hayek and Carlson seem to preclude any appeal to nonhistoricist ethical first principles.

On the positive side, recall Simon's discussion of the principle of autonomy. It is unjust, it is paternal, not to give each part of a community the liberty in which to exercise its powers, to actualize its own self. Even if some activity can be done more effectively by centralized authority than by some other association, the presumption is in favor of the smaller association. To be concrete and to employ Schrecker's model, even if training in speaking were better done in a centralized, coercive fashion by experts, the family, according to the principle of autonomy, ought to perform that task. Again employing Schrecker (and Oakeshott), in the teaching of language or of any tradition, imitation is crucial, not the learning of explicit rules. For the child, the most intimate model follows naturally from a most intimate relationship: that of child to parent. Following Hayek, no central planner can know the special needs of each child or have the specific concern that the parent possesses. If centralized, coercive education replaces the parent, then, the while "spontaneous order" of language and of tradition (including its "inner form") would be subjugated to the limited horizons of the planner. Mistakes made would be more difficult to correct via the transmission of tradition than they would be in the decentralized scheme involving such transmission through many families.

Needless to say, the family can transmit many different kinds of traditions, not all of which are ethically defensible. But implicit in the family structure is a set of norms hostile to the totalitarian mind. And something must be said about the healthiness of the norms, which Carlson commends, communicated by the "bourgeois family": discipline, promptness, initiative. Why not substitute a multitude of schools, of kibbutz-type settings for the family? Normally, only a parent has the incentive to attend to the time-consuming demands of the child, as Aristotle notes.

In conclusion, since Plato's *Republic* has been referred to so often in this essay, I would like to reflect upon Aristotle's philosophically principled correction of his friend. It is true that, for Aristotle, the family is much more plastic an institution than it is for, say, Simon; much more justifiably subject to political shaping than it ought to be for Hayek; much less of a community than it is for Nisbet, yet Aristotle emerges as a friend of the family and of its corollary private property.[104] Unlike most of our modern theorists, Aristotle's defense of the family appeals to nature. Human love, for Aristotle, is connected with familiarity. The strongest kind of love is love of that which is one's own. Make property communal and, though everybody "owns" it, nobody really does and, therefore, nobody cares for that property. Any common room in an American university bespeaks that point. The same is true, though, for children. If I am the Platonic "father" to a thousand children, or one of the many "mothers" in a kibbutz, Aristotle says that I am less likely to care for my children than I would for the limited number of my nephews or nieces in conventional society.[105]

What Aristotle is referring to is not simply biological parenthood. After all, my godchild may mean quite a bit to me. Rather, my "fund" of affection is limited: The wider I attempt to extend affection, the less intense it becomes, the less I care about the object of that affection. The human child needs intense affection. Or, perhaps, the parent requires powerful incentive to spend so much time and energy on a child.[106] The love of one's own appears to be the sole sure source for such energy. The family, above all else, is the nature-given channel for what I have termed the love of one's own. Its place cannot be vacant as long as "sun and man" cooperate to reproduce the human race. If the principles of a free society are going to be effective, they must become connected with the love of one's own. The defense of a free society, therefore, necessitates the defense of the family.

CONCLUSION

We began our discussion with the observation that unlike previous periods in political philosophy, contemporary mainstream political

104. Ernest Barker, ed., *The Politics of Aristotle* (New York: Oxford University Press, 1972), bk. 1. Chaps. 2, 3, and 1269a26–1270a8, 1272a21.

105. Ibid., 1261a33–1264b25.

106. Michael Novak, "Freedom and the Family," *The Human Life Review* 6, (no. 3 Summer: 1980) 52–53.

thought either pays scant attention to the family or betrays an overt hostility to that institution. We have suggested that this phenomenon is clearly foreshadowed in Kant's notion of the nature of philosophy. For Kant, the realm previously staked out for philosophy as her sphere dissolves into the domains of pure and of practical reason. Pure reason investigates affairs involving a restricted sort of formal, efficient, and material causality. This domain is the home of empirical science. Although there is a place in that sphere for final causation, for purposive explanation, the domain of the "ought" is restricted by Kant to the realm of practical reason. What would be commonly termed "values" are comprehensible in a purely formal way, detached from any substantive specification by, say, nature.

Contemporary theory, the apparent "cutting edge" (if you will) of political thought, preserves that Kantian distinction. In the case, say, of Rawlsian theory, it interests itself in a pure form, that of justice or, more important, of equality. Such equality, though, as we have seen, is inimicable to the preservation of the family. Passing from ethical theory to empirical "social science," in accordance with Kantian norms, we find much description of the family from all sorts of sociological, psychological, or economic perspectives, but no real ground for either an attack upon or a defense of that institution. Here, though, is where the historicist school in its neo-Marxist form comes in. Formal values, so the historicist would argue, always have a substance. That concrete substance is derived not from nature but from "history." History displays the changing features of all institutions, including the family. If, as neo-Marxists contend, history is moving toward the classless and propertyless society, the family will disappear along with property and its disappearance will be a good thing.

Where the family is given attention and even viewed as defensible is in conservative and classical liberal theories. I suggest that this is so because both conservative and classical liberal theory have preserved a notion of nature (natural right, natural law, natural rights) as a ground for political philosophizing. We have suggested the strengths and weaknesses of the views of representatives of these latter schools. An eclectic argument appears to me constructable from the resources of the aforementioned schools, but one with ancient precedents. This argument involves the consideration that, like any other unplanned phenemenon, the family performs a multitude of tasks that may not be performed well, if at all, by some centralized social body like the state. Some of these family functions, like the functions of language, may not be either fully known or even discoverable by that central authority. The analogue here is that of language or custom or the market place, where the limitations of what any one actor or group of actors knows or can know make concrete overall planning seemingly impossible, if not dangerous.

Even if some of the functions of the family could be more effectively performed by the state, the value of self-actualization would be lost in state assumption of familial privilege. Simon's principle of autonomy, usually termed subsidiarity, links up the defense of the family to a venerable ethical and metaphysical tradition in this way. That tradition is again apparent in our concluding remarks about a human capacity we term *spiritedness*. We have contended that the love of one's own, the capacity for an angry response to injuries, threats, and other manifestations of injustice, is in as much need of cultivation as any other strictly human feature of our psychic constitution, including reason. The need for self-actualization requires, I believe, attention to spiritedness. The family, we contend, is the most appropriate setting for the development and exercise of that capacity. It comes as no surprise, therefore, that the enemies of individuality have been as hostile to the family as they have been inimicable to property.

2

THE FAMILY AND THE STATE: A THEORETICAL FRAMEWORK

Barry W. Poulson

INTRODUCTION

The economic analysis of the family is both one of the oldest and newest fields of research. Economic historians have for a very long time recognized the role of the family as an economic organization. In societies with self-sufficient agricultural units, the family functioned as an economic organization in making decisions regarding planting, harvesting, improving the land, etc. With the onset of the Industrial Revolution, the family continued to function as an economic organization. The early putting out system in the textile industry required the contribution of each family member. While the father wove the woolen cloth, the mother might spin and the children card the raw wool. Even when textile production shifted from the home to the factory, the family often entered the early factories as an economic unit performing similar functions within the factory.[1]

Early businesses in manufacturing, trade, services, etc., were usually organized as family enterprises. For business historians, the early phases of the Industrial Revolution were essentially histories of dif-

1. For an excellent discussion of the role of the family as an economic organization during the Industrial Revolution, see Neil J. Smelser, *Social Change in the Industrial Revolution: An Application of Theory to the British Cotton Industry* (Chicago: University of Chicago Press, 1959).

ferent family businesses; invention, innovation, and operation of firms were identified with individual families. The vitality of the family as an economic organization is seen in the ubiquitous role of family enterprises right down to the present day. Business history is one of the oldest branches of research in economic history and business, and business historians have developed a rich literature that provides insights into the role of the family as an economic organization.[2]

While there is a wealth of information on the role of the family in business and economic history, a theory of the family as an economic organization has only recently been developed. Economists have begun to construct an economic theory of the family to explore the unique characteristics of decision making within the family, in contrast to other economic organizations such as the modern corporation.[3] In this study we will review this economic theory of the family, not as a comprehensive survey of this literature, but rather as a basis for analyzing the relationship between the family and the state. The latter requires an extension of the economic theory of the family to encompass the role of the family as its members' agent vis-à-vis other institutions, including the state. We will also introduce a dynamic theory of the family to explain how changes within the family and in the family environment affect the decision process of the family over time.

THE ECONOMIC THEORY OF THE FAMILY

A Conceptual Framework

The family, for our purposes, consists of a group of individuals related by blood, marriage, or adoption. Transactions within the family take place within the framework of rules for behavior that define the role of each family member and govern members' interactions. Such rules are rarely defined in terms of a formal written contractual agreement, but rather evolve mainly through custom and traditions within the family and in the broader society.

2. The role of the family in the early development of business enterprise is explored in Burton Benedict, "Family Firms and Economic Development," *Southwestern Journal of Anthropology* 24 (Spring 1968): 1–19.

3. See, for example, Theodore W. Schultz, ed., *Economics of the Family: Marriage, Children, and Human Capital,* published for the National Bureau of Economic Research (Chicago: University of Chicago Press, 1973); Gary S. Becker, *A Treatise on the Family* (Cambridge: Harvard University Press, 1981).

Transactions within the family, just as transactions in other economic organizations, involve the interaction of two or more individuals in the exchange or transfer of property rights. However, family transactions are uniquely influenced by several characteristics: (1) transactions between family members do not necessarily involve an equivalent exchange of property rights in the sense that market transactions do, but often involve transfers of property rights; (2) the family members engage in a wide range of interdependent transactions; (3) the family represents its members as an agent involving transactions with other institutions in the society; (4) family transactions involve a dynamic sequence of transactions over long periods of time.

The characteristic of the family that most distinguishes it from other forms of economic organization is the unique identity and interdependence of family members. In the analysis of market transactions, economists traditionally assume an economic organization in which the identity of the transacting parties is unknown; transactions by anonymous individuals in a competitive market is the foundation of economic analysis. Recently economists have applied the tools of economic analysis to nonmarket transactions in which the identity of the transacting parties influences the outcome, for example, in the analysis of clubs, labor unions, insurance societies, etc. The family is distinguished from these organizations by the predominance of personal identity and personal interaction in the transactions between family members.[4]

The Family as a Welfare-Maximizing Institution

Traditionally economists have viewed the family as a collection of individuals in which the individual family members' utility is assumed to be independent of the utility of other family members. The total utility of the family is simply the sum of the utility of each member of the family, with no interdependence in their utility functions. This assumption simplifies analysis because then the decision making of individuals within the family is no different from their decisions as separate individuals. However, this approach eliminates the most important characteristic of the family, namely, the interdependence of the welfare of the different family members.

---

4. These unique characteristics of family transactions are explored in Yoram Ben-Porath, "The F-Connection: Families, Friends, and Firms and the Organization of Exchange," *Population and Development Review* 6 (no. 1, March 1980): 1–31.

The family is a complex institution in which the welfare of the individual family members is not independent from that of the other members of the family. Interdependence of the welfare of individual family members results in decision making that is unique to the family as an economic institution. The welfare function of the family is not simply the aggregation of the individual utility functions of its members, but emerges from a decision process that reflects interdependent utility functions. In recent years, economists have begun to develop a new economic theory of the family as a welfare-maximizing institution in which this more complex decision process can be analyzed.[5]

In this new economic theory, the family is viewed as analogous to a firm. While the objective of the firm is to maximize profits, the goal of the family is to maximize family welfare. The family's happiness or well-being is a function of "family goods" such as health, nutrition, education, recreation, entertainment, etc. Family welfare also depends upon services that are often unique to the family, such as companionship and love between family members, and upon the care provided to family members at different stages of the life cycle, such as care for the young and the aged. The family often provides a form of insurance to family members in such times of stress as illness, death, and unemployment. Note the distinction here between family goods and services on the one hand and market goods and services on the other. The latter affect the family's welfare in the sense that they are inputs in the production of more basic "family goods."

Just as a business firm is a production unit in combining certain inputs to produce market goods and services, the family is viewed as a production unit combining inputs to produce "family goods." The resource inputs available to the family include not only market goods and services, but also the time of the family members. Before a market good such as food can yield a family good such as nutrition, it must be combined with the time of family members in purchasing, preparing, cooking, and eating the food. In the production process, the food may also generate other family goods and services besides

---

5. This approach to an economic theory of the family is developed in Theodore W. Schultz, ed., *n*. 3; see especially the work in that volume by Gary S. Becker, "A Theory of Marriage," and Robert J. Willes, "Economic Theory of Fertility Behavior." See also the following works by Gary Becker, "A Theory of the Allocation of Time," *Economic Journal* 75 (Sept. 1965); *Human Capital: A Theoretical and Empirical Analysis with Special Reference to Education*, published for the National Bureau of Economic Research (New York: Columbia University Press, 1964); *A Treatise on the Family, n. 3*.

nutrition, such as health, and more esoteric family services, such as companionship, friendship, love, caring, and so forth.

The inclusion of time as an input into the family production process implies a major reformulation of the economic theory of the family. The family faces a resource constraint that is set not only by the limited income and wealth available to consume or save, but also by the time available to family members. In the traditional economic theory, the time utilized by family members in producing family goods is productive in the same sense that time spent in the labor force generating income is productive. In order to maximize family welfare, each family member must allocate his or her time between market activities that generate income, and family activities that produce family goods. The objective of each family member is to maximize the family goods that they consume. However, in the new economic theory of the family, love and caring between family members leads to intrafamily transfers of market goods and services and allocation of time between market activities and family activities so as to maximize the welfare of the family as a whole. The assumption of interdependence of welfare functions among family members leads to a quite different allocation of the family's limited resources than would occur with independent welfare functions.

Each family's ability to maximize family welfare depends upon its ability to produce family goods. We can think of a production function for the family analogous to the production function of the firm, relating the welfare of the family to the resource inputs of market commodities and the time of family members. That relationship will be determined by the technology available to the family for converting market goods and services into family goods and the productivity of each family member in producing family goods. An understanding of this family technology is essential, not only in understanding how each family member allocates his or her time, but also in explaining the very existence of the family as an institution. The family exists because the welfare of individuals within the family exceeds their welfare independent from a family relationship. These benefits may accrue to family members for a number of reasons, which we will briefly survey.

Specialization and Division of Labor

One potential source of benefit in a family relationship is through specialization and division of labor. If each family member—male or female, adult or child—has the same attributes so that each is a perfect substitute for other family members, then their utility as family members might be no greater than that as separate individuals. However, it is unlikely that each individual has the same attributes as other members of the family. Individuals may differ because of heredity and biological factors that affect their innate abilities and because of education and other forms of human capital investment, family upbringing, and social conditioning that affect their preferences and abilities. These individual differences permit each family member to specialize in the allocation of time between various market and family activities based upon their comparative advantage. Individuals with relatively higher productivity in generating a wage will allocate more time to the labor market, while individuals with relatively higher productivity in the production of family goods will allocate more time to family activities. Within the family we expect each individual to allocate time to the production of family goods such as nutrition, health, recreation, education, etc., based upon their comparative advantage. The greater the differences in the productivity of individuals in these different activities, the greater the potential benefits to the family through specialization and division of labor based upon comparative advantage.

Economies of Scale

Another source of benefit to the family accrues through economies of scale. Economies of scale will result when the production of family goods increases proportionately more than an increase of factor inputs in the family production function. Very simply, economies of scale exist when two can live more cheaply together than separately. For example, the fixed costs of housing and transportation and time-consuming activities such as shopping and cooking may be spread over a number of individuals in a multiperson household. However, economies of scale are available to multiperson households other than families; the explanation of the family as an economic organization must go beyond the benefits of economies of scale.

Joint Production and Consumption

A third potential benefit of a family relationship derives from joint production and joint consumption. These benefits are likely to occur in the production and consumption of family goods such as entertainment, recreation, nutrition, etc. A simple example would be a family's participation in a game like Trivial Pursuit. The family members jointly produce and consume a family good, i.e., entertainment, in playing the game. It would be possible for each individual to play the game separately, but the utility derived from a game like Trivial Pursuit requires cooperation between family members in the joint production and consumption of this form of entertainment. Similar arguments could be made for the family's joint participation in other activities, for example, travel, or going to a ballgame or the theater. The benefits accruing to the family through joint production and consumption of family goods is likely to be greater when family members share similar traits. Similarities in such traits as innate intelligence, levels of education, and similar preferences based upon family upbringing and social conditions, permit family members to share in the production and consumption of family goods that they each enjoy.[6]

Children as a Family Good

For many individuals the desire to have their own children is a major motivation to marry and form a family relationship. In this sense we can think of children as a family good. The services of children yield utility to their parents, just as do other family goods. Indeed, in the new economic theory of the family, children are treated as a consumer durable good. When the couple combines children with market goods and services and their own time, they generate a flow of services from children that gives them utility or satisfaction. The amount of utility they receive depends upon the number of children, the quality of children, and the parents' tastes or desires for child services. The parents may increase their welfare by increasing the number of children and/ or increasing the quality of children by allocating more market goods and services and more of their own time to their children.[7]

The new economic theory of the family yields some important in-

6. There may be benefits to the family in jointly producing and consuming family goods where the family members differ in their individual personality traits, e.g., dominance, possessiveness, maturity. Very little work has been done to determine when these benefits accrue to the family. See for example, R. F. Winch, *The Modern Family*, rev. ed. (New York: Holt, Rinehart and Winston, 1964).

7. One of the important reasons for persons with similar traits to marry is to raise children with those same traits. In population genetics, the mating of individuals with similar traits such as race, intelligence, height, etc., increases the probability that children of that union will have similar traits. In raising children the couple is likely to benefit from specialization, division of labor, and economies of scale in the family.

sights about children—for example, predicting fertility rates, family size, and so forth. However, the role of children in the family is part of a complex relationship; to understand that relationship, we must go beyond the economic theory of children as a family good. Children must be incorporated into the family's production function and welfare function, as noted previously in our discussion. We incorporate children into the production function for the family because the time of the children, like that of their parents, may be utilized to produce family goods. Children, like their parents, may also enter the labor force to earn a wage, which contributes to the family's disposable income. Particularly in rural agricultural families, we expect that the time of the children is an important resource input in the family's production function. In the new economic theory of the family, children may even be perceived as a producer durable rather than a consumer durable good. If the value of the time of children as an input in the family's production function exceeds the value of the time of their parents plus the value of other resources consumed in raising the children, then children may be viewed as producer durables within the family. Empirical studies suggest that in some developing countries children are producer durables in this sense. In this country, the evidence suggests that children are a consumer durable, and it is doubtful if children were ever a producer durable in the above sense, even in our early history.

We introduce children into the family's welfare function by assuming that total family welfare is the sum of the welfare of the parents and their children. It is surprising that the new economic theory of the family has done little to explore the role of children as a component in family welfare.[8] Most of the research has focused upon the role of children in the family production function, either as a family good or as an input in the production of family goods. Note the distinction here that children affect the family decision process, not only because they affect the welfare of their parents, but also because their own welfare is part of the total family welfare to be maximized. In particular we expect the parents to make decisions designed to improve their children's welfare as well as their own welfare. In order

8. While many economists would not object to the notion of the family as an agency for maximizing the welfare of its members, some take exception to this view. See Richard Easterlin, "Population Change and Farm Settlement in the Northern U.S.," *Journal of Economic History* 36 (March 1976): 45–76.

to understand this interdependence of welfare between family members, we must explore the role of love and caring in the family decision-making.

Love and Caring

The existence of love or caring in the family means that the welfare of family members is interdependent. We cannot assume that total family welfare is the simple aggregation of the separate welfare of individual family members because the welfare of one family member affects that of the others. In fact, when each family member cares as much about other family members as about himself or herself, then we must add the welfare of all other family members to that of each family member to determine his total welfare. Even when there is not full love or caring, in this sense, we expect the individual family member to take into account the welfare of other family members in maximizing his or her own welfare.

The existence of love and caring results in altruistic behavior that alters the transactions between family members. Family goods will be allocated among family members in such a way as to maximize total family welfare. We can define intrafamily transfers as transfers of family goods within the family from some initial distribution of family goods based upon each family member's marginal productivity in producing family goods. The most obvious example, of course, is the transfer of family goods from parents to their children. The parents produce family goods such as nutrition, shelter, health, recreation, nurturing, etc., which are consumed by their children. Note that the production of such family goods requires the time of parents as well as market goods. Once the time and market goods are combined to produce family goods, the latter may be transferred within the family so as to maximize family welfare. Intrafamily transfers may also occur between parents, from children to their parents, and from one child to another child.

Love and caring will also affect the production process within the family. Without love, one individual in the family must spend time in policing the activities of other family members, that is, making sure that they do not shirk their responsibilities or consume more than their marginal product of family goods. That is a waste of the limited resources available to the family in producing family goods. When family members care for each other, they have less incentive to shirk their responsibilities or consume more than their marginal product, because that will reduce their welfare as well as the total family welfare.

Family Goods as Collective Goods

It should be clear from the previous discussion that at least some family goods are collective goods in terms of the family's consumption. In order for a family good to qualify as a collective good for the family, it must satisfy two criteria. One criterion is that of unlimited joint consumption, i.e., the benefit any one family member receives from consuming the good does not diminish the value of the good to other family members. A second criterion is the impossibility of applying the exclusion principle, i.e., assuming that the family wished to exclude one family member from the consumption of the good; it would be impossible for them to do so. This rationale for collective goods in the family is analogous to that for collective goods in the context of other institutions.[9] A good example of family goods that satisfy these criteria for collective goods is either housing or entertainment. When the family chooses to improve the quality of housing—lighting, heating, air conditioning, etc.—one family member's consumption of these housing benefits does not preclude another family member from enjoying the same benefits, and it would be difficult or impossible to exclude one family member from such benefits. Other aspects of housing would be considered private goods, for example, building a bedroom for an additional child, to the extent that the benefits of the bedroom accrue to the child to the exclusion of other family members. Note that even in the latter case, the additional bedroom may be a collective good in that the welfare of all family members is increased by the increased welfare of the child.

When we move from family goods involving tangibles such as housing and entertainment to family goods involving intangibles such as companionship, friendship, nurturing, and security, an even stronger case can be made for viewing family goods as collective goods. The unique quality of these intangibles is that they are produced and consumed by the family collectively and cannot be duplicated by other social and economic institutions. Day-care centers provide an alternative to child care within the family, but they are not substitutes for

9. For a discussion of the concept of collective goods see Barry W. Poulson, "Is Collective Bargaining a Collective Good," *Journal of Labor Research* 4 (no. 4, Fall 1983): 348–65.

the unique nurturing relationship that exists between parent and child. We can view nurturing as a collective family good in the sense that all family members benefit from a nurturing family environment.

In economic theory the expectation is that collective goods will not be produced at an optimum level. When the benefits of a good accrue in a collective manner and it is not possible to exclude individuals from the consumption of the good, there may not be sufficient incentive for individuals to incur the cost of producing the good. If one person does produce the good, others will "free ride" by enjoying the benefits of the good without contributing to its cost. Therefore, all individuals have an incentive to free ride and none will incur the cost of producing the good. This problem is somewhat different for collective family goods. The existence of interdependent welfare functions due to love and caring will provide an incentive for family members to produce family goods, even when the benefits accrue to other family members. In other words, there is less incentive to free ride in the consumption of family goods, in contrast to the free rider problem that exists in the consumption of nonfamily goods.

THE FAMILY AS A BUSINESS ENTERPRISE

The Family as a Monitoring Agent

As a business enterprise the family may function in the same way that a firm functions, that is, as the monitoring agent in the firm's production function. The functions performed by the family acting as a monitoring agent include metering input productivity and metering rewards.[10] The benefit of the family as a monitoring agent in this sense is the superiority of family metering versus that provided by other forms of economic organizations, such as the market or the capitalist firm. One source of these benefits may accrue to the family because of the cooperative relationship that exists between family members working as a team in the production process. Such benefits may also accrue to other nonfamily forms of economic organization, such as the firm. In both cases the cooperation of individuals as members of a production team does not yield identifiable, separate products that can be summed to measure total output. Further, the

---

10. Metering here refers to both measuring output and apportioning output among family members. See Armen A. Alchian and Harold Demsetz, "Production, Information Costs, and Economic Organization," *American Economic Review* 62 (Dec. 1972): 777–95.

cooperating individuals may use resource inputs that are jointly owned. The use of joint inputs and the production of a joint output creates a metering problem. In nonfamily forms of economic organization, the metering problem requires some means of measuring the marginal productivity of the cooperating individuals and making payments to them equal to the value of their marginal product. The market as a form of economic organization may perform well if metering costs are low and individuals receive their value marginal product in the form of market wages. When metering costs are high owing to the existence of joint ownership of inputs and/or joint production, then nonmarket forms of economic organization are likely to emerge.

The capitalist firm provides an alternative form of economic organization in metering the production process. The owners of the firm may hire a monitor who performs a metering function in measuring output, observes the marginal productivity of the factor inputs, and apportions rewards based upon marginal productivity. The monitor is in a position to alter contracts with the cooperating factor inputs to reflect changes in their marginal productivity. This reward system provides an incentive to cooperating individuals to increase their productivity and a disincentive to shirk responsibilities as cooperating inputs in the production process. As Alchian and Demsetz have argued:

> Two necessary conditions exist for the emergence of the firm on the prior assumption that more than pecuniary wealth enter utility functions: (1) It is possible to increase productivity through team-oriented production, a production technique for which it is costly to directly measure the marginal outputs of the cooperating inputs. This makes it more difficult to restrict shirking through simple market exchange between cooperating inputs. (2) It is economical to estimate marginal productivity by observing or specifying input behavior. The simultaneous occurrence of both these preconditions leads to the contractual organization of inputs, known as the classical capitalist firms with (a) joint input production, (b) several input owners, (c) one party who is common to all the contracts of the joint inputs, (d) who has rights to negotiate any inputs' contract independently of contracts with other input owners, (e) who holds the residual claim, and (f) who has the right to sell his contractual residual status.[11]

(Note that the removal of (b) converts the argument from that for a capitalist proprietary firm to an explanation for a socialist firm organization.)

11. Alchian and Demsetz, *n.* 10, p. 783.

To the extent that the family satisfies these conditions, we can view the rationale for the family as a business enterprise, analogous to that for the capitalist firm. The question is, What distinguishes the family from the firm as an economic organization? It is possible for a family to organize as a capitalist firm and hire a monitor who meters the production process and who claims a residual return; and it is also possible for family members to be hired on a contractual basis. Although most family enterprises are not organized on such a formal contractual basis, the family has functioned, and continues to function, as a viable business enterprise.

The Metering Function

One explanation for the success of the family as a business enterprise is the nature of family organization. Family members usually enjoy an intimacy of contact on a long-term basis that facilitates the metering function of the family. Individual family members' contributions in the production process are readily observable so that it is easy to detect shirking of responsibilities. When shirking does occur, the family has available to it a system of penalties and rewards not available to the capitalist business firm. The worker who shirks his responsibilities in a business firm may receive reduced pay or be fired. He may also be ostracized by co-workers who can make it uncomfortable for him to continue shirking. The intimacy of contact in the family not only makes it easier to detect shirking, but also to ostracize family members for such behavior. The family usually does not enter into formal contracts specifying the responsibilities of family members, yet those responsibilities emerge from the day-to-day interaction of family members, and the individual family member is not likely to shirk those responsibilities without detection and ostracism from other members of the family.

This discussion implies that the family may use methods of punishment for shirking not available to the business firm. An authoritarian relationship between parent and child, and between husband and wife, may provide negative inducements to motivate family members to assume their responsibilities without shirking. Corporal punishment is still condoned in many families as a negative inducement. However, this tyrannical view of the family is relevant in the United States to a small and declining range of family relationships. The personal rights of individuals within the family are recognized and protected in modern societies, and as family members mature over the life cycle of the family, those authoritarian relationships are not likely to endure. This suggests that the success of the family as a business enterprise is based, not upon the negative inducements, but rather the positive incentives for family members to assume their responsibilities. Specifically, it is the benefit of increased productivity through cooperation between family members that provides a positive inducement to the role of the family as a business enterprise.

A related explanation for the role of the family as a business enterprise is the success of the family in combining the heterogeneous inputs of different family members into an efficient production process. Again, the self-sufficient family farm provides the best illustration of those benefits. The small family farm had to rely on the inputs of all family members to survive as an economic organization. Children would be expected to contribute their labor at an early age in caring for animals, cutting firewood, and contributing during periods of planting and harvesting when there was a heavy demand for labor. Farm wives contributed to these activities as well as doing the household chores. The family farm successfully adapted this heterogeneous labor supply to the variety of tasks required on the farm, blurring any distinction between the role of the family as a business enterprise and other functions of the family.

The Role of Affective Relationships

At this point the argument is that the intimate long-term contact among family members facilitates the role of the family as a business enterprise. This does not assume affective relationships among family members; however, it is the existence of love and caring that distinguishes the family as a business enterprise as well as a welfare-maximizing institution. When the welfare of other family members is part of the welfare of individual family members, each family member will be motivated to assume his or her responsibilities in family production. As a result, there is less need for the family to perform a monitoring function at all in order to maximize family welfare. If each family member is motivated to contribute to the family's welfare, there is no need to measure his or her marginal productivity, or to allocate the family's output based upon marginal productivity. At least within the family, the Marxian dictum, "from each according to his ability, to each according to his needs," may be a better description of the decision process than a neoclassical theory of the family based upon marginal productivity theory. It is important to emphasize that this is true to the extent that affective relationships are the basis of decision making within the family.

We must also note the existence of negative affective relationships as well as love and caring in the family. Evidence of such negative affective relationships is abundant in modern society—battered family members, high divorce rates, and so forth. Negative affective relationships, of course, tend to undermine not only the role of the family as a business enterprise but the very existence of the family. In the absence of love and caring, the major advantage of the family as a business enterprise would disappear. The family would have to incur monitoring costs in measuring the marginal productivity of individual family members, and be forced to rely upon an explicit set of penalties and rewards based upon marginal productivity in order to motivate family members to assume their responsibilities.

We should also emphasize that affective relationships are evident in other forms of economic organization as well as in the family.[12] It is difficult to think of any functioning economic organization in which there is an absence of caring and in which the organization has to rely completely upon a specialized monitor. Even the most authoritarian forms of economic organization, such as the slave plantation, were not based entirely on an explicit monitoring system. Negative inducements existed in actual or threatened punishment of slaves, yet some economic historians maintain that the slave plantation was a highly efficient and productive form of economic organization, primarily because of the cooperation between the factors of production.[13] Cooperation was achieved through positive inducements to slave productivity, including the maintenance of the slave family, as well as through negative inducements and coercion. While this is a controversial argument, it suggests that economists have tended to overlook the role of affective relationships as a source of motivation in nonfamily as well as family forms of economic organization.

The existence of love and caring as the motivating factor in the

---

12. Alternatives to the family such as the Israeli kibbutz apparently function well as economic organizations in similar circumstances, suggesting that they share similar attributes with a family organization.

13. Robert Fogel and Stanley Engerman, *Time on the Cross* (Boston: Little, Brown & Co., 1974).

family reduces and, in the extreme, eliminates the need for a monitoring function within the family. Further, it permits each family member to be a residual claimant to the family's output. Each family member may share in the benefits of increased output accruing through cooperation among family members. The best analogy with the family as a business enterprise is that of a profit-sharing partnership. Alchian and Demsetz point out that characteristics evident in the family are also found in profit-sharing partnerships like law firms and other professional partnerships. These shared characteristics tend to be found in small teams where it is easy to monitor performance of team members and where the cost of a specialized monitor is large relative to the benefits of increased productivity due to cooperation among the partners.[14] Profit sharing provides a superior incentive system, leaving each partner a great deal of leeway in contributing to the output of the partnership. In the same sense, each family member is motivated to contribute to the family as a business enterprise because he is a residual claimant of the output.

The Family as a Long-Term Contract

There is a final important distinction between the family and the firm as an economic organization. Recent research has begun to explore the long-term contractual relationship between the firm and its employees. A firm may have an informal obligation to provide a job for its employees over their lifetime, but such an obligation is qualitatively different from the obligation of the family to its members.[15] Historically, the family has allocated returns to family members over their lifetime, to some extent independent of the contribution of individual family members to production. The care of older or sick family members who may contribute little, if anything, to production was primarily a family obligation. Such long-term obligations motivated individuals to cooperate within the family and distinguished the family from other forms of economic organization such as the firm.

In the course of modern economic growth the family has emerged as a more specialized institution. A small percentage of families continue to operate family farms, and even these farms are often organized as corporate firms. With industrialization, the family as a business

---

14. Alchian and Demsetz, n. 10, pp. 785–86.
15. The best analogy would be the lifetime employment obligation in Japanese firms.

enterprise has tended to be displaced by other forms of economic organization such as the corporate firm. However, modernization has at the same time required an expanded role for the family in relating to this more complex social and economic environment. In order to relate to the new economic environment of business firms and labor markets, and to the new social and political institutions, the family has increasingly assumed a role as its members' agent.

THE FAMILY AS ITS MEMBERS' AGENT

The Family and Environmental Institutions

The new economic theory of the family takes environmental constraints as given, focusing upon the decision process within the family. A logical extension of this economic theory of the family is to relax the assumption of a given set of environmental constraints to explore the interaction of the family and other institutions.[16] When the family represents its members vis-à-vis these environmental institutions, it is acting as its members' agent. The role of the family as its members' agent in relating to environmental institutions involves a somewhat different decision process from that which takes place in the internal decision of the family. The crucial issue in the analysis of the role of the family as its members' agent is again the interaction of family members. When we assume interdependence of family members, then the relationship between the family and environmental institutions takes on a unique character. The welfare of individual family members may be increased if the family acts as their agent in dealing with environmental institutions.

It is important here to distinguish between an authoritarian relationship between family members versus a cooperative relationship. Traditionally, sociologists have characterized the family by the controls exercised over family members, such as parents and children, by authority or by disciplinary action. While an authoritarian relationship may characterize some types of family decisions, we do not need to assume such a relationship in viewing the family as its members' agent. If the family *qua* agent is based upon voluntary choice rather than on authoritarian relationship, members of the family will

---

16. The environmental constraint is made explicit in a formal theory of the family being developed by the author.

choose to have the family represent them vis-à-vis environmental institutions when this maximizes their individual and family welfare. The fact that family members choose to be represented by the family in our modern society suggests that this assumption is valid for a wide range of family decisions. Husbands and wives may opt out of their family relationship and children may achieve economic independence at a relatively early age. Yet, they usually maintain interdependent family relationships throughout the family's life cycle. This suggests that it is the benefits of the family acting as its members' agent rather than any authoritarian relationship which motivates family members to choose an interdependent family relationship over the family life cycle. The economic literature suggests several ways in which the family, by acting as their agent, may improve the welfare of family members.

The Voice Function

The function performed by the family as its members' agent is analogous to a political process; the preferences and interests of family members must be coordinated in order to maximize the family welfare function. The goal that the family attempts to maximize at any given time may not be identical with that of all or even a majority of family members. The family utilizes the political mechanism that Albert Hirschman terms *voice*.[17] *Voice* refers to the use of direct communication to bring actual and desired conditions closer together. The nature of family relationships facilitates communication among family members for maximizing family welfare. The communication that takes place between spouses and between parents and children is unique to the family. The intimacy of contact and long-term relationship between family members permit each family member to build a stock of knowledge about the other members of the family and about the family's welfare, and this knowledge enables each member of the family to make rational decisions designed to maximize family welfare. The love and caring that exist within the family permit an honesty in communication among family members that is not likely to take place outside the family. The voice function enables the family to resolve differences among family members in order to maintain the

---

17. See the discussion of this "voice" function in connection with labor unions acting as their members' agent in Richard B. Freeman and James L. Medoff, "The Two Faces of Unionism," *The Public Interest* 52 (Fall 1979): 69–93.

family as an organization. Hirschman provides the example of couples discussing marital problems rather than going to the divorce court. However, the voice function of the family entails more than simply resolving day-to-day conflicts among family members; fundamentally, it is that function which permits the family to aggregate the interests of its different members so that the family can act as the agent in maximizing the welfare of the family as a whole.

The Family as a Bargaining Agent

The analogy with the family as its members' agent is the modern labor union, which performs a similar function for union members.[18] The union acts as its members' agent, representing workers and communicating with management through collective bargaining. In an earlier era, these services were performed for family members by the family acting as its members' agent. These bargaining services of the family vis-à-vis employers were collective goods to the individual family members. If a family struck a good bargain with a potential employer, all members of the family benefited. Such bargaining services were subject to unlimited joint consumption of each family member, and when the output of the family was a joint product, it was difficult or impossible to exclude one family member from the benefits of the family's bargaining services. Note that we distinguish here between the bargaining services of the family as its members' agent and the outcome of that bargaining in the form of wages and other job benefits. The latter might accrue to individual family members, and thus not satisfy our criteria for collective goods. At this point, we want to expand the concept of the family as its members' agent beyond this analogy with the collective bargaining activities of labor unions. The family may represent its members as an agent, not only with business firms but with other economic, social, and political organizations that form the environment within which the family functions.

The Family as a Centralized Contractual Agent

When a family head exercises great authority and influence over other family members, the role of the family as its members' agent is often enhanced. Family decisions relating to other institutions are trans-

---

18. For a discussion of the role of labor unions as their members' agent, see Poulson, *n.* 9.

mitted through a family head who represents the family as a whole. The family head is in a position to induce behavior from other family members that maximizes total family welfare, both through example and through the discipline and authority imposed upon other family members. The benefits to nonfamily members include the saving in transactions costs in dealing with one person (rather than a number of individual family members) and also in the perception of the family head as responsible for all family members' transactions.[19]

The Family Name as a Public Good

Acting as its members' agent, the family can exploit the potential benefits of the family's name or reputation in its dealings with environmental institutions. In this sense the family name is not unlike a brand name established by business corporations. The family name may be distinguished by the substance of the transactions made by the family and/or by the perception of those transactions by others in the society. A "good" family name established by a reputation for honesty and fairness in transactions by family members may affect a wide range of transactions outside the family. This is especially evident at an early stage in economic development characterized by imperfect markets for labor and capital. The family may best represent its members in labor markets, signaling to potential employers information regarding the efficiency and integrity of family members as employees. Further, the family may substitute for both labor and management institutions in training and monitoring performance of family members and allocating rewards and penalties based upon performance. Over time the family name is enhanced or diminished by the performance of individual family members and the role of the family as its members' agent changes accordingly. The same arguments hold for capital and product markets when the family acts as its members' agent. The family name influences people's perception of the risk in lending and the quality of products produced by a family, as well as the quality of its labor services.[20]

The family may act as its members' agent in relation to both private and public institutions. The relationship between the family as its members' agent and the state is largely unexplored. The public choice

19. Ben-Porath, *n*. 4, pp. 12–14.
20. Ibid.

literature provides a framework for this analysis, but little work has been done in exploring the decision process of the family as it relates to the state. In the next section, we will discuss how the public choice paradigm can be extended to encompass family decision-making.

THE FAMILY AND THE STATE IN A PUBLIC CHOICE PARADIGM

The Public Choice Paradigm

The origins of the public choice paradigm can be traced to the major writers in classical liberal political economy: Thomas Hobbes, John Locke, Jean-Jacques Rousseau, and Edmund Burke. These writers provided the ideological foundations for the public choice paradigm centered on the Lockean concept of natural rights and the contract theory of the state.[21]

In the "natural order" each individual has certain natural rights. He has the rights to his own body and to the fruits of his own labor. When the individual applies his labor to other property, he creates private property. Thus, private property rights are an extension of natural rights, and this bundle of property rights exists prior to the organization of individuals into society and prior to the existence of the state. An individual's economic rights are a logical extension of personal rights. If we accept that an individual has rights to his person, including freedom of expression, association, religion, etc., then we must also accept the rights of the individual to apply his faculties to improve his welfare. He is then entitled to claim property rights in the fruits of his labor. Thus, the freedom to enter into a calling or trade necessitates the freedom to own real property in the form of land, buildings, and other forms of capital.

In this public choice paradigm, individuals enter into a constitutional contract with each other to form a civil society. Individuals voluntarily agree to surrender certain rights to the state in order to secure their individual property rights. The locus of power in this contractarian view is the individual, that is, sovereignty resides in the people rather than in the state. The power vested in the state exists only so long as the individuals in the society will it.

---

21. See the discussion of this ideology in Barry W. Poulson, "Ideology and Labor Law," *Journal of Social, Political and Economic Studies* 8 (no. 1, Spring 1983): 43–80.

There are certain rules of the game that must be established to protect individual property rights, whether those rules are established by statute, i.e., written law emanating from the government, or by common law, i.e., previous court decisions that have the force of law. Individual property rights must be defined and enforced so as to protect individual freedom. Individuals must have recourse to adjudication of disputes over property rights with reference to a rule of law that is understandable and enforceable. They must be protected from abuse of property rights, whether by other individuals or groups, or by the coercive power of government, or by judges and courts that make arbitrary decisions inconsistent with a rule of law. These individual rights are violated when a person is denied, against his will, the exclusive possession and control of himself or the fruits of his labor. Such violation occurs through acts of aggression: initiation of physical force against person or property; threats to initiate such force; theft, fraud, breach of contract; activities involving a high risk that the person or property of another is interfered with in any of these ways. When an individual is wronged in any of these ways, but only on that condition, he has a moral right to respond with force in defense of his person or property. The use of force or coercion in any other circumstance is an act of aggression and is morally wrong. When these moral rights are codified into law, they also become legal rights.

Legal rights determine when the government acting as the agent of individuals within the society may respond with force. The circumstances that permit a government to respond with coercion are no different from those that justify the individual use of force, that is, to defend individuals and their property from acts of aggression. When the government uses coercion in any other circumstances, those acts are not morally justifiable and the government is committing acts of aggression. Individuals have a moral right and obligation in a free society to protect themselves from acts of aggression by government as well as by other individuals.

The Family as a Private Voluntary Contract

Within the framework of this fundamental constitutional contract, individuals may enter into private voluntary contracts for the production and exchange of goods and services. A wide range of private postconstitutional contracts is possible, among which is the marriage contract, entered into by a husband and a wife when they form a family.

The nature of the marriage contract itself varies from a simple agreement to own and use their property in common, to very complex marriage contracts specifying in detail the rights and obligations of each individual in his use of real and personal family property. However, marriage contracts have a common characteristic with all private contractual relationships in that they are voluntary, as opposed to involuntary or coercive contracts.

In a public choice paradigm the contractual basis for the family is a private voluntary contract. As in all private voluntary contracts, we assume that rational individuals enter into a marriage contract and form families only when this improves their welfare. Production and exchange take place within the family, and the family acts as the agent for family members. The production of family goods and services increases the welfare of family members and maximizes the welfare of the society as a whole. No party to such private voluntary decisions can be left worse off; in economic terminology the results are positive sum and Pareto optimal.

Family Contracts With the State

As members of the polity, the family enters into a contractual relationship with the state. In addition to the primary contractual relationship embodied in the Constitution, the family enters into postconstitutional contracts with the state. The family contracts with the state for the provision of public goods and services. In addition to these contracts for the provision of public goods and services, the family may also contract with the state for transfers of income and wealth. Virtually every decision made by the government has some impact on the distribution of income and wealth, but some decisions, such as progressive income taxes, inheritance taxes, and transfer payments, are specifically designed to redistribute income and wealth.

Postconstitutional contracts between the family and the state, in contrast to private postconstitutional contracts, involve some element of coercion. The family may participate in the decision process that determines its relationships to the state, as befits a democracy, but unless a family-state (public) contract is based upon unanimous agreement among all citizens, the state's relationship with at least some of its clients will involve coercion. Even when families support a contractual relationship with the state, the actual outcome may not be the anticipated outcome. In that event, a decline in social welfare would result. While it is true that private contracts may have such unanticipated results, there is a significant difference between the risks of private and public contracts in this regard. If an unanticipated result of a private contract diminishes the welfare of one of the contracting parties, that party may opt out of the contract, incurring some costs in the process. For example, the partners to a marriage contract may (and at an increasing rate, do) opt out of the contract, with certain real and psychological costs to family members. In contrast, the family generally cannot opt out of a contractual relationship with the state, or can do so only at a prohibitive cost. Individuals may choose not to pay their taxes or not to obey the law, but the cost in terms of fines, imprisonment, and other penalties prohibits most individuals from exercising these options. Even when many individuals, and perhaps a majority of the people, oppose a public contract, the costs of mobilizing support for a change in public policies may prohibit people from taking such action. Thus, the risks of getting stuck with unwanted public contracts entail costs not encountered in private voluntary contracts. This element of coercion distinguishes the contractual relationship between the family and the state from private voluntary contracts.

The Impact of the State on Family Welfare

Because of the element of coercion, we cannot predict the effect of contracts with the state on the family's welfare. The expectation is that private voluntary contracts are positive sum and Pareto optimum. But the outcome of involuntary public contracts may be positive sum, zero sum, or negative sum, and therefore may or may not improve the welfare of the family. Some public contracts are likely to be positive sum and increase the welfare of the family. The definition and enforcement of private property rights is an essential condition for the production and exchange of goods and services in private voluntary contracts. Activities of the state that have the effect of more clearly defining and enforcing private property rights will affect the distribution of income and wealth, but such activities are likely to increase the welfare of the society as a whole. Other public contracts, such as government transfer activities, are likely to be negative sum in diminishing the welfare of the society. When the government redistributes income and wealth through transfer activities, the welfare of some interest group is improved, but the welfare of the society as a whole is likely to diminish. Such transfers require taxes or other means of expropriating the income and wealth of some members of the society—diminishing their welfare. Further, the incentives created by such public transfers will lead members of the society to shift resources from productive activities to transfer activities. Different interest groups will allocate more resources to political activities designed to obtain special interest legislation and other public contracts to benefit that interest group. As resources are shifted from productive activities to transfer activities, the welfare of the society as a whole is diminished.

The Constitutional Contract

The purpose of the constitutional contract with the state is not only to establish the legal basis for governmental powers, but also to set limits to that power. The rights of the family are protected from the coercion of the state to the extent that those rights are defined and protected by law. This assumes not only a written constitution, but also an independent judiciary capable of enforcing the law. If the judiciary merely sanctions governmental powers, there are no limits to the power the government may exercise over the family. Without limits to the coercive power of government to redistribute income and wealth, there can be no private property rights. The personal as well as economic liberties bound up in such property rights will be eroded as the power of government expands.

Thus, a constitutional democracy establishes a unique relationship, grounded in private property rights, between the family and the state. The objective is to maximize social welfare, not in terms of some abstract social welfare function independent of the welfare of the individual, but rather in terms of the welfare of each individual in the society. The assumption is that social welfare is maximized by establishing a rule of law defining and protecting property rights in such a way that the family is free to maximize its own welfare. It is not an appropriate function of government to do something for the family because it is in their best interests. Rather, it is up to the family to determine what is in its best interests. The function of government and the rule of law is to make sure that the family is able to pursue its self-interest, free from coercion by others and by the institutions of the state. The objective of a rule of law is an equitable society in the sense that each family's property rights are defined, enforced, and protected.

TOWARD A DYNAMIC ECONOMIC THEORY OF THE FAMILY

Dynamic Change in the Role of the Family

A dynamic economic theory of the family must encompass changes in the role of the family in terms of the functions that we have explored, as an institution maximizing the welfare of family members in the production of "family" goods and services, as a business enterprise producing market goods and services, and as its members' agent in relating to environmental institutions, including the state. We find that these functions often overlap within the family, and that the success or failure of the family in performing one of these functions influences its performance of other functions. The family is only one of a variety of institutional arrangements that can perform these functions. Historically, we observe the role of the family changing as some functions are shifted to other private or public institutions, while other functions of the family are expanded. The task of a dynamic economic theory of the family is to explain the relationship between the different functions performed by the family and the changing role of the family in relation to alternative institutional arrangements over time.

The Family Life Cycle

One source of change in the role of the family is due to dynamic changes that take place within the family itself. Over the family's life cycle the composition of the family and the age of family members change. As individual family members pass through the family life cycle, their roles within the family change as well. The goals of the family and the decision process within the family reflect these changes in family structure. The concept of the *life cycle* has long been an important foundation for economic analysis.[22] The individual is assumed to pass through a life cycle that influences the economic decisions he makes. As an individual ages, he makes different choices

---

22. See the review of this approach to a dynamic theory of the family by historians in Tamara Hareven, "Cycles, Courses and Cohorts: Reflections on Theoretical and Methodological Approaches to the Historical Study of Family Development," *Journal of Social History* 12 (no. 1, Fall 1978): 97–110.

regarding work versus leisure, consumption versus savings, education and other investments in human capital, etc. Usually the individual and the family are assumed to be synonymous in order to facilitate the analysis. When we relax this assumption, then we must distinguish between an individual's life cycle and the family's life cycle.

The family cycle refers to changes in the family as an institution over time. Some historians identify stages in the family cycle over the life of its members. From its formation with marriage to its dissolution with death of the head of the household, the family cycle follows the stages of parenthood: family formation, child rearing, launching of the children and survival—with the first marriage still intact or broken by separation or divorce. This concept of stages in the family cycle is a useful construct in developing a dynamic economic theory of the family. However, like most "stage" formulations, it has important limitations. Different families vary in terms of the stages through which the members pass, and the family cycle for a whole population varies over time from one generation to the next. In the nineteenth century the combination of a later age of marriage, higher fertility rate, and earlier age at death meant that parenthood encompassed the entire time span of the family. Fathers rarely survived beyond the marriage of their second child. Frequently the youngest child would be starting his or her education at about the time that the oldest child was marrying. Thus, the demarcation between stages in the family life cycle was less clear in nineteenth century families. The final or "empty nest" stage typical of twentieth century families was not typical for nineteenth century families.

The family cycle concept introduces a dynamic element into an economic theory of the family. An individual's decisions will reflect both the individual's life cycle and the family cycle. Over time, the role of each individual in the family changes as his or her life cycle synchronizes with the family cycle. In fact, the individual has an interdependent relationship with several family units. One is first a member of one's parents' family and kinship group; when the individual marries, not only is a new family unit created, but new interdependencies develop between the family of procreation (the family of origin) and the family of one's spouse. The termination of a family through death or divorce does not end this interdependence, but creates a new set of relationships between the surviving family members and their kinship groups.

The Family Life Course

Historians have begun to develop a rich literature on the meshing of individual careers with the family unit as it changes over time. This field of research is referred to as life course analysis, to distinguish it from the narrower life cycle analysis. The synchronization of individual and family transitions is found to affect a wide range of decisions such as schooling, entry into the labor force, marriage and family formation, retirement, and inheritance. Particularly, as we explore family decision-making earlier in our history, we see a dynamic process in which individual decisions are coordinated with those of other family members, and their roles within the family change over time so as to maximize family welfare. The decisions that individuals make at one point in time reflect their life course experience in the past and their expected life course in the future.

Over the life course, the preferences and interests of family members change, and the goals of the family shift. Changes in the composition and age structure also bring about such changes. The voice function requires that the family respond to these dynamic changes over the life course. It will not be possible to satisfy all the family members' interests and pursue all of their goals at a given time, but in order to maximize family welfare, the family must make choices that reflect changing interests. Let us illustrate this voice function with reference to the choice of family members in the allocation of their time.

Traditionally, economists distinguished between the time allocated between work and leisure. In the new economic theory of the family, time is allocated between market and family activities, and all time is productive with reference to the family welfare function. Family members must choose how much time they will allocate to the labor market, which generates the income necessary to purchase market goods and services. They must also allocate their time to family activities such as child rearing, education, and the preparation of food, in order to maximize family welfare in the production of family goods. We expect those decisions in the allocation of time to change over the life course. When a couple first marry, they are likely to allocate much of their time to market activities in order to generate an income necessary to finance the purchase of consumer durable and nondurable goods. The decision to have children requires a significant reallocation of time from market activities to family activities focused around child rearing. As the children grow up, they are expected to contribute their time to both market and family activities so as to maximize the family's welfare. In low-income families, a significant part of the family's earned income may be generated by children. The role of children as sources of family income depends upon the amount of education they receive, the age at which they enter the labor force, and the age at which they depart from their parents' family. Over the life course, as the parents age and the children mature, a reallocation of time takes place. The parents may choose to allocate less time to market activities and eventually to withdraw from the labor market altogether. When parents enter their retirement years, they may be dependent upon their children for financial and other support. The life course of the family involves a constantly changing reallocation of time by the different family members, reflecting their changing roles. The voice function of the family involves communication of the changing preferences and abilities of the family members over time, and the adjustment of their allocation of time between market activities and family activities so as to maximize family welfare. This illustrates only one of the many dynamic changes affecting the family.

Dynamic Change in the Family Environment

A dynamic economic theory of the family must also relate changes in the environment to family decision-making. In a sense, we move to higher levels of aggregation in the analysis of the individual life cycle, the family cycle, life course analysis of the interaction of individual and family decisions, and finally to the interaction between family decision-making and the demographic, social, political, and economic changes in the family environment. An economic theory of the family must provide a framework for analyzing the impact of economic, political, and social change on family decision-making. For example, the political environment may introduce new opportunities and constraints on a wide range of family decisions including age of entry and exit from the labor force, education, employment, inheritance, tax and subsidy of family income, etc. It is at this stage of analysis of family decision-making that economic theory is most limited. We do not as yet have a theoretical framework that captures the complex interaction between the family and changing environmental institutions. What we have is an economic theory of the family that provides at least a starting point for this area of research.[23]

CONCLUSION

An economic theory of the family must encompass the role of the family in performing a number of different functions: as a business enterprise producing market goods and services; as an institution for maximizing the welfare of family members in the production of family goods and services; and as the family members' agent in interacting with environmental institutions. That theory must be based upon the unique characteristics of the family as an institution, in particular the love and caring between family members that results in interdependent utility functions. A dynamic theory of the family must take into account changes in the individual family members' life cycle, changes in the family cycle, and changes in the family course tracing the interaction of individual and family decision-making. Finally, a dynamic economic theory must relate family decision-making to the dynamic changes occurring in the social, political, and economic environment.

The family is only one of a number of possible institutional arrangements for performing a given function. Economic theory suggests that when the cost/benefit ratio for alternative institutional arrangements exceeds that for family decision-making, then alternative institutional arrangements will be substituted for the family. For example, the role of the family as a business enterprise has declined as alternative forms of economic organization, such as the corporation, have displaced the family. The dynamic changes in the size, scale, and complexity of economic organization that accompanied the Industrial Revolution tended to erode the role of the family as a business enterprise. However, the analysis of the role of the family as an economic organization reveals that this transition did not occur in a continuous and ubiquitous manner during the Industrial Revolution. There were technological changes, such as power spinning, that actually enhanced the role of the family as a business enterprise during

---

23. This approach to institutional change is developed by Lance E. Davis and Douglass C. North in *Institutional Change and American Economic Growth* (Cambridge, Mass.: Cambridge University Press, 1971).

the "putting out" stage of the textile industry. In some sectors of the economy, such as agriculture and retail services, the family has continued as a viable form of business enterprise right down to the present day.

In the course of modern economic growth, the family has emerged as a more specialized institution. With industrialization, individual family members increasingly entered labor markets in which they offered their labor services independent from those of other family members. In agriculture the family farm increasingly gave way to commercial agricultural organizations that are difficult to distinguish from other business firms. As a result, the family has functioned less as a business enterprise, and a clearer distinction has emerged between the time allocated by family members to market activities and time allocated to family activities. The role of the family became increasingly specialized as an institution maximizing the welfare of its members, involving the allocation of time and resources to produce family goods. With modernization came an increasingly complex set of social institutions that have had a major impact on the family, requiring an expanded role for the family as its members' agent.

The family performed an important function as its members' agent in negotiations with employers during the early Industrial Revolution. As individual family members began to enter the labor market independent from other family members, the function of bargaining agent shifted to labor unions. Yet, labor unions have always represented a minority of workers in the labor force. The family has continued to perform an important function as its members' agent in bargaining with employers in many sectors of the economy, such as the southern textile industry, right down to the twentieth century. Since the 1930s, the government has intervened extensively in labor markets in support of labor unions as the collective bargaining agent for workers. The displacement of the family as the bargaining agent for its members by labor unions in this more recent period reflects the legislative and legal constraints within which the bargaining process takes place, as well as the benefits and costs of alternative institutional arrangements for bargaining between employees and employers.

One of the most dramatic changes that has occurred in the role of the family is in the education of children. In the preindustrial era, the primary responsibility for education was with the family. By the early nineteenth century, the educational system had evolved into a diverse mix of public and quasi-public schools, and church-related and other private schools. That educational system was responsive to the desires of families acting as their members' agent regarding local schools. With the "Common School Movement" after 1840, there was a dramatic expansion in public schools, which to some extent replaced private schools. The educational system became less responsive to the desires of families and more influenced by a politicized state educational system. This changing role of the family vis-à-vis the state in the education of children can be understood only in the context of public choice theory. The expanded role of the state in education cannot be explained by a cost/benefit analysis of alternative educational institutions; that transition reflected the coercive nature of contractual arrangements between the family and the state, and the dynamic institutional changes that resulted in an expanded role for the state during the Industrial Revolution.

It is clear that the dynamic changes that have occurred in the relationship between the family and the state in America are complex, and that we do not yet have an economic theory capable of explaining all of these changes. In this chapter, we have suggested some refinements that provide a broader theoretical framework for the analysis of the family and the state.

3

TOWARD A NEW THEORY OF THE FAMILY

Lyla H. O'Driscoll

INTRODUCTION

American social and legal institutions reflect our fundamental uncertainty regarding the moral status of children. In some contexts, we confidently ascribe to them moral rights identical to those of adults, and we regard these rights as equally worthy of legal protection. To defend children from maiming, murder, or enslavement, for example, we readily appeal to their rights and to their status as "persons" in our morality.

In other contexts, with equal assurance, we deny that children have the same rights as adults. To defend their lesser liberty in matters such as the determination of their day-to-day activities and associates, for example, we readily characterize them as undeveloped and dependent beings needing adult protection. Children, it seems, are not on a par with adults after all; they are not to be accorded exactly the rights adults enjoy because they lack "experience," "rationality," "the capacity for choice," or some other "adult" faculty or attribute.

It would appear, then, that we think children are persons—but not-quite-persons. Our legal and social institutions reflect this uncertainty by making children citizens and bearers of rights, but second-class citizens whose social and legal status is inferior to that of adults. The lesser liberties of children fall into three categories: their subjection to the will and authority of adults, including their parents; their liability to arrest and incarceration for acts that are not offenses if committed by adults; and their legal disabilities, including restrictions such as laws making them ineligible to vote.

In this essay, I explore some moral aspects of such institutions of unequal liberty. My general concern is the justification of adult dominion over children. To bring the topic into sharper focus, I consider one fundamental case of unequal liberty: the institution of the family. Thus, although the legal disabilities of minors and their liability to arrest for "status" offenses are also important and interesting features of children's lesser liberty, I will not be directly concerned with these.

To forestall possible misunderstanding, let me point out that I am not assuming that arrangements of unequal liberty cannot be warranted. There *may* be considerations sufficient to establish the permissibility of some such structures in various circumstances. The propriety of such arrangements cannot be taken for granted, however; it must be shown.

Arrangements of unequal liberty seem to collide with formidable moral considerations. First, justice requires relevantly similar treatment of relevantly similar cases. If the disparities between the liberties granted adults and those permitted children are justified, there must be substantial and pertinent differences between the two groups.

Moreover, a society that values freedom—either for its own sake or as a means to some further end—must demand a justification for the legal subjection of members of one group to the will of members of another. The problem is particularly acute when, as in the present case, those who occupy the role of lesser liberty do not choose it and lack the legal capacity to remove themselves from it.

At the root of this inquiry is a concern about the compatibility of the family with fundamental moral principles. Although the basic theme is ethical, many of the issues addressed are conceptual: To assess the moral legitimacy of "the family," it is necessary in the first place to be clear about what the family is.

In the next section, I characterize the family as a social and legal institution, and identify some of the key elements of an adequate theory of the family.

The third section briefly reviews the family structure as it is embodied in contemporary American law, and outlines four conceptions of the family as a social and legal institution: the authoritarian, the sentimental, the paternalistic, and the economic. Each, to some degree or another, is embedded in American legal and social practices.

In the fourth section, I suggest a conception of the family that employs modified versions of the authoritarian and sentimental views.

THE FAMILY AS AN INSTITUTION

In this discussion, I highlight some conceptual issues concerning the family as a social and legal institution, and put various moral questions about the family into a broader context.

Let me emphasize at the outset that my subject is the family as a social and legal institution, and not the biological connections between parent and child.

To be a member of the social and legal structure which is the family is to occupy a role in an institutional arrangement, a position that carries with it (and indeed is in a sense defined by) certain rights, duties, powers, and immunities. In many legal systems, the role of (legal) parent falls in the first instance to the biological parent. But we cannot identify legal with biological parenthood. In the first place, a biological parent can relinquish, or be removed from, the role, and someone can occupy the legal role without being a biological parent. Moreover, we would recognize as a family an institutional arrangement that assigned, say, to the maternal aunt, the rights, duties, powers, and immunities we associate with the parental role, or even a structure that did not invest biological relationships with social meaning, but used some other criterion to place adults and children in the social and legal roles of parent and child.

Nor can we suppose that the rights and duties of legal parenthood follow simply and directly from the facts of biological parenthood. At a minimum, some mediating consideration must be employed to connect the biological fact and some moral principle underlying the legal institution.

Philosophers and social theorists have suggested various principles for this purpose. Some contend that the biological parents have the right and duty to accept the role of legal parent because their voluntary acts have created a being who is dependent on others for survival.[1] Others seem to suggest that parents, having created a child, have a limited property interest in it and therefore the right (though

---

1. Frederick A. Olafson, "Rights and Duties in Education," in J. Doyle, ed., *Educational Judgments: Papers in the Philosophy of Education* (London: Routledge & Kegan Paul, 1973), pp. 173–95, cited by Francis Shrag, "Children: Their Rights and Needs," in W. Aiken and H. LaFollette, eds., *Whose Child? Children's Rights, Parental Authority and State Power* (Totowa, N.J.: Littlefield, Adams & Co., 1980), pp. 237–53.

perhaps not the duty) to accept the role of legal parent.[2] Still others base the assignment of legal parenthood to biological parents on the right of adults to form intimate relationships or on the supposition that these arrangements are the most likely to serve the child's best interests.[3]

My objective here is not to resolve the conflicts among such conceptions of the moral basis of parents' legal rights and duties, but simply to stress that the biological ties are not moral connections and need not be social bonds. By themselves, biological facts do not establish a legal and social role defined by rights, duties, immunities, and powers.

The family as a social and legal institution, in short, is not an array of biological relationships. It is a package of roles related to the function of caring for and rearing children. In it, some (legal) adult takes general legal and social responsibility for rearing some (legal) child (i.e., occupies the parental role with respect to that child).

The family is not the only social and legal structure that might evolve or be designed to execute this function. It is distinguished from certain other possible arrangements by being relatively more private and autonomous.

To see the privacy and autonomy accorded the family, imagine by way of contrast a society in which the child-rearing function is executed in an institution fully as public as courts, legislatures, and prisons. In this society, all newborns are thought "orphans," so to speak; that is, they are thought not to "belong" to anyone, not to be the particular responsibility of any identifiable individual. Instead, the legal and social responsibility for the care and rearing of all children, the "parental" role, is assigned to professional caretakers who represent, and are in the service of, the community at large.

Like other public officials such as judges, legislators, and wardens, these caretakers exercise certain defined powers and can be held accountable in public to public standards of competence and conduct. The judge, for example, on pain of possible removal from office, cannot decide to punish an offender in the absence of evidence or in a manner not prescribed by law.

---

2. Murray N. Rothbard, *The Ethics of Liberty* (Atlantic Highlands, N.J.: Humanities Press, 1982), p. 99.

3. Feradinand Schoeman, "Rights of Children, Rights of Parents, and the Moral Basis of the Family," *Ethics* 91 (1980): 6–19.

In the imagined society, every aspect of a caretaker's official conduct is subject to similar public scrutiny, for the manner in which children are reared is wholly a public concern.

Families are more private and autonomous institutions than this imagined communal arrangement. Families are less subject to scrutiny by those not party to the relationship: Within broad limits, parents are at liberty to determine what their child's good is and how it is to be pursued. Activities in the family are thought in large measure legitimately removed from public view, knowledge, and control.

This is not to say, of course, that families enjoy total autonomy or freedom from public scrutiny. If parents flagrantly, excessively, and repeatedly act outside of certain limits—if, for example, they neglect or abuse their children—they may come under public scrutiny and receive public rebuke, and might even be deprived of the parental role. Within rather broad limits, however, parents are at liberty to tell someone who might criticize their child-rearing practices that the matter is their private concern and none of his.

The family, then, is a relatively private and autonomous institution having the function of caring for and rearing children. It must have some minimal autonomy and privacy in order to be distinguished from a public and communal structure having the same function. Beyond that, however, there is no particular level of autonomy and privacy that it must enjoy in order to be a family. In some societies or during certain epochs, the family will have these attributes to a greater degree than in others. It is often thought, for example, that the colonial American family had greater privacy and autonomy than the American family has today.

This suggests that one task of an adequate theory of the family will be to make a case for an institution with a level of privacy and autonomy that distinguishes it from public and communal arrangements. A secondary task will be to develop a rationale for any requisite privacy and autonomy beyond this minimum.

Yet another task is the specification of the rights, obligations, powers, and immunities attached to the roles of parent and child. Different forms of the family involve different characterizations of these roles and relationships. The family of ancient Rome, for example, had a different arrangement of rights and duties from that found in the family of modern Japan. Both structures, nonetheless, are families.

Families may differ in size as well as structure. A family might consist of mother, father, and their offspring, the familiar "nuclear family"; it might be a larger group, the "extended family" in one form or another; it might be smaller, as in a "single-parent family." All of these forms fall under the same concept.

A theory that defends the family, that is, a private, relatively autonomous social and legal institution having certain functions, need not commit itself exclusively to one or another of these possible forms or sizes. If it does, it must offer a rationale for the preferred form or size.

In addition, an adequate theory of the family will be coherent: It will exhibit a unity or continuity among the considerations employed in addressing these issues. The unity or continuity can take one of several forms. One kind of unity is that which obtains when several or all of the considerations flow from a single central principle.

An example of a theory having this unity is one that bases biological parents' duty to accept the parental role on their voluntary acts, which created beings who are dependent on others for their survival. The basic theme suggests a rationale for assigning the parental role to particular individuals; the biological parents, and not others, are to take the legal and social role because they, not others, voluntarily created a dependent being. (It appears, moreover, that in the case of conception resulting from an involuntary act, only the initiating party has an obligation to take the parental role.) The basic theme also suggests that parental obligations may be limited to the responsibility of assuring the survival of the offspring and that the obligations cease when the dependency ceases.

A second kind of unity prevails in a theory that employs several independent principles to address the various issues, and does not derive them from a single central consideration. If one holds, for example, that a biological parents have a limited property right in their children, it seems that one must adduce additional principles to explain how and why this interest terminates—irrespective of the parents' wishes—when the child reaches some particular age or level of development. The notion of property addresses the issue of acquisition of parental rights but does not identify the basis for limiting the scope and duration of these rights.

A theory employing several considerations might simply be structured around a plurality of independent principles deemed equally fundamental; or it might have a unity arising when the analysis is placed in some broader theoretical context.

For our purposes, the main point to keep in mind is that an adequate theory of the family will have accounts of the various normative and conceptual aspects of the institution, and these accounts will be consistent in themselves and will cohere with one another to form a unified whole.

Judged by the standards just described, the theory of the family embedded in American social and legal institutions is less than adequate. As will be shown in the next section, there are at least four conceptions of the family embodied in our legal and social practices. These are not linked to one another and applied in such a way that they form a comprehensive vision of the family as a unitary institution defined and governed by a coherent set of principles. Instead, as we move from one context to another, we have abrupt shifts of focus, with no discernible underlying rationale for the choice of perspective in any particular context. In short, the elements are combined *ad hoc,* not structured to form a unified theory.

FOUR CONCEPTIONS OF THE FAMILY

In this section, I describe four conceptions of the family, each of which coheres with certain aspects of our legal and social practices. The *authoritarian* conception emphasizes the parents' right to command and the child's duty to obey. The *sentimental* view focuses on the emotional and psychological aspects of the relationship between parent and child. The paternalistic outlook stresses the parents' role in limiting the child's liberty in order to secure his good. The *economic* vantage point emphasizes the role of financial factors in the family structure.[4]

The differences among these outlooks are often matters of emphasis or focus. A theory can stress one consideration, the sentimental, for example, and also incorporate another, say, paternalism.

A *caveat* about this classification may be in order. Placing a theory within one of these groups does not locate it on a political spectrum. Theories in different categories may have similar policy implications: Both the authoritarian and the sentimentalist, for example, may strongly oppose (for different reasons, to be sure) state intervention in the family. Also, theories from a single category may differ sharply in their policy implications. Among the paternalists, for example, there are

---

4. Yet another conception, one that treats children as property of their parents, occasionally appears in the context of adoption or in custody disputes related to divorce.

those who favor (or at least would allow) a rather extensive governmental role in the family, and those who would advocate far less intervention.

As background to the presentation of these four conceptions, I shall briefly summarize some aspects of contemporary American family law.

The Family in Contemporary American Law

Judicial pronouncements have been more emphatic than clear about the basis of parental rights, that is, about the grounds for assigning to biological parents the legal role of parent. In leading decisions, the courts have held that the right to conceive and raise one's children is "essential" and one of the "basic civil rights of man." Other decisions state, "It is cardinal with us that the custody, care and nurture of the child reside first with the parents, whose primary function and freedom includes preparation for obligations the state can neither supply nor hinder." Another decision characterized the right to marry and raise a family as "of similar order and magnitude as the fundamental rights specifically protected by the Constitution" and described familial ties as being "as old as civilization itself." Constitutional bases for parental rights have been found in the due process and equal protection clauses of the Fourteenth Amendment and in the Ninth Amendment.[5]

While the courts recognize "a private realm of family life which the state cannot enter," they also unhesitatingly assert a governmental authority to regulate the family "in the public interest." Thus, they hold that "acting to guard the general interest in youth's well-being, the state as *parens patriae* may restrict the parents' control by requiring school attendance, regulating or prohibiting the child's labor and in many other ways." Indeed, it is held that "the state has a wide range of power for limiting parental freedom and authority in things affecting the child's welfare," and that this authority is broader than the state's authority over like actions of adults.[6]

The legal rights of family privacy are thus primarily the rights of parents (against the state) to act as they see fit in exercising their

---

5. The cases are *Meyer* v. *Nebraska, Skinner* v. *Oklahoma, Prince* v. *Massachusetts,* and *Griswold* v. *Connecticut.* See Homer H. Clark, Jr., *Cases and Problems in Domestic Relations,* 2d ed. (Saint Paul, Minn.: West Publishing Co., 1974), pp. 50, 54, 444–46, 222.

6. *Prince* v. *Massachusetts.* See Clark, *n.* 5, pp. 445–46.

rights over their children and in discharging their legal responsibilities for them.

Under current practices, parents are legally responsible for the care, education, and support of their children and may have a legal right to the services and earnings of the child. Parents may also enjoy legal immunity from suits concerning actions that would be torts against the child (e.g., battery) in nonfamilial contexts.[7]

Children are thus under broad parental control in matters of religion, education, domicile, associates, and recreation. A child's parents can choose vegetarianism for him, or pantheism; they can forbid him to associate with other children or with adults of whom they disapprove. Parents can compel a child to practice the cello; forbid him to learn physics; prevent him from getting a job, taking a spouse, or establishing a separate domicile. The child can be subjected to corporal punishment (whereas even the convicted adult felon is protected by law from such treatment).

Parental authority is sufficiently extensive that a child who has developed firm and deeply held religious convictions that happen to be at odds with those of his parents may find himself the target of a lawful and systematic attempt to eradicate his beliefs. His parents can legally limit his access to reading material, restrict his associates, and prevent his participation in the religious services of the disapproved denomination. With respect to his parents' wishes, the child enjoys no freedom of religion.

Parents can also lawfully thwart the ambitions of a child who has an exceptional talent in music or mathematics and a commitment to building a career around that ability: They have no legal obligation to provide the opportunity that would make achievement of these objectives possible, even if it lies well within their means to do so.

The child has little legal recourse against the exercise of parental authority that seems to him arbitrary or unfair. In general, he is not legally empowered to seek, accelerate, or effect a termination of his subjection to his parents. If he "votes with his feet" and leaves the parental domicile to find more acceptable living conditions, the par-

---

7. Homer H. Clark, Jr., *Law of Domestic Relations in the United States* (Saint Paul, Minn.: West Publishing Co., 1968), pp. 240, 245, 551–59. See also Sanford N. Katz, William A. Schroeder, and Lawrence R. Sidman, "Emancipating Our Children—Coming of Legal Age in America," *Family Law Quarterly* 7 (1973): 214–15; William L. Prosser, *The Law of Torts*, 4th ed. (Saint Paul, Minn.: West Publishing Co., 1971), pp. 864–69.

ents can deny permission for him to relocate and force him to return. Should he contemplate a law suit demanding parental recognition of his freedom of religion or his right to pursue the vocation of his choice, he would most likely find himself without legal standing or counsel.

In short, a child generally lacks the legal capacity to free himself from parental control. The end of parental authority can come through the passage of time, the initiative of the parents, or the initiative of others. If the parents exceed the somewhat indeterminate bounds set by laws governing abuse and neglect, others can initiate suits to remove the child from their control. The parents themselves can relinquish their rights and make the child available for adoption, or they can renounce their duties and "emancipate" the child. In the absence of such actions, however, the passage of time is the only certain solution to the conflict. When he reaches some legally specified age, eighteen in most jurisdictions, a person ceases to be a (legal) child and is no longer subject to parental control.

With this summary of some aspects of contemporary family law in mind, we can proceed to an examination of four conceptions of the family.

The Authoritarian Family

A comprehensive account of the authoritarian conception of the family can be found in the writings of James Kent, nineteenth century American jurist and scholar. Many features of his view, which was based on common law, survive in our current legal system.

The authoritarian conception emphasizes the parents' right to issue commands and to punish disobedience, and the child's duty to obey. The essential points of the theory, as articulated by Kent, are that children cannot maintain themselves, that parents have a natural duty to maintain and educate their children, and that parents' rights to exercise control and to discipline their children are derived from their duty to maintain and educate them.

Kent offers the following characterization of the common law regarding the rights of parents and the duties of children:

> The duties of parents to their children, as being their natural guardians, consist in maintaining and educating them during the season of infancy and youth, and in making reasonable provision for their future usefulness and happiness in life, by a situation suited to their habits, and a competent provision for the exigencies of that situation.
>
> The wants and weaknesses of children render it necessary that some

person maintain them, and the voice of nature has pointed out the parent as the most fit and proper person. . . . The obligation on the part of the parent to maintain the child continues until the latter is in a condition to provide for its own maintenance, and it extends no further than to a necessary support. . . .

And in consequence of the obligation of the father to provide for the maintenance, and, in some qualified degree, for the education of his infant children, he is entitled to the custody of their persons, and to the value of their labor and services. . . .

The rights of parents result from their duties. As they are bound to maintain and educate their children, the law has given them a right to such authority; and in support of that authority, a right to exercise such discipline as may be requisite for the discharge of their sacred trust.[8]

A contemporary account follows Chancellor Kent in deriving parental rights from parental duties:

As a result of statutory and common law developments, the American parent is generally held responsible for his child's financial support, health, education, morality, and for instilling in him respect for people and authority. To facilitate the performance of these obligations, the parent is vested with the custody and control of the child, including the requisite disciplinary authority. And, under a heritage of the past, the parent is also entitled to the child's services and, by derivation, to his or her earnings.[9]

Historically, the authoritarian family has been patriarchal. As it existed in traditional society, this patriarchal structure has been thought to have these features: "It was founded almost exclusively on economic and pragmatic considerations . . . . It was low in affect or psychological commitment, and was characterized by formality and distance rather than by intimacy. It was not sharply separated from the outside world of the community and did not place much value on privacy."[10]

The Sentimental Family

In contrast with the authoritarian conception, the sentimental view emphasizes the potential intimacy and psychological intensity of the personal aspects of familial ties; it also stresses family privacy.

---

8. James Kent, *Commentaries on American Law,* in Bremner, ed., *Children and Youth in America: A Documentary History,* vol. 1, 1600–1865 (Cambridge: Harvard University Press, 1970), pp. 363–64.

9. Katz, et al., *n.* 7, p. 214 (footnotes omitted). See also Clark, *n.* 7, p. 240.

10. Susan Moller Okin, "Women and the Making of the Sentimental Family," *Philosophy and Public Affairs* 11 (1982): 73.

This conception draws attention to the possibility—and the importance—of affectionate personal relationships. In many of our dealings with others, it is acceptable to adopt a distant and impersonal attitude, and to regard our activities with them as instrumentally valuable (if at all) but not worthwhile in themselves. This is not to say that we may properly be rude, callous, or malicious—only that we need attach no particular value to dealing with *this* individual rather than someone else who could perform the desired tasks equally well. Paradigmatic of these activities is a one-time commercial transaction. Mutual affection is not an essential ingredient in the relationship between merchant and customer, but mutual regard for rights and duties is.

Our lives would be impoverished, however, if all of our relationships were similarly impersonal. Fortunately, we are capable of forming attachments to one another, relationships in which we value individuals primarily, if not exclusively, for themselves and not simply for their usefulness to us. Friendship is one such relationship; familial ties, in the sentimentalist view, can be another.

The affection characteristic of such relationships is not to be confused with regard for one another's virtues, merits, or accomplishments—or for any other attributes. It attaches to a particular being and involves a commitment to him. This attitude survives changes in virtue or merit that he might undergo and is not necessarily elicited by another person who possesses similar (or even superior) attributes.[11]

The sentimental family, like the authoritarian, has been patriarchal. The role of sentiment in the family has been adduced as a reason for entrusting adult males with leadership responsibilities within the family as well as in the larger community. Husbands and fathers, it is argued, "can safely be entrusted with representing their families' interests in the political realm" because "the interests of the family are totally united," and "family relations, unlike those outside, are based only on love."[12]

---

11. See Lyla H. O'Driscoll, "On the Nature and Value of Marriage," in M. Vetterling-Braggin, F. Elliston, and J. English, eds., *Feminism and Philosophy* (Totowa, N.J.: Littlefield, Adams & Co., 1977), pp. 249–63. See also Gregory Vlastos, "Justice and Equality," in R. Brandt, ed., *Social Justice* (Englewood Cliffs, N.J.: Prentice-Hall, Inc., 1962), pp. 43–44.

12. Okin, *n*. 10, p. 74. She points out that philosophers otherwise as disparate as Mill (in his early writings), Hegel, Rousseau, and Betham united in accepting such a conception of the family and a concomitant limitation of the political role of women and children.

According to the sentimental conception, the family is a private relationship. It is not private simply in the sense of subsisting between "private individuals" rather than public officials: A commercial arrangement can be private in that sense. Rather, it is private in a stronger sense: The environment is which personal ties are formed and can flourish is one which is broadly protected from intervention by those not party to the relationship. Family activities are thus legitimately removed from public view, knowledge, and control, according to the sentimental conception, for the sake of the intimacy that can be achieved in such circumstances.

Versions of this conception of the family have recently been advanced by Ferdinand Schoeman and Francis Shrag.

Schoeman argues that the "right" to a private and autonomous relationship with one's biological children stems from the importance of intimate relationships in general."[13] He suggests that talk of children's rights can be hazardous:

> As persons, children ought to be thought of as possessing rights; but as infants in relationship to their parents, they are to be thought of primarily as having needs, the satisfaction of which involves intimate and intense relationships with others. As against society, we might yet think of infants and parents as having rights to conditions which permit or encourage, or at least do not discourage, the social and material conditions conducive to parent-child intimacy.[14]

Shrag finds talk of rights out of place in the context of the family, warning that "we must be watchful lest our pervasive preoccupation with rights, even with children's rights, impair our ability to give children what they need," particularly the love and affection critical to the development of self-esteem.[15]

The Paternalistic Family

Numerous theories of the family are paternalistic. What they have in common is the view that parents may legitimately limit the child's

---

13. Schoeman, *n*. 3, p. 6.
14. Ibid., p. 9.
15. Shrag, *n*. 1, pp. 237–53. Elsewhere, Shrag argues that "the perspective required by justice is different from and opposed to that required for intimate relations." See Francis Shrag, "Justice and the Family," *Inquiry* 19 (1976): 193–208. It is instructive to note that, *mutatis mutandis*, these comments repeat warnings against ascribing equal legal rights to spouses and against talk, within a marriage, of the rights of spouses.

liberty "for his own good" and the supposition that adults—parents in particular—are likely to know better than the child what is in his interest. The claim of legitimate limitation is usually grounded in further beliefs concerning children's lack of experience, rationality, or some other feature thought to differentiate fundamentally between children and adults.

A case in point in Gerald Dworkin's view:

> What justifies us in interfering with children? The fact that they lack some of the emotional and cognitive capacities required in order to make fully rational decisions. It is an empirical question to just what extent children have an adequate conception of their own present and future interests but there is not much doubt that there are many deficiencies. For example, it is very difficult for a child to defer gratification for any considerable period of time. Given these deficiencies and given the very real and permanent dangers that may befall the child, it becomes not only permissible but even a duty of the parent to restrict the child's freedom in various ways. There is however an important moral limitation on the exercise of such parental power which is provided by the notion of the child eventually coming to see the correctness of his parent's interventions. Parental paternalism may be thought of as a wager by the parent on the child's subsequent recognition of the wisdom of the restrictions. There is an emphasis on what could be called future-oriented consent—on what the child will come to welcome, rather than on what he does welcome.[16]

Paternalistic views differ from one another regarding the proper basis for adult intervention. They also differ regarding the proper form and scope of intervention (e.g., about the propriety of coercive rather than persuasive methods, about whether limitations can be properly imposed in any area of the child's activity or only in a narrow range, and about the criterion to be used in determining when the intervention ceases to be proper).[17]

16. Gerald Dworkin, "Paternalism," in ed., R. Wasserstrom, *Morality and the Law* (Belmont, Calif.: Wadsworth Publishing Co., 1971), pp. 118–19.

17. *Whose Child?*, cited in *note* 1 above, includes several paternalistic views. See Ann Palmeri, "Childhood's End: Toward the Liberation of Children," pp. 105–23 and Joel Feinberg, "The Child's Right to an Open Future," pp. 124–52. See also O. O'Neill and W. Ruddick, eds., *Having Children* (New York, Oxford University Press, 1979). For critiques of various forms of parental paternalism, see Howard Cohen, *Equal Rights for Children* (Totowa, N.J.: Littlefield, Adams & Co., 1980) and Laurence D. Houlgate, *The Child and the State: A Normative Theory of Juvenile Rights* (London and Baltimore: Johns Hopkins University Press, 1980).

Some forms of paternalism will issue the same injunction regarding parental behavior as, say, the sentimental conception of the family. Much depends on how the particular version of paternalism conceives the grounds of legitimate intervention and the nature of the child's well-being.

Paternalistic views, along with the sentimental conception, have influenced our social norms for parental conduct. The paternalistic view, particularly versions appealing to "the child's best interest," has shaped policy and practice in such matters as adoption, removal of "neglected" children and their placement in foster care, and the assignment of custody in the event of divorce.[18]

The Economic Conception

Legal discussions of the emancipation of minors treat the family primarily as a network of rights and duties in financial matters. The "emancipated" minor is essentially one who is financially independent of his parents—earning a living, maintaining himself in a separate residence, managing his own affairs.[19] A parent has a duty to support an unemancipated minor, a right to retain that minor's earnings, or sue for the loss of his services.

The underlying principle of the family as so conceived seems to be "he who pays the piper calls the tune," and this maxim applies in three ways. First, the person who supports a minor is thought to control him in a way that would make it inappropriate to permit the minor to sue his parents for torts. Second, he who supports a minor is entitled to control him: He ought to be recognized as having a right to exercise disciplinary control, to retain the minor's earnings, to determine the minor's domicile, and to sue for damages in the event that the minor's services are lost. Third, he who does not pay the

18. See Cohen, *n.* 17, pp. 1–14 on what he terms the "caretaker ideology."

19. See Henry H. Foster, A *"Bill of Rights" for Children* (Springfield, Ill.: Charles C. Thomas Publisher, 1974), p. 48, and Clark, *n.* 7, p. 240. See also the Institute for Judicial Administration–American Bar Association (IJA–ABA) Joint Commission on Juvenile Justice Standards, *Standards Relating to Rights of Minors* (Cambridge, Mass.: Ballinger Publishing Co., 1980), p. 21. In a recommendation approved by the American Bar Association House of Delegates in 1977, the commission proposed legislation authorizing "a finding of emancipation when a child, prior to the age of majority, has established a residence separate from that of his or her family, whether or not with parental consent or consent of a person responsible for his or her care, and is managing his or her own financial affairs."

piper is thought to have no right to call the tune: The parent who abandons a child loses his claim to the child's earnings.[20]

TOWARD A NEW THEORY OF THE FAMILY

Each of these conceptions of the family is to some degree reflected in American social and legal practices. A kind of authoritarianism undergirds our confident assertion that the biological parents have a "natural dominion" over their child. Sentimentalism and paternalism influence our social and legal norms for judging parental conduct. The economic conception shapes our views on the termination of parental rights and responsibilities.

Since the outlooks these conceptions represent may simply indicate differences in emphasis, a theory of the family may employ more than one of these considerations without internal contradiction. There is, however, risk of conflict or paradox in a theory that incorporates more than one of these principles. The potential for conflict between the sentimental and the authoritarian views is evident.

Indeed, the sentimentalist, it will be recalled, warns against stress on the family as a structure defined by rights and duties, and governed by justice. Some authoritarians reject sentiment as an element of family life. Chancellor Kent says little about sentiment or affection in familial relations. More recently, Robert Nisbet has emphasized familial authority and has disavowed the more modern notion of family bonds as emotional.

The family Nisbet extols is "the longitudinal family of generations in time, the family of blood line, of tradition and history, of ancestors and planned-for posterity," not "the small household group that is customarily the referent in our time." This structure "extended itself into all aspects of individual life—economic, political, legal, cultural, psychological, and biological," and "in political terms was a government itself, monarchy or republic, with no nonsense about equality of membership."[21]

---

20. See Clark, *n.* 7, p. 240. This "economic" conception of the family is not to be identified with analyses such as those advanced by Gordon Tullock, Richard B. McKenzie, and Gary S. Becker. See Gary S. Becker, *A Treatise on the Family* (Cambridge: Harvard University Press, 1981) and Richard B. McKenzie and Gordon Tullock, *The New World of Economics* (Homewood, Ill.: Irwin, 1975), pp. 95–123.

21. Robert Nisbet, *Prejudices: A Philosophical Dictionary* (Cambridge: Harvard University Press, 1982), p. 111.

According to Nisbet, "justice, not equality was the sovereign value" of this family. Further, the family in this "large and historic sense of the word has no more to do with love and romance than do state and church. The fundamental cement of family is duty or obligation, not love. The test of brotherhood or virtue is response to duty, not love or even friendship."[22]

In this section, I want to dispel some of the air of paradox characteristic of a theory that employs both the idea of parental authority and the ideal of sentimental ties. I begin with the idea of familial roles as defined by rights, duties, powers, and immunities, and familial relations as governed by principles of justice.

I adopt, without argument here, a principle of justice for social institutions according to which each person is entitled to the most extensive liberty compatible with a like liberty for all.[23] I assume, then, a family structure governed by this principle, one in which neither parent nor child is gratuitously deprived of liberty. Both parent and child are seen as bearers of rights—fundamentally, the right to maximal equal liberty. In addition, their roles in the social institution are defined by a complex of rights, duties, powers, and immunities.

I also adopt, again without argument here, several principles of justice for individuals.[24] These can be thought of as "natural duties," requirements that apply without regard to an individual's voluntary acts and that have no necessary connection with institutions and social practices. They hold between persons regardless of their institutional relationships; they hold between all persons and in this sense are not owed to definite individuals. The two I shall employ here are the natural duty to support and to comply with just institutions that exist and apply to us, and the natural duty of mutual respect. The latter involves acknowledging others as having, either in potential or in actualized form, a sense of justice and a conception of the good. We show this respect in various ways, including our willingness to view matters from another's point of view and our readiness to give reasons for our actions when they affect another's interests.[25]

The nature, scope, and legitimate exercise of parental authority are governed by these principles of justice. Parents do not exercise au-

---

22. Ibid.
23. See John Rawls, *A Theory of Justice* (Cambridge: Harvard University Press, 1971).
24. Ibid., pp. 114–17, 333–42.
25. Ibid., p. 337.

thority over their children by virtue of their biological connection: They do so because the social or legal structure that assigns them that authority is just. Children do not owe unquestioning and unqualified obedience to their parents: They owe obedience to just institutions.

Parental authority is inherently limited by principles of institutional and individual justice. Parents are not entitled to be despots; children have rights, and parents who act justly recognize their rights. Military command and the power of the absolute monarch are not appropriate models for parental authority. Parents do not have the right to issue any command, however arbitrary, and are not owed unquestioning obedience.

In showing regard for the child's rights, the parents foster the child's self-respect, his "sense of his own value, his secure conviction that his good, his plan of life, is worth carrying out."[26]

One way to see the connection between seeing oneself as having rights and having self-respect is to imagine a person who believes that he has no rights. If he acts, it is on the basis of a revocable privilege or favor granted by another, not because he believes he has a claim against others that they not interfere with his actions. If he seeks a benefit from others, it is again a request or a plea for a favor; he does not believe that others are obligated to give it, or that they wrong him if they refuse it.

The hallmarks of someone who believes he has no rights are humility, deference, and servility—not self-respect.[27] To teach a child that he has no rights is to teach him self-contempt.

When parental authority is seen as limited by children's rights and the principles of justice, and its exercise is seen as guided by mutual respect, the apparent conflict between authority and sentiment diminishes.

The sentimental conception, it will be recalled, regards the family as a structure in which we are to realize our potential to form affec-

---

26. Ibid., p. 440.

27. See Thomas E. Hill, Jr., "Servility and Self-Respect," *Monist* 57 (1973):87–104; Richard A. Wasserstrom, "Rights, Human Rights and Racial Discrimination," in A. Melden, ed., *Human Rights* (Belmont, Calif.: Wadsworth Publishing Co., 1970), pp. 96–110; Joel Feinberg, "On the Nature and Value of Rights," *Journal of Value Inquiry* 4 (1970): 243–57; Bernard R. Boxill, "Self-Respect and Protest," *Philosophy and Public Affairs* 6 (1976): 58–69; Lyla H. O'Driscoll, "Abortion, Property Rights and the Right to Life," *The Personalist* 58 (1977): 99–114; Lyla H. O'Driscoll, "The Quality of Mercy," *The Southern Journal of Philosophy* 21 (no. 2, Summer 1983): 229–50.

tionate personal relationships. On this view, the members of a family are to regard one another, their relationships, shared activities, and their commitments, as valuable in themselves. Family members thwart the development of such a valuation if they are absorbed in a legalistic specification of each person's rights and duties.[28]

In addition, the sentimental conception holds that appeals to rights, justice, duty, and the like are appropriate in public contexts, or in situations in which there is a psychological distance between the parties involved. It holds such appeals to be incongruent with an intimate private relationship characterized by mutual affection and shared commitment.

I believe that the sentimental conception correctly emphasizes the family as a social unit capable of fostering relationships characterized by intimacy, trust, and mutual affection. I do not suggest, however, that the family is a uniquely suitable environment for developing these relationships, or that individual families are uniformly successful in fostering them.

I also think that the sentimentalist is correct in claiming that a broad measure of familial privacy is necessary if these relationships are to develop and thrive.

But I would add some substantial qualifications to the conception's insight concerning the possible incongruity of appeals to rights, justice, duty, and the like in intimate private relationships of shared affection commitment. I believe it is possible to have a relationship which is, on the one hand, founded on principles of justice and defined by roles that specify rights and duties, and which is, on the other hand, characterized by intimacy, trust, and mutual respect.

The sentimentalist's strictures against appeals to rights and duties seem to apply best to an intimate relationship that satisfies the principles of justice and that the involved parties regard as just and valuable in itself. In the everyday workings of such a relationship, there is typically little need for the involved parties to dwell on their rights and duties to one another, or on the principles that underlie their association. They accept those principles and regard their roles in the relationship as fair, and they value their association for its own sake. Their affection for one another and their regard for the bond between

---

28. Similarly, they would forestall the development of such a valuation if they were absorbed in assessments of the various instrumental values of the relationship, and this includes its economic worth.

them incline each to meet the standards set by these principles, to confer the benefits and to undertake the burdens associated with his role in this relationship, and to do more as well.

Too broadly construed, however, the sentimentalist insight obscures the priority of justice in these relationships. These principles govern the structures of personal relationships and provide standards for judging the conduct of participants in the relationship. Moreover, these are standards to which the participants themselves may have recourse. Even in an intimate relationship, one may have occasion to criticize another for failing to discharge the duties that partly define his role in that association. Further, one might appeal to the principles of justice as grounds for changes in the definition of the roles within an association. In short, the participants in an intimate relationship may object to the structure of their relationship, or to conduct that fails to satisfy the requirements of a role within the relationship; in either case they can ground their complaint in the principles of justice.

The sentimentalist view, then, should not be construed as denying the individuality of parties to an intimate relationship. They remain aware of themselves as distinct persons, as individuals who have shared concerns but who also have separate interests, identities, and rights. This cognizance is not incompatible with the attitudes that characterize intimate personal relationships: to acknowledge that they are different individuals does not imply distance and mutual distrust.

What does collide with mutual affection and trust, however, is *excessive* focus on rights, duties, and the like—and *inordinate* appeal to these grounds in matters large and small. Someone intoxicated by the consciousness of having rights may become, in Narveson's phrase, "*pushy* . . . crabby, thin-skinned, cantankerous, touchy, and quite possibly bitchy."[29] Someone who thus pursues his rights in a personal relationship exhibits a distrust that belies the existence of affection and that can undermine the bond.

What is excessive or inordinate, of course, will depend in part on such factors as the degree of intimacy in the relationship and the importance or frequency of the infraction. In public matters or in private relationships, however, it is appropriate to reserve appeals to justice and rights for weightier matters rather than to employ them in trivial spheres, and to consider the strategic as well as the moral aspects of

29. Jan Narveson, "Commentary on Feinberg's 'On the Nature and Value of Rights,'" *Journal of Value Inquiry* 4 (1970): 259.

the use of this rather blunt weapon. If, for example, one wishes to sustain a congenial relationship, some methods of achieving recognition of one's rights will be more effective than others.

What should not be overlooked, however, is that someone can be excessively attentive—or excessively inattentive—to his rights. In personal or impersonal relationships, an attitude of self-effacing deference, unwillingness to acknowledge one's own rights and their importance, involves the vice of servility.[30]

What seems sound in the sentimentalist's view, then, is the recognition in an intimate relationship, or attentive in a way that is incompatible with underlying attitudes of affection. This must not be exaggerated, however, or taken to mean that it is appropriate or required that participants in intimate relationships be inattentive to their rights and duties with respect to one another.

CONCLUSION

In this discussion, I have sought to identify and to clarify some of the issues that must be addressed by an adequate theory of the family. I have not argued that the family, in any form, is preferable to alternative arrangements, nor have I tried to show that the inequality of rights found in most family structures is just. I have indicated a way in which two apparently discordant conceptions of the family— the authoritarian and the sentimental—might be reconciled with each other. I have tried to make intelligible the idea of the family as a social structure governed by justice, defined by rights and duties, and animated by love.

---

30. Hill, *n*. 27.

SELECTED BIBLIOGRAPHY
PART I

Alchian, Armen A., and Harold Demsetz. "Production, Information Costs, and Economic Organization." *American Economic Review* 62 (December 1972):777–95.

Anderson, Michael. *Family Structure in Nineteenth Century Lancashire.* London: Cambridge University Press, 1971.

Asher, Shirley J., and Bernard L. Bloom. "Geographic Mobility as a Factor in Adjustment to Divorce." *Journal of Divorce* 6 (Summer 1983):69–84.

Barker, Ernest, ed. *The Politics of Aristotle.* New York: Oxford University Press, 1972.

Becker, Gary S. *Human Capital: A Theoretical and Empirical Analysis With Special Reference to Education.* New York: Columbia University Press for National Bureau of Economic Research, 1964.

———. "A Theory of the Allocation of Time." *Economic Journal* 75 (September 1965):493–517.

———. "A Theory of Marriage." In T. Schultze, ed., *Economics of the Family: Marriage, Children, and Human Capital,* pt. 3, pp. 299–345. Chicago: University of Chicago Press, 1974.

———. "Altruism, Egoism and Genetic Fitness." *Journal of Economic Literature* 14 (September 1976):817–26.

———. *A Treatise on the Family.* Cambridge: Harvard University Press, 1981.

Ben-Porath, Yoram. "Family Functions and Structure and the Organization of Exchange." In *Economic and Demographic Change: Issues for the 1980s,* pp. 51–64. Vol. 3. Liege, Belgium: IUSSP, 1979.

————. "The F-Connection: Families, Friends, and Firms and the Organization of Exchange." *Population and Development Review* 6 (no. 1, March 1980):1–31.

————. "Economics and the Family—Match or Mismatch? A Review of Becker's 'A Treatise on the Family'." *Journal of Economic Literature* 20 (March 1982):52–64.

Berger, Brigitte, and Peter L. Berger. *The War Over the Family: Capturing the Middle Ground.* Garden City, N.Y.: Anchor Press, 1983.

Bishop, John H. "Jobs, Cash Transfers and Marital Instability: A Review and Synthesis of the Evidence." *Journal of Human Resources* 15 (Summer 1980):301–34.

Blumstein, Philip, and Pepper Schwartz. *American Couples.* New York: William Morrow, 1983.

Carlson, Allan. "Taxes and Families." *Human Life Review* 9 (Winter 1983):38–45.

————. "The Family and Liberal Capitalism." *Modern Age* 26 (1982):366–71.

————. "Families, Sex, and the Liberal Agenda." *Human Life Review* 6 (Summer 1980):30–48.

Demos, John, and Sarane Spence Boocock, eds. "Turning Points: Historical and Sociological Essays on the Family." *American Journal of Sociology,* Supplement 84 (1978).

Easterlin, Richard. "Population Change and Farm Settlement in the Northern U.S." *Journal of Economic History* 36 (March 1976):45–76.

Fogel, Robert, and Stanley Engerman. *Time on the Cross.* Boston: Little, Brown & Co., 1974.

Gilder, George. *Wealth and Poverty.* New York: Basic Books, 1980.

Greene, William H., and Aline O. Quester. "Divorce Risk and Wives' Labor Supply Behavior." *Social Science Quarterly* 63 (March 1982):16–27.

Hannan, Michael T. "Families, Markets, and Social Structures: An Essay on Becker's 'A Treatise on the Family'." *Journal of Economic Literature* 20 (March 1982):65–72.

Hareven, Tamara. "Cycles, Courses and Cohorts: Reflections on Theoretical and Methodological Approaches to the Historical Study of Family Development." *Journal of Social History* 12 (no. 1, Fall 1978):97–110.

Hayek, Friedrich A. *The Constitution of Liberty.* Chicago: University of Chicago Press, 1960.

Huber, Joan, and Glenna Spitze. "Considering Divorce: An Expansion of Becker's Theory of Marital Instability." *American Journal of Sociology* 86 (July 1980):75–89.

Kant, Immanuel. "Fundamental Principles of the Metaphysic of Morals." In T. Greene, ed., *Kant Selections,* pp. 268–89, 296–323, 334-38. New York: Charles Scribner's Sons, 1957.

Laslett, Peter. *Household and Family in Past Time.* Cambridge: Cambridge University Press, 1972.

Manser, Marilyn, and Murray Brown. "Marriage and Household Decision Making: A Bargaining Analysis." *International Economic Review* 21 (February 1980):31–44.

Marx, Karl. "The German Ideology." In R. Tucker, ed., *The Marx-Engels Reader,* pp. 146–203. New York: W. W. Norton, 1978.

Moen, Phyllis. "Unemployment, Public Policy and Families: Forecasts for the 1980s." *Journal of Marriage and the Family* 45 (November 1983):751–60.

Moynihan, Daniel P. *The Negro Family: The Case for National Action.* Washington, D.C.: U.S. Department of Labor, March 1965.

Murray, Charles. *Losing Ground: American Social Policy, 1950–1980.* New York: Basic Books, 1984.

Nerlove, Marc. "Household and Economy: Toward a New Theory of Population and Economic Growth." *Journal of Political Economy* 83 (part 2, March/April 1974):200–18.

Nisbet, Robert A. *The Quest for Community.* New York: Oxford University Press, 1953.

———. *Tradition and Revolt.* New York: Random House, 1968.

Novak, Michael. "Freedom and the Family." *Human Life Review* 6 (Summer 1980):49–59.

Oakeshott, Michael. *Rationalism in Politics.* New York: Methuen, 1981.

Pollak, Robert A. "A Transaction Cost Approach to Families and Households." *Journal of Economic Literature* 23 (June 1985):581–608.

Pollak, Robert A., and Michael L. Wachter. "The Relevance of the Household Production Function and Its Implications for the Allocation of Time." *Journal of Political Economy* 83 (part 2, April 1975):255–77.

Poster, Mark. *Critical Theory of the Family.* New York: Seabury Press, 1978.

Rawls, John. *A Theory of Justice.* Cambridge: Harvard University Press, 1981.

Schrecker, Paul. "The Family: Conveyance of Tradition." In R. Nanda Ashen, ed., *The Family: Its Function and Destiny,* chap. 23, pp. 488–510. New York: Harper & Brothers, 1959.

Schultz, Theodore W., ed. *Economics of the Family: Marriage, Children, and Human Capital.* Chicago: University of Chicago Press for National Bureau of Economic Research, 1973.

Simon, Yves R. *Philosophy of Democratic Government.* Chicago: University of Chicago Press, 1958.

Steiner, Gilbert Y. *The Futility of Family Policy*. Washington, D.C.: Brookings Institution, 1981.

Strauss, Leo. *Natural Right and History*. Chicago: University of Chicago Press, 1971.

Thompson, Kenneth S. *The Divorce Profile: Differential Social Correlates in 1952 and 1972*. San Francisco: R & E Research Associates, 1978.

Wilkson, Kenneth P., et al. "Divorce and Recent Net Migration Into the Old West." *Journal of Marriage and the Family* 45 (May 1983):437–45.

Zimmerman, Carle C., and Lucius F. Cervantes. *Successful American Families*. New York: Pageant Press, 1960.

THE NINETEENTH- AND EARLY TWENTIETH- CENTURY EXPERIENCE

4

THE PROGRESSIVE ERA AND THE FAMILY

Murray N. Rothbard

While the "Progressive Era" used to be narrowly designated as the period 1900–1914, historians now realize that the period is really much broader, stretching from the latter decades of the nineteenth century into the early 1920s. The broader period marks an era in which the entire American polity—from economics to urban planning to medicine to social work to the licensing of professions to the ideology of intellectuals—was transformed from a roughly laissez-faire system based on individual rights to one of state planning and control. In the sphere of public policy issues closely related to the life of the family, most of the change took place, or at least began, in the latter decades of the nineteenth century. In this paper we shall use the analytic insights of the "new political history" to examine the ways in which the so-called progressives sought to shape and control selected aspects of American family life.

ETHNORELIGIOUS CONFLICT AND THE PUBLIC SCHOOLS

In the last two decades, the advent of the "new political history" has transformed our understanding of the political party system and the basis of political conflict in nineteenth century America. In contrast to the party systems of the twentieth century (the "fourth" party system, 1896–1932, of Republican supremacy; the "fifth" party system, 1932–? of Democratic supremacy), the nineteenth century political parties were not bland coalitions of interests with virtually the same amorphous ideology, with each party blurring what is left of its image during campaigns to appeal to the large independent center. In the nineteenth century, each party offered a fiercely contrasting ideology, and political parties performed the function of imposing a common ideology on diverse sectional and economic interests. During campaigns, the ideology and the partisanship became fiercer and even more clearly demarcated, since the object was not to appeal to independent moderates—there were virtually none—but to bring out the vote of one's own partisans. Such partisanship and sharp alternatives marked the "second" American party system (Whig versus Democrat, approximately 1830 to the mid-1850s) and the "third" party system (closely fought Republican versus Democrat, mid-1850s to 1896).

Another important insight of the new political history is that the partisan passion devoted by rank-and-file Democrats and Republicans to national economic issues, stemmed from a similar passion devoted at the local and state level to what would now be called "social" issues. Furthermore, that political conflict, from the 1830s on, stemmed from a radical transformation that took place in American Protestantism as a result of the revival movement of the 1830s.

The new revival movement swept the Protestant churches, particularly in the North, like wildfire. In contrast to the old creedal Calvinist churches that stressed the importance of obeying God's law as expressed in the church creed, the new "pietism" was very different. The pietist doctrine was essentially as follows: Specific creeds of various churches or sects do not matter. Neither does obedience to the rituals or liturgies of the particular church. What counts for salvation is only each individual being "born again"—a direct confrontation between the individual and God, a mystical and emotional conversion in which the individual achieves salvation. The rite of baptism, to the pietist, therefore becomes secondary; of primary importance is his or her personal moment of conversion.

But if the specific church or creed becomes submerged in a vague Christian interdenominationalism, then the individual Christian is left on his own to grapple with the problems of salvation. Pietism, as it swept American Protestantism in the 1830s, took two very different forms in North and South, with very different political implications.

The Southerners, at least until the 1890s, became "salvationist pietists," that is, they believed that the emotional experience of individual regeneration, of being born again, was enough to ensure salvation. Religion was a separate compartment of life, a vertical individual-God relation carrying no imperative to transform man-made culture and interhuman relations.

In contrast, the Northerners, particularly in the areas inhabited by "Yankees," adopted a far different form of pietism, "evangelical pietism." The evangelical pietists believed that man could achieve salvation by an act of free will. More particularly, they also believed that it was *necessary* to a person's *own salvation*—and not just a good idea—to try his best to ensure the salvation of everyone else in society:

> "To spread holiness," to create that Christian commonwealth by bringing all men to Christ, was the divinely ordered duty of the "saved." Their mandate was "to transform the world into the image of Christ."[1]

Since each individual is alone to wrestle with problems of sin and salvation, without creed or ritual of the church to sustain him, the evangelical duty must therefore be to use the state, the social arm of the integrated Christian community, to stamp out temptation and occasions for sin. Only in this way could one perform one's divinely mandated duty to maximize the salvation of others.[2] And to the evangelical pietist, sin took on an extremely broad definition, placing the requirements for holiness far beyond that of other Christian groups. As one antipietist Christian put it, "They saw sin where God did not." In particular, sin was any and all forms of contact with liquor, and doing anything except praying and going to church on Sunday. Any

---

1. The quotations are, respectively, from the *Minutes of the Ohio Annual Conference of the Methodist Episcopal Church, 1875*, p. 228; and the *Minutes of the Annual Meeting of the Maine Baptist Missionary Convention, 1890*, p. 13. Both are cited in Paul Kleppner, *The Third Electoral System, 1853–1892: Parties, Voters, and Political Cultures* (Chapel Hill: University of North Carolina Press, 1979), p. 190. Professor Kleppner is the doyen of the "new political," also known as the "ethnocultural," historians. See also his *The Cross of Culture: A Social Analysis of Midwestern Politics, 1850–1900* (New York: The Free Press, 1970).

2. In contrast to previous Christian groups, which were either amillennial (the return of Jesus will bring an end to human history) or premillennial (the return of Jesus will usher in a thousand-year reign of the Kingdom of God on earth), most evangelical pietists were postmillennialists. In short, whereas Catholics, Lutherans, and most Calvinists believed that the return of Jesus is independent of human actions, the postmillennialists held that Christians must establish a thousand-year reign of the Kingdom of God on earth as a necessary *precondition* of Jesus' return. In short, the evangelicals will have to take over the state and stamp out sin, so that Jesus can then return.

forms of gambling, dancing, theater, reading of novels—in short, secular enjoyment of any kind—were considered sinful.

The forms of sin that particularly agitated the evangelicals were those they held to interfere with the theological free will of individuals, making them unable to achieve salvation. Liquor was sinful because, they alleged, it crippled the free will of the imbibers. Another particular source of sin was Roman Catholicism, in which priests and bishops, arms of the Pope (whom they identified as the Antichrist), ruled the minds and therefore crippled the theological freedom of will of members of the church.

Evangelical pietism particularly appealed to, and therefore took root among, the "Yankees," i.e., that cultural group that originated in (especially rural) New England and emigrated widely to populate northern and western New York, northern Ohio, northern Indiana, and northern Illinois. The Yankees were natural "cultural imperialists," people who were wont to impose their values and morality on other groups; as such, they took quite naturally to imposing their form of pietism through whatever means were available, including the use of the coercive power of the state.

In contrast to evangelical pietists were, in addition to small groups of old-fashioned Calvinists, two great Christian groups, the Catholics and the Lutherans (or at least, the high-church variety of Lutheran), who were "liturgicals" (or "ritualists") rather than pietists. The liturgicals saw the road to salvation in joining the particular church, obeying its rituals, and making use of its sacraments; the individual was not alone with only his emotions and the state to protect him. There was no particular need, then, for the state to take on the functions of the church. Furthermore, the liturgicals had a much more relaxed and rational view of what sin really was; for instance, *excessive* drinking might be sinful, but liquor per se surely was not.

The evangelical pietists, from the 1830s on, were the northern Protestants of British descent, as well as the Lutherans from Scandinavia and a minority of pietist German synods; the liturgicals were the Roman Catholics and the high-church Lutherans, largely German.

Very rapidly, the political parties reflected a virtually one-to-one correlation of this ethnoreligious division: the Whig, and later the Republican, party consisting chiefly of the pietists, and the Democratic party encompassing almost all the liturgicals. And for almost a century, on a state and local level, the Whig/Republican pietists tried desperately and determinedly to stamp out liquor and all Sunday activities except church (of course, drinking liquor on Sunday was a heinous double sin). As to the Catholic church, the pietists tried to restrict or abolish immigration, since people coming from Germany and Ireland, liturgicals, were outnumbering people from Britain and Scandinavia. Failing that and despairing of doing anything about adult Catholics poisoned by agents of the Vatican, the evangelical pietists decided to concentrate on saving Catholic and Lutheran youth by trying to eliminate the parochial schools, through which both religious groups transmitted their precious religious and social values to the young. The object, as many pietists put it, was to "Christianize the Catholics," to force Catholic and Lutheran children into public schools, which could then be used as an instrument of pietist Protestantization. Since the Yankees had early taken to the idea of imposing communal civic virtue and obedience through the public schools, they were particularly receptive to this new reason for aggrandizing public education.

To all of these continuing aggressions by what they termed "those fanatics," the liturgicals fought back with equal fervor. Particularly bewildered were the Germans who, Lutheran and Catholic alike, were accustomed to the entire family happily attending beer gardens together on Sundays after church and who now found the "fanatic" pietists trying desperately to outlaw this pleasurable and seemingly innocent activity. The pietist Protestant attacks on private and parochial schools fatally threatened the preservation and maintenance of the liturgicals' cultural and religious values; and since large numbers of the Catholics and Lutherans were immigrants, parochial schools also served to maintain group affinities in a new and often hostile world—especially the world of Anglo-Saxon pietism. In the case of the Germans, it also meant, for several decades, preserving parochial teaching in the beloved German language, as against fierce pressures for Anglicization.

In the last three decades of the nineteenth century, as Catholic immigration grew and the Democratic party moved slowly but surely toward a majority status, the Republican, and—more broadly—pietist pressures became more intense. The purpose of the public school, to the pietists, was "to unify and make homogeneous the society." There was no twentieth century concern for separating religion and the public school system. To the contrary, in most northern jurisdictions only pietist-Protestant church members were allowed to be teachers in the public schools. Daily reading of the Protestant Bible, daily Protestant prayers and Protestant hymns were common in the public schools, and school textbooks were rife with anti-Catholic propaganda. Thus, New York City school textbooks spoke broadly of "the deceitful Catholics," and pounded into their children, Catholic and Protestant alike, the message that "Catholics are necessarily, morally, intellectually, infallibly, a stupid race."[3]

Teachers delivered homilies on the evils of Popery, and also on deeply felt pietist theological values: the wickedness of alcohol (the "demon rum") and the importance of keeping the Sabbath. In the 1880s and 1890s, zealous pietists began working ardently for antialcohol instruction as a required part of the public-school curriculum; by 1901, every state in the Union required instruction in temperance.

Since most Catholic children went to public rather than parochial schools, the Catholic authorities were understandably anxious to purge the schools of Protestant requirements and ceremonies, and of anti-Catholic textbooks. To the pietists, these attempts to de-Protestantize the public schools were intolerable "Romish aggression." The whole point of the public schools was moral and religious homogenization, and here the Catholics were disrupting the attempt to make American society holy—to produce, through the public school and the Protestant gospel, "a morally and politically homogeneous people." As Kleppner writes:

> When they [the pietists] spoke of "moral education," they had in mind principles of morality shared in common by the adherents of gospel religion, for in the public school *all* children, even those whose parents were enslaved by "Lutheran formalism or Romish supersitition," would be exposed to the Bible. That alone was cause for righteous optimism, for they believed the Bible to be "*the* agent in *converting* the soul," "the volume that makes human beings *men*."[4]

In this way, "America [would] be Saved Through the Children."[5]

The pietists were therefore incensed that the Catholics were attempting to block the salvation of America's children—and eventually of America itself—all at the orders of a "foreign potentate." Thus, the New Jersey Methodist Conference of 1870 lashed out with their deepest feelings against this Romish obstructionism:

---

3. Cited in David B. Tyack, *The One Best System: A History of American Urban Education* (Cambridge: Harvard University Press, 1974), pp. 84–85.

4. Kleppner, *Third Electoral System, n.* 1, p. 222.

5. *Our Church Work* (Madison, Wis.), July 17, 1890. Cited in ibid., p. 224.

Resolved, That we greatly deprecate the effort which is being made by "Haters of Light," and especially by an arrogant priesthood, to exclude the Bible from the Public Schools of our land; and that we will do all in our power to defeat the well-defined and wicked design of this "Mother of Harlots."[6]

Throughout the nineteenth century, "nativist" attacks on "foreigners" and the foreign-born were really attacks on liturgical immigrants. Immigrants from Britain or Scandinavia, pietists all, were "good Americans" as soon as they got off the boat. It was the diverse culture of the *other* immigrants that had to be homogenized and molded into that of pietist America. Thus, the New England Methodist Conference of 1889 declared:

We are a nation of remnants, ravellings from the Old World. . . . The public school is one of the remedial agencies which work in our society to diminish this . . . and to hasten the compacting of these heterogeneous materials into a solid nature.[7]

Or, as a leading citizen of Boston declared, "the only way to elevate the foreign population was to make Protestants of their children."[8]

Since the cities of the North, in the late nineteenth century, were becoming increasingly filled with Catholic immigrants, pietist attacks on sinful cities and on immigrants both became aspects of the antiliturgical struggle for a homogeneous Anglo-Saxon pietist culture. The Irish were particular butts of pietist scorn; a New York City textbook bitterly warned that continued immigration could make America "the common sewer of Ireland," filled with drunken and depraved Irishmen.[9]

The growing influx of immigrants from southern and eastern Europe toward the end of the nineteenth century seemed to pose even greater problems for the pietist progressives, but they did not shrink from the task. As Elwood P. Cubberley of Stanford University, the nation's outstanding progressive historian of education, declared, southern and eastern Europeans have

served to dilute tremendously our national stock, and to corrupt our civil

---

6. *Minutes of the New Jersey Annual Conference of the Methodist Episcopal Church, 1870,* p. 24. Cited in ibid., p. 230. Similar reactions can be found in the minutes of the Central Pennsylvania Methodists in 1875, the Maine Methodists in 1887, the New York Methodists of 1880, and the Wisconsin Congregationalists of 1890.

7. *Minutes of the Session of the New England Annual Conference of the Methodist Episcopal Church, 1889, p. 85.* Cited in ibid., p. 223.

8. Tyack, *n.* 3, p. 84.

9. Tyack, *n.* 3, p. 85.

life. . . . Everywhere these people tend to settle in groups or settlements, and to set up here their national manners, customs, and observances. Our task is to break up these groups or settlements, to assimilate and amalgamate these people as a part of our American race and to implant in their children . . . the Anglo-Saxon conception of rightousness, law and order, and popular government . . .[10]

PROGRESSIVES, PUBLIC EDUCATION, AND THE FAMILY: THE CASE OF SAN FRANCISCO

The molding of children was of course the key to homogenization and the key in general to the progressive vision of tight social control over the individual via the instrument of the state. The eminent University of Wisconsin sociologist Edward Alsworth Ross, a favorite of Theodore Roosevelt and the veritable epitome of a progressive social scientist, summed it up thus: The role of the public official, and in particular of the public school teacher, is "to collect little plastic lumps of human dough from private households and shape them on the social kneadingboard."[11]

The view of Ross and the other progressives was that the state must take up the task of control and inculcation of moral values once performed by parents and church. The conflict between middle- and upper-class urban progressive Anglo-Saxon Protestants and largely working-class Catholics was sharply delineated in the battle over control of the San Francisco public school system during the second decade of the twentieth century. The highly popular Alfred Roncovieri, a French-Italian Catholic, was the elected school superintendent from 1906 on. Roncovieri was a traditionalist who believed that the function of schools was to teach the basics, and that teaching children about sex and morality should be the function of home and church. Hence, when the drive for sex hygiene courses in the public schools got under way, Roncovieri consulted with mothers' clubs and, in consequence, kept the program out of the schools.

By 1908, upper-class progressives launched a decade-long move-

10. Ellwood P. Cubberley, *Changing Conceptions of Education in America* (Boston: Houghton, Mifflin, 1909), pp. 15–16.

11. Edward Alsworth Ross, *Social Control* (New York, 1912). Cited in Paul C. Violas, "Progressive Social Philosophy: Charles Horton Cooley and Edward Alsworth Ross," in C. J. Karier, P. C. Violas, and J. Spring, eds., *Roots of Crisis: American Education in the 20th Century* (Chicago: Rand McNally, 1973), pp. 40–65.

ment to oust Roncovieri and transform the nature of the San Francisco public school system. Instead of an elected superintendent responding to a school board elected by districts, the progressives wanted an all-powerful school superintendent, appointed by a rubber-stamp board that in turn would be appointed by the mayor. In other words, in the name of "taking the schools out of politics," they hoped to aggrandize the educational bureaucracy and maintain its power virtually unchecked by any popular or democratic control. The purpose was threefold: to push through the progressive program of social control, to impose upper-class control over a working-class population, and to impose pietist Protestant control over Catholic ethnics.[12]

The ethnoreligious struggle over the public schools in San Francisco was nothing new; it had been going on tumultuously since the middle of the nineteenth century.[13] In the last half of the nineteenth century, San Francisco was split into two parts. Ruling the city was a power elite of native-born old Americans, hailing from New England, including lawyers, businessmen, and pietist Protestant ministers. These comprised successively the Whig, Know-Nothing, Populist, and Republican parties in the city. On the other hand were the foreign-born, largely Catholic immigrants from Europe, Irish, Germans, French, and Italians, who comprised the Democratic party.

The Protestants early tried to use the public schools as a homogenizing and controlling force. The great theoretician and founder of the public school system in San Francisco, John Swett, "the Horace Mann of California," was a lifelong Republican and a Yankee who had taught school in New Hampshire before moving West. Moreover, the Board of Education was originally an all–New England show; consisting of emigrants from Vermont, New Hampshire, and Rhode Island. The mayor of San Francisco was a former mayor of Salem, Massachusetts, and every administrator and teacher in the public schools was a transplanted New Englander. The first superintendent of schools was not exactly a New Englander, but close: Thomas J. Nevins, a

12. The cities were already beginning to reach the point where class and ethnic divisions almost coincided, where, in other words, few working-class Anglo-Saxon Protestants resided in the cities.

13. For an excellent study and analysis of the ethnoreligious struggle over the San Francisco public schools from the mid-nineteenth through the first three decades of the twentieth century, see the neglected work of Victor L. Shradar, "Ethnic Politics, Religion, and the Public Schools of San Francisco, 1849–1933" (Ph.D. dissertation, School of Education, Stanford University, 1974).

Yankee Whig lawyer from New York and an agent of the American Bible Society. And the first free public school in San Francisco was instituted in the basement of a small Baptist chapel.

Nevins, installed as superintendent of schools in 1851, promptly adopted the rule of the New York City schools: Every teacher was compelled to begin each day by a Protestant Bible reading and to conduct daily Protestant prayer sessions. And John Swett, elected as Republican state superintendent of public instruction during the 1860s, declared that California needed public schools because of its heterogeneous population: "Nothing can Americanize these chaotic elements, and breathe into them the spirit of our institutions," he warned, "except the public schools."[14]

Swett was keen enough to recognize that the pietist educational formula meant that the state takes over jurisdiction of the child from his parents, since "children arrived at the age of maturity belong, not to the parents, but to the State, to society, to the country."[15]

A seesaw struggle between the Protestant Yankees and Catholic ethnics ensued in San Francisco during the 1850s. The state charter of San Francisco in 1855 made the schools far more responsive to the people, with school boards being elected from each of a dozen wards instead of at large, and the superintendent elected by the people instead of appointed by the board. The Democrats swept the Know-Nothings out of office in the city in 1856 and brought to power David Broderick, an Irish Catholic who controlled the San Francisco as well as the California Democratic party. But this gain was wiped out by the San Francisco Vigilance Movement, a private organization of merchants and New England-born Yankees, who, attacking the "Tammany" tactics of Broderick, installed themselves in power and illegally deported most of the Broderick organization, replacing it with a newly formed People's party.

The People's party ran San Francisco with an iron hand for ten years, from 1857 to 1867, making secret nominations for appointments and driving through huge slates of at-large nominees chosen at a single vote at a public meeting. No open nomination procedures, primaries, or ward divisions were allowed, in order to ensure election

14. Shradar, *n.* 13, p. 14.
15. Rousas John Rushdoony, "John Swett: The Self-Preservation of the State," in *The Messianic Character of American Education: Studies in the History of the Philosophy of Education* (Nutley, N.J.: Craig Press, 1963), pp. 79–80.

victories by "reputable" men. The People's party promptly reinstalled an all-Yankee school board, and the administrators and teachers in schools were again firmly Protestant and militantly anti-Catholic. The People's party itself continually attacked the Irish, denouncing them as "micks" and "rank Pats." George Tait, the People's party–installed superintendent of schools in the 1860s, lamented, however, that some teachers were failing to read the Protestant Bible in the schools, and were thus casting "a slur on the religion and character of the community."

By the 1870s, however, the foreign-born residents outnumbered the native-born, and the Democratic party rose to power in San Francisco, the People's party declining and joining the Republicans. The Board of Education ended the practice of Protestant devotions in the schools, and Irish and Germans began to pour into administrative and teaching posts in the public school system.

Another rollback began, however, in 1874, when the Republican state legislature abolished ward elections for the San Francisco school board, and insisted that all board members be elected at large. This meant that only the wealthy, which usually meant well-to-do Protestants, were likely to be able to run successfully for election. Accordingly, whereas in 1873, 58 percent of the San Francisco school board was foreign-born, the percentage was down to 8 percent in the following year. And while the Irish were approximately 25 percent of the electorate and the Germans about 13 percent, the Irish were not able to fill more than one or two of the twelve at-large seats, and the Germans virtually none.

The seesaw continued, however, as the Democrats came back in 1883, under the aegis of the master politician, the Irish Catholic Christopher "Blind Boss" Buckley. In the Buckley regime, the post-1874 school board dominated totally by wealthy native-born, Yankee businessmen and professionals, was replaced by an ethnically balanced ticket with a high proportion of working-class and foreign-born. Furthermore, a high proportion of Irish Catholic teachers, most of them single women, entered the San Francisco schools during the Buckley era, reaching 50 percent by the turn of the century.

In the late 1880s, however, the stridently anti-Catholic and anti-Irish American party became strong in San Francisco and the rest of the state, and Republican leaders were happy to join them in denouncing the "immigrant peril." The American party managed to oust the Irish Catholic Joseph O'Connor, principal and deputy superintendent, from his high post as "religiously unacceptable." This victory heralded a progressive Republican "reform" comeback in 1891, when none other than John Swett was installed as superintendent of schools in San Francisco. Swett battled for the full reform program: to make everything, even the mayoralty, an appointive rather than an elective office. Part of the goal was achieved by the state's new San Francisco charter in 1900, which replaced the twelve-man elected Board of Education by a four-member board appointed by the mayor.

The full goal of total appointment was still blocked, however, by the existence of an elective superintendent of schools who, since 1907, was the popular Catholic Alfred Roncovieri. The pietist progressives were also thwarted for two decades by the fact that San Francisco was ruled, for most of the years between 1901 and 1911, by a new Union Labor party, which won on an ethnically and occupationally balanced ticket, and which elected the German-Irish Catholic Eugene Schmitz, a member of the musician's union, as mayor. And for eighteen years after 1911, San Francisco was governed by its most popular mayor before or since, "Sunny Jim" Rolph, an Episcopalian friendly to Catholics and ethnics, who was pro-Roncovieri and who presided over an ethnically pluralistic regime.

It is instructive to examine the makeup of the progressive reform movement that eventually got its way and overthrew Roncovieri. It consisted of the standard progressive coalition of business and professional elites, and nativist and anti-Catholic organizations, who called for the purging of Catholics from the schools. Particular inspiration came from Stanford educationist Elwood P. Cubberley, who energized the California branch of the Association of Collegiate Alumnae (later the American Association of University Women), led by the wealthy Mrs. Jesse H. Steinhart, whose husband was later to be a leader in the Progressive party. Mrs. Steinhart got Mrs. Agnes De Lima, a New York City progressive educator, to make a survey of the San Francisco schools for the association. The report, presented in 1914, made the expected case for an "efficient," business-like, school system run solely by appointed educators. Mrs. Steinhart also organized the Public Education Society of San Francisco to agitate for progressive school reform; in this she was aided by the San Francisco Chamber of Commerce.

Also backing progressive reform, and anxious to oust Roncovieri, were other elite groups in the city, including the League of Women Voters, and the prestigious Commonwealth Club of California.

At the behest of Mrs. Steinhart and the San Francisco Chamber of Commerce, which contributed the funds, Philander Claxton of the U.S. Office of Education weighed in with *his* report in December 1917. The report, which endorsed the Association of Collegiate Alumnae study and was extremely critical of the San Francisco school system, called for all power over the system to go to an appointed superintendent of schools. Claxton also attacked the teaching of foreign languages in the schools, which San Francisco had been doing, and insisted on a comprehensive "Americanization" to break down ethnic settlements.

The Claxton Report was the signal for the Chamber of Commerce to swing into action, and it proceeded to draft a comprehensive progressive referendum for the November 1918 ballot, calling for an appointed superintendent and an appointed school board. This initiative, Amendment 37, was backed by most of the prominent business and professional groups in the city. In addition to the ones named above, there were the Real Estate Board, elite women's organizations such as the Federation of Women's Clubs, wealthy neighborhood improvement clubs, and the San Francisco *Examiner*. Amendment 37 lost, however, by two to one, since it had little support in working-class neighborhoods or among the teachers.

Two years later, however, Amendment 37 passed, aided by a resurgence of pietism and virulent anti-Catholicism in postwar America. Prohibition was now triumphant, and the Ku Klux Klan experienced a nationwide revival as a pietist, anti-Catholic organization. The KKK had as many as 3,500 members in the San Francisco Bay Area in the early 1920s. The anti-Catholic American Protective Association also enjoyed a revival, led in California by a British small businessman, the anti-Irish Grand Master Colonel J. Arthur Petersen.

In opposing Amendment 37 in the 1920 elections, Father Peter C. Yorke, a prominent priest and Irish immigrant, perceptively summed up the fundamental cleavage: "The modern school system," he declared, "is not satisfied with teaching children the 3 Rs . . . it reaches out and takes possession of their whole lives."

Amendment 37 passed in 1920 by the narrow margin of 69,200 to 66,700. It passed in every middle- and upper-class Assembly District, and lost in every working-class district. The higher the concentration of foreign-born voters in any district, the greater the vote against. In the Italian precincts 1 to 17 of the 33rd A.D., the Amendment was beaten by 3 to 1; in the Irish precincts, it was defeated by 3 to 1 as well. The more Protestant a working-class district, the more it supported the Amendment.

The bulk of the lobbying for the Amendment was performed by the ad hoc Educational Conference. After the victory, the conference happily presented a list of nominees to the school board, which now consisted of seven members appointed by the mayor, and which in turn appointed the superintendent. The proposed board consisted entirely of businessmen, of whom only one was a conservative Irish Catholic. The mayor surrendered to the pressure, and hence, after 1921, cultural pluralism in the San Francisco school system gave way to unitary progressive rule. The board began by threatening to dock any teacher who dared to be absent from school on St. Patrick's Day (a San Francisco tradition since the 1870s), and proceeded to override the wishes of particular neighborhoods in the interest of a centralized city.

The superintendent of schools in the new regime, Dr. Joseph Marr Gwinn, fit the new dispensation to a tee. A professional "scientist" of public administration, his avowed aim was unitary control. The entire package of typical progressive educational nostrums was installed, including a department of education and various experimental programs. Traditional basic education was scorned, and the edict came down that children should not be "forced" to learn the 3 Rs if they didn't feel the need. Traditional teachers, who were continually attacked for being old-fashioned and "unprofessional," were not promoted.

Despite continued opposition by teachers, parents, neighborhoods, ethnic groups, and the ousted Roncovieri, all attempts to repeal Amendment 37 were unsuccessful. The modern dispensation of progressivism had conquered San Francisco. The removal of the Board of Education and school superintendent from direct and periodic control by the electorate had effectively deprived parents of any significant control over the educational policies of public schools. At last, as John Swett had asserted nearly sixty years earlier, schoolchildren belonged "not to the parents, but to the State, to society, to the country."

ETHNORELIGIOUS CONFLICT AND THE RISE OF FEMINISM

Women's Suffrage

By the 1890s, the liturgically oriented Democracy was slowly but surely winning the national battle of the political parties. Culminating the battle was the Democratic congressional victory in 1890 and the Grover Cleveland landslide in the presidential election of 1892, in which Cleveland carried both Houses of Congress along with him (an unusual feat for that era). The Democrats were in way of becoming the majority party of the country, and the root was demographic: the fact that most of the immigrants were Catholic and the Catholic birthrate was higher than that of the pietist Protestants. Even though British and Scandinavian immigration had reached new highs during the 1880s, their numbers were far exceeded by German and Irish immigration, the latter being the highest since the famous post-potato-famine influx that started in the late 1840s. Furthermore, the "new immigration" from southern and eastern Europe, almost all Catholic—and especially Italian—began to make its mark during the same decade.

The pietists became increasingly embittered, stepping up their attacks on foreigners in general and Catholics in particular. Thus, the Reverend T. W. Cuyler, President of the National Temperance Society, intemperately exclaimed in the summer of 1891: "How much longer [will] the Republic . . . consent to have her soil a dumping ground for all Hungarian ruffians, Bohemian bruisers, and Italian cutthroats of every description?"

The first concrete political response by the pietists to the rising Catholic tide was to try to restrict immigration. Republicans successfully managed to pass laws partially cutting immigration, but President Cleveland vetoed a bill to impose a literacy test on all immigrants. The Republicans also managed to curtail voting by immigrants, by getting most states to disallow voting by aliens, thereby reversing the traditional custom of allowing alien voting. They also urged the lengthening of the statutory waiting period for naturalization.

The successful restricting of immigration and of immigrant voting was still not enough to matter, and immigration would not really be foreclosed until the 1920s. But if voting could not be restricted sharply enough, perhaps it could be *expanded*—in the proper pietist direction.

Specifically, it was clear to the pietists that the role of women in the liturgical "ethnic" family was very different from what it was in the pietist Protestant family. One of the reasons impelling pietists and Republicans toward prohibition was the fact that, culturally, the lives of urban male Catholics—and the cities of the Northeast were becoming increasingly Catholic—revolved around the neighborhood saloon. The men would repair at night to the saloon for chitchat, discussions, and argument—and they would generally take their political views from the saloonkeeper, who thus became the political powerhouse in his particular ward. Therefore, prohibition meant breaking the political power of the urban liturgical machines in the Democratic party.

But while the social lives of liturgical males revolved around the saloon, their wives stayed at home. While pietist women were increasingly independent and politically active, the lives of liturgical women revolved solely about home and hearth. Politics was strictly an avocation for husbands and sons. Perceiving this, the pietists began to push for women's suffrage, realizing that far more pietist than liturgical women would take advantage of the power to vote.

As a result, the women's suffrage movement was heavily pietist from the very beginning. Ultrapietist third parties like the Greenback and the Prohibition parties, which scorned the Republicans for being untrustworthy moderates on social issues, supported women's suffrage throughout, and the Populists tended in that direction. The Progressive party of 1912 was strongly in favor of women's suffrage; theirs was the first major national convention to permit women delegates. The first woman elector, Helen J. Scott of Wisconsin, was chosen by the Progressive party.

Perhaps the major single organization in the women's suffrage movement was the Women's Christian Temperance Union, founded in 1874 and reaching an enormous membership of 300,000 by 1900. That the WCTU was also involved in agitating for curfew, antigambling, antismoking, and antisex laws—all actions lauded by the women's suffrage movement—is clear from the official history of women's suffrage in the nineteenth century:

> [The WCTU] has been a chief factor in State campaigns for statutory prohibition, constitutional amendment, reform laws in general and those for the protection of women and children in particular, and in securing anti-gambling and anti-cigarette laws. It has been instrumental in raising the "age of protection" for girls in many States, and in obtaining curfew laws in 400 towns and cities. . . . The association [WCTU] protests against the legalization of all crimes, especially those of prostitution and liquor selling.[16]

Not only did Susan B. Anthony begin her career as a professional

---

16. Susan B. Anthony and Ida H. Harper, *The History of Woman Suffrage,* Vol. 4 (Rochester: Susan B. Anthony, 1902), pp. 1046–47.

prohibitionist, but her two successors as president of the leading women's suffrage organization, the National American Woman Suffrage Association—Mrs. Carrie Chapman Catt and Dr. Anna Howard Shaw—also began their professional careers as prohibitionists. The leading spirit of the WCTU, Frances E. Willard, was prototypically born of New England–stock parents who had moved westward to study at Oberlin College, then the nation's center of aggressive, evangelical pietism, and had later settled in Wisconsin. Guided by Miss Willard, the WCTU began its prosuffrage activities by demanding that women vote in local option referendums on prohibition. As Miss Willard put it, the WCTU wanted women to vote on this issue because "majorities of women are against the liquor traffic. . . ."[17]

Conversely, whenever there was a voters' referendum on women's suffrage, the liturgicals and the foreign-born, responding to immigrant culture and reacting against the pietist-feminist support of prohibition, consistently opposed women's suffrage. In Iowa, the Germans voted against women's suffrage, as did the Chinese in California. The women's suffrage amendment in 1896 in California was heavily supported by the bitterly anti-Catholic American Protective Association. The cities, where Catholics abounded, tended to be opposed to women's suffrage, while pietist rural areas tended to favor it. Thus, the Oregon referendum of 1900 lost largely because of opposition in the Catholic "slums" of Portland and Astoria.

A revealing religious breakdown of votes on an 1877 women's suffrage referendum was presented in a report by a Colorado feminist. She explained that the Methodists (the most strongly pietistic) were "for us," the (less pietistic) Presbyterians and Episcopalians "fairly so," while the Roman Catholics "were not all against us"—clearly they were expected to be.[18] And, testifying before the U.S. Senate Judiciary Committee in favor of women's suffrage in 1880, Susan B. Anthony presented her own explanation of the Colorado vote:

> In Colorado . . . 6,666 men vote "Yes." Now, I am going to describe the men who voted "Yes." They were native-born men, temperance men, cultivated, broad, generous, just men, men who think. On the other hand, 16,007 voted "No." Now, I am going to describe that class of voters. In the southern part of that State are Mexicans, who speak the Spanish lan-

17. Cited in Eleanor Flexner, *Century of Struggle: The Woman's Rights Movement in the United States* (New York: Atheneum, 1970), p. 183.

18. Anthony and Harper, *n.* 15, Vol. 3, p. 724.

guage. . . . The vast population of Colorado is made up of that class of people. I was sent out to speak in a voting precinct having 200 voters; 150 of those voters were Mexican greasers, 40 of them foreign-born citizens, and just 10 of them were born in this country; and I was supposed to be competent to convert those men to let me have so much right in this Government as they had . . .[19]

A laboratory test of which women would turn out to vote occurred in Massachusetts, where women were given the power to vote in school board elections from 1879 on. In 1888, large numbers of Protestant women in Boston turned out to drive Catholics off the school board. In contrast, Catholic women scarcely voted, "thereby validating the nativist tendencies of suffragists who believed that extension of full suffrage to women would provide a barrier against further Catholic influence."[20] During the last two decades of the nineteenth century "the more hierarchical the church organization and the more formal the ritual, the greater was its opposition to women suffrage, while the democratically organized churches with little dogma tended to be more receptive."[21] The key, we might add, was the basic attitude toward ritual and creed, rather than the form of church organization.

Four mountain states adopted women's suffrage in the early and mid-1890s. Two, Wyoming and Utah, were simply ratifying, as new states, a practice they had long adopted as territories: Wyoming in 1869 and Utah in 1870. Utah had adopted women's suffrage as a conscious policy by the pietistic Mormons to weight political control in favor of their polygamous members, who contrasted to the Gentiles, largely miners and settlers who were either single men or who had left their wives back East. Wyoming had adopted women's suffrage in an effort to increase the political power of its settled house-

19. Quoted in Alan P. Grimes, *The Puritan Ethic and Woman Suffrage* (New York: Oxford University Press, 1967), p. 87.

20. Jane Jerome Camhi, "Women Against Women: American Antisuffragism, 1880–1920" (Ph.D. dissertation in history, Tufts University, 1973), p. 198. See also James J. Kenneally, "Catholicism and Woman Suffrage in Massachusetts," *Catholic Historical Review* 53 (April 1967): 253. Joining in the demand that only Protestants be elected to the Boston school board were, in addition to British-American clubs and numbers of Protestant ministers, the WCTU, the Loyal Women of American Liberty, the National Women's League, and the League of Independent Women Voters. See Kleppner, *Third Electoral System*, *n.* 1, p. 350. See also Tyack, *n.* 3, pp. 105–6; and Lois Bannister Merk, "Boston's Historic Public School Crisis," *New England Quarterly* 31 (June 1958): 172–99.

21. Camhi, *n.* 20, p. 200. Hierarchically organized pietist churches, like the Methodist or the Scandinavian Lutheran, were no less receptive to women's suffrage than the others.

holders, in contrast to the transient, mobile, and often lawless single men who peopled that frontier region.

No sooner had Wyoming Territory adopted women's suffrage, than it became evident that the change had benefited the Republicans, particularly since women had mobilized against Democratic attempts to repeal Wyoming's Sunday prohibition law. In 1871, both houses of the Wyoming legislature, led by its Democratic members, voted to repeal women's suffrage, but the bill was vetoed by the Republican territorial governor.

Two additional states adopting women's suffrage in the 1890s were Idaho and Colorado. In Idaho the drive, adopted by referendum in 1896, was led by the ultrapietistic Populists and by the Mormons, who were dominant in the southern part of the state. The Populist counties of Colorado gave a majority of 6,800 for women's suffrage, while the Republican and Democratic counties voted a majority of 500 against.[22]

It may be thought paradoxical that a movement—women's suffrage—born and centered in the East should have had its earliest victories in the remote frontier states of the Mountain West. But the paradox begins to clear when we realize the pietist-Anglo-Saxon-Protestant nature of the frontiersmen, many of them Yankees hailing originally from that birthplace of American pietism, New England. As the historian Frederick Jackson Turner, that great celebrant of frontier ideals, lyrically observed:

> In the arid West these pioneers [from New England] have halted and have turned to perceive an altered nation and changed social ideals. . . .If we follow back the line of march of the Puritan farmer, we shall see how responsive he has always been to *isms.* . . . He is the Prohibitionist of Iowa and Wisconsin, crying out against German customs as an invasion of his traditional ideals. He is the Granger of Wisconsin, passing restrictive railroad legislation. He is the Abolitionist, the Anti-mason, the Millerite, the Woman Suffragist, the Spiritualist, the Mormon, of Western New York.[23]

---

22. Furthermore, in the Colorado legislature that submitted the women's suffrage amendment to the voters in 1893, the party breakdown of voting was as follows: Republicans, 19 for women's suffrage and 25 against; Democrats, 1 in favor and 8 against; Populists, 34 in favor and 4 against. See Grimes, *n.* 19, p. 96 and passim.

23. Frederick Jackson Turner, "Dominant Forces in Western Life," in *The Frontier in American History* (New York: Holt, Rinehart & Winston, 1962), pp. 239–40. Quoted in Grimes, *n.* 19, pp. 97–98.

Eugenics and Birth Control

Thus the women's suffrage movement, dominated by pietist progressives, was not directed solely to achieving some abstract principle of electoral equality between males and females. This was more a means to another end: the creation of electoral majorities for pietist measures of direct social control over the lives of American families. They wished to determine by state intervention what those families drank and when and where they drank, how they spent their Sabbath day, and how their children should be educated.

One way of correcting the increasingly pro-Catholic demographics was to restrict immigration; another to promote women's suffrage. A third way, often promoted in the name of "science," was eugenics, an increasingly popular doctrine of the progressive movement. Broadly, eugenics may be defined as encouraging the breeding of the "fit" and discouraging the breeding of the "unfit," the criteria of "fitness" often coinciding with the cleavage between native, white Protestants and the foreign born or Catholics—or the white-black cleavage. In extreme cases, the unfit were to be coercively sterilized.

To the founder of the American eugenics movement, the distinguished biologist Charles Benedict Davenport, a New Yorker of eminent New England background, the rising feminist movement was beneficent provided that the number of biologically superior persons was sustained and the number of the unfit diminished. The biologist Harry H. Laughlin, aide to Davenport, associate editor of the *Eugenical News,* and highly influential in the immigration restriction policy of the 1920s as eugenics expert for the House Committee on Immigration and Naturalization, stressed the great importance of cutting the immigration of the biologically "inferior" southern Europeans. For in that way, the biological superiority of Anglo-Saxon women would be protected.

Harry Laughlin's report to the House Committee, printed in 1923, helped formulate the 1924 immigration law, which, in addition to drastically limiting total immigration to the United States, imposed national origin quotas based on the 1910 census, so as to weight the sources of immigration as much as possible in favor of northern Europeans. Laughlin later emphasized that American women must keep the nation's blood pure by not marrying what he called the "colored races," in which he included southern Europeans as well as blacks:

for if "men with a small fraction of colored blood could readily find mates among the white women, the gates would be thrown open to a final radical race mixture of the whole population." To Laughlin the moral was clear: "The perpetuity of the American race and consequently of American institutions depends upon the virtue and fecundity of American Women."[24]

But the problem was that the fecund women were not the pietist progressives but the Catholics. For, in addition to immigration, another source of demographic alarm to the pietists was the far higher birthrate among Catholic women. If only they could be induced to adopt birth control! Hence, the birth control movement became part of the pietist armamentarium in their systemic struggle with the Catholics and other liturgicals.

Thus, the distinguished University of California eugenicist, Samuel J. Holmes, lamented that "the trouble with birth control is that it is practiced least where it should be practiced most." In the *Birth Control Review,* leading organ of the birth control movement, Annie G. Porritt was more specific, attacking "the folly of closing our gates to aliens from abroad, while having them wide open to the overwhelming progeny of the least desirable elements of our city and slum population."[25] In short, the birth controllers were saying that if one's goal is to restrict sharply the total number of Catholics, "colored" southern European or no, then there is no point in only limiting immigration while the domestic population continues to increase.

The birth control and the eugenics movement therefore went hand in hand, not the least in the views of the well-known leader of the birth control movement in the United States: Mrs. Margaret Higgins Sanger, prolific author, founder and long-time editor of the *Birth Control Review.* Echoing many of the various strains of progressivism, Mrs. Sanger hailed the emancipation of women through birth control as the latest in applied science and "efficiency." As she put it in her *Autobiography:*

In an age which has developed science and industry and economic efficiency to their highest points, so little thought has been given to the development of a science of parenthood, a science of maternity which could

24. Cited in Donald K. Pickens, *Eugenics and the Progressives* (Nashville, Tenn.: Vanderbilt University Press, 1968), p. 67.

25. Annie G. Porritt, "Immigration and Birth Control, an Editorial," *The Birth Control Review* 7 (Sept. 1923):219. Cited in Pickens, *n.* 24, p. 73.

prevent this appalling and unestimated waste of womankind and maternal effort.[26]

To Mrs. Sanger, "science" also meant stopping the breeding of the unfit. A devoted eugenicist and follower of C. B. Davenport, she in fact chided the eugenics movement for not sufficiently emphasizing this crucial point:

> The eugenists wanted to shift the birth control emphasis from less children for the poor to more children for the rich. We went back of that and sought first to stop the multiplication of the unfit. This appeared the most important and greatest step toward race betterment.[27]

GATHERED TOGETHER: PROGRESSIVISM AS A POLITICAL PARTY

Progressivism was, to a great extent, the culmination of the pietist Protestant political impulse, the urge to regulate every aspect of American life, economic and moral—even the most intimate and crucial aspects of family life. But it was also a curious alliance of a technocratic drive for government regulation, the supposed expression of "value-free science," and the pietist religious impulse to save America—and the world—by state coercion. Often both pietistic and scientific arguments would be used, sometimes by the same people, to achieve the old pietist goals. Thus, prohibition would be argued for on religious as well as on alleged scientific or medicinal grounds. In many cases, leading progressive intellectuals at the turn of the twentieth century were former pietists who went to college and then transferred to the political arena, their zeal for making over mankind, as a "salvation by science." And then the Social Gospel movement managed to combine political collectivism and pietist Christianity in the same package. All of these were strongly interwoven elements in the progressive movement.

All these trends reached their apogee in the Progressive party and its national convention of 1912. The assemblage was a gathering of businessmen, intellectuals, academics, technocrats, efficiency experts and social engineers, writers, economists, social scientists, and leading representatives of the new profession of social work. The Pro-

26. Quoted in Pickens, *n.* 24, p. 80.
27. Ibid., p. 83.

gressive leaders were middle and upper class, almost all urban, highly educated, and almost all white Anglo-Saxon Protestants of either past or present pietist concerns.

From the social work leaders came upper-class ladies bringing the blessings of statism to the masses: Lillian D. Wald, Mary Kingsbury Simkhovitch, and above all, Jane Addams. Miss Addams, one of the great leaders of progressivism, was born in rural Illinois to a father, John, who was a state legislator and a devout nondenominational evangelical Protestant. Miss Addams was distressed at the southern and eastern European immigration, people who were "primitive" and "credulous," and who posed the danger of unrestrained individualism. Their different ethnic background disrupted the unity of American culture. However, the problem, according to Miss Addams, could be easily remedied. The public school could reshape the immigrant, strip him of his cultural foundations, and transform him into a building block of a new and greater American community.[28]

In addition to writers and professional technocrats at the Progressive party convention, there were professional pietists galore. Social Gospel leaders Lyman Abbott, the Reverend R. Heber Newton, and the Reverend Washington Gladden were Progressive party notables, and the Progressive candidate for governor of Vermont was the Reverend Fraser Metzger, leader of the Inter-Church Federation of Vermont. In fact, the Progressive party proclaimed itself as the "recrudescence of the religious spirit in American political life."

Many observers, indeed, reported in wonder at the strongly religious tone of the Progressive party convention. Theodore Roosevelt's acceptance address was significantly entitled, "A Confession of Faith," and his words were punctuated by "amens" and by a continual singing of Christian hymns by the assembled delegates. They sang "Onward, Christian Soldiers," "The Battle Hymn of the Republic," and finally the revivalist hymn, "Follow, Follow, We Will Follow Jesus," except that "Roosevelt" replaced the word "Jesus" at every turn.

The *New York Times* of August 6, 1912, summed up the unusual experience by calling the Progressive assemblage "a convention of fanatics." And, "It was not a convention at all. It was an assemblage of religious enthusiasts. It was such a convention as Peter the Hermit

---

28. See Paul C. Violas, "Jane Addams and the New Liberalism," in Karier et al., eds., *Roots of Crisis, n.* 11, pp. 66–83.

held. It was a Methodist camp following done over into political terms."[29]

Thus the foundations of today's massive state intervention in the internal life of the American family were laid in the so-called "progressive era" from the 1870s to the 1920s. Pietists and "progressives" united to control the material and sexual choices of the rest of the American people, their drinking habits, and their recreational preferences. Their values, the very nurture and education of their children, were to be determined by their betters. The spiritual, biological, political, intellectual, and moral elite would govern, through state power, the character and quality of American family life.

SIGNIFICANCE

It has been known for decades that the Progressive Era was marked by a radical growth in the extension and dominance of government in America's economic, social, and cultural life. For decades, this great leap into statism was naively interpreted by historians as a simple response to the greater need for planning and regulation of an increasingly complex economy. In recent years, however, historians have come to see that increasing statism on a federal and state level can be better interpreted as a profitable alliance between certain business and industrial interests, looking for government to cartelize their industry after private efforts for cartels and monopoly had failed, and intellectuals, academics, and technocrats seeking jobs to help regulate and plan the economy as well as restriction of entry into their professions. In short, the Progressive Era re-created the age-old alliance between Big Government, large business firms, and opinion-molding intellectuals—an alliance that had most recently been embodied in the mercantilist system of the sixteenth through eighteenth centuries.

Other historians uncovered a similar process at the local level, especially that of urban government beginning with the Progressive Era. Using the influence of media and opinion leaders, upper-income and business groups in the cities systematically took political power away from the masses and centralized this power in the hands of urban government responsive to progressive demands. Elected officials, and decentralized ward representation, were systematically replaced either by appointed bureaucrats and civil servants, or by centralized at-large

29. Cited in John Allen Gable, *The Bull Moose Years: Theodore Roosevelt and the Progressive Party* (Port Washington, N.Y.: Kennikat Press, 1978), p. 75.

districts where large-scale funding was needed to finance election races. In this way, power was shifted out of the hands of the masses and into the hands of a minority elite of technocrats and upper-income businessmen. One result was an increase of government contracts to business, a shift from "Tammany" type charity by the political parties to a taxpayer-financed welfare state, and the imposition of higher taxes on suburban residents to finance bond issues and redevelopment schemes accruing to downtown financial interests.

During the last two decades, educational historians have described a similar process at work in public, especially urban, school systems. The scope of the public school was greatly expanded, compulsory attendance spread outside of New England and other "Yankee" areas during the Progressive Era, and a powerful movement developed to try to ban private schools and to force everyone into the public school system.

From the work of educational historians, it was clear that the leap into comprehensive state control over the individual and over social life was not confined, during the Progressive and indeed post-Progressive eras, to government and the economy. A far more comprehensive process was at work. The expansion of compulsory public schooling stemmed from the growth of collectivist and anti-individualist ideology among intellectuals and educationists. The individual, these "progressives" believed, must be molded by the educational process to conform to the group, which in practice meant the dictates of the power elite speaking in the group's name. Historians have long been aware of this process.[30] But the accruing insight into progressivism as a business cartelizing device led historians who had abandoned the easy equation of "businessmen" with "laissez faire" to see that all the facets of progressivism—the economic and the ideological and educational—were part of an integrated whole. The new ideology among business groups was cartelist and collectivist rather than individualist and laissez faire, and the social control over the individual exerted by progressivism was neatly paralleled in the ideology and practice of progressive education. Another parallel to the economic realm, of course, was the increased power and income accruing to the technocratic intellectuals controlling the school system and the economy.

---

30. For further discussion of education, see Robert B. Everhart, ed., *The Public School Monopoly: A Critical Analysis of Education and the State in American Society* (San Francisco: Pacific Institute for Public Policy Research, 1982).

If the action of business and intellectual elites in turning toward progressivism was now explained, there was still a large gap in the historical explanation and understanding of progressivism and therefore of the leap into statism beginning in the early twentieth century. There was still a need to explain mass voting behavior and the ideology and programs of the political parties in the American electoral system. This chapter applies the illuminating findings of recent "ethnoreligious historians" to significant changes that took place during the Progressive Era in the power of government over the family. In particular, we discuss the movement to expand the power of the public school and the educationist elite over the family, as well as the women's suffrage and eugenics movement, all important features of the Progressive movement. In every case, we see the vital link between these intrusions into the family and the aggressive drive by Anglo-Saxon Protestant "pietists" to use the state to "make America holy," to stamp out sin and thereby assure their own salvation by maximizing the salvation of others. In particular, all of these measures were part and parcel of the long-standing crusade by these pietists to reduce if not eliminate the role of "liturgicals," largely Roman Catholics and high-church Lutherans, from American political life. The drive to stamp out liquor and secular activities on Sundays had long run into successful Catholic and high-church Lutheran resistance. Compulsory public schooling was soon seen as an indispensable weapon in the task of "Christianizing the Catholics," of saving the souls of Catholic children by using the public schools as a Protestantizing weapon. The neglected example of San Francisco politics was urged as a case study of this ethnoreligious political battle over the schools and hence over the right of Catholic parents to transmit their own values to their children without suffering Anglo-Saxon Protestant obstruction. Women's suffrage was seized upon as a means of increasing Anglo-Saxon Protestant voting power, and immigration restriction as well as eugenics was a method of reducing the growing demographic challenge of Catholic voters.

In sum, recent insights into the cartelizing drive of various business interests have provided an important explanation of the rapid growth of statism in the twentieth century. Ethnoreligious history provides an explanation of mass voting behavior and political party programs that neatly complement the cartelizing explanation of the actions of business elites.

5

EDUCATION AND THE FAMILY DURING THE INDUSTRIAL REVOLUTION

Barry W. Poulson

INTRODUCTION

The period of the "common school movement" beginning in about 1840, represents a discontinuous change in the American educational system. The magnitude of resources allocated to education and the share of those resources allocated through the public sector increased after 1840. While all of the developed countries increased resources allocated to education during the Industrial Revolution, the common school movement in America was unique in many respects.

The common school movement occurred at a very early stage of the Industrial Revolution in this country, and the magnitude of the increase in public resources allocated to education was unprecedented. In contrast, the British were much further along in the process of modern economic growth, and yet the British did not significantly expand public education until later in the nineteenth century. Even then, the magnitude of the shift in resources allocated toward education through the public sector in England was not comparable to that which occurred in America beginning with the common school movement.

To understand the common school movement in America, we must go beyond the traditional economic arguments based upon external benefits of education. There is no question that increased investments in human capital contributed to higher rates of economic growth. However, we must be careful not to simply translate increased expenditures for education into increased productivity in the early phase of the Industrial Revolution. While there is ample evidence that investments are tied to increased productivity in the twentieth century, the evidence for the initial stages of the Industrial Revolution suggests that productivity was tied primarily to age and experience rather than to formal schooling.

The implication of the externalities argument is that without an expanded role for public education through the common school movement, Americans would have underinvested in education. Yet the private and quasi-private educational system that preceded the common school movement had achieved remarkable success in terms of levels of literacy and resources allocated to education. Moreover, with the expansion in tax-supported public educational institutions, there was some displacement of private expenditures for education and, at least in some areas and levels of schooling, a net decrease in expenditures. It is reasonable to conclude that without the common school movement, resources allocated to education would still have increased, and levels of literacy would have increased and become more widely distributed throughout the population.

Support of the common school movement cannot be explained, at least for some interest groups, in terms of the social benefits of higher levels of literacy and education. Even for so-called public-spirited educators of the day like Horace Mann, the objective was not just increased literacy but rather the use of education to achieve welfare objectives as they perceived them. This social engineering came into conflict with the desires of individuals and families and with their ability to maximize the welfare of their children through control over the educational system. As education began to shift from the family and local institutions to state-dominated educational institutions, the role of the family changed from the primary provider of educational services to that of agents for children vis-à-vis the state. As might be expected, educational decisions began to reflect less the welfare of individual families and more the goals of the state. This conflict between the desires of families and those supporting an expanded role for the state in education was one of the most hotly debated political issues of the nineteenth century. It was also reflected by a broader set of institutional changes affecting the relationship between the family and the state. This analysis explores these issues in the common school movement to better understand the debate regarding public and private education, which has continued down to the present day, and to gain insight into this crucial discontinuous change in the relationship of the family to the state.

EDUCATION IN THE PREINDUSTRIAL ERA

Up to the early nineteenth century, most of the child's education took place within the family or in an apprenticeship system. Although basic literacy skills were included, education was oriented toward vocational skills. This role of the family carried over into the early factories, where children were often trained by their parents in some vocational skills.[1]

Education outside the home played a relatively small part in the lives of most American children in the preindustrial era. There were church-supported schools in the colonial and early national period, and formal education was provided by "dame" schools, which were really an extension of the family system of education. A literate woman would offer elementary education in her own home, usually her kitchen, for neighborhood children. "Writing schools" were also organized in the urban areas, offering basic literary and computational skills. These writing schools were often offered in the evening for working children and young people. Some factories established their own evening schools and Sunday schools for children. For example, Samuel Slater set up a Sunday school in his home for the children working in his textile mill, at first teaching it himself, later securing as instructors students from Rhode Island College (now Brown University).

In most of the literature written about education in the preindustrial era, the system is viewed as a failure. Bernard Bailyn remarks that "within a remarkably short time after the beginnings of settlement, it was realized that the family was failing in its more obvious educational functions."[2] Another historian notes that the "old picture of every village with its free school and a population athirst for learning is a pure figment of the imagination."[3] Contemporaries of the period criticized the lack of educational facilities, particularly in rural areas, and the widespread illiteracy among the population.

1. Forest Chester Ensign, *Compulsory School Attendance and Child Labor* (New York: Arno Press, 1969); and Lee Soltow and Edward Stevens, *The Rise of Literacy and the Common School in the United States: A Socioeconomic Analysis to 1870* (Chicago: University of Chicago Press, 1981).

2. Bernard Bailyn, *Education in the Forming of American Society: Needs and Opportunities for Study* (Chapel Hill: University of North Carolina Press, 1960), p. 26.

3. Soltow and Stevens, *n.* 1, p. 30.

In 1798 Reverend Samuel Knox lamented, "In every corner or portion of the state how many hundreds of our youth are deprived of the means of instruction suitable to the offspring of free and independent citizens."[4]

In the early nineteenth century criticism of the educational system reached a peak. Educators expressed concern especially for the children of the laboring classes in rapidly growing industrial centers, an increasing proportion of whom were immigrants. Horace Mann cited the "frightful evidence of the number of children who either do not go to school at all or go so little as not to be reckoned scholars."[5] James G. Carter maintained that the common schools "have most certainly not kept up with the progress of society in other respects . . . and there never was a time, since the settlement of our country, when the common schools were farther in the rear of the improvements of the age . . . than they are at the present moment."[6]

In assessing these criticisms of American education, we should first note the rise in the literacy rate from the colonial period to the end of the early national period. Lockridge's data for New England show an increase in male literacy rates from 60 percent to 90 percent over the period 1650 to 1795. The literacy rates for females increased from 30 percent to 45 percent over that period. Literacy rates in other parts of the country with similar population density were apparently comparable to those in New England. In the less populated areas and especially the frontier areas, the literacy rates were much lower. In the early nineteenth century literacy rates improved substantially. In the North literacy rates rose from about 75 percent in 1800 to between 91 percent and 97 percent in 1840. In the South literacy rates rose from about 50 percent or 60 percent to 81 percent over that same period. It is important to emphasize that this period preceded the rapid growth and systematization of the public schools system that occurred after 1840. The pre-1840 era is best described as one in which the primary reliance for education rested with the family; it was a period when private schooling played a major role in the educational system and the financial support and control of public schools rested in local communities and school districts.[7]

4. Ibid., p. 47.
5. Ensign, *n*. 1, p. 46.
6. Ibid., p. 47.
7. Soltow and Stevens, *n*. 1, pp. 34–57.

From the standpoint of the families living in this preindustrial era, the levels of education and literacy of the American population were a remarkable achievement. No other country in the world, with the possible exception of Great Britain, had achieved comparable levels of education and literacy per capita. In terms of efficiency, American families produced higher levels of education and literacy per dollar spent than any other country, including Great Britain. The share of resources allocated to education relative to total national income was as high in America as in any other country.[8]

It is important to evaluate the educational system in the early nineteenth century, not only from the standpoint of educators like Mann who were critical of the system, but also from the standpoint of the families who assumed the major burden of educating and training their children. The important question from the standpoint of the family was whether the benefits of educating their children outweighed the costs. If the child was educated at home, the out-of-pocket costs were limited to the few books, primers, and other supplies the family might purchase. The major cost was the opportunity cost of the parent who spent time educating and training the child, and of the child, who might otherwise allocate that time to work. The benefits of education accrued not only to the child but to the family—in terms of increased productivity and higher levels of satisfaction from the human capital embodied in their children.

From the family's standpoint, there was an important difference between vocational skills and the elementary education that determined literacy. The overwhelming evidence is that American families from the very outset provided the vocational and social skills that enabled their children not only to function, but to achieve higher levels of income and wealth than their parents. No one disputes the success of the family in providing these utilitarian skills, whether through the family, the apprenticeship system, or the early factory system. The criticism is rather that the family failed to provide formal education as measured by literacy.

Let us discount the problem of defining literacy and let us accept the definition "ability to read and write in a language." The vast majority of Americans had achieved that level of literacy by 1840. A minority of the population failed to achieve literacy, but for many of

---

8. Barry W. Poulson, *Economic History of the United States* (New York: Macmillan, 1981), pp. 469–95.

these people, literacy was not a prerequisite to their material success. Farmers, laborers, and artisans often prospered without being able to read and write. Outside the urban areas, illiteracy did not present a problem to merchants who plied their commerce on the rivers and roads of the interior of the country. The famous Yankee peddler could function quite well without the skill to read and write. Illiteracy did not preclude American families from participating in the political and social affairs of the community. Evidence from signatures on wills, ballots, and other political documents reveals that the illiterate who signed by marking rather than writing their signatures participated actively in political affairs. The illiterate could rely on the assistance of literate family members, friends, and professionals such as lawyers to conduct the few transactions requiring reading and writing skills. Illiteracy did not, as it does today, mark a person as necessarily inferior or preclude that person from active participation in society.[9]

Literacy and the ability to do simple calculations were more important in the skilled occupations and in the commerce of the urban areas. That level of education could be achieved with a few years of elementary schooling, and as the previous evidence suggests, all but a small minority of Americans living in the urban areas acquired that level of education. Education beyond the elementary level was a prerequisite to only a few highly skilled and professional occupations such as accounting, teaching, law, the clergy, etc. The composition of the children enrolled in school reflected these occupational differences. The children of the poorer class of farmers and laborers received limited formal education; most of their education took place in the family or apprenticeship system. The middle class of farmers, workers, merchants, etc., generally provided an elementary education and, in the more populated areas where such facilities existed, a secondary education. A college education was a luxury provided to the wealthy few who wished their children to assume a higher status in life, such as one of the professions. Except in sparsely populated rural areas of the country, the resources allocated to formal edcation were probably consistent with these objectives. As the frontier areas grew in population, they were able to generate the private and public resources necessary to establish elementary and secondary schools, similar to those already operating in the older sections of the country.

---

9. Soltow and Stevens, *n.* 1, pp. 28–57.

While the amount of formal education one received reflected economic class, race, sex, and ethnic background, this did not preclude upward mobility for the able, ambitious, and lucky. Americans achieved a mobility by region, industry, occupation, and social class that seemed remarkable to contemporary observers. De Tocqueville commented on the acquisitive spirit in America: "In no country in the world is the love of property more active and anxious than in the United States, nowhere does the majority display less inclination for those principles which threaten to alter, in whatever manner, the laws of property."[10]

THE COMMON SCHOOL MOVEMENT

The educational system in the early nineteenth century was viewed as a failure, not by the majority of families, but rather by a minority in the society. The latter group, dissatisfied with the pace of educational development, initiated the common school movement, which called for a major reallocation of resources to education through the public sector. We must understand the motives of the minority group initiating the common school movement in order to understand the change in our educational system that occurred in this period.

There were several different groups advocating educational reform in the early nineteenth century. The most vocal of these groups were the educators themselves, who wanted to improve the welfare of educators in the public sector. The greater the allocation of resources to education through the public sector, the higher the expected income for educators. For people who, like Horace Mann, were in administrative positions, the expectation would be for an expanded bureaucracy with a corresponding increase in power and income. The educators of course did not advocate educational reform on these grounds, but rather cloaked their arguments in the moral and ethical garb of maximizing social welfare.[11]

These arguments found a receptive ear among the factory owners and propertied interests in the society. It was an industrialist, Edmund Dwight, who persuaded Horace Mann to accept the position of secretary of the Massachusetts Board of Education.[12] The support given

---

10. Barry W. Poulson, "Ideology and Labor Law," *Journal of Social, Political, and Economic Studies* 8 (no. 1, Spring 1983): 43–80.

11. Ensign, *n.* 1, pp. 46–86; and Soltow and Stevens, *n.* 1, pp. 58–88.

12. Samuel Bowles and Herbert Gintis, *Schooling in Capitalist America, Educational Reform and the Contradictions of Economic Life* (New York: Basic Books, 1976), p. 165.

by industrialists to an expanded public education system also reflected their self-interest. Factory owners like Slater were quite willing to support public education for the labor force in their textile mills. Such educational services were attractive to families and young people, and expenditures for education were an important nonwage benefit necessary to attract labor into the factories, given the primitive state of the labor market. Most important, the factory owners could be reasonably sure that the benefits of such expenditures would accrue to them in terms of a better quality of workers and a more stable labor force. While there was some migration between factories and some employers raided the employees of their competitors, these practices involved only a small share of the labor force. The industrialists who supported public education in the early nineteenth century believed that education directly affected the productivity of their work force. As an agent for a cotton textile mill wrote in 1841:

> From my observations and experience, I am perfectly satisfied that the owners of manufacturing property have a deep pecuniary interest in the education and morals of the help, and I believe the time is not distant when the truth of this will appear more and more clear. And as competition becomes more close, and small circumstances of more importance in turning the scale in favor of one establishment over another, I believe it will be seen that the establishment, other things being equal, which has the best educated and most moral help will give the greatest production at least cost per pound.[13]

We must qualify this argument in an important respect. There is no evidence of a direct link between education and productivity of workers in the early factories comparable to that found in recent investigations of labor force productivity. The cognitive skills taught in formal education had little to do with the productivity of children as workers. Most of the work in the early textile mills required not literacy but manual dexterity and skill. Even a skilled position, such as that of machinist, did not require literacy, although skilled workers were more likely to be educated and literate than the unskilled labor force. Productivity in industry in general was tied to age and experience rather than to level of education and literacy of the work force. It should not be surprising that formal education played such a small

13. Ibid., p. 162.

part in the total education and training of the work force in the industrial as well as the agricultural sector. The benefits of education to the factory owner were not so much in terms of direct increases in the productivity of educated workers, but rather in the indirect effects of education in attracting a more stable and industrious group of workers into the factory.

Toward the middle of the nineteenth century, the industrialists began to view education quite differently. The expansion of the labor supply in more mature labor markets meant that industrialists did not have to offer nonwage benefits such as education to attract workers into their factories. Since that labor force was increasingly mobile, expenditures for education did not always accrue to the factory owner and very often ended up benefiting his competitor. The influx of immigrants and other workers into urban labor markets presented another kind of problem for the industrialist, one that was shared by other propertied interests. They were concerned about the impact of a large illiterate segment of the population concentrated in the urban areas. They attributed problems such as unemployment, alcoholism, crime, and poverty to the increased numbers of uneducated people crowded into the cities. The propertied interests viewed the illiterate and uneducated as a threat to political and social stability in their communities. Factory owners were willing to share with other property owners the costs of educating these groups, but they were less willing to provide that support through private expenditures. They viewed education as a "public good" that if left to the private sector, would not be adequately financed. In order to eliminate free riders who would benefit from educating the uneducated without incurring the costs, they demanded an increase in resources allocated to education through the public sector—this increase to be underwritten by a coercive tax system on all property owners.

Another conspicuous group in support of the common school movement was the clergy. That support had a long tradition extending back to the Puritan laws requiring compulsory education. During the Great Awakening of the early nineteenth century, religious groups such as the Methodists saw in public education a vehicle for proselytizing their faith. They disseminated low-priced books and pamphlets in the sparsely populated regions of the country. Their Sunday schools were devoted to the teaching of basic literacy as well as Bible literacy. Other denominations viewed expanded education and liter-

acy as prerequisites to the missionary activities of evangelical Protestantism. They supported public education along with their private
support of education through secondary schools, the dissemination of
religious literature, etc. The public schools usually included religious
as well as secular instruction. Since the majority of the population
was Protestant and the religious instruction in the public schools was
biased toward Protestant theology, the Protestant sects saw no great
problem in this combination of religious and secular instruction in the
schools. Over time the schools became more secular in character,
relegating religious instruction to a minor role. The church relied on
the schools to teach basic literacy and concentrated more on Bible
literacy and religious training.[14]

Another group that supported the common school movement in the
nineteenth century was organized labor. To understand the motives
of labor unions we should point out that early compulsory education
laws were really laws restricting child labor. For example, in Rhode
Island labor unions supported compulsory schooling legislation as early
as 1800. Those efforts were unsuccessful until 1840, when a law was
passed requiring that no child under twelve years of age be permitted
to work in any factory unless he had attended school for three months
during the preceding year. However, no provision was made for the
enforcement of the law, and it was universally disregarded. The
Working Men's party in Pennsylvania supported a bill that provided
for an investigation into "the extent and increase of manufactures in
the state and to exclude from them all children between twelve and
eighteen years of age unless either receiving instruction or able to
produce a certificate signed by a respectable schoolmaster or by two
reputable citizens of the county testifying to their ability to read and
write the English, German, or some other foreign language." That
bill was opposed by manufacturing interests in the state on the grounds
that it was unnecessary, undemocratic, and foreign to the spirit of
American government. In its first constitution the American Federation of Labor declared itself in favor of the complete abolition of the
employment of children under fourteen years of age. Clearly, the early
labor unions were primarily interested in restricting the employment
of children and only indirectly concerned with their schooling. Labor
unions supported schooling legislation because it restricted employ-

14. Soltow and Stevens, *n*. 1, pp. 48–49.

ment opportunities for children in an era in which child labor legislation was viewed as unconstitutional.[15]

Finally, we should point out the role of private philanthropic groups in support of public education. The first public free schools were established by charitable institutions. They were first provided to children of the impoverished and to orphans; only in the nineteenth century were these schools opened to families working in the factories. This transition is apparent in 1805 when the New York Schools Society, an organization that had privately supported free public schools for the poor for almost half a century, petitioned the legislature for public support on the grounds that "the rich having ample means of educating their offspring . . . it must be apparent that the laboring poor— a class of citizens so evidently useful—have a superior claim to public support."[16] Philanthropic groups included a diverse assortment of intellectuals, newspaper editors, social reformers, etc., which to some extent overlapped with the previous groups mentioned. However, we should distinguish the motives of philanthropic groups such as the New York Schools Society, who were genuinely interested in the level of education and literacy of children, from the other groups mentioned who stood to gain some benefits from an expanded public educational system, regardless of the impact on the education of the young.

Whatever their motives, these different interest groups coalesced in the early nineteenth century to support educational legislation that laid the foundations for the common school movement in America. Beginning in Massachusetts and spreading to other states, enabling legislation was passed that essentially transferred to the state the primary responsibility for education—a responsibility that had hitherto belonged to the family and other private institutions such as the church and business. While these statutes varied from state to state, they had common features that have characterized public education right down to the present day:

1. Educational services were provided through public institutions: common schools for elementary education and state-supported secondary schools and colleges.
2. The financing of education was through general taxes, primarily taxes on private property.

15. Ensign, *n.* 1, pp. 30–45.
16. Ibid., p. 44.

3. Educational services at the elementary and secondary level were provided free to all school-age children.
4. Enrollment and attendance in public schools was made compulsory for children and later for adolescents below a minimum age.
5. The administration and provision of educational services was organized in an increasingly hierarchical bureaucracy. Responsibility and control of education shifted from the local communities and school districts to state boards of education and, later, to the federal bureaucracy. State officials, usually the secretary of education, assumed positions of leadership in setting the goals and allocating resources to the educational system.
6. The content of the curriculum became standardized and reflected the politization of the schools in achieving social objectives.
7. Education became increasingly secular, reflecting division between church and state.
8. Recruitment of teachers was based upon objective criteria such as completion of a given level of education or certification by a state board of education.
9. Failure to comply with educational requirements for their children subjected the family to state-imposed penalties.
10. Failure to comply with educational requirements of local schools and local school districts subjected those school systems to state-imposed penalties (later, penalties were imposed by the federal government on state governments that failed to comply with federal requirements).

THE IMPACT OF THE COMMON SCHOOL MOVEMENT

The common school movement resulted in a massive reallocation of resources to education through the public sector. The numbers of school-age children increased and expenditures per child increased. Between 1840 and 1860, the period of rapid growth in public schools, total expenditures for education increased from $9 million to $35 million. By the end of the nineteenth century, educational expenditures totaled $290 million, 80 percent of which was financed through the public sector. Private schooling continued to expand over that period, especially at the elementary and university levels, but much of private schooling was displaced by public education.[17]

The impact of this rapid growth in public schools can be measured and evaluated in a number of ways. In Massachusetts the percentage of people under the age of twenty enrolled in both public and private schools fell slightly from 46 percent in 1837 to 43 percent in 1860. However, Massachusetts was unique in that respect; for the country as a whole, the percentage of school-age children enrolled in schools increased. Attendance at private schools decreased absolutely as well as relative to attendance at public schools. The common school was clearly displacing private education.[18]

The objective most often cited by educational reformers of that era was to reduce illiteracy. The illiteracy rate declined from about 9 percent in 1840 to 7 percent in 1860, but rose to 9 percent again in 1870. It is not clear why the illiteracy rate increased from 1860 to 1870. The Civil War had a disruptive effect on schooling, particularly in the South. But changes took place in the measurement of illiteracy between those two census years, making the illiteracy rates on those two dates not comparable. What is clear from this evidence is that the major reduction in illiteracy occurred prior to 1840. The educational reformers had made some progress in expanding the common school in the early nineteenth century, but the rapid growth in public education occurred after 1840.[19]

The major issues surrounding the debate over common school reform in the early nineteenth century were not just the problem of illiteracy, but also the quality of literacy and the extent to which schooling reached different ethnic groups and socioeconomic classes in the population. In the North where basic literacy was almost universal, the educational reformers were more concerned with the amount and quality of schooling available in the rural sector and the problem of lack of attendance, particularly by the poor and immigrant groups in the urban areas. In the South where illiteracy was more widespread, edu-

17. Poulson, *n.* 8, pp. 476–83.

18. Maris Vinovskis, "Trends in Massachusetts Education," *History of Education Quarterly* 12 (no. 4, Winter 1972): 501–29; Michael B. Katz, *The Irony of Early School Reform* (Boston: Beacon Press, 1970); Alexander James Field, "Educational Reform and Manufacturing Development in Mid Nineteenth Century Massachusetts" (Ph.D. dissertation, Stanford University, 1974).

19. Soltow and Stevens, *n.* 1, pp. 188–201.

cational reform was aimed at basic literacy as well as the quality of schooling received by different segments of the population.

Reforms aimed at equalizing educational opportunities between the rural and urban sectors of the North had a significant impact. A Gini coefficient measuring disparities in literacy rates by county in the North declined from .63 in 1840 to .52 in 1850 and .34 in 1870. Significant differences in literacy between rural and urban areas persisted, but it is clear that public education was an important factor in the convergence of literacy rates in different regions of the North.[20]

Regional differences in literacy between the North and South persisted over this period. The proximate cause of this North-South difference in literacy was the larger share of the population in the South living in rural agricultural areas. The quality and quantity of schooling available to rural populations, especially in frontier regions, was significantly lower than that available to the urban population. The rural areas lacked the economic base necessary to finance schooling at levels comparable to those of the urban commercial and industrial areas. Even if the farm population had had the financial resources necessary to achieve educational parity with the urban population, they would not have chosen to do so. As we have argued, the demand for education and literacy among the farm population was less than that of the urban population for any given level of wealth and income. Education and literacy were less important to material success in agriculture, and the opportunity cost for farm children to acquire an education was greater than that for their urban counterparts.

In addition to these differences in benefits and costs, the taste for education differed between the rural and urban population. This taste for education, like that for other consumer durable goods, reflected the exposure of the population to the media and alternative life-styles. There were substantial differences in the access to such information, whether through printed material or other means, that resulted in different tastes and consumption patterns for the rural population. Whatever the relative importance of these different factors, the rural population continued with higher rates of illiteracy than the urban population, and in some pockets of rural America such as the Appalachian plateau, illiteracy rates remained significantly above those of the rest of the population.

20. Ibid., pp. 190–191.

The expansion in public schooling at the elementary level provided more equal educational opportunities to different socioeconomic groups in the nineteenth century. Elementary education provided basic training in reading and writing essential for literacy. Public schools did not provide elementary education as a free good, but they reduced the cost of that education, making it attractive to the population as a whole. Public education at the elementary level was egalitarian to the extent that it offset differences in literacy by wealth and occupation. However, this was not true for public education at the intermediate and secondary levels. Education at these more advanced levels was highly unequal in distribution. Children enrolled in these schools were more likely to come from families who were in the middle- and upper-income groups. It is fair to say that public education was egalitarian in terms of basic literacy skills that could be achieved through elementary schooling, but public education was inegalitarian in terms of advanced literacy skills taught at the intermediate and secondary levels.[21]

Illiteracy did not preclude those at the bottom of the income and wealth distribution from upward mobility. But with the spread of public education and literacy, it became more difficult for the illiterate to improve their wealth and maintain their position in the total wealth distribution. By the second half of the nineteenth century, there was evidence of a causal relationship between literacy and wealth; upward economic mobility was directly related to the level of education and literacy. The quality of literacy as measured by the level of education completed was becoming more important as a criterion for access to higher-paying occupations.[22]

Differences in literacy rates between men and women originated in the colonial and early national period and persisted throughout the nineteenth century. However, women were moving toward parity with men in literacy, particularly in the urban areas. Public education, at least at the primary levels, contributed to this convergence in literacy rates by sex. The labor force participation rate was lower for women than for men in the nineteenth century. To the extent that education was viewed as an investment in human capital designed to generate a higher income in the labor market, we would expect lower levels of schooling for women compared to men, based upon differences in labor force participation rates alone. However, differences in school-

21. Ibid., pp. 200–201.
22. Ibid.

ing by sex reflected the broader differentiation in roles for men and women in the society as well.[23]

Convergence in the levels of schooling and literacy rates for the foreign born with those of the native born was not achieved until the twentieth century. The educational decisions of immigrant families were tied to other decisions designed to maximize the family's welfare. The foreign born rather quickly emulated consumption patterns of the native-born population. Since wage rates for the foreign born were, on average, below those of the native born, the only way that immigrants could maintain high levels of consumption was by supplementing family income through earnings of other family members. Wives of the foreign born, as well as the native born, had low labor-force participation rates; they tended to enter the labor market only in periods of family emergency such as the loss of income by the male head of the household. Wives might supplement family income by taking in boarders or doing other work in their homes, but that income formed a small part of total income for most families.

The major supplement to family income came from the earnings of children. The typical pattern in immigrant families was for older children to enter the labor market at an early age to supplement family income. That income would be used in part to support the education of younger children in the family. Throughout this period, immigrant families had higher fertility rates and lower levels of education and literacy than those of the native-born population. Expansion in the public schools system may have altered their decisions by making education cheaper for immigrant as well as native-born families. However, the convergence of immigrant education levels and literacy rates, as well as fertility rates, with those of the native-born population awaited the twentieth century, when wage rates for these two groups also converged.[24]

A COUNTERFACTUAL HYPOTHESIS

We can pose a counterfactual hypothesis that assumes a continuation of the patterns of schooling from the preindustrial era through the Industrial Revolution. This assumes a continuation of the educational system that characterized the pre-1840 era. In that system, the pri-

23. Ibid., pp. 191–92.
24. Ibid., p. 199.

mary responsibility for education rested with the family. Although common schools were an important part of that system, they were responsive to the influence of the family and the community at the local level, in contrast to the systematization of public education after 1840, which increasingly shifted the responsibility and control of education to a hierarchical government at the state and later at the federal level.

When we speculate about that counterfactual educational system, it is fair to conclude that levels of education and literacy would have improved, even without the rapid expansion of public schooling associated with the common school revival after 1840. As Kaestle and Vinovskis have argued, the educational institutions of the late eighteenth and early nineteenth centuries had the capacity "to increase the extent of schooling in the decades prior to the common school revival." [25] We may also infer that such schooling would have reached a broader cross-section of the population in terms of region of residence, occupation, income and wealth, ethnicity, and sex.

Whether or not the pace of education and literacy and the rate of diffusion through the population would have been lower in this counterfactual educational system than that which actually occurred due to the common school movement is a debatable issue. It is important to point out that private education was to a great extent displaced by public education. Particularly in urban areas where families could not afford to support private schools as well as public schools, private support declined. There is some evidence that at least during the early phase of the common school movement, the decline in private support may have been greater than the increase in public support, resulting in a net decrease in expenditures per child. Clearly, private expenditures for education would have grown more rapidly in the absence of the common school movement.

Even if private expenditures for education would have expanded at a faster pace, this would not have satisfied the supporters of the common school movement. Their criticism was that the traditional educational system was deficient, not only with respect to the level of educational expenditures, but also in terms of the content of the curriculum.

25. Carl F. Kaestle and Maris A. Vinovskis, *Education and Social Change in Nineteenth Century Massachusetts* (Cambridge: Cambridge University Press, 1980).

THE HIDDEN AGENDA OF THE COMMON SCHOOL MOVEMENT

Underlying the demands for educational reform was a hidden agenda for the common school movement. That hidden agenda included a diverse range of goals to be achieved by shifting responsibility for education from the family to the state. The particular goals, of course, depended upon the interest group concerned. Some of those goals were narrowly defined in terms of interest groups that stood to benefit directly from an expanded public education system; however, a broader set of goals was to be achieved by those who advocated the politization of the educational system.

For educational reformers in the nineteenth century, public education was to be a vehicle for "social progress." They viewed the disparities in education between the rural and urban sectors as a threat to national and political cohesion. The concentration of low-income families, particularly immigrant families in urban areas, was seen as a threat to social and political stability. The educational system that had emerged by the early nineteenth century was considered inadequate to the task; the diverse mix of public schools, quasi-public schools and private schools, private church-related schools, and private educational institutions was viewed as inconsistent with maximizing "social welfare" in the eyes of educational reformers. Whether these reformers defined "social progress" in terms of economic prosperity, a more egalitarian society, fervent nationalism, or spiritual well-being, they felt that social progress could be achieved only through the transmission of ideas in the public schools. This meant a curriculum that conveyed an entire ideology and culture consistent with "social progress"; education was to acquire all of the trappings of social engineering in which performance was measured by conformity to a set of values or norms consistent with "social progress." Most important, education was to perform an integrative function in bringing different ethnic groups into the mainstream of American culture. The ideology of literacy through public education was spelled out in detail by Horace Mann. His objective was "the removal of vile and rotten parts from the structure of society as fast as salutary and sound ones can be prepared to take their place." Education, he wrote, would become "the balance wheel of the social machinery," to produce "sober, wise, good men to prepare for coming events, to adjust society to the new relations it is to fill, to remove the old, and to substitute a new social edifice, without overwhelming the present occupants in ruin.[26]

It is interesting to note that Mann perceived the extent to which the public schools would displace the family in the transmission of values and the socialization of children. Indeed, Mann argued that in order to transmit ideas through the public schools, the latter should rely on the same motives that influence family members in maximizing family welfare. In response to a critic who argued for more school discipline, he wrote:

> Here then is the philosophy of School Discipline. Authority, Force, Fear, Pain! The ideas of Childhood and Punishment indissolubly associated together. . . . Authority, Force, Fear, Pain! These motives, taken from the nethermost part of the nethermost end of the scale of influences, are to be inscribed on the lintels and doorposts of our school houses and embroidered on the phylacteries of the teachers' garments. . . . Conscience is nowhere referred to as one of the motive powers in the conduct of children. . . . That powerful class of motives which consists of affection for parents, love for brothers and sisters, . . . justice and the social sentiment toward schoolmates, respect for elders, the pleasures of acquiring knowledge, the duty of doing as we would be done by, the connection between present conduct and success, estimation, eminence in future life, the presence of an unseen eye—not a syllable of all these is set forth with any earnestness or insisted upon as the true source and spring of human actions.[27]

THE CONFLICT BETWEEN THE FAMILY AND THE STATE IN THE COMMON SCHOOL MOVEMENT

The educational reformers did not implement their plans for politicizing the educational system without conflict. Lower-income groups in both the rural and urban sector opposed the increased levels of taxation required to finance the expanded public school system. Laborers in the urban areas fought compulsory schooling as a restriction on their parental rights. The Irish and other immigrant groups boycotted (and in a few instances, burned down) the public schools that were displacing their Catholic educational institutions. The rights of individual families to make decisions regarding education of their

26. Bowles and Gintis, *n.* 12, p. 166.
27. Ibid., p. 170.

children were sacrificed in the politicization of education associated with the common school revival. As the public schools reflected the distinction between church and state, religious instruction was removed and the curriculum became more secular in character. Some clergymen saw the secular instruction in the common schools as complementary to religious instruction in the church and home; but other clergymen viewed with alarm this compartmentalization of education and the growing dominance of the secular values inculcated through the public school system.

It was impossible for the public schools to be neutral with respect to major social issues confronting the society; in some cases such as racial segregation, these schools embodied official public policies. Horace Mann accepted racially segregated education and admonished schoolmasters who spoke out publicly on that issue, although as a member of the U.S. House of Representatives, he later adopted the antislavery cause. Abolitionists in New England were critical of Mann's position and the official policy of racial segregation in public schools. The extent to which the public schools had become politicized and had antagonized different groups in the society is revealed by the defeat by a close margin of a bill in the Massachusetts House of Representatives to halt the development of common schools and abolish a State Board of Education.

Similar battles were fought between the supporters of educational reform and the critics of public education in other states. A major debate over public education occurred in the Pennsylvania Constitutional Convention of 1837–1838. The debate over public schools in New York City continued over the entire first half of the nineteenth century. There were many issues and different interest groups involved in these debates, as we have noted, but the fundamental issue was whether education would continue to reflect the influence and control of the family and the local community, or whether that influence and control would shift to the state through an increasingly bureaucratized and politicized public school system. It was clear that the latter could not take place without state intervention in the rights of the family to determine how their children would be educated. Educational reformers who perceived this conflict with the rights of families argued that violation of those rights was justified by the "social progress" achieved through state intervention in the educational system. Samuel Harrison Smith wrote in 1798 that the success of a stable government required that society must establish the right to educate, and acknowledge the duty of having educated, all children:

It is the duty of a nation to superintend and even to coerce the education of children, and . . . high consideration for expediency not only justify, but dictate the establishment of a system, which shall place under a control, independent of, and superior to, parental authority, the education of children.[28]

The state was increasingly viewed as an institution to achieve "social progress" even when this conflicted with the rights of the family. Public education was to be an instrument for "social progress," and to accomplish that goal, the state not only came into conflict with the family, but had to displace an important role for the family in educating their children. As long as the common schools reflected the influence and control of the family at the local level, as they had through the early nineteenth century, they were consistent with the maximization of family welfare. The family, as its members' agent, organized formal education as a public, quasi-public, or private institution depending upon the interests of the family involved. When that decision did result in public education through the common school movement, the education was responsive to the interests of family and the local community. When the common schools failed to satisfy the families' wishes as its members' agent, families could mobilize support, as they did in Lowell, Massachusetts, to throw out the school board and put in members more responsive to their wishes. If families were still dissatisfied with the common school, they often had the option of private schooling.

The existence of general taxes to support the common school involved some sacrifices for families who chose private schooling for their children, but the levels of taxation were modest. The rapid growth of public education after 1840 had a different impact on the family. As the control of common schools shifted to a state bureaucracy, the schools became less responsive to the interests of the family as its members' agent. When the common schools implemented a social policy through the curriculum dictated by the state government, the family had little influence over those decisions. Families and local communities were not likely to throw out a school board that was the instrument of state policy. For example, the selection of text materials, the curriculum of instruction, and the method of evaluating teachers and students were increasingly determined in a hierarchical manner from a state secretary of education down to the common school, rather than by the local community.

---

28. Soltow and Stevens, *n.* 1, p. 48.

The result of this politicization of the educational system was a growing conflict between the common school as the instrument of state policy and the wishes of the family and the local community. When families disagreed with the policies of state-supported educational institutions, they had fewer options. State schools displaced the private schools—particularly in poorer school districts where working-class people could not afford to both support a private educational institution and pay taxes to finance the state-supported common schools. The result was an alienation between the family, as its members' agent, and the state-supported educational institutions, which no longer reflected the family's influence or control. This conflict between the family and the state over education was the first in a series of conflicts over the growing incursion by the state into the decisions of the family. The role of the state expanded during the Industrial Revolution, not only in the field of education, but also in a broader range of decisions that had been vested in the family. These incursions into the family and constraints on the rights of the family to maximize the welfare of its members were justified on the grounds of "social progress."

CONCLUSION: IDEOLOGY AND THE COMMON SCHOOL MOVEMENT

The success of reformers in transferring control of education from the family to the state reflected changes in ideology and philosophy that coincided with the Industrial Revolution. The fundamental presuppositions of the preindustrial era, based upon the Lockean concepts of social contract and natural rights, were gradually discarded during the Industrial Revolution. In the mid-nineteenth century, Jeremy Bentham, John Stuart Mill, and other utilitarian philosophers provided an ideology more in tune with the rapid social and economic changes that accompanied the Industrial Revolution in America.

The previous generation identified justice with equality of opportunity and with procedural safeguards for individual property rights, i.e., an entitlement theory of justice. If the family acquired property by lawful means, the outcome was just—even though equality of opportunity resulted in substantial inequalities in the distribution of property. The only criterion for intervening in the exercise of property rights was when property laws were violated, that is, when individuals acquired or exercised property rights through illegal or fraudulent means.

Utilitarians established a new rationale for the just society to maximize the total welfare or utility of the society. If we assume that there is an objective criterion for measuring welfare, then we can judge a specific case with reference to that objective criterion of welfare. The nineteenth century writers in political economy attempted to define a social welfare function independent of the welfare of families. They began not with the presupposition of classical liberalism based upon an entitlements theory of justice, but with an abstract theory of justice: enhancing the wealth of the community, creating an egalitarian society, etc. This implied social goals such as economic growth or economic equality to be achieved by government intervention, even when this was in conflict with the rights of the family. Conflicts between the family and the state had to yield to governmental decision-making designed to maximize some objective social welfare function. The criterion for court decisions was no longer the rights of the family, but social welfare—however that was perceived by the justices. For Bentham and the utilitarians, the calculus of pleasure and pain could be refined to mathematical precision as a tool for adjudicating cases in order to maximize social welfare. The result was that rule by man replaced rule of law.

Once a social welfare function was specified independent of the welfare of families, the ideological foundations for collectivism was provided. The criterion for the law in a collectivist society is based upon the principle of the greatest good for the greatest number. If a particular law or judicial decision increases social welfare in this utilitarian sense, then, in a collectivist political system, encroaching on the rights of the family is justified.

While elements of collectivism were evident in preindustrial America, it was during the Industrial Revolution that a collectivist political system began to dominate. Legislation was passed involving government infringement on the rights of families—on the grounds of maximizing social progress. Judicial decisions shifted from the protection of the rights of families to positivist law designed to maximize some social objective. Democracy legitimized the incursions of the state into the family's affairs on the utilitarian grounds that this reflected majority vote rule. The courts sanctioned this expansion of government as a legitimate exercise of the police powers of the state. Legislation and judicial reasoning was cloaked in the moral and ethical garb of altruism with reference to social welfare and social progress. However, the outcome was an increasingly collectivist society in which the rights of the family were sacrificed for the "good" of the community. What was a laissez-faire economy began to look more like a collectivist state.[29] The deep-seated changes wrought during that pivotal period pervaded every aspect of life—the state, the economy, education, the family. For better or for worse, none have been the same since.

29. Poulson, *n*. 10.

SELECTED BIBLIOGRAPHY
PART II

Bailyn, Bernard. *Education in the Forming of American Society: Needs and Opportunities for Study*. Chapel Hill: University of North Carolina Press, 1960.

Bowles, Samuel, and Herbert Gintis. *Schooling in Capitalist America, Educational Reform and the Contradictions of Economic Life*. New York: Basic Books, 1976.

Bullough, William A. *Cities and Schools in the Gilded Age: The Evolution of an Urban Institution*. New York: Kennikat, 1974.

———. *The Blind Boss and His City: Christopher Augustine Buckley and Nineteenth-Century San Francisco*. Berkeley: University of California Press, 1979.

Ensign, Forest Chester. *Compulsory School Attendance and Child Labor*. New York: Arno Press, 1969.

Everhart, Robert B., ed. *The Public School Monopoly: A Critical Analysis of Education and the State in American Society*. San Francisco: Pacific Institute for Public Policy Research, 1982.

Field, Alexander James. "Educational Reform and Manufacturing Development in Mid Nineteenth Century Massachusetts." Ph.D. dissertation, Stanford University, 1974.

Grimes, Alan P. *The Puritan Ethic and Woman Suffrage*. New York: Oxford University Press, 1967.

Hays, Samuel P. "The Politics of Reform in Municipal Government in the Progressive Era." *Pacific Northwest Quarterly* 55 (1964):157–69.

Jensen, Richard. *The Winning of the Midwest: Social and Political Conflict, 1888–1896.* Chicago: University of Chicago Press, 1971.

Kaestle, Carl F., and Maris A. Vinovskis. *Education and Social Change in Nineteenth Century Massachusetts: Quantitative Studies.* Cambridge: Cambridge University Press, 1980.

Kahn, Alfred J., and Sheila B. Kamerman. *Helping America's Families.* Philadelphia: Temple University Press, 1982.

———. "Developments in the Law—The Constitution and the Family." *Harvard Law Review* 93 (no. 6, April 1980): 1157–1383.

Katz, Michael B. *The Irony of Early School Reform.* Boston: Beacon Press, 1970.

———. *Class, Bureaucracy, and Schools: The Illusion of Educational Change in America.* New York: Praeger, 1975.

Kleppner, Paul. *The Cross of Culture: A Social Analysis of Midwestern Politics, 1850–1900.* New York: Free Press, 1970.

———. *The Third Electoral System, 1853–1892: Parties, Voters, and Political Cultures.* Chapel Hill: University of North Carolina Press, 1979.

Lazerson, Marvin. *Origins of the Urban School: Public Education in Massachusetts, 1870–1915.* Cambridge: Harvard University Press, 1971.

Pickens, Donald K. *Eugenics and the Progressives.* Nashville, Tenn.: Vanderbilt University Press, 1968.

Platt, Anthony M. *The Child Savers: The Invention of Delinquency.* Chicago: University of Chicago Press, 1969.

Poulson, Barry. *Economic History of the United States.* New York: Macmillan, 1981.

———. "Ideology and Labor Law." *Journal of Social, Political, and Economic Studies* 8 (no. 1, Spring 1983): 43–80.

Rushdoony, Rousas John. *The Messianic Character of American Education: Studies in the History of the Philosophy of Education.* Nutley, N.J.: Craig Press, 1963.

Shradar, Victor L. "Ethnic Politics, Religion, and the Public Schools of San Francisco, 1849–1933." Ph.D. dissertation, School of Education, Stanford University, 1974.

Soltow, Lee, and Edward Stevens. *The Rise of Literacy and the Common School in the United States: A Socioeconomic Analysis to 1870.* Chicago: University of Chicago Press, 1981.

Spring, Joel H. *Education and the Rise of the Corporate State.* Boston: Beacon Press, 1972.

Tyack, David B. *The One Best System: A History of American Urban Education.* Cambridge: Harvard University Press, 1974.

Vinovskis, Maris A. "Trends in Massachusetts Education." *History of Education Quarterly* 12 (no. 4, Winter 1972): 501–29.

Violas, Paul C. "Jane Addams and the New Liberalism." In C. Karier, P.

Violas, and J. Spring, eds., *Roots of Crisis: American Education in the 20th Century*, pp. 66–83. Chicago: Rand McNally, 1973.

————. "Progressive Social Philosophy: Charles Horton Cooley and Edward Alsworth Ross." In C. Karier, P. Violas, and J. Spring, eds., *Roots of Crisis: American Education in the 20th Century*, pp. 40–65. Chicago: Rand McNally, 1973.

THE LEGAL STATUS OF PERSONAL RELATIONSHIPS

6

PHILOSOPHIC ASSUMPTIONS OF SOME CONTEMPORARY JUDICIAL DOCTRINES

Henry Mark Holzer

[Marriage] is an institution, in the maintenance of which in its purity the public is deeply interested, for it is the foundation of the family and of society, without which there would be neither civilization nor progress.[1]

The altruist-collectivist ethics and their political-legal corollary, statism, have always been the basic assumption of United States Supreme Court jurisprudence. As a result, the Court's decisions have consistently exalted government power at the expense of individual rights. The Court's decisions affecting the family have been no exception, and it is some of those decisions which this chapter will examine. But first, three basic concepts.

ALTRUISM, COLLECTIVISM, STATISM

Popularly, *altruism* is understood to mean simply being nice to people, for example, supporting an artist, helping the poor, contributing to medical research. In strictly ethical terms, however, the meaning of altruism is quite different. It is "the doctrine that the welfare of society is the proper goal of an individual's actions," not his or her

---

1. *Maynard v. Hill*, 125 U.S. 190, 209 (1888).

own happiness.[2] Political philosopher Ayn Rand addressed the concept more fundamentally, holding that altruism was "the ethical theory which regards man as a sacrificial animal, which holds that man has no right to exist for his own sake, that service to others is the only justification of his existence, and that self-sacrifice is his highest moral duty."[3]

Closely related to the concept of altruism is that of collectivism. Contrary to popular understanding, collectivism has nothing to do with voluntarism, or with the fact that people inhabit the same geographical areas. On the contrary, collectivism "holds that the individual has no rights, that his life and work belong to the group (to 'society,' to the tribe, the state, the nation) and that the group may sacrifice him at its own whim to its own interest."[4]

Because altruism and collectivism are ethical doctrines, and because the only way to implement them against nonconsenters is by force, they necessarily have a familiar political-legal corollary: statism, "the principle or policy of concentrating extensive economic, political, and related controls in the state at the cost of individual liberty."[5]

THE SUPREME COURT'S PREMISES

That altruist-collectivist ethics have consistently been the motivational base of Supreme Court decision-making, that in consequence the Court has consistently upheld ever increasing statist government power at the expense of the individual—these are established facts, no longer open to question. Lest anyone be misled by a justice's occasional expression of solicitude for individual rights, it must be understood that such sentiments not only have been few and far between, but they have always been quite superficial and highly selective. In terms of individual rights, it is not easy to take seriously a liberal justice's

2. *Webster's New World Dictionary of the American Language,* 2d College Edition (New York: Simon and Schuster, 1982).

3. Ayn Rand, "The Objectivist Ethics," in *The Virtue of Selfishness* (New York: New American Library, 1965), pp. 32–33. [*Editors' note:* Closely related to the doctrine of altruism is utilitarianism, which maintains that what is right is whatever contributes to "the greatest good of the greatest number," individual sovereignty notwithstanding. See Jeremy Bentham, *An Introduction to the Principles of Morals and Legislation* (London: Methuen and Co., 1982).]

4. Ayn Rand, "Racism," in ibid., p. 175.

5. *The American College Dictionary* (New York: Random House, 1957).

protestation about government's censorship of speech, when he supports government's intrusive regulation of business. For the same reason, one must wonder about the depth of a conservative justice's opposition to government's control of property through zoning, when he approves of government's regulation of contraception.

To the extent that there has been disagreement between the justices of our Supreme Court, it has not been over the fundamental principle of whether government *should* control our personal value choices, but merely over the details of how, when, and to what extent our personal value choices *will* be controlled. Regrettably, because the confines of this article do not allow an examination of the hundreds of Supreme Court decisions that relentlessly attest to the truth of this proposition, only the briefest summary will have to suffice. Among other things, the High Court has upheld the constitutionality of laws that did the following:

- Regulated the working hours of women because "healthy mothers are essential to vigorous offspring, [and] the physical well-being of woman becomes an object of public interest and care in order to preserve the strength and vigor of the race."[6]

- Limited the amount of wheat some farmers could grow for their own consumption, in order to keep wheat scarce and thus help other farmers by keeping the price high.[7]

- Allowed Congress to establish racial quotas in awarding funds for public works contracts, because "[i]t is because of a legacy of unequal treatment that we now must permit the institutions of this society to give consideration to race in making decisions about who will hold the positions of influence, affluence, and prestige in America."[8]

- Opened private property to the use of uninvited protesters, because "neither property rights nor contract rights are absolute. . . . Equally fundamental with the private right is that of the public to regulate it in the common interest."[9]

---

6. *Muller* v. *Oregon,* 208 U.S. 412, 421 (1908).
7. *Wickard* v. *Filburn,* 317 U.S. 111 (1942).
8. *Fullilove* v. *Klutznick,* 448 U.S. 453, 522 (1980).
9. *Prune Yard Shopping Center* v. *Robins,* 447 U.S. 74 (1980).

- Nullified a contract between a private creditor and debtor, relieving the latter of a substantial obligation, because "of public needs and . . . the necessity of finding a ground for a rational compromise between individual rights and public welfare."[10]

- Jailed male Mormons for exercising the religiously mandated duty of entering into polygamous marriages, because "[p]olygamy has always been odious among the Northern and Western Nations of Europe, and, until the establishment of the Mormon Church, was almost exclusively a feature of the life of Asiatic and of African people."[11]

- Censored speech because it was "no essential part of any exposition of ideas, and . . . of such slight social value as a step to truth that any benefit that may be derived from them is clearly outweighed by the social interest in order and morality."[12]

- Punished certain consensual sexual practices because they violated "the laws of society, designed to secure its peace and prosperity, and the morals of its people. . . ."[13]

- Sterilized alleged mental defectives, against their will, because it was "better for all the world, if . . . society can prevent those who are manifestly unfit from continuing their kind. . . ."[14]

There are many more such decisions, growing from the same altruist-collectivist ethical base and thus allowing rampant statism to ceaselessly violate individual rights.[15] In light of those decisions, it is hardly surprising that when the Supreme Court of the United States has been called upon to assess the constitutionality of laws affecting family relationships and interests, the same premises have led to the same results.

"FAMILY"

When considering the vast quantity of laws enacted by local and state governments and by Congress, many of which are brought to various

10. *Home Building & Loan Ass'n.* v. *Blaisdell,* 290 U.S. 398 (1938).

11. *Reynolds* v. *United States,* 98 U.S. 145, 164 (1878).

12. *Chaplinsky* v. *New Hampshire,* 315 U.S. 568, 571–572 (1942).

13. *State* v. *Rhinhart,* 424 P.2d 906, 910 (Wash., 1967), quoting *Davis* v. *Beason,* 133 U.S. 333 (1890).

14. *Buck* v. *Bell,* 274 U.S. 200, 205 (1927).

15. See Henry Mark Holzer, *Sweet Land of Liberty? The Supreme Court and Individual Rights* (New York: Common Sense Press, 1982).

state and federal courts for interpretation and constitutional scrutiny, and when considering the very large number of topics embraced in those laws and legal decisions, it quickly becomes obvious that hard-and-fast categorization of topics is extremely difficult. For example, does a state law dealing with the estate taxes of intestate unmarried male veterans leaving illegitimate children readily fall into the legal category of taxation, intestacy, or illegitimacy? Or two categories? Or just one? Or perhaps none of them? Or perhaps the real category, in context, is one dealing with the sharing of legislative power between the federal and state governments.

This simple illustration points up the problem in facilely shoving legal issues into seemingly convenient categories. Indeed, under the rubric of "family law" issues, one could legitimately include such diverse legal topics as marriage, dissolution of marriage, procreation (including sterilization, contraception and abortion), definition of "nuclear" and other types of "family," children's rights, parental duties, illegitimacy, termination of parental status, the role of the state, and much more. Although analysis of scores of Supreme Court decisions on these topics (as well as others) would be interesting thematically, doing so within the confines of this chapter is obviously not possible. Nor is it necessary. Simply examining three major areas where government has been deeply involved in the family—marriage, definition of the family, and procreation—amply demonstrates how statism has significantly and consistently interfered with individual rights in this most important of human relationships. Indeed, examination of the following decisions of the Supreme Court of the United States shows conclusively that the legal relationship between men, women, and children has become purely a creature of society's values, defined by government and unwaveringly imposed by it on men, women, and children alike.

MARRIAGE

Back in the early 1900s a federal statute prohibited the importation into the United States of any female "for the purpose of prostitution, or for any other immoral purpose."[16] Under that statute, one John Bitty was indicted in the New York federal court for bringing a woman from England to the United States to live with him as his concubine.

---

16. 34 Stat. at L.898, chap. 1134, U.S. Comp. Stat. Supp. 1907, p. 389; *U.S.* v. *Bitty*, 208, U.S. 393, 398 (1908).

The Supreme Court of the United States, in sending Bitty to trial, accepted the following definition of *concubinage:* "illicit intercourse, not under the sanction of a valid or legal marriage."[17] In doing so, the Court made some noteworthy observations about individual rights, societal values, government power, and the nature and permissible limits of marriage:

> [The Court endorsed] the idea of the family as consisting in and springing from the union for life of one man and one woman in the holy estate of matrimony; the sure foundation of all that is stable and noble in our civilization; the best guaranty of that reverent morality which is the source of all beneficent progress in social and political improvement. . . . Congress, no doubt [passed the law believing] that contact with society on the part of [loose] women . . . would be hurtful to the cause of sound private and public morality and to the general well-being of the people.[18]

The Supreme Court's nakedly collectivist-statist view of the institution of marriage was nothing new. Thirty years before, the Court had said and decided much worse in ruling on the constitutionality of a federal law set against plural marriage.

The Mormon Church—officially named the Church of Jesus Christ of Latter-day Saints—was founded in the United States in 1830, and many of its adherents settled in Utah. Since Utah was a territory prior to its 1896 admission to the Union, federal laws governed there. One of those laws, enacted in 1862, provided that

> every person having a husband or wife living, who marries another, whether married or single, in a Territory, or other place over which the [federal government has] jurisdiction, is guilty of bigamy, and shall be punished by a fine of not more than $500, and by imprisonment for a term of not more than 5 years.[19]

Set squarely against this federal antibigamy statute was the religious familial duty of male Mormons to practice polygamy.

Indeed, even the Supreme Court of the United States had acknowledged that this duty was enjoined by different books which [Mormons] believed to be of divine origin . . . that the members of the Church believed that the practice of polygamy was directly enjoined

17. Id. at 401.
18. Id. at 401.
19. *Reynolds* v. *United States*, 98 U.S. 145, 153 (1878).

upon the male members thereof by the Almighty God . . . that the failing or refusing to practice polygamy by such male members . . . would be punished, and that the penalty . . . would be damnation in the life to come.[20]

With the federal antibigamy law pushing at him from one side, and his familial religious duty to practice polygamy pushing from the other, Utah Mormon George Reynolds was in a vise. If he rendered unto Caesar, he affronted God and was damned. If he rendered unto God, Caesar would surely imprison him.

God won the first round. Reynolds, within the ritual of his church, took a second bride. Caesar, however, was not amused. The federal government indicted Reynolds for violation of its antibigamy statute. He defended the charge by asserting that the First Amendment guaranteed him the right freely to exercise his religion. Convicted in the territorial courts, Reynolds's case reached the Supreme Court of the United States in 1878. There, though Chief Justice Waite's enunciation of the issue for the Court was a bit fuzzy (". . . whether religious belief can be accepted as a justification of an overt act made criminal by the law of the land"),[21] the issue itself was clear. The Chief Justice was really asking whether, in light of the free exercise guarantee, a statute could outlaw the required Mormon religious practice of polygamy—an issue of family central to the Mormon faith.

The Court's answer was another victory for Caesar. It unanimously held the federal antibigamy law constitutional, and the religious duty required of Reynolds by his God had to take a back seat to secular considerations. Why?

To support its decision that the nineteenth century American conception of the family did not allow for polygamy, the Court in *Reynolds v. United States* invoked English history—but inadequately. England (a country with its own national church) had never enjoyed a guarantee of free exercise of religion, nor even a written constitution, for that matter. The Court invoked the supposed intention of the guarantee's original sponsors—but that was equivocal at best. The court even resorted to "nose-counting"—with a clear racist implication—to buttress its conclusion that "polygamy has always been odious among the Northern and Western Nations of Europe, and, until the establishment of the Mormon Church, was almost exclusively a

20. Id. at 161.
21. Id. at 162.

feature of the life of Asiatic and of African people."[22] Mongoloid and Negro families could practice polygamy, but not American.

All camouflage, English history, and snide racist references aside, the real reason the Court reached its conclusion—the real reason that society took its view of family out on Mormon George Reynolds's back—is contained in portions of just two sentences in the Court's 24-page opinion. In one, the Court observed that Congress was "free to reach actions which were in violation of social duties. . . ."[23] In the other, the court noted that ". . . there never has been a time in any State of the Union when polygamy has not been an offense against society. . . ."[24]

The common denominator here is apparent. What did the Court mean by the traditions of "society"—specifically the majority of Americans whose antipolygamy attitudes and different views of family spurred Congress to enact the law, the president to approve it, and various courts (up to and including the Supreme Court) to uphold it? By "society," the Court meant the "collective." "Society" (lots of other people, but not the Mormons) opposed polygamy; therefore, society's values had to prevail. Since Mormon values, then, were to be sacrificed, the Court was doing so in the name of altruism. Though polygamy involved consenting adults exercising a religious duty whose exercise was guaranteed by the First Amendment, the altruist-collectivist ethics prevailed. The Mormans were not allowed to organize their families as they (and their God) saw fit.

The threat that plural marriage posed to society's view of a "proper" marital relationship was again before the Supreme Court nearly three-quarters of a century later. Unfortunately, nothing much had changed—except that this time (not 1878, but 1946), the Court's opinion was written not by arch-conservative Chief Justice Waite but by arch-liberal Justice William O. Douglas.

Cleveland v. *United States*[25] involved the prosecution of practicing Mormon polygamists under the so-called Mann Act, which punished transporting in interstate commerce "any woman or girl for the purpose of prostitution or debauchery." Cleveland and other defendants had been convicted of transporting their plural wives across state lines.

22. Id. at 164.
23. Id. at 164.
24. Id. at 165.
25. *Cleveland* v. *United States*, 329 U.S. 14 (1946).

In affirming the convictions, Douglas's opinion for the Court perpetuated the collectivist-statist view of marriage enunciated in earlier cases:

> The organization of a community for the spread and practice of polygamy is, in a measure, a return to barbarism. It is contrary to the spirit of Christianity and of the civilization which Christianity has produced in the western world. . . . The establishment or maintenance of polygamous households is a notorious example of promiscuity.[26]

It could not be clearer that *Bitty, Reynolds* and *Cleveland* (and other uncited cases that make the same point) stand for the same proposition—one as firmly entrenched today as it was in the 1870s when society and the government turned Mormon polygamist George Reynolds into a criminal for his unwillingness to betray his unconventional religious values. That point is painfully simple: *Society deems the institution of monogamous marriage to be a sacred cornerstone of Christian civilization, and through the majority's agent, government, it has used the law to institutionalize that value to the exclusion of competing views of marriage—to the extent that a minority's contrary, yet profoundly religious, duty will be criminalized. In sum, marriage is what collectivism-statism says it is, and woe unto individual rights if they get in the way.*

But the state does not stop there. It goes well beyond mandating the nature of the husband-wife relationship. On occasion, it has even attempted to define, and actually *has* defined, the nature of the family itself.

"FAMILY" DEFINED

The Village of Belle Terre, Long Island, was a tiny community of some 220 homes not far from a state university. As an anti-rooming-house measure, Belle Terre enacted an ordinance prohibiting "groups of more than two unrelated persons, as distinguished from groups consisting of any number of persons related by blood, adoption, or marriage, from occupying a residence within the confines of the town."[27] The ordinance accomplished this by its definition of "family":

> [o]ne or more persons related by blood, adoption, or marriage, living and cooking together as a single housekeeping unit, exclusive of household

26. Id. at 19.
27. *Village of Belle Terre* v. *Boraas*, 416 U.S. 1, 12 (1974).

servants. A number of persons but not exceeding two (2) living and cooking together as a single housekeeping unit though not related by blood, adoption, or marriage shall be deemed to constitute a family.[28]

The ordinance's definition of "family" was attacked on various grounds, including that, in effect, government had no legitimate power to define "family"—not even for purposes of implementing the state's unquestioned power to enact zoning laws. But the argument went nowhere. If to accomplish what the Village considered proper zoning a restrictive definition of "family" was required, the Supreme Court of the United States was not going to interfere. Why not? Because:

. . . boarding houses, fraternity houses, and the like present urban problems. More people occupy a given space; more cars rather continuously pass by; more cars parked; noise travels with crowds.

A quiet place where yards are wide, people few and motor vehicles restricted are legitimate guidelines in a land-use project addressed to family needs. This goal is a permissible one. . . . The police power is not confined to elimination of filth, stench, and unhealthy places. It is ample to lay out zones where family values, youth values, and the blessings of quiet seclusion and clean air make the area a sanctuary for people.[29]

In other words, if society decides that it wants tranquility, government can provide it—even at the cost of statutorily defining the family in the most restrictive manner possible.

The *Belle Terre* case was by no means aberrational. Countless local ordinances throughout the country, often for zoning and related land-use purposes, have defined the "family." For example, Section 1341.08 (1966) of the Housing Code of the City of East Cleveland, Ohio, provided as follows:

"Family" means a number of individuals related to the nominal head of the household or to the spouse of the nominal head of household living as a single housekeeping unit in a single dwelling unit, but limited to the following:

(a) Husband or wife of the nominal head of the household.

(b) Unmarried children of the nominal head of the household or of the spouse of the nominal head of the household, provided, however, that such unmarried children have no children residing with them.

(c) Father or mother of the nominal head of the household or of the spouse of the nominal head of the household.

28. Id. at 2.
29. Id. at 9.

(d) Notwithstanding the provisions of subsection (b) hereof, a family may include not more than one dependent married or unmarried child of the nominal head of the household or of the spouse of the nominal head of the household and the spouse and dependent children of such dependent child. For the purpose of this subsection, a dependent person is one who has more than fifty percent of his total support furnished for him by the nominal head of the household and the spouse of the nominal head of the household.

(e) A family may consist of one individual.

For violating East Cleveland's idea of what a "family" consisted of, Mrs. Inez Moore was prosecuted, convicted, and sentenced to five days in jail and a $25 fine. Her offense? Allowing one too many grandsons to live with her. The intermediate Ohio appellate court affirmed Mrs. Moore's conviction, and the Ohio Supreme Court refused even to take her case. Finally, she reached the Supreme Court of the United States. There, although Mrs. Moore won, her victory was no cause for celebration for those who would keep government out of strictly family affairs.

Although the Court's majority concluded that by some unstated criteria the East Cleveland ordinance went "too far" in pursuance of legitimate municipal interests (preventing overcrowding, minimizing traffic, relieving congestion), unlike Belle Terre whose ordinance was "reasonable," the *Moore* decision's underlying premises nevertheless recognized the continued existence of statist power to define the "family" and to advance its interests. Indeed, even in invalidating the East Cleveland ordinance, the Court pointedly observed: "Of course, the Family is not beyond regulation."[30] The *principle* of government interference in the family having thus been acknowledged, the only remaining questions were when, why, and how much will the state be allowed to intrude.

The *Moore* Court provided a clear answer. Acknowledging that the government possesses the power to intrude on the family generally and "on choices concerning family living arrangements"[31] in particular, the Court set up a test for that power's exercise: ". . . the importance of the governmental interests advanced and the extent to which they are served by the challenged regulation."[32] So, basically, the

---

30. Id. at 499.
31. Id. at 499.
32. Id. at 499.

Moore Court was setting up a balancing equation. On the one side was government interference in the family, justified by sufficiently important statist concerns—like the quality of life in the Village of Belle Terre. What was on the other side? Individual rights? Basic principles of free association? Voluntary choice? Not at all. In helping out Inez Moore, the *Moore* Court's acceptance of some notion of "family rights" rested not on any proper, defensible theory of family, but on naked, traditional collectivism:

> Our decisions establish that the Constitution protects the sanctity of the family because the institution of the family is deeply rooted in this Nation's history and tradition. It is through the family that we inculcate and pass down many of our most cherished values, moral and cultural.
>
> Ours is by no means a tradition limited to respect for the bonds uniting the members of the nuclear family. The tradition of uncles, aunts, cousins, and especially grandparents sharing a household along with parents and children has roots equally venerable and equally deserving of constitutional recognition. [Footnote omitted.] Over the years millions of our citizens have grown up in just such an environment, and most, surely, have profited from it.[33]

Taken together, *Belle Terre* and *Moore* stand for at least three propositions. First, that no concept of individual rights lies at the base of official government thinking about how the "family" is to be defined. Second, that what is at the base are traditional collectivist-statist principles. Third, that therefore when the Court is asked to review state definitions of, and/or other intrusions into, the family, the determinative criterion will be the importance of the state interest involved.

If, as we have seen, collectivist-statist principles are the roots of government's attitude toward the institution of marriage and the definition of family, surely it is no surprise that those same principles—not any notion of individual rights—control the state's view of the "right" to *have* a family.

PROCREATION

Once, by means of anticontraceptive laws, the state virtually assured conception, and by means of antiabortion laws it virtually assured birth. For the moment at least, the state has *lost* that power. But just as Inez Moore's win over East Cleveland was no victory for individ-

---

33. Id. at 503–505.

ual rights, neither was the Supreme Court's restoration of procreational freedom. The two principal cases—*Griswold* v. *Connecticut* and *Roe* v. *Wade*—themselves make quite clear that little was gained for the *right* to procreate or not.

Connecticut law provided as follows:

> Any person who uses any drug, medicinal article or instrument for the purpose of preventing conception shall be fined not less than fifty dollars or imprisoned not less than sixty days nor more than one year or be both fined and imprisoned.[34]

> Any person who assists, abets, counsels, causes, hires or commands another to commit any offense may be prosecuted and punished as if he were the principal offender.[35]

Estelle T. Griswold was executive director of the Planned Parenthood League of Connecticut. Dr. Buxton, a licensed physician and a professor at the Yale Medical School, served as the league's medical director at its center in New Haven. Both Mrs. Griswold and Dr. Buxton each "gave information, instruction, and medical advice to married persons as to the means of preventing conception. They examined the wife and prescribed the best contraceptive device or material for her use. Fees were usually charged, although some couples were serviced free."[36] Mrs. Griswold and Dr. Buxton were arrested, charged as accessories to their clients' crime (using contraceptives), and found guilty. Their convictions were affirmed, first by an appeals court in Connecticut, then by that state's highest court.

The United States Supreme Court reversed the convictions. But— and it is a profoundly important "but"—the Griswold decision is a mass of contradictory reasoning, from its multiple concurring opinions to its multiple dissents. And worse: The decision as a whole stands as testament to government's power to regulate morality in general and the family in particular.

Justice Douglas spoke for the majority. But in his zeal to legalize the use of contraceptives by married persons, he constructed out of whole cloth a previously unheard-of constitutional right—"the right of privacy." And in the process, he clearly implied that, while he disapproved of outlawing the use of contraceptives (as in Connecti-

---

34. General Statutes of Connecticut (1958 rev.), Section 53-32.
35. Id. at Section 54-196.
36. *Griswold* v. *Connecticut,* 381 U.S. 479, 480 (1965).

cut), he might well rule constitutional a law regulating the "manu-facture or sale"[37] of contraceptives!

The Goldberg-Warren-Brennan concurring opinion concluded that Connecticut's anticontraceptive statute was unconstitutional—but not because of some amorphous, ill-defined "right of privacy." Their ra-tionale, instead, was based on an amorphous, ill-defined, concept of "fundamental rights."

The fact that the three concurring justices voted against the statute is outweighed by the altruist-collectivist premises they revealed in the process. These were the very premises that had made the Connecticut statute possible in the first place. Said Goldberg:

> In determining which rights are fundamental, judges are not left at large to decide cases in light of their personal and private notions. Rather, they must look to the "traditions and [collective] conscience of our people" to determine whether a principle is "so rooted [there] . . . as to be ranked as fundamental. . . ."[38]

A modest disclaimer. But while confessing that a judge's values are not the litmus paper by which "fundamental rights" are revealed, Goldberg openly defers to "the traditions and [collective] conscience of our people"—an admission that rights (family or any other kind) are neither absolute nor anchored in the Constitution: Rights are what-ever society decides they are. Goldberg further incriminates himself by his view of what Connecticut society had already "decided" in related areas of sexual conduct:

> The State of Connecticut does have statutes, the constitutionality of which is beyond doubt, which prohibit adultery and fornication. . . .
>
> Finally, it should be said of the Court's holding today that it in no way interferes with a State's proper regulation of sexual promiscuity or misconduct.[39]

Goldberg, Warren, and Brennan were, of course, motivated by al-truism-collectivism-statism—principles about as controllable as a loose cannon on a rolling deck. How else to explain why they denied Con-necticut the power to interfere with use of contraceptives (by married persons), while simultaneously granting the state the power to inter-fere with adultery, fornication, sexual promiscuity, and "miscon-

---

37. Id. at 485.
38. Id. at 493.
39. Id. at 498–499.

duct"? How else to explain why, with the following words, they implicitly endorsed even *a forced sterilization program for married persons:*

> . . . . the Government, absent a showing of a compelling subordinate state interest, could not decree that all husbands and wives must be sterilized after two children have been born to them.[40]

So much for "fundamental rights," let alone family rights.

Justice Harlan's concurring opinion was cast in the same mold, although Harlan's constitutional litmus paper was neither "right of privacy" nor "fundamental rights." In his view, "basic values 'implicit in the concept of ordered liberty'"[41] rendered Connecticut's anticontraception statute unconstitutional. Like his colleagues, Harlan embraced, in other respects, the very principles that made the Connecticut statute possible.[42] He started out, at least, by grasping the underlying issue:

> Precisely what is involved here is this: the State is asserting the right to enforce its moral judgement by intruding upon the most intimate details of the marital relation with the full power of the criminal law.[43]

But in addressing himself to an argument that statutes barring (as immoral) the use of contraceptives were based on an "irrational" premise, and that such statues subjected people "in a very important matter to the arbitrary whim of the legislature, and that it does so for no good purpose . . . ,"[44] Harlan bared his collectivist soul:

> Yet the very inclusion of the category of morality among state concerns indicates that society is not limited in its objects only to the physical well-being of the community, but has traditionally concerned itself with the moral soundness of its people as well. Indeed to attempt a line between public behavior and that which is purely consensual or solitary would be to withdraw from community concern a range of subjects with which every society in civilized times has found it necessary to deal. The laws regarding marriage which provide both when the sexual powers may be

---

40. Id. at 496–497.

41. Id. at 500.

42. Harlan's belief that Connecticut's anticontraception law violated "basic values 'implicit in the concept of ordered liberty'" was based on "reasons stated at length in [his] dissenting opinion of *Poe* v. *Ullman*," 367 U.S. 497 (1961). Harlan's quotations below are from that dissent.

43. *Poe* v. *Ullman* 367 U.S. 497, 548 (1961).

44. Id. at 497, 545.

used and the legal and societal context in which children are born and brought up, as well as laws forbidding adultery, fornication and homosexual practices which express the negative of the proposition, confining sexuality to lawful marriage, form a pattern so deeply pressed into the substance of our social life that any Constitutional doctrine in this area must build upon that basis. . . .[45]

Though the order in which Harlan made his points was a bit convoluted, *what* he was saying was not. He was clearly saying that any attempt to isolate in people's lives an area of purely private conduct—in or outside the family—is necessarily to infringe on areas where society has long had its own interests. Translation: Don't try to draw a line between your "private" activities and those over which society may claim an interest—no clear distinction exists.

Harlan was saying that tradition justifies society's concern "with the moral soundness of its people." Harlan was saying that society rightly manifests that concern through marriage laws regulating "when the sexual powers may be used," and through "laws forbidding adultery, fornication and homosexual practices" which confine "sexuality to lawful marriage."

Harlan, clearly enamored of this theme—the state's power to regulate morality—could not resist restating it:

> The right of privacy most manifestly is not an absolute. Thus, I would not suggest that adultery, homosexuality, fornication and incest are immune from criminal enquiry, however privately practiced. So much has been explicitly recognized in acknowledging *the State's rightful concern for its people's moral welfare.* . . .
>
> Adultery, homosexuality and the like are sexual intimacies which the State forbids altogether, but the intimacy of husband and wife is necessarily an essential and accepted feature of the institution of marriage, an institution which the State must not only allow, but which always and in every age it has fostered and protected. . . .
>
> [R]equiring husband and wife to render account before a criminal tribunal of their uses of that intimacy, is surely a very different thing indeed from punishing those who establish intimacies which the law has always forbidden and which can have no claim to social protection.[46]

In view of the troublesome constitutional guarantee that no one shall be deprived of life, liberty, or property without "due process of

45. Id. at 545–546.
46. Id. at 552–553 (emphasis added).

law," however, Harlan apparently felt compelled to "justify" himself:

> Due process has not been reduced to any formula; its content cannot be determined by reference to any code. The best that can be said is that through the course of this Court's decisions it has represented the balance which our Nation, built upon postulates of respect for the liberty of the individual, has struck *between that liberty and the demands of organized society.*[47]

There it was, again: the blind belief that whenever individual liberty—personally expressed, or expressed in a family or other context—clashes with society's demands, a balance somehow can be struck between the two; the blind refusal to recognize that America's constitutional history is littered with the casualities of government's doomed attempts at an impossible balancing act.

Justice White wrote his own concurring opinion, voting to invalidate the Connecticut statute. But he, too, agreed that Connecticut's "policy against all forms of promiscuous or illicit sexual relationships, be they premarital or extramarital, [was] concededly a permissible and legitimate legislative goal."[48]

Justices Black and Stewart both dissented, not because they agreed with Connecticut's anticontraceptive law personally, (they opposed it), but because they saw no way the Supreme Court could strike it down—not without a specific provision of the Constitution they could literally point to. Perhaps a provision that read, "Congress shall make no law interfering with a person's right to use contraceptives!" And, once again, both dissents echoed the sentiments of their concurring brethren: that government possesses the power to regulate sexual morality and, presumably, morality in general. And the family.

The fact that *Griswold* v. *Connecticut* is popularly considered a victory for individual rights—and thus, by implication, for family rights—is due to a combination of misinformation, context dropping, and wishful thinking. *Griswold* constitutes a mishmash of altruism-collectivism-statism at its worst and most revealing.

Eight years later, another case understandably received the same popular accolade as *Griswold*—based on the same misconception. The case was *Roe* v. *Wade;* the issue, abortion.

A Texas statute, like statutes in a majority of the states, had out-

---

47. Id. at 542 (emphasis added).
48. *Griswold* v. *Connecticut,* 381 U.S. 479, 505 (1965).

lawed abortion, except to save the mother's life. One effect, of course, was to create unwanted families. Jane Roe (a pseudonym), unmarried and pregnant, sued in a federal court to declare the Texas antiabortion statute unconstitutional. Relying principally on the *Griswold* case and the Fourteenth Amendment's concept of "due process," Roe claimed that the statutes abridged her right of personal privacy and her right to personal liberty. She cited no other source, constitutional or otherwise, in defense of her right to an abortion.

The Supreme Court's decision in *Roe* was, to say the least, fragmented—even more than *Griswold* had been.

In his majority opinion, Blackmun ruled the Texas antiabortion statute unconstitutional. How did he reach that momentous decision?

First, by canvassing a wide variety of sources—he was seeking their attitudes about abortion. He examined ancient views concerning abortion, but they proved inconclusive. He discovered that the Hippocratic Oath's rigid antiabortion stand had been unpopular even at the time it was formulated.[49] He examined English common law and hit pay dirt: Apparently, even under the early statutes, abortion to save the mother's life was not considered a criminal act. According to Blackmun, "abortion performed before 'quickening'—the first recognizable movement of the fetus in utero, appearing usually from the sixteenth to the eighteenth week of pregnancy—was not an indictable offense."[50] Blackmun discovered further that in those days, even abortion of a quick fetus had not been a felony—merely a lesser offense; that, though the "quickening" distinction once existed in England, it had vanished in 1837, reappeared in 1861, and remained until 1967, when the law was greatly liberalized. Blackmun did not fare as well in his survey of American law. He found that it had followed the preexisting English common law's "quickening" distinction only until the mid-nineteenth century—after which the distinction gradually began to disappear until "[b]y the end of the 1950s, a large majority of the jurisdictions banned abortion, however and whenever performed, unless done to save or preserve the life of the mother."[51]

Summarizing his survey of the past, Blackmun observed:

---

49. L. Edelstein, *The Hippocratic Oath;* see *Roe* v. *Wade*, 410 U.S. 113, 130, and 93 S.Ct. 705, 715 (footnote) (1973).

50. *Roe* v. *Wade*, 410 U.S. 113, 132 (1973).

51. Id. at 139.

It is thus apparent that at common law, at the time of the adoption of our Constitution, and throughout the major portion of the 19th century, abortion was viewed with less disfavor than under most American statutes currently [1973] in effect. Phrasing it another way, a woman enjoyed a substantially broader right to terminate a pregnancy than she does in most States today. At least with respect to the early stage of pregnancy, and very possibly without such a limitation, the opportunity to make this choice was present in this country well into the 19th century. Even later, the law continued for some time to treat less punitively an abortion procured in early pregnancy.[52]

Next, Blackmun turned his attention to medical views, past and prevailing. The American Medical Association, since the mid-nineteenth century, had bitterly condemned abortion, only to ameliorate its harsh view in the mid-1960s. More pay dirt. In viewing the American Public Health Association's proabortion position, he noted that just the year before, the American Bar Association had approved a Uniform Abortion Act prepared by the prestigious Conference of Commissioners on Uniform State Laws. Blackmun's potpourri of current views now included legal as well as medical.

What was Blackmun seeking from all this opinion-gathering? Some kind of justification. If, historically, abortion had received equivocal treatment, the Court's task—coming up with a favorable abortion ruling—would be easier; the justices could write, as it were, on a clean slate. What they wrote was, in turn, equivocal:

> We, therefore, conclude that the right of personal privacy includes the abortion decision, but this is not unqualified and must be considered against important state interests in regulation.[53]

The Court had before it a case going to the heart of so fundamental a personal (and, indirectly, a family) choice that one might have expected to find a United States Supreme Court opinion that was a dazzling array of legal/constitutional arguments (some did exist), adorned with impeccable reasoning and irrefutable logic. We find, instead, as sole constitutional justification for its decision, the amorphous, Douglas-invented "right of personal privacy" borrowed from *Griswold.*

Even Blackmun had to concede that "privacy" was nowhere to be found in the Constitution. So, following Douglas's earlier lead, he

---

52. Id. at 140–141.
53. Id. at 113, 154.

tried to weave a "privacy" pattern into the Bill of Rights by borrowing threads where he could. Even so, Blackmun's entire 54-page opinion—which would invalidate antiabortion laws nationwide—contained a single paragraph devoted to the constitutional basis for the Court's conclusion:

> The Constitution does not explicitly mention any right of privacy. In a line of decisions, however, going back perhaps as far as . . . 1891 . . . the Court has recognized that a right of personal privacy, or a guarantee of certain areas or zones of privacy, does exist under the Constitution. In varying contexts, the Court or individual Justices have, indeed, found at least the roots of that right in the First Amendment . . . in the Fourth and Fifth Amendments . . . in the penumbras of the Bill of Rights . . . in the Ninth Amendment . . . or in the concept of liberty guaranteed by the first section of the Fourteenth Amendment. . . . These decisions make it clear that only personal rights that can be deemed "fundamental" or "implicit in the concept of ordered liberty" . . . are included in this guarantee of personal privacy. They also make it clear that the right has some extension to activities relating to marriage . . . procreation . . . contraception . . . family relationships . . . and child rearing and education. . . . [54]

Blackmun's constitutional pastiche spawned reactions from two of his colleagues; both are instructive.

Justice Stewart, in his concurring opinion, flatly rejected the "right of privacy" rationale:

> There is no [federal] constitutional right of privacy, as such. "[The Fourth] Amendment protects individual privacy against certain kinds of governmental intrusion, but its protections go further, and often have nothing to do with privacy at all. Other provisions of the Constitution protect personal privacy from other forms of governmental invasion. But the protection of a person's general right to privacy—his right to be let alone by other people—is, like the protection of his property and of his very life, left largely to the law of the individual states." [55]

Stewart believed the Texas antiabortion statute should be tested and found wanting—but by a standard with more substance: "Several decisions of this Court make clear that freedom of personal choice in matters of marriage and family is one of the liberties protected by the Due Process Clause of the Fourteenth Amendment." [56]

54. Id. at 152–153.
55. Id. at 168.
56. Id. at 169.

Justice Rehnquist also flatly rejected the "right of privacy" rationale, underscoring, in dissent, that the majority opinion lacked a constitutional foundation:

> I have difficulty in concluding . . . that the right of "privacy" is involved in this case. Texas . . . bars the performance of a medical abortion by a licensed physician on a plaintiff such as [Jane] Roe. A transaction resulting in an operation such as this is not "private" in the ordinary usage of that word. Nor is the "privacy" that the Court finds here even a distant relative of the freedom from searches and seizures protected by the Fourth Amendment . . . which the Court has referred to as embodying a right to privacy.
>
> If the Court means by the term "privacy" no more than that the claim of a person to be free from unwanted state regulation of consensual transactions may be a form of "liberty" protected by the Fourteenth Amendment, there is no doubt that similar claims have been upheld in our earlier decisions on the basis of that liberty. . . . But that liberty is not guaranteed absolutely against deprivation, only against deprivation without due process of law. The test traditionally applied in the area of social and economic legislation is whether or not a law such as that challenged has a rational relation to a valid state objective. [Citing a Supreme Court case, *Williamson* v. *Lee Optical Co.*, authored by Douglas.]

Rehnquist and Stewart had made the same telling points: there was no such thing as a *Griswold-Roe* "right of privacy"; the antiabortion laws should have been tested by the usual due process/liberty standard, that is, whether the legislation had a rational relation to a valid state objective.

Although Rehnquist parted company with Stewart on what constituted a valid state objective, and both justices parted company with the majority on the correct constitutional test to be applied, *every justice on the Bench agreed that under no circumstances did a woman have an absolute right to an abortion.* Always, there were other factors to be considered. What did society feel about abortion? What important state interests were at stake? Indeed, when the technical aspects and the historical review that make up the bulk of Blackmun's majority opinion are pared away, virtually all that remains is a preoccupation with *state interests:*

> . . . a State may properly assert important interests in safeguarding health, in maintaining medical standards, and in protecting potential life. At some

57. Id. at 172–173.

point in pregnancy, these respective interests become sufficiently compelling to sustain regulation of the factors that govern the abortion decision.[58]

And the particular state interest that seemed to interest Blackmun most, judging from the frequency with which it was mentioned in his opinion, was the state's "important and legitimate interest in preserving and protecting the health of the pregnant woman."[59]

Arch-liberal Douglas agreed—in spades: "While childbirth endangers the lives of some women, voluntary abortion at any time and place regardless of medical standards would impinge on a rightful concern of society. The woman's health is part of that concern; as is the life of the fetus after quickening."[60] Whence comes this seemingly unchallengeable absolute? Why is society's interest strongly asserted, never explained, and deemed to require not even a modicum of proof? Doubtless, Douglas and his brethren were operating on the basic premise of *Muller* v. *Oregon,* that solidly liberal decision with its Hitlerian overtones: ". . . as healthy mothers are essential to vigorous offspring, the physical well-being of woman becomes an object of public interest and care in order to preserve the strength and vigor of the race.[61]

A necessary corollary of avowed state interest in the pregnant woman is state interest in her unborn child—an interest Blackmun could hardly ignore. The Court made a series of findings: "the word 'person' as used in the Fourteenth Amendment, does not include the unborn,"[62] "the unborn have never been recognized in the law as persons in the whole sense,"[63] [we do not] "resolve the difficult question of when life begins."[64] But the "potential life" issue had yet to be dealt with. Blackmun "dealt" with it in two sentences: "[T]he State's important and legitimate interest in potential life is at viability. This is so because the fetus then presumably has the capability of meaningful life outside the mother's womb."[65]

---

58. Id. at 154.
59. Id. at 162.
60. Id. at 215.
61. *Muller* v. *Oregon,* 208 U.S. 412, 421 (1908). Indeed, the *Roe* Court's explicit endorsement of the state's interest in "the preservation and protection of maternal health" (*Roe* v. *Wade,* 410 U.S. 113, 163 [1973]) clearly echoes *Muller.*
62. *Roe* v. *Wade,* 410 U.S. 113, 158 (1973).
63. Id. at 162.
64. Id. at 159.
65. Id. at 163.

On the basis of such specious and almost offhand "reasoning," the Supreme Court of the United States came up with the following mixed bag:

Because the Court judged abortions within the first trimester to be as medically safe (in 1973) as, or even safer than, normal childbirth, abortions in the first three months of pregnancy "must be left to the medical judgment of the pregnant [woman and her] attending physician."[66]

Because the Court assumed a state interest in the health of the pregnant woman, abortions during "the stage subsequent to approximately the end of the first trimester" could be regulated "in ways that are reasonably related to maternal health"[67] (e.g., licensed physicians, adequate facilities).

Because the Court asserted a state interest in potential life, "[f]or the stage subsequent to viability [approximately during the final trimester], the state . . . may, if it chooses, regulate, and even proscribe, abortion except where it is necessary, in appropriate medical judgment, for the preservation of the life or health of the mother."[68]

Perhaps because too many Americans have come to think of their rights as conditional, and themselves as less than wholly free, it was to be expected that *Roe* v. *Wade* would be greeted as a victory not just for women's rights, but for individual (and, by implication, for family) rights as well. Perhaps a small, even Pyrrhic victory in a long, losing war assumes significance. Perhaps most people have lost sight of the fact that rights flow, not from accommodation, compromise, or "balancing," but from defensible moral principle. Whatever the reasons, the Supreme Court's abortion decision is regarded, by friend and foe, as a giant liberalizing step forward. In a practical sense and in the short run, the cause of free-choice abortion has been advanced; women can abort—at least for now. But in principle and over the long run, the cause of freedom has been pushed a giant step backward.

Few people realize that *Roe* v. *Wade* opened a Pandora's box when the Supreme Court legitimized a "state interest" in pregnant women and their unborn children, and thus in the family. This time around— in this case—antiabortion laws have been struck down and some women permitted to have abortions. Next time around—in some future case—

66. Id. at 164.
67. Id. at 164.
68. Id. at 164–165.

188 THE AMERICAN FAMILY AND THE STATE

antiabortion laws may be upheld and no women permitted to have abortions. The time after next—depending on the current "state interest"—women may even be *compelled* to abort. A far-fetched notion? Science fiction? Not if we accept the ultimate logic of *Roe* v. *Wade* as seen from the perspective of a 1977 Supreme Court case.

The states, in the wake of *Roe* v. *Wade,* had to revise not only their abortion laws, but also a considerable number of related laws directly and indirectly affected by that decision, such as criminal laws and Medicaid (which, prior to *Roe* v. *Wade,* had funded certain childbearing experiences).

Connecticut Welfare Department regulations, which paid for childbirth expenses, limited state Medicaid benefits for first trimester abortions to those which were "medically necessary." So in 1977 the Supreme Court was asked to decide "whether the Constitution requires a . . . State to pay for . . . [non-medically necessary] abortions when it pays for childbirth."[69] In other words, did Connecticut have a constitutional right to a Medicaid funding policy that treated birth and abortion differently?

Before answering that question, the Court felt obliged to point out what *Roe* v. *Wade* had not held: "*Roe* did not declare an unqualified 'constitutional right to an abortion.' . . . It implies no limitation on the authority of a State to make a value judgment favoring childbirth over abortion, and to implement that judgment by the allocation of public funds."[70]

(Presumably, then, "[it] implies no limitation on the authority of the State to make a value judgment favoring abortion over childbirth."

The Court in *Maher,* like the State of Connecticut, clearly favored childbirth over abortion. But following the 6–3 majority's statement that "[t]he State unquestionably has a 'strong and legitimate interest in encouraging normal childbirth,' . . . an interest honored over the centuries," there appeared a footnote as astonishing as it was ominous:

> In addition to the direct interest in protecting the fetus, a State may have legitimate demographic concerns about its rate of population growth. Such concerns are basic to the future of the State and in some circumstances could constitute a substantial reason for departure from a position of neutrality between abortion and childbirth.[71]

69. *Maher* v. *Roe,* 432 U.S. 464, 466 (1977).
70. Id. at 473–474.
71. Id. at 478.

How reminiscent of that democratic state in modern India—"demographic concerns about its rate of population growth" prompted it to depart "from a position of neutrality between abortion and childbirth"—by a program of forced sterilization.

Three members of the Court dissented in *Maher*, two of them the Court's remaining "liberals." One might have expected a ringing denunciation from Brennan and Marshall of the majority's naked assertion that, should population grow too large or food become too scarce, society could forcibly dump the unborn.

No denunciation was forthcoming. Indeed, nearly half a century earlier the Supreme Court had endorsed another governmental approach to preventing birth and thus limiting families.

Seventeen-year-old Carrie Buck was allegedly

> . . . a feeble-minded white woman who was committed to the State [mental hospital]. She [was] the daughter of a feeble-minded mother in the same institution, and the mother of an illegitimate feeble-minded child.[72]

A Virginia statute back in the 1920s provided that the health of certain types of individuals, and the welfare of society generally, could be promoted by the sterilization of mental defectives. Carrie Buck was ordered sterilized, Virginia having found that she was "the probably potential parent of socially inadequate offspring, likewise afflicted, that she may be sexually sterilized without detriment to her general health and that her welfare and that of society will be promoted by her sterilization."[73] The Virginia Supreme Court upheld the statute, observing that it "was not meant to punish but to protect the class of socially inadequate citizens from themselves and to promote the welfare of society by mitigating race degeneracy and raising the average standard of intelligence of the people of the state."[74]

Eventually, the question of the Virginia law's constitutionality reached the United States Supreme Court. While the opinion of the legendary Justice Oliver Wendell Holmes for an 8–1 Court contained some familiar ideas and minced no words, those words still have the power to shock:

> We have seen more than once that the public welfare may call upon the best citizens for their lives. It would be strange if it could not call upon

72. *Buck* v. *Bell*, 274 U.S. 200, 205 (1927).
73. Id. at 207.
74. *Buck* v. *Bell*, 143 Va. 310, 130, S.E. 516, 519 (1925).

those who already sap the strength of the State for these lesser sacrifices, often not felt to be such by those concerned, in order to prevent our being swamped with incompetence. It is better for all the world, if instead of waiting to execute degenerate offspring for crime, or to let them starve for their imbecility, society can prevent those who are manifestly unfit from continuing their kind. The principle that sustains compulsory vaccination is broad enough to cover cutting the Fallopian tubes. . . . Three generations of imbeciles are enough.[75]

The underlying principles in which the Court's opinion is rooted—represented by concepts like "public welfare," "sacrifices," "better for all the world," "society"—should, by now, require no elaboration. But the idea worth pursuing here is that in the name of those principles, in the name of avoiding socially inadequate offspring, promoting society's welfare, mitigating race degeneracy, raising the average intelligence of Virginians, and not sapping the strength of the state, a woman's procreative capacity—her ability ever to have a family—was extinguished by state-mandated and state-executed involuntary sterilization.

So was that of some 8,299 other persons who were involuntarily sterilized in Virginia between 1924 and 1972. So were some 65,000 persons throughout America in the first half of this century. None could ever have a family.

In Virginia, deceit played a role; some of those sterilized were told that an appendectomy or other comparable operation was being performed. Some victims were merely retarded. Some, according to Dr. K. Ray Nelson (now Director of Lynchburg, Virginia's and America's largest institution for the retarded), "would not be admitted to this institution today."[76]

Carrie Buck was one of them. Her sister Doris was another. The sister, at age seventeen, had been involuntarily sterilized, then told she had undergone an appendectomy. According to Dr. Nelson, Doris Buck, who is alive today and married, "was not particularly retarded."[77] According to the account in the *New York Times*,

For years, [Dr. Nelson] said, she and her husband . . . could not understand why she could not bear children. "This is one of the tragedies,"

75. *Buck* v. *Bell*, 274 U.S. 200, 205 (1927).
76. *New York Times*, 23 Feb. 1980.
77. Ibid.

Dr. Nelson said. He said the statistical probability of their having a retarded child was no greater than for the general population.

"I broke down and cried," [she] told the [newspaper]. "My husband and me wanted children desperate—we were crazy about them. I never knew what they done to me."[78]

Doris Buck did not seem consoled by the knowledge that her "lesser sacrifice" (a barren life) had been made for the "welfare of society . . . and [to] rais[e] the average intelligence of the people of the state."

Her sister Carrie fared worse, in a way; she had been used. The Virginia physician who started the state's sterilization program in 1924 considered Lynchburg "a cleaning house," existing to "give these young women education, industrial and moral training, sterilize them and send them out to earn their own living."[79] Facing litigation over previous sterilizations, the physician needed a test case—judicial sanction to legitimize his work in eugenics. Carrie Buck was his guinea pig, the alleged linchpin in "[t]hree generations of imbeciles." (What would Justice Holmes do, one wonders, with the fact that Carrie Buck, alive as recently as 1980 and living in abject poverty in Virginia, had led a reasonably normal life for half a century, as had her sister, Doris, and that Carrie Buck's daughter, whom Virginia authorities had characterized as "slow" and whom Holmes and his Court had characterized as an "imbecile," had actually been considered a "bright child" by her second-grade teachers?)

Carrie Buck was sterilized, although Holmes's assumption of hereditary imbecility, which surely would be challenged today, was open to serious doubt even in 1924.

Lest optimists write off these tragic and fearsome examples of altruism-collectivism-statism run amok as regrettable ancient history, they should know that today fully half of the states in America (including Virginia) still have laws on their books allowing for the involuntary sterilization of "incompetents." Not only has *Buck* v. *Bell* not been overruled, but fifteen years after it was decided, the Supreme Court pointedly declined an invitation to do so. Instead, the Court did just the opposite, resurrecting the principles upon which *Buck* v. *Bell* rested.

78. Ibid.
79. Ibid.

The case was *Skinner* v. *Oklahoma*,[80] involving that state's Habitual Criminal Sterilization Act. Assuming that certain "criminal tendencies" were transmissible genetically (how is that for a literally collectivist judgment?), the act provided that "habitual criminals were to be sterilized if the procedure could be accomplished "without detriment to his or her general health."[81]

The Oklahoma act was struck down by the Supreme Court. Although Justice Jackson observed, "[t]here are limits to the extent to which a legislatively represented majority may conduct biological experiments at the expense of the dignity and personality and natural powers of a minority—even those who have been guilty of what the majority define as crimes,"[82] the act was not held unconstitutional for this reason. What the Court disapproved of was Oklahoma's arbitrary classification of which criminal acts were "moral turpitude" felonies and which were not, since this would result in an arbitrarily administered sterilization program. Indeed, Douglas's opinion for a unanimous Court, as well as the two concurring opinions (by Chief Justice Stone and Justice Jackson [the Chief Prosecutor at Nuremberg!]) clearly implied that not all involuntary sterilization laws were unconstitutional. Stone went so far as to agree that

> Undoubtedly a state may, after appropriate inquiry, constitutionally interfere with the personal liberty of the individual to prevent the transmission by inheritance of his socially injurious tendencies. [citing] *Buck* v. *Bell.* . . .[83]

Buck and *Skinner* make clear that the Supreme Court has openly and consistently endorsed the state's power to involuntarily sterilize certain individuals and thus deprive them of ever having children. No comfort can be found in the fact that, so far, government has approved sterilization programs for so-called mental defectives and habitual criminals. The important, inescapable point is now how far these sterilization statutes have gone, but that they exist and have been upheld.

---

80. *Skinner* v. *Oklahoma*, 316 U.S. 535 (1942).
81. A habitual criminal was one who, having been convicted two or more times for crimes "amounting to felonies involving moral turpitude" either in an Oklahoma court or in a court of any other state, was thereafter convicted of such felony in Oklahoma and was sentenced to a term of imprisonment in an Oklahoma penal institution.
82. *Skinner* v. *Oklahoma*, 316 U.S. 535 (1942).
83. Id. at 544.

CONCLUSION

It is not a pleasant story, this relentless violation of individual (and, by implication, family) rights by the principal institution sworn to uphold them—this utilization by the Supreme Court of altruist-collectivist ethics to create statist control over what marriage is, how the family relationship is to be defined, who may procreate and under what conditions, and more. But it is a fact of ethical, political, and legal life. Some of the most important choices we make as human beings are being significantly controlled by the government in the name of others' values. And they will continue to be—until we replace that government control with an unyielding commitment to individual rights. Then, and only then, we will have truly free choice— not merely in family matters, but in every other aspect of our lives.

7

MARRIAGE, DIVORCE, AND PROPERTY RIGHTS: A NATURAL RIGHTS FRAMEWORK

Roger A. Arnold

INTRODUCTION

There are some subjects that scholars are inclined to deal with on a piecemeal basis rather than as a whole. Marriage and divorce is one example. As a subject of study, marriage and divorce is extremely interesting. First, it is "real world" enough to get most people's attention. Second, once put under the microscope for examination, it is rich in unexpected nooks and crannies. One would think it a subject already studied from every conceivable angle.

Unfortunately not. Except for the work of a few scholars, marriage and divorce, as a subject of study, has only been pecked at and not studied in its totality. Minor subjects within the entire subject area have been looked at, but the whole has been largely untouched.

The objective of this paper is to provide a framework within which marriage and divorce may be analyzed, and one hopes, better understood. Once a proper framework of analysis is delineated, one's focus is heightened and with this come answers to previously hard-to-answer questions.

A BRIEF HISTORY OF FAMILY AND MARRIAGE

In order to understand more about marriage and divorce, one must understand the family of yesterday. In short, we are in need of an explanation of why the institution of the family came to be.

Both Gary Becker and Richard Posner hold that families arose out of a need in primitive society to cope with uncertainty and ignorance (or better yet, high information costs). Becker says: "The family— or more accurately, the kinship group—is important in traditional societies in large measure because it protects members against uncertainty."[1]

The idea here is rather simple. In a primitive society neither the present nor the future is as well understood as in a modern society. Characteristically, ignorance of the way things operate would be high and uncertainty would be great. Individuals would thus be inclined to guard against the two through the means of the family, sometimes the extended family.[2] Having other members of society around you, people with whom you had a personal and intimate relationship, reduced the risks of everyday life. As Becker says, "A kinship group is a reasonably effective 'insurance company.'"[3] Also, the functional relationships between family members were different from those of today. For instance, older persons in a family were held in greater respect, not so much because of their age, but because they possessed knowledge that was particularly profitable in a society where change took place very slowly.

Additionally, because the family in a primitive society was more than the "insurance company" that it is today, and because new members coming into it were of greater importance to all existing members, parents played an active role in selecting their children's mates.[4] Since it affected so many people, marriage was not viewed as an individual matter. In economic terms, it was a relationship that had spillover effects for third parties—most notably parents—and the parents' strong opinion as to a proper mate may be seen as an attempt to get a child to incorporate the "third party effects" into his decision-making.[5]

---

1. Gary Becker, *A Treatise on the Family* (Cambridge: Harvard University Press, 1981), p. 238. See also Richard Posner, "A Theory of Primitive Society, with Special Reference to Law," *Journal of Law and Economics* 23, (no. 1, April 1980): 1–53

2. We say "sometimes the extended family" because there appears to be evidence that the family before the twentieth century was not as extended as is commonly thought. On this point, see Peter Laslett, *The World We Have Lost* (New York: Charles Scribner's Sons, 1965), pp. 89–90.

3. Becker, *n.* 1, p. 238.

4. To call a family an "insurance company" does not mean to imply that the family was formed exclusively to function as such; the term merely points out that the insurance function was more important in primitive society than it is in modern society.

5. Providing insurance for themselves was not the only reason parents influenced the se-

Within the family framework, it is important to speak of marriage. Although many different marriage arrangements appear throughout history, three main categories may be distinguished: group marriage (consisting of at least two members of each sex), polygamy (multiple spouses of one sex with one member of another sex), and monogamy (two persons).

McLennan, Engels, Bachofen, and Briffault argue that sexual promiscuity preceded group marriage, although there does not appear to be any good evidence that any society for any substantial length of time practiced group marriage.[6] Murstein makes the point that many times persons who thought group marriage was being practiced actually misunderstood the situation.[7] He cites an Eskimo custom as a case in point: An Eskimo whose wife was ill, pregnant, or nursing a child when he had to go on a long trip, would accept a neighbor's offer of his own wife for the duration of the journey. Later, should the circumstances be reversed, the Eskimo would reciprocate the favor and offer his wife to the neighbor. Since this was not a common occurrence, it cannot be said to be illustrative of group marriage.

There are a few isolated examples of group marriage, but these tend to be short in duration. It would appear that group marriage is an extremely unstable institution, probably because of the difficulty in establishing a satisfactory set of property rights. Because it appears that the "jealousy factor" is quite high between members of the same sex in a group marriage, the property-rights question is a difficult one to settle; thus, group marriage often dissolves into either polygamy—the two forms of which are polygyny (one man and several wives) and polyandry (one woman and several husbands)—or monogamy.

Polyandry has been found to exist among many groups, including the Todas, Tibetans, Marquesans, Karaites, and Jats.[8] Murstein states that it is usually associated with "severe economic hardship and with

---

lection of their children's mates. Sometimes the advice was motivated by a baser reason—such as envy. In some cultures, parents felt treated disrespectfully if their children made a better marriage than they had, or did better financially. For a complete work on this subject, see Helmut Schoeck, *Envy: A Theory of Social Behavior* (New York: Harcourt, Brace & World, 1969).

6. J. F. McLennan, *Studies in Ancient History* (New York: Macmillan, 1896); F. Engels *The Origin of the Family, Private Property and the State* (Chicago: Charles H. Kerr, 1910); J. J. Bachofen, *Das Mutterrecht* (Stuttgart: Krais and Hoffman, 1861); R. Briffault *The Mothers,* 3 vols. (New York: Macmillan, 1927).

7. Bernard Murstein, *Love, Sex, and Marriage through the Ages* (New York: Springer, 1974), p.11.

8. Ibid., p. 15.

the attendant practice of female infanticide."[9] The problem that has arisen in polyandrous marriages is trying to establish paternity. There have been different ways of coping with this problem—for instance, among the Todas, the eldest brother claimed paternity, whether or not it was the case—but none have been satisfactory. A plausible reason for the general unpopularity of polyandry might be this difficulty in determining property rights in children.

Polygyny, of course, doesn't have this problem of establishing paternity since each wife has sexual relations with only one man. Historically, polygyny is found more often than is polyandry.[10] There are numerous explanations, both simple and complex, for this phenomenon. One explanation states that polygyny benefits men more than polyandry does, and thus men, being physically superior to women, chose the institutional framework that benefited them. This has some ring of truth to it until we realize that in many societies polygyny was demanded by women and their families.[11] The families of the women sometimes pushed for polygyny because they predicted, it turned out correctly, that polygyny led to a higher bride price (a monetary settlement) being paid to the family of the bride.

Another nongeneralized explanation holds that polygyny became common in societies in which women outnumbered men (perhaps because of a war that killed off many of the men). In such a setting, women are said to gain from polygyny, for the alternative is often no marriage at all. In earlier societies, where women were not economically independent of men, being husbandless was a fate most women tried to avoid.[12]

---

9. Ibid.

10. Becker notes that polygyny has appeared in early Jewish societies, in Moslem societies, in many parts of ancient Greece, in much of Africa, and in Chinese societies. See Becker, *n*. 1, p. 43.

11. For instance, Becker states: "My analysis of efficient, competitive marriage markets indicates, however, that the income of women and the competition by men for wives would be greater when polygyny is greater if the incidence of polygyny had been determined mainly by the relative marginal contribution of women to output. This view is supported by the fact that bride prices are more common and generally higher in societies with a greater incidence of polygyny." Becker, *n*. 1, p. 56.

12. As Murstein states: "Polygyny has quite a few advantages. Where women outnumbered men, it assured that all women would marry and have the opportunity to bear children— a vital consideration for societies in constant need of warriors and labor. For the woman, overburdened with pregnancies, backbreaking toil in the fields, and a lack of companionship in the home, there were manifold benefits: relief from successive pregnancies, a longer time to nurse her child, someone with whom to share the domestic chores, and companionship."

In the United States polygyny has been practiced mostly by Mormons. There does not appear to be any strictly economic reason for this, only a religious one. There is some talk (as one would expect) that the founder of Mormonism, Joseph Smith, advanced polygyny for personal reasons. He was said to have been a man who "played around with the ladies,"[13] and is alleged to have said, "Wherever I see a pretty woman I have to pray for grace."[14]

Smith gave religious legitimacy to the practice of polygyny by noting that Abraham, Jacob, Moses, David, and Solomon had practiced polygyny. (Solomon is said to have practiced it quite extensively, having had 700 wives.) Perhaps to advance Joseph Smith's position, the Mormon theologian, Orson Pratt, reasoned that Jesus had had several wives.[15]

Polygyny among the Mormons ceased to exist for reasons quite different from those that caused its demise in most other societies. In most other societies it ceased because of natural reasons—a change in the ratio of men to women, a change in preferences, or the difficulty of establishing property rights (in some cases). In the case of the Mormons, however, it was the United States government that effectively abolished (with a few minor exceptions) the practice of polygyny.[16] In any case, whether the state is involved or not, there has been a movement toward monogamy.

Monogamy does not have many of the problems encountered in group marriage, polyandry, and polygyny. Of particular importance,

---

Murstein, *n.* 7, p. 16. It should also be noted that in societies where polygyny was practiced, it was most often practiced by men of wealth.

13. Ibid., p. 352.

14. F. M. Brodie, *No Man Knows My History: The Life of Joseph Smith, the Mormon Prophet* (New York: Alfred A. Knopf, 1946), p. 297.

15. Pratt says, "There were several holy women that greatly loved Jesus—such as Mary, and Martha her sister, and Mary Magdalene; and Jesus greatly loved them, and associated with them much; and when he arose from the dead, instead of first showing himself to his chosen witnesses, the Apostles, he appear first to these women, or at least to one of them namely Mary Magdalene. Now it would be very natural for a husband in the resurrection to appear first to his own dear wives, and afterwards show himself to his other friends." Quoted in K. Young, *Isn't One Wife Enough* (New York: Holt, 1954), p. 30.

16. Within Mormonism it is noted that Mormons gave up polygyny voluntarily—or for religious reasons—when President Woodruff declared that it was revealed to him that polygyny should no longer be permissible practice for Mormons. Others have speculated that the revelation would not have come had the federal government not been jailing Mormons, and had there been no public outcry against polygyny. With respect to the latter, the Republican party in 1856 called for the abolition of the relics of barbarism: slavery and polygyny.

it does not have the property rights problems (especially as they relate to children) that exist in group marriages and polyandry, and it does not have the high costs (of supporting numerous wives) that exist for the male in polygyny.[17] M. Osmond has noted that monogamy, as a marriage institution, and the complexity of society appear to be highly correlated.[18] While correlation does not necessarily imply causation, in this case it makes reasonable sense to believe that the changing of society—here, toward increased complexity—would influence marriage institutions (to what degree and over what time span is a broadly defined empirical question).

THE MARRIAGE CONTRACT AND THE STATE

The nature of marriage and the state-imposed marriage contract has changed substantially over the last hundred years. In a way, this is a difficult time to be writing an essay on marriage, divorce, the marriage contract, and property rights within marriage, because matters that relate to these subjects are in flux. To give but one example, in past years judges were much more likely than they are today to advance a "public policy" argument as to why they could not enforce the private provisions of a marriage contract between two individuals. The sentiments expressed in the Supreme Court decision of *Maynard* v. *Hill* (1888) for a long time have held sway and, to a lesser degree, still do today. In that decision the Supreme Court said:

17. Whether the high cost of supporting numerous wives will be undertaken by the male depends on whether the benefits of having numerous wives outweigh the cost. Perhaps for a host of reasons—ranging from a movement from a largely rural to an urban society to greater rights for women—the benefits of polygyny seemed to have decreased while the costs of polygyny have increased. A full explanation of what factors have specifically lowered the benefits of polygyny and increased costs is beyond the scope of this paper. One point should be made, though, since my position on why polygyny gave way to monogamy is both like and unlike Becker's position on this subject. Becker notes: "The incidence of polygyny has declined substantially over time until no more than 10 percent of the world's population lives today in polygynous societies. The decline has been attributed to the spread of Christianity and the growth of women's rights, but I am skeptical of these explanations. Doctrines encouraging monogamy are attractive only when the demand for polygyny is weak." Becker, *n*. 1, p. 39.

The Becker position, while it rightly sees that the net benefits of polygyny have to decrease (relative to other marriage structures) before fewer individuals will enter into it, seems to ignore that such things as the "spread of Christianity and the growth of women's rights" may very well affect one's perceived net benefits of polygyny.

18. M. Osmond, "Toward Monogamy: A Cross-Cultural Study of Correlates of Types of Marriage," *Social Forces* 44:8–16 (1965)

"Other contracts may be modified, restricted, or enlarged, or entirely released for the consent of the parties. Not so with marriage. The relation once formed, the law steps in and holds the parties to various obligations and liabilities. It is an institution, in the maintenance of which in its purity the public is deeply interested, for it is the foundation of the family and of society, without which there would be neither civilization nor progress."[19]

Two things are noted. First, the Court speaks to "various obligations and liabilities" in a marriage, and secondly, to the idea that the public has an interest in the marriage. For a long part of the history of marriage and divorce in this country, and to some degree today, both of these sentiments have been voiced by the courts. A case in point is *Carlson* v. *Carlson,* in which the court ruled that the marriage contract imposes upon the wife the obligation to reside where her husband wishes to reside.[20] Historically, the chief obligation of the wife has pertained to matters that relate to home and to family; the chief obligation of the husband has pertained to matters of producing income.[21]

As far as the "public policy doctrine" goes, courts have had a history of ruling on matters of marriage and divorce with one eye open—if not two—to the effects on the public. They have, without any embarrassment whatsoever, been willing to state that society has a decision-making role to play with respect to the marriage between two individuals. Consider the words spoken by the court in *Graham* v. *Graham:*

"Under the law, marriage is not merely a private contract between the two parties, but creates a status in which the state is vitally interested and under which certain rights and duties incident to the relationship come into being, irrespective of the wishes of the parties."[22]

The so-called public policy doctrine has also been applied to prohibit husband and wife from shaping their marriage in a way that attempts to circumvent the state-drawn marriage contract. This is particularly noticeable where antenuptial (prenuptial) agreements are concerned. While things are easing up today, courts still look negatively upon those antenuptial agreements that relieve one or the other

19. *Maynard* v. *Hill,* 125 U.S. 190 8 S. Ct. 723, 31 LEd 654 (1888).
20. Carlson *v.* Carlson, 256 P.2d 249 (1953).
21. For much more on this see Lenore Weitzman, "Legal Regulation of Marriage: Tradition and Change," *California Law Review,* 62 (no. 4):1169–1288.
22. 33 F. Supp. 929, 938 (F. D. Mich. 1940).

spouse of a particular obligation the court feels is imposed upon him or her because of the state-drawn marriage contract and that contain any provisions relating to divorce. As Charles Gamble notes: "The attitude of the courts toward antenuptial contracts is so restrictive, indefinite and unpredictable as to preclude widespread and consistent use."[23]

Many courts have been particularly reluctant to enforce antenuptial agreements that in any way speak of divorce, their reasoning being that the contemplation of divorce makes divorce more likely and the court in no way should undertake actions that make divorce more likely.

It is, of course, not difficult to see how the court's attitude toward antenuptial agreements that speak of divorce often makes for fewer marriages. Consider, for example, the case of a rich woman and a poor man who are contemplating marriage. The poor man, we assume, has been married before and is presently paying alimony. Fearful that his marriage to the rich woman might end in divorce and add to his financial burdens, he asks his rich wife-to-be to sign an antenuptial agreement stating that in case of a divorce no claims will be made by her on his property or income. She gladly consents. Along comes an attorney and tells the poor man that there is no guarantee that the court will enforce the antenuptial agreement because it is contrary to the public policy rule. The attorney cites a few cases as examples. Given this piece of news, the poor man is less likely to enter into marriage with the rich woman. The conclusion, then, is that the attitude of the courts toward enforcing such antenuptial agreements sometimes reduces the likelihood of marriage—which, if we note closely, is also contrary to the public policy rule. After all, courts state that they should not do anything that will make it more difficult for individuals to get married.

What courts have not seemed to realize is that whatever they do, they contravene a particular version of the public policy rule. As noted above, the version that says a court must not do anything to encourage divorce leads the court into promoting activity that increases the probability there will be fewer marriages. The version that says a court should not do anything to upset the duties and obligations each spouse has to the other, as loosely specified in the state-drawn marriage con-

23. Charles W. Gamble, "The Antenuptial Contract," *University of Michigan Law Review*" 26 (no. 4, Summer 1972): 693.

tract, increases the likelihood that prospective spouses will not be able to shape their marriage the way they want to and thus increases the likelihood that they will not get married.

There is also another way of looking at this. Most courts decide matters of marriage and divorce based on "typical cases," or "the modal case."[24] For instance, since typically the man in a marriage earns more income than does the woman, duties and obligations that relate to income support seem to fall to the man. Couples that are not typical (nonmodal) in this respect usually have a difficult time of changing the duties and obligations imposed upon them by the state-drawn marriage contract.

Another example illustrates this point. There is a general feeling among courts, and among most laypersons, that antenuptial agreements most often benefit the man more than the woman—sometimes even exclude the woman's interests. This is partly for the reason that men most often come into a marriage with greater assets and income than do women. The typical case cannot be argued with, but not all couples are typical. Once again, atypical couples have a difficult time of restructuring things to their own needs.

An observation presents itself here that can best be explained by way of example. Suppose there are two couples; Couple A and Couple B. Couple A is a typical couple that goes before the court; it is a "modal" couple. Couple B is an atypical couple; it is a "nonmodal" couple. Couple A is more likely to have information relevant to it considered by the court than is Couple B.[25] This being the case, we come to the conclusion that courts naturally bias their decisions against

---

24. For more on this, see Weitzman, *n.* 21. In lay language, it is said that courts decide cases based on "averages." This is not correct, since there is no such thing in reality as an "average" case. It is perhaps easier to the ear to use the word "average" rather than "mode," but it is the modal, or typical, case that courts look to in reaching decisions. For an explanation of why courts do this, see footnote 25.

25. There is a microeconomic reason why a state court system is likely to base its decisions on information that relates to typical cases. Specifically, a decision by a court is a public good; this being so, we will probably have an underinvestment of information-gathering on the part of the court in "producing" the public good. One consequence of underinvestment in information-gathering will be seen in courts trying to lower their costs of gathering information. A way to do this is to base decisions on information that is already available. Information that flows from typical cases is more readily available, and cheaper to generate, than information that is connected with atypical cases. For more on the point that court decisions are public goods and subject to an underinvestment in information-gathering, see Gordon Tullock, "Public Decisions as Public Goods," *Journal of Political Economy* 79 (July-Aug. 1971): 913–18.

atypical couples. When it comes to marriage and divorce, it is costly to be different.[26]

Economics would tell us that this higher cost of being different will translate itself into a higher percentage of atypical couples not getting married than typical couples not getting married—in much the same way that a small percentage of atypical individuals will buy insurance that is based on what typically happens than will typical individuals. This appears to be an application of the *lemons law*.

George Akerlof first spoke of the lemons law with respect to the market for used cars.[27] Within the market for used cars there are, of course, some "lemons." The potential buyer of a used car knows this, but does not know whether the car he is considering buying is a lemon. The seller, though, does know. Because of the lack of information on the part of the buyer, he will only pay a price for the used car that reflects the average frequency of lemons in the used car market. Suppose that for a particular model and year, this is $5,000. Further suppose that the car that is being considered is not a lemon, but only the seller knows this. It follows that $5,000 is too low a price for the particular car under consideration. What happens, then, is that the seller will be unwilling to sell his car for a price that takes into account the lemons that others are selling. A sale that would have occurred if things had not been decided on the "average" does not occur.

The situation sheds some light on our discussion of marriage. If the courts are going to base their decisions on typical cases—just as the buyer of the used car bases his behavior on the average frequency of lemons in the used car market—then individuals who find the typical case unrepresentative of their case will be less likely to get married.

To return to Akerlof's example, it is possible for the buyer and the seller in the example to make an exchange if the seller, knowing that

---

26. Someone will probably argue at this point that it would be too costly for courts to decide cases in a way other than on the mode. Information being costly, it is unrealistic to think they can—or taxpayers would want them to—generate complete information on couples that come before them. Reference is often made to insurance companies, which set premiums based on what occurs "on average." The point is, however, that the insurance analogy is irrelevant to court decisions in matters of marriage and divorce. The courts do not have to base their decisions on "averages," nor do they have to generate full information, as long as they allow married couples to structure their marriage/divorce in a way they believe is right for them. Once this is allowed there will be no bias shown against the "nonmodal" couple, nor any shown against the "modal" couple. This would appear to be a Pareto-superior move.

27. George A. Akerlof, "The Market for 'Lemons': Quality Uncertainty and the Market Mechanism," *The Quarterly Journal of Economics* 84 (no. 3, Aug. 1970): 488–500.

his car is not a lemon and knowing that the buyer does not know this, is allowed to offer the buyer a guarantee for some period of time. In short, if the seller of the nonlemon is allowed to prove to the buyer that his car is not a lemon, then the probability increases that an exchange between the two will occur. In terms of marriage, the analogue is to allow atypical couples to write their way out of a judicial system that considers them typical.

It is important to see whether Coasian-type thinking provides any insights into this area. When the court decides matters on typical cases it is setting property rights assignments that may not be warranted in the case of atypical couples. The Coasian question that arises, though, is, Do the property rights assignments matter to the atypical couple? The answer is that in some cases they do, and in other cases they do not. Let us explain by way of example.

In the case of *Carlson* v. *Carlson*,[28] the court ruled that the wife has the obligation to reside where the husband resides; in other words, the husband has the exclusive property right to decide residency. Consider it the typical case that the husband values determining residency more so than does the wife. To add numbers, let us assume that the husband values determining residency by $1,000 (he would pay $1,000 to determine residency) and the wife values determining residency by $500. Given the numbers above, the husband would stand to gain by paying more than $500 (to his wife) to determine residency if, in fact, his wife had the exclusive right to determine residency. If this is, in fact, the typical case and the court finds it out over time, then if the court followed efficiency standards it would grant the husband the property right to determine residency.

Now let an atypical couple come along. Let us suppose that the wife values determining residency by $1,000, and the husband values determining residency by $500. If the court treats this couple as the typical couple, it will decide that the property right for determining residency goes to the husband. This property rights assignment will mean nothing, though, because the wife in this case will quickly buy out her husband's property right for something more than $500. We will end up with the wife determining residency. In summary, the atypical couple will be able to structure its married life in such a way as to not allow the court to affect it adversely.

---

28. See *Carlson* v. *Carlson*, n. 20.

But consider another example where we do not have such a happy ending. Suppose that for the typical couple the husband wants the right to write an antenuptial agreement that specifies only X, Y and Z, and wants it to a greater degree than the wife wants the right to write an antenuptial agreement that specifies only A, B and C. Assume that the court is all-knowing and adopts the efficiency standard, with the result that only X, Y and Z can be specified in a legally binding antenuptial agreement.[29] This will not be different from what the typical couple itself would have done.

Now suppose that an atypical couple comes along. The husband wants the right to write an antenuptial agreement that specifies only X, Y and Z, and wants it to a lesser degree than the wife wants the right to write an antenuptial agreement that specifies only A, B, and C. If the court decides such things by looking to typical cases, as is likely, then it will say that only an antenuptial agreement that specifies X, Y and Z is legally binding. The husband would be willing to sell to his wife the right to write an antenuptial agreement specifying only A, B and C, but the sale really has no meaning once the court has said it will not enforce such an antenuptial agreement. In this case, property rights assignments do matter to the outcome; specifically, they prevent an efficient outcome from being reached.[30]

This outcome could be changed if either (1) in addition to allowing for antenuptial agreements, courts also allowed for the unlimited mutual exchange of rights within them; or (2) there were more than one court system; that is, if there were competing courts. With competing courts, when couples contemplated certain provisions of their antenuptial agreement, it is likely that they would, at the same time, agree on a court to enforce their antenuptial agreement, if the need arose. If it is really true that it is inefficient to deny individuals the right to put anything they wish into their antenuptial agreement, then it is likely that in a competing court system, there will be courts that will enforce antenuptial agreements, no matter what.

---

29. Some scholars believe that courts do follow efficiency standards. See Richard Posner, *Economic Analysis of the Law* (Boston: Little, Brown and Company, 1972), pp. 10–40.

30. In a way, the outcome here can be compared to what happens when zoning is enforced. With zoning, there is effectively a law that says X, Y and Z can go on this piece of land, but not A, B and C. Zoning, we know, lowers the probability that resources will flow to where they are most highly valued; thus it decreases the likelihood of achieving efficiency. So it is with a court that allows only certain provisions to be written into an antenuptial agreement.

At this point the argument can be made that we already have competing courts within a government court system. Reference is often made to the fact that courts do not always decide matters in the same way.[31] While it is true that courts do not always decide matters in the same way, it should not be inferred from this that they are in competition with each other. The difference in opinions, far from being illustrative of competition, is a result of judges in different courts weighing factors in a case differently. For instance, while one court might give great weight to "public policy doctrine" when deciding a divorce case that deals with an antenuptial agreement, another might give this doctrine only slight consideration. This difference can and does cause great uncertainty for persons who go before government courts.

DIFFERENT WAYS OF LOOKING AT MARRIAGE AND DIVORCE

Obviously there are different ways of looking at marriage and divorce—and the numerous matters encompassed by them. As noted above, when the subject is antenuptial agreements, some individuals take the position that individuals about to be married should have the right to enter into such agreements. Others disagree. And just as there are differences when it comes to antenuptial agreements, so there are differences when it comes to other topics. For instance, the marriage contract itself.

While some believe that the state-imposed contract should be enforced, others put forth the case that "freedom of contract" should rule when it comes to marriage. Those who hold to the single, state-imposed marriage contract usually make the argument that this contract has been honed over many years, that it properly takes into account public policy issues that marriage is concerned with, and that it is not subject to problems like "unequal bargaining power" which would naturally arise if freedom of contract were allowed.

Those who hold to freedom of contract make a number of points: First, they say that the state-imposed contract is not well understood by most married couples. For example, Lenore Weitzman states: "The

---

31. This point can be illustrated by the fact that many cases are appealed to higher courts, where decisions are overturned. For an interesting case in point, see one of the most important cases concerned with antenuptial agreements: *Posner* v. *Posner*, 233 So 2d 381.

marriage contract is unlike most contracts: its provisions are unwritten, its penalties are unspecified, and the terms of the contract are typically unknown to the 'contracting' parties."[32] The implication here is that there is more than the "optimum" amount of uncertainty present when it comes to the state-imposed marriage contract.

Second, the point is often made that the state-imposed marriage contract has provisions that relate to status (duties and obligations that are sex-based), and is concerned with public policy issues, both of which have no place in a relationship that concerns two people. With respect to the latter point, it is noted that the "externality argument" (which holds that the courts must regulate marriage because it has third-party effects, beyond those of children) is no more than a rationale for the state, or for special-interest groups, to interfere where they have no right.

Third, many persons make the point that the state-imposed marriage contract is outdated; that it reflects a period in time no longer with us. Gregg Temple makes the point well when he says: "If marriage has lost many of the economic and social functions that defined the traditional marriage terms, it follows that the state's interest in regulating marriage has lessened. Since the new function of marriage is happiness and fulfillment of the individuals, it also follows that personal preferences as to the substance of the marriage should be honored. Our society is based on diversity and tolerance of that diversity. If marriage has truly become a personal rather than a social institution, we should defer to personal, private ordering of the relationship."[33]

Fourth, the so-called "unequal bargaining power" problem that arises when there is absolute freedom to contract is said by freedom-to-contract advocates to be no more than a rationale for state involvement. They note that unequal bargaining power is something like "fairness": it is impossible to define, and difficult to notice, even when it is staring one right in the face.

To a large degree, the major differences between the ways marriage and divorce are viewed bring into the discussion some of the same arguments that are made on totally different topics. For instance, the unequal-bargaining-power argument is not made only when speaking

---

32. Weitzman, *n*. 21, p. 1170.
33. Gregg Temple, "Freedom of Contract and Intimate Relationships," *Harvard Journal of Law and Public Policy* 8 (no. 1): 151.

of the marriage contract but also when consumers' rights are discussed, or when contracts, in general, are discussed. Also, to take another example, state involvement based on "protecting third parties" or "dealing with externalities" is not used only when speaking of marriage and divorce—it is used in thousands of other areas as well. It would appear, then, that such discussions are not unique to the topic of marriage and divorce; arguments made with reference to them are made with reference to many other topics. It would seem to behoove us, instead of speaking about the particulars of marriage and divorce, to seek a larger (and proper) framework within which to discuss them—as well as many other topics of interest. We propose to do that here. The framework will be that of natural rights. We hope to show that it is a framework that offers many insights into the topics of marriage and divorce, and that when compared to other non-natural-rights frameworks, it is superior.

Before we proceed, it is perhaps important to explain how our approach to marriage, divorce, and the family is both different from and an addition to the major work in this area done by Gary Becker. Becker's approach to these topics differs from the one to be outlined here, not so much because we disagree with the scientific approach Becker takes in dealing with the subject matter, but because we are focusing on different aspects of the subject matter. Becker is interested in the maximizing behavior of individuals when it comes to marriage, divorce, and the family.[34] We, on the other hand, are not disputing the axiom that individuals attempt to maximize (utility)—no matter who they are, what they are doing, or where they are. In this sense, we are "Beckerites." It is simply that the discussion here relates to our intent to outline a framework different from the one most commonly used for viewing and discussing matters that relate to marriage, divorce, and the family.

MARRIAGE AND DIVORCE WITHIN A NATURAL RIGHTS FRAMEWORK

Criticism of natural rights, and natural law, usually comes from those who (1) do not believe that natural rights can be found through reason—they do not believe that objective law and rights exist—or (2) who wish to use the state to meet some end or purpose—either in-

---

34. See, for instance, Gary Becker, *n.* 1.

dividual or group-oriented. As far as the latter group is concerned, there is not much that can be said to convince them otherwise, for their advocacy of the state is a rationale for what it is they want. It is doubtful that any amount of rational discourse will sway these persons.

As to the first group, those who do not believe that natural rights can be found through reason, much has been written.[35] This is not the place to wage a full-scale discussion on natural rights theory; in fact, the objective here is not so much to prove that natural rights exist, but rather to develop within a natural rights framework some implications for marriage and divorce, and, as stated above, to address some of the differences between natural rights theory with respect to marriage and divorce and other non-natural-rights theories. We begin by outlining the natural rights framework.

The heritage of the natural rights framework used here is Lockean individualist, where "every man has a property in his own person. This nobody has any right to but himself. The labour of his body, and the work of his hands, we may say, are properly his. Whatsoever then he removes out of the state that nature hath provided, and left it in, he hath mixed his labour with, and joined to it something that is his own, and thereby makes it his property."[36]

This Lockean tradition of natural rights has perhaps best been elucidated and developed by Murray Rothbard.[37] Rothbard has noted that natural rights consist of the following:

1. The right to self-ownership.
2. The right to previously unowned natural resources that a person first occupies and brings into use.[38]

---

35. See, for example, Murray Rothbard, *The Ethics of Liberty* (Atlantic Highlands, N.J.: Humanities Press, 1982), pp. 1–26.

36. John Locke, "An Essay Concerning the True Origin, Extent and End of Civil Government," in P. Laslett, ed., *Two Treatises of Government* (Cambridge: Cambridge University Press, 1960), p. 305.

37. See Rothbard, *n.* 34, pp. 1–155.

38. "There are two fundamental principles upon which the libertarian theory of just property rests: (a) Everyone has absolute property right over his or her own body; and (b) everyone has an absolute property right over previously unowned natural resources (land) which he first occupies and brings into use (in the Lockean phrase, "mixing his labor with the land"). Murray Rothbard, "Law, Property Rights, and Air Pollution," *The Cato Journal* 2, (no. 1, Spring 1982): 76–77.

Given 1 and 2, we can say that a person has a property right in himself and in those things he first occupies and brings into use. From this we conclude that a person also has

3. The right to make contracts that concern his property.[39]

These rights are sometimes popularly referred to as the self-ownership right, the homesteading right, and the freedom-to-contract right, respectively. Together they make up the core of what is called natural rights. For purposes of this paper, we shall be most interested in the third of the three: the freedom-to-contract right; all, however, will be necessary to the discussion at hand. Within this natural rights framework we wish to discuss some important points often voiced in any discussion of marriage and divorce and peripheral areas.

The Externality Argument

As noted above, government courts have in some cases, both past and present, decided on matters that relate to marriage and divorce by taking into account third-party effects.[40] Is this consistent with natural rights? The answer is a definite no. Within a natural rights framework, where each individual has the right to self-ownership, it follows logically that each individual is free to do as he pleases as long as he does not infringe upon the natural rights of others.[41] It is important to stipulate, "as long as he does not infringe upon the natural rights

39. "The right of property implies the right to make contracts about property: to give it away or to exchange titles of ownership for the property of another person." Rothbard, *n.* 34, p. 133.

40. Some will say that courts should concern themselves with third-party effects if, for example, the third parties are children (within the marriage). There is little disagreement with this. However, many of the third-party effects that courts have dealt with have had nothing to do with children (within the marriage).

41. While this oft-referred to libertarian principle, "Each individual is free to do as he pleases as long as he does not infringe upon the natural rights of others," stems from the self-ownership right, it is possible that this principle might be chosen within a contractarian paradigm. Consider, for example, a Rawlsian setting where individuals are behind the veil-of-ignorance in the original position where all parties are rational adults who do not know what position they will occupy in society once the veil is removed. Is it so far-fetched to believe that natural rights might be agreed to by the participants? Inasmuch as natural rights has a long tradition and is quite popular today when versed in the terms, "You can do whatever you want as long as you do not physically harm anyone," it seems reasonable to believe that natural rights might be one of the top contenders in the Rawlsian original position.

of others," instead of, "as long as he does not harm anyone," because "harm" is something that anyone can claim at any time. For example, if Jones opens up a restaurant across the street from Smith's restaurant, Smith can claim that Jones's behavior has harmed him. Assume that it has; assume that Smith is worse off with Jones's restaurant across the street from him than he was without it. Is this then reason enough for Smith to take things into his own hands—to try to prevent Jones from operating a restaurant or to take the matter to the courts? The answer is no. The reason is simple: Jones, by setting up a restaurant, has not infringed upon the natural rights of Smith. He has not denied Smith the right to self-ownership; he has not infringed upon Smith's homesteading right; he has not interfered with Smith's freedom to contract. He has, we can assume, harmed Smith, but this is quite different from denying Smith any basic rights. The point is that it is possible to make someone worse off without infringing upon his natural rights.[42]

Once we understand that the "externality argument" makes little sense unless it can be proved that natural rights are infringed upon, we realize that the long-held view that courts should uphold public policy standards is no more than an intrusion on natural rights itself. Looking over a large number of court decisions, Weitzman notes: "The courts, however, have maintained two basic limitations on the enforceability of contracts between husbands and wives. Courts will not enforce contracts (1) that alter the essential elements of the marital relationship, or (2) that are made in contemplation of divorce."[43] Courts have acted this way essentially because they have accepted the "externality argument": they have accepted the idea that marriage and divorce affects third parties, that it has public policy ramifications, and that it is the task of the courts to watch over the public. Courts have not always realized that if they are going to watch over the public on the basis of the iffy externality argument, they will undoubtedly infringe upon the natural rights of both partners in the marriage.

To illustrate, let us consider the following hypothetical, but still realistic, case. John and Mary decide they want to marry. John would

---

42. To say that one person's actions or presence makes another person "worse off" should not imply that the first person's actions or presence was intended to have this outcome. It could be a consequence of the second person being particularly sensitive to the actions or presence of the first person.

43. Weitzman, *n*. 21, p. 1259.

like Mary to sign an antenuptial agreement stating that in the event they decide to divorce, she will not ask for any alimony. Mary is content to sign the antenuptial agreement.

For her part, Mary would like John to agree, in writing, that he will not take any of their children to his church. John says he will agree to this if Mary agrees to pay him $25 a month. Mary agrees, providing, however, that if John ever does take a child to his church, he will refund all the money Mary has paid to him up until that point in time.[44]

Given this agreement between John and Mary, we must remind ourselves that more than mere promises are made: Titles to property are exchanged, and we cannot be certain if a court will enforce this contract.[45] If a court today wanted, it could easily find precedent that speaks to the nonenforceability of antenuptial agreements that contemplate divorce, and to the "selling of property in a child" for money. No doubt many courts would simply say that the contract between John and Mary contravenes public policy, and that is that. End of discussion.

This being the case, and it very well could be, the natural rights of John and Mary would have been infringed upon. They would have been denied the right to freedom of contract in a case where the matters dealt with in their contract denied no other individual his natural rights. By entering into an antenuptial agreement that addresses divorce, John and Mary do not deny the right to self-ownership to anyone; they do not deny the homesteading right to anyone; they do not deny the freedom to contract to anyone.

And what about the case where the child is concerned? Here, once again, there is no infringement upon anyone's natural rights. The child, at least until a certain age, is the property of the parents—if not theirs, then whose?—and they can do with the child as they see fit, as long as they do not infringe upon his or her natural rights. It is doubtful

---

44. My assumption here is that both John and Mary have a property right in any children they might have, and that John can trade his property in his child for other property (at least until the children are of an age to say otherwise).

45. We wish to emphasize the point that more than a mere promise has been made, that titles to property have been exchanged, inasmuch as the enforcing of a contract based on a mere promise is not derivable from any of the three natural rights spoken of earlier. On this point, and on the "title-transfer" theory of contracts, see Williamson Evers, "Toward a Reformulation of the Law of Contracts," *Journal of Libertarian Studies* 1 (Winter 1977): 3–13; and Rothbard, *n.* 34, pp. 133–48.

that an agreement between mother and father not to have the child attend the father's church is an infringement upon the child's natural rights.[46,47]

The Unequal Bargaining Power Argument

The argument has been made that there needs to be one state-imposed marriage contract, that without it—in short, with perfect freedom to contract—marriage contracts will be unfair because of the unequal bargaining power of the parties writing the contract. Put bluntly, if freedom to contract is allowed, one person is going to have greater bargaining power than the other, sometimes much greater, and thus the contract is likely to be unfair.[48]

This is, of course, the extreme position. A notch down from this extreme position is the position that holds that it is permissible for individuals to modify the state-imposed marriage contract slightly as long as there is no evidence that unequal bargaining power was present in the contractual modifications. Courts have usually adopted this less extreme position, but not without making errors of judgment.

Courts have readily jumped to the conclusion that unequal bargaining power is proved if the agreement under consideration is termed "unfair." As Temple correctly states: "Some courts look at the fairness of the agreement itself. Some presume wrongdoing when the division of property is disproportionate."[49] Thus, a disproportionate property division is automatically termed unfair and assumed to have

---

46. If the child when older expresses a desire to attend the father's church and if his father and mother prevent him from doing so because of their contract, then we could in clear conscience say they were infringing upon his natural right of self-ownership. At this point in time the contract between the mother and the father should be deemed unenforceable.

47. John and Mary's natural right to "freedom of contract" is not as likely to be infringed upon if they could opt out of the state court system and have their contract ruled upon by a private court. It is reasonable to believe that because of competition, a private court would be less likely to frustrate the desires of buyers of their service.

48. This "unequal bargaining power" argument is often spoken of in terms of employee-employer bargaining where the employer is usually posited as having greater bargaining power. "Unequal bargaining power" between employee and employer is said to work to the detriment of the employee, in that without some offset to this unequal bargaining power—such as collective bargaining—the employee will be exploited. For a devastating critique of this, see William H. Hutt, *The Theory of Collective Bargaining* (Glencoe, Ill.: The Free Press, 1954).

49. Temple, *n.* 33, p. 131.

been the result of unequal bargaining power, or some other type of wrongdoing.[50]

The logic here is slippery. Why, we are entitled to ask, does a disproportionate property settlement mean unfairness? Might not the disproportionate property settlement be only one side of a broadly defined exchange, the other side being invisible to the court? It does not seem unreasonable to believe that a disproportionate property settlement is the "price" someone has paid for something he values more than an equal property settlement.

Putting aside the issue of whether a disproportionate property settlement means unfairness, there is the question of whether the existence of unequal bargaining power in the real world is enough of a reason to warrant the abrogation of the freedom to contract. There are a number of problems tied up with this issue.

First, there is this question: Can unequal bargaining power be identified? It was shown above that an outcome—namely, a disproportionate property settlement—is not proof positive that unfairness exists, or that unequal bargaining power might have been the reason for the supposed unfairness. We conclude that it is impossible to prove unequal bargaining power based on an observed outcome. But if not an outcome, what then?

We are left with trying to determine, on the basis of observation of the two parties involved in making the agreement or writing the contract, whether unequal bargaining power exists. It is obvious that this is not an objective way to decide whether unequal bargaining power exists or not. What might to one person appear to be unequal bargaining power might be no more than a difference in styles between two people, or a difference in, say, educational backgrounds— a difference that the observer mistakenly believes must necessarily imply unequal bargaining power. Consider, for example, a man with a doctorate in political science who is about to marry a woman with only a high school education. Suppose the two decide to write their own marriage contract. Given the information presented, is there any reason to assume unequal bargaining power? Should we assume that because the man has more education than the woman, there is unquestionably unequal bargaining power? We think not. But even if

---

50. To most courts, an unfair contract implies wrongdoing, of which "unequal bargaining power" is one variety.

there were, the possession of unequal bargaining power does not mean that it will be used.

The "unequal bargaining power" argument has too long been the rationale for negating the absolute freedom to contract. But not only can unequal bargaining power not be proved, even if we assume that it does exist in certain cases, this is no reason to abrogate the absolute freedom to contract. In a world where freedom to contract were allowed, individuals planning marriage would no doubt write their own contracts—but not usually without expert assistance.

Let us postulate the case of two persons, one of whom is not only much more capable of drawing up a marriage contract in his favor, but guaranteed to do so. We will call the person with greater bargaining power, Richard; the one with far less bargaining power, Alice. Question: In a world where the absolute freedom of contract is upheld, will it be the case that Richard will take advantage of Alice if the two write their own marriage contract? The quick, and wrong, answer is yes. This, though, overlooks the likelihood that in a world of absolute freedom to contract, there will be marriage-contract lawyers who can be retained to assure a contracting party that he or she is not making a mistake by agreeing to the terms of a marriage contract. So, the presence of unequal bargaining power (assuming that it does exist) is no reason to deny individuals the absolute freedom to contract. After all, even individuals who feel they are on the short end of the bargaining-power stick know they can buy expert advice.

The criticism may be made, however, that the person who feels he is on the short end of the bargaining-power stick might be too poor to hire expert advice. What then? it is asked. The reply is simply that before the contract is agreed to, both parties can exercise the option of turning it down. In short, if one party feels that the contract is not advantageous to him and that hiring expert advice (to change it or to help him understand all its ramifications) is too costly, then all he has to do is refuse to sign it. Exercising this course of action leaves the person no worse off.

Obligation to Disclose Information

Marriage contracts entered into under duress, with incompetents, or as a result of fraud, are not enforceable within a natural rights framework. The reason is simple: In each case the essence of contract, namely exchange, is subverted, and the probability of the contract being used as an instrument to steal is enhanced.[51] Related to this is the belief, recently put into effect by many courts, that a contract is unenforceable if one of the parties did not disclose pertinent information that would enable the other party to make an informed decision. Some have argued the point that under the law individuals should have the obligation to disclose information in a contractual setting if it is casually acquired, but not if it is deliberately acquired.[52] The difference in treatment is warranted on efficiency grounds. With deliberately acquired information, there are usually high costs of generating the information; these costs will not be incurred—and thus the information will not come to the surface—unless individuals are allowed to profit from the information.

An example serves to illustrate. Suppose Clark has undertaken months of study to determine whether or not there is oil under Smith's land. Finally, he concludes that the probability of striking oil is quite high. He makes Smith a monetary offer greater than any offer Smith has received to date. Smith accepts the offer. Months later, Smith finds out that Clark knew of the high probability of oil under the land and sues Clark for not disclosing information. In this case, since the information was deliberately, not casually, acquired by Clark, the ruling, based on efficiency grounds, should be that Clark did not have the obligation to disclose information. The rationale is that requiring individuals to disclose deliberately acquired information will lead to a reduction in the amount of information thus acquired and, as can be seen from this example, to a lesser probability of resources flowing to where they are most highly valued.

This would not be the case with obligating individuals to disclose casually acquired information. Casually acquired information—information that individuals did not invest substantial resources into acquiring—can be placed into the hands of any party without affecting

51. The ticklish issue in all this is determining what exactly constitutes duress, incompetence, and fraud. Of the three, perhaps incompetence and fraud are easier to prove than duress. For instance in *Norris* v. *Norris* 624 P. 2d 636 (51 Or. App. 43 1981) the court denied the enforceability of a contract the wife agreed to en route to her wedding. While this may seem as if duress were present at the time the contract was made, it is not obviously clear that it was. In any case, outside the obvious duress case, "Your money or your life," things become fuzzy. For a clear discussion of the misuse of the so-called doctrine of unconscionability, see Richard Epstein, "Nonconscionability: A Critical Reappraisal," *Journal of Law and Economics* 18 (no. 2, Oct. 1975): 293–315.

52. See Anthony T. Kronman, "Mistake, Disclosure, Information, and the Law of Contracts," *Journal of Legal Studies* 7 (no. 1, Jan. 1978): 1–34.

the allocation of resources. Here, then, requiring an individual to disclose casually acquired information does not reduce the probability of resources flowing to where they are most highly valued.

If we examine this concept vis-à-vis marriage, we would conclude that the groom-to-be can be held responsible for not disclosing casually acquired information—or information available without further expenditure of resources—to his wife-to-be at the time they were writing their marriage contract—especially where failure to disclose the information results in the wife-to-be agreeing to something she might otherwise not have agreed to.[53]

Obligating an individual to disclose information is imposing a positive obligation upon that person, something that is definitely not consistent with natural rights. It appears that the courts not only have gone against natural rights when obligating individuals to make informational disclosures, but they have also overlooked the fact that even without an informational disclosure the essence of contract—that is, to make oneself better off through exchange—is left undisturbed.

Put more simply, we might reasonably look at it this way: (1) The essence of contract is exchange of property;[54] (2) It would seem logical to conclude that the only valid reason for deeming a contact unenforceable is either where property is not concerned, or where the exchange process obviously cannot be consummated;[55] (3) The courts, by deeming a contract unenforceable in those cases where property is concerned but where information is not disclosed, are implicitly assuming that exchange has been negated in some way by one of the parties to the contract—and perhaps replaced by something else (theft). This is not necessarily, or even likely to be, the case. Simply because information is not disclosed, simply because a person might act differently in a case where information was disclosed, is not reason enough to assume that individuals are not making themselves better off through contract.

For example, let us suppose that Jane and Donald have recently gotten married. Jane, a rich widow, chose not to disclose information

---

53. That courts require disclosure of information in marriage cases has been well documented. See, for example, *Burgess* 646 P.2d 908 (Okla Ct. App. 1982). Also see the Uniform Premarital Agreements Act (UPAA).

54. For the development of this point, see Murray Rothbard, *For a New Liberty* (New York: Macmillan, 1978), 39–42.

55. An example, once again, of a case in which contract may not be concerned with exchange is one in which duress, incompetence, or fraud is present.

about her finances to Donald, either before or after the marriage. Before the marriage, though, Jane asked Donald to sign an agreement stating that both he and she preferred to live under separate property rules rather than under community property rules.[56] Let us suppose that Donald went along with the agreement.

Years pass, and Donald learns that Jane is wealthy and that she withheld this information from him. He sues on grounds that Jane did not disclose pertinent information necessary to his making an informed decision with respect to the agreement.

It is not at all clear what a modern-day court would rule. Within a natural rights framework, though, what it should rule is that Donald has absolutely no case against Jane. First, she does not have a positive obligation to disclose information Donald feels is necessary to his decision-making.

But, more important, the reason the court should not rule in Donald's favor is because he has made gains through the agreement he made earlier with Jane—or else he wouldn't have made it. This seems to be proof positive that the nature of contract—namely exchange—is not disturbed in any way by lack of disclosure of certain information.

It is not the case that Donald would not have married Jane had he known of her finances; it is only that he might have negotiated for better "terms of exchange."[57] The point is that there is a difference between holding back true information and stating incorrect information. The latter, when it comes to negotiating agreements or contracts, is properly deemed fraudulent behavior and is thus proper grounds for denying the enforceability of a contract; the former is not fraudulent—it does not negate the existence of benefits derived through the exchange process, and therefore should not be a reason for denying the enforceability of a contract.

Consider another example that may serve to further clarify the point. Suppose John would really have been willing to pay as much as $400

56. It is possible today for a couple in a community property state to write themselves out of it and into a separate property agreement. The exception is Texas. See Gamble, *n.* 23., p. 701. The relevant statement is, "The important point, however, is that both Spanish and French community property systems were grounded upon an optional basis."

57. The point has been made before by numerous others, but somehow it needs repeating periodically: There is a difference between "exchange" and the "terms of exchange." Upon the consummation of most exchanges, there exists another (and different) set of terms of exchange that would have benefited one party to the exchange to a greater degree than did the original terms. This fact, though, does not imply that the exchange was not beneficial to the party in question.

for the good he purchased from Bill for only $3. We can say that John withheld information about himself from Bill. Days after the exchange and quite by chance, John discloses this information. Bill claims that he was taken advantage of because John withheld information from him.

Such a claim would of course be nonsense. In that he accepted John's offer on the basis of information in his possession, Bill was no doubt made better off by the exchange. In that he could have been made even better off had he known John's top price is not reason enough to say that John took advantage of him by not disclosing certain information.

There is no evidence of fraud here. It is not the case that Bill has had his rights violated by accepting John's offer of $3. It is only the case that the "terms of exchange" could have been more in Bill's favor had John disclosed information he chose not to. Given this, there would appear to be no good reason for somehow invalidating the exchange that was made by the two persons, or by forcing John to pay Bill some dollar amount more than $3 but less than $400.

The same logic holds for marriage contracts. Where property is concerned, there does not seem to be any reason for denying enforceability to an agreement or contract because information was not disclosed by one or both parties: In such a case the *essence* of contract— exchange—is not disturbed by the failure to disclose information.[58]

ENFORCEABILITY OF CONTRACTS

If government courts were to move toward allowing the absolute freedom of contract, or were we to move to a system of competing private

---

58. Someone will no doubt make the following point: When information is not disclosed but comes to the surface later, the exchange process can be disturbed inasmuch as the exchange might not have been made had the information been available. While this is possible when the exchange does not involve property, it is extremely unlikely to be the case where it does, and only the latter case is of concern here. Nonproperty exchanges—"I will do the dishes for you on Tuesday if you do the dishes for me on Thursday"—are not deemed enforceable within a natural rights framework because failure to uphold them does not involve theft of property. More on this later.

For those interested, the reason exchanges dealing with property are unlikely not to be made once previously undisclosed information is disclosed is because individuals naturally tend to withhold information that relates to their having more property than others think they have, and not the reverse. This is like saying that the only time John will hold back information concerning an exchange with Bill is when he is willing to pay more for what Bill has than he (John) thinks he will end up paying. This being the case, our marriage contract case is analogous to the John-Bill exchange spoken of in the text.

courts, the question would naturally be asked: What contracts should be deemed unenforceable within a natural rights framework?

Consider, for example, a contract in which the husband says he will take out the garbage every day, and the wife says that in return she will cook dinner every night. The husband, let us say, decides not to take out the garbage every day. Does the wife now have legal recourse? The answer is no. The reason is simple: The contract was only promissory in nature; there was no implicit theft that occurred as a result of one party deciding not to do what he had promised to do. In the example above, the wife can quite easily decide not to cook dinner as a response to her husband deciding not to take out the garbage. In short, she has lost nothing because her husband failed to live up to his promise.

Consider another case. Suppose the situation is one where one party would lose something if the other party failed to keep a promise. For example, John promises Joe that when he (Joe) is 21 years old, he (John) will give him a million dollars. Joe, now 17 years old, decides not to attend college because he feels that with a million dollars soon coming his way college is unnecessary.

Four years pass and Joe turns 21 years old. He goes to John and asks for the million dollars. John tells Joe that he has reconsidered; he has now decided, he says, not to give Joe the money. Here, then, we have a case where Joe has given up the opportunity to go to college between the ages of 17 and 21 because of a promise made by John. Within a natural rights framework, would Joe have grounds upon which to take legal action against John? Once again, no. At issue here is a promise. Granted, it is a promise that has been broken, but within the natural rights framework failure to keep a promise does not warrant legal punishment. It might be morally reprehensible, but legally it is not punishable. Before legal punishment is appropriate in connection with "breaking" a contract, it is necessary for implicit theft to be present.

To illustrate this, consider Jones, who states that he will pay $10,000 to Smith one year from now if Smith lends him $9,000 today. Suppose that Smith does lend Jones $9,000. In short, Smith gives up his title to $9,000 today for the opportunity to receive title to $10,000 one year from today. If Jones does not pay Smith $10,000, as he agreed to, then Jones is subject to legal punishment. Within natural rights theory, this contract entered into by Jones and Smith is enforceable, because failure to enforce it will result in Jones being able to steal from Smith.

This is an implication of the "title-transfer" theory of contracts,[59] which holds that contracts are enforceable only if not enforcing them would involve implicit theft (of property). Within this theory of contracts there is also light shed on what kinds of property can and cannot be transferred. For instance, one's property right in his will and in his body is not transferable; this property right is inalienable. However, one's property right in his material property—his house, his car, his money—is transferable; this property right is alienable.[60] In the context of a marriage contract, for instance, a wife who contracted with her husband to provide him with sexual services in return for financial support would be attempting to alienate her will—something that cannot be alienated. If she at some later point in time decided to break the "contract," she has that right, since what she promised was impossible to transfer. The "contract" was in the realm of a promise, and the breaking of a promise is not, in the "title-transfer" theory of contracts, grounds for legal punishment.

HOMESTEADING IN CHILDREN

In the family setting, and from the point of view of the parents, children are quasi-public goods that are jointly produced. Given that the production of a child requires two parties, one wonders if this necessitates equal property right in the child. If not, then what is it that warrants something other than equal property rights?

These are not unimportant questions; the answers to them are relevant to numerous divorce cases and to the writing of marriage contracts in a world where the absolute freedom to contract exists. Consider some of the problems that might arise if property rights in children were not established.

Once again, an example is used to illustrate the relevant points. Joe and Mary are about to be married. They want to write their own marriage contract. One of the important provisions in it concerns whom the children will live with in case there is a divorce. Now before such an agreement can be made, it is necessary to determine who has just title over the children. This is important for purposes of the "title-transfer" theory of contracts: Without knowing whether a person has

---

59. Evers, *n*. 44, pp. 3–13

60. The discussion here follows that in Rothbard's *The Ethics of Liberty*, *n*. 34, pp. 134–35.

title to property, we cannot know if the contract is enforceable or not. Two difficult questions present themselves: One, are children, in fact, property? And if so, who holds the property rights to them?

We begin with the easier question: Are children property? The answer here is yes. Children, up until a certain age, cannot own themselves the way adults can own themselves. A three-month-old baby, for example, cannot be said to own herself. After all, for the most part she does not even know she exists.

Well, if the child cannot own herself, who then owns her? We are left with one or both of the parents—or would it be some third party? The third party would seem to be the wrong answer: Obviously, the third party had nothing to do with the creation of the child—that is, there is no homesteading right in the child held by a third party.

There is, of course, a homesteading right held by the parents.[61] The parents did create the child, but not, we should note, to the same degree. Individuals today commonly make the correct point that "it takes two" to make a child. What is then overlooked, though, is that the mother of the child "homesteads" the child for nine months while the father does not. While it is true that neither the man nor the woman can create a child alone—and so on this point there is equality—once we have passed the point where the egg and sperm have united, we realize that the gestation period to birth is nine months, the full time of which the united egg and sperm are incubated in the body of the mother. On homesteading grounds, the major property right to the child would seem to go to the mother.[62] Whether the property right to the child should be 75 percent mother, 25 percent father; or 80 percent mother, 20 percent father, no one can answer. All that is being said is that there appears to be a good reason why it should not be 50–50 and why the weighting factor for the mother should be generally greater than that for the father.[63] We have established, then, that a child is property—that is, someone can own him—and that the

---

61. Parents are not absolute owners, but simply trustee owners. The distinction is an important one, because if parents were absolute owners, they could do anything they wanted to with their children. Since children are potential adults and, as such, full possessors and exercisers of natural rights, they cannot be owned in an absolute sense, even during that time when they cannot exercise their own natural rights.

62. I would like to thank Murray Rothbard for bringing this point to my attention.

63. When we state that the father should have some below-50 percent property right in the child, we are assuming that the father can unequivocally be identified. Obviously it is easier to identify the mother of a child than it is to identify the father.

parents have property rights in the child up until a certain age (essentially until he can exert self-ownership in himself), and that the
property rights are held unequally by the parents—the majority share
generally being held by the mother.

The fact that both parents, not one, have property rights in a child
implies that both parents will have to agree before actions that relate
to the child can be taken. A priority there would appear to be reason
for giving greater control over the child to the mother than to the
father, but it is difficult to see how this would work itself out. Would
the mother, for example, always be the one who has the right to decide what the child will do, or what will be done with the child,
simply because she is the majority shareholder in the child? If so,
then this completely ignores the fact that the father has a property
right in the child.

There are three other possibilities: The father always decides, the
mother decides the majority of the time, or the mother and father
jointly decide in all cases. The first possibility, the father always decides, would clearly—on the basis of homesteading principles—be
wrong. The second possibility, while it sounds like the right way to
proceed, would be extremely difficult to put into practice. Since we
do not know how much more than 50 percent of the child the mother
owns, we do not know what percentage of the time she should have
control over the child. The third possibility, while not strictly in accordance with the fact that the mother owns the child to a greater
degree than does the father, seems to be the only workable and most
nearly equitable way of deciding things. Because of the problems inherent in the joint, yet unequal, ownership of the child by the parents,
we hold that both parents must agree before a course of action that
relates to the child can be taken. Realistically, this turns out to mean
that when the mother is alone with the child, she will decide what
the child will do; when the father is alone with the child, he will
decide what the child will do; and when both the mother and the father
are with the child, both must agree on the course of action for the
child to take. Put differently, when both mother and father are with
the child, each has absolute veto power.

Now consider what "joint ownership with unequal weightings" means
in the case of child custody. Obviously it implies that the mother
should have the right to have the child live with her, and that the
father should have visiting rights. The rationale here is simple: Since
the mother is majority owner in the child, it stands to reason that in

the case of a divorce custody should go to the mother, with the strict provision that the father has visiting rights.[64]

This is, of course, what many courts have decided, and to that extent, they have followed natural rights doctrine. Some courts, however, have awarded child custody to the father; in some other cases, where child custody is awarded to the mother, the father has been denied visiting rights. Both these types of decisions are inconsistent with natural rights doctrine.

As to the first, the awarding of child custody to the father: This is inconsistent with the fact that the mother has a greater homesteading right in the child than does the father. It is often argued that child custody should not depend upon "who homesteaded the child more" but on who is the better parent for the child to reside with. For instance, if the mother is deemed by the court to be less than a good parent, perhaps because of her lifestyle, then the father, assuming he lives a life preferred by the court, is given custody. This is an example where the court overlooks property rights and practices paternalism. Paternalism is sometimes justified on the grounds that the child, in this example, needs someone to act in his best interest when he cannot.[65] Such reasoning, though, forgets that no third party can own the child; therefore paternalism by the court, or anyone else, is unjustified on natural rights grounds if it goes against the wishes of the natural property-rights holder.

The latter case, where the father is denied visiting rights, is also contrary to natural rights doctrine. Here the court's reasoning is the same as above. The father is denied visiting rights when he is deemed an unfit parent. Once again, paternalism is placed above property rights. The father has a homesteading right in his child; given this, if he is denied visiting rights, his natural rights are being infringed upon. The court, in this instance, would then be the destroyer, not the preserver, of natural rights.[66]

---

64. Once again, we have the problem of deciding how often the father should have the right to visit—how much time he should be allowed with the children. A priori, we know he should get less than 50 percent of the time, but how much less is unclear.

65. For a discussion on paternalism, and one that brings up this point, see John Hospers "Libertarianism and Legal Paternalism," *Journal of Libertarian Studies* 4 (no. 3, Summer 1980): 255–65. Also see David Gordon's "Comment on Hospers," *Journal of Libertarian Studies* 4 (no. 3 Summer 1980): 267–72.

66. The only instance where the father should be given custody of the child, or where the

SUMMARY AND CONCLUSIONS

The courts have a history of deciding matters that relate to marriage and divorce outside a natural rights framework. "Public policy doctrine," "the externality argument," "unequal bargaining power," and much more have been employed as rationalizations for court decisions and for state involvement in a relationship that basically involves only two individuals. This has not gone without consequences—the main one being that numerous individuals have had their natural rights infringed upon.

Viewing marriage and divorce within a natural rights framework yields certain conclusions, some of which can be stated as follows:

1. Individuals contemplating marriage have the absolute freedom to contract, thus implying that they have a right to structure their marriage as they see fit. "Externality arguments" and arguments based on promoting the "public interest" are not only weak but if put into practice, infringe upon persons' natural rights.

2. Unequal bargaining power cannot be proved, but even if it could be, there is no reason to negate one's absolute freedom to contract: The existence of unequal bargaining power does not necessarily imply use of it, nor does it prohibit one from counterbalancing it through the purchase of expert advice in the market.

3. Individuals have no obligation to disclose information. In many cases where information has not been disclosed, there is no reason not to enforce a contract because the essence of contract—exchange—might not have been thwarted—only the terms of exchange might have been affected.

4. Marriage contracts that deal with property and alienable transfers of just titles, and do not involve theft (as the result of fraud, etc.) or infringe upon the natural rights of third parties, are deemed enforceable.

5. Children are the property of their parents up until the time they are able to exert self-ownership of themselves.

6. Parents must not treat their children in ways that violate the children's natural rights.

---

father should be denied visiting rights, is where it can be proved that the mother (in the first case) or the father (in the second case) has attempted to physically harm the child, i.e., where the natural rights of the child are in danger.

7. The mother generally has a greater homesteading right in her children than does the father.
8. Courts generally violate natural rights when they give (a) child custody to the father, or (b) if having given it to the mother, proceed to deny the father visiting rights. In so doing courts practice paternalism and, as a consequence, deny the natural right of ownership over the child to the homesteaders—the parents—of the child.

What is necessary in the area of marriage and divorce is a greater respect for, and a strict application of, natural rights by the courts. Marriage and divorce basically involves relationships—human relationships—and as such, it is amenable to study and to understanding within a property rights framework. We hold that it is incumbent upon the courts to find the "best" property rights framework and then apply it with dedication and consistency. We offer the natural rights framework for consideration, debate, and, we hope, acceptance.

8

FREEDOM OF CONTRACT AND THE FAMILY: A SKEPTICAL APPRAISAL

Paul Horton and Lawrence Alexander

The movement of the progressive societies has been uniform in one respect. Through all its course it has been distinguished by the gradual dissolution of family dependency, and the growth of individual obligation in its place. The individual is steadily substituted for the Family as the unit of which civil laws take account. . . . Nor is it difficult to see what is the tie between man and man which replaces by degrees those forms of reciprocity in rights and duties which have their origin in the Family. It is Contract. . . .

All the forms of Status taken notice of in the law of Persons were derived from, and to some extent are still coloured by, the powers and privileges anciently residing in the Family. If then we employ Status . . . to signify these personal conditions only, and avoid applying the term to such conditions as are the immediate or remote result of agreement, we may say that the movement of the progressive societies has hitherto been a movement from *Status* to *Contract.*[1]

Sir Henry Maine wrote these words in 1864, near perhaps the zenith of contract worship in the western world. In the more than century that has followed, individualists like Maine have taken quite a beating. Even as Maine's words were written, the main collectivist theories that were to hold sway in the next century—fascism, social-

1. Henry Maine, *Ancient Law* (Boston: Beacon Press, 1963), pp. 163–65.

229

ism, the Soviet version of communism, and the welfare state—were in bare-root form. The institution of Contract itself, developed with such missionary zeal by nineteenth century British and American scholars, has come under such severe attack in the last fifty years or so that much recent debate is centered on whether Contract is dead already or only mortally wounded.[2]

One important area, however, has given individualists cause for rejoicing. Within Family itself—the social institution posed as Contract's antithesis by Henry Maine—the apparent trend in recent years has been that of withdrawal on the part of government regulation. Although the trend seems clearest with regard to the husband-wife relationship, aspects of the parent-child relationship have also evinced a withdrawal of the state-imposed regulatory framework that Maine associated with the Status concept.

With this withdrawal of state overt control in these areas of family regulation, many commentators have assumed that the domain of Contract has been opened wide to husbands and wives, and perhaps to parents and children. In the last decade or so, these commentators— who are found primarily in the fields of law and the social sciences— have been joined by the popular press in proclaiming the arrival of the Age of Contract for the Family.[3]

---

2. See, for example, Patrick Atiyah, *The Rise and Fall of Freedom of Contract* (Oxford: Clarendon Press, 1979), pp. 405–19; Charles Fried, *Contract as Promise* (Cambridge: Harvard University Press, 1981); Lawrence Friedman, *Contract Law in America* (Madison: University of Wisconsin Press, 1965); Grant Gilmore, *The Death of Contract* (Columbus: Ohio State University Press, 1974); Ian Macneil, *The New Social Contract* (New Haven: Yale University Press, 1980); Jeffrey O'Connell, "The Interlocking Death and Rebirth of Contract and Tort," *Michigan Law Review* 75 (1977):659.

3. See, for example, Lenore J. Weitzman, *The Marriage Contract: Spouses, Lovers, and the Law* (New York: The Free Press, 1981); Joan M. Krauskopf, ed., *Marital and Non-Marital Contracts: Preventive Law for the Family* (Chicago: American Bar Association, Section of Family Law, 1979); Marjorie Maguire Schultz, "Contractual Ordering of Marriage: A Model for State Policy," *California Law Review* 70 (1982):204; Richard W. Bartke, "Marital Sharing—Why Not Do It by Contract," *Georgetown Law Review* 67 (1979):1131; Homer H. Clark, "Antenuptial Contracts," *University of Colorado Law Review* 50 (1979):141; Joan M. Krauskopf and Rhonda C. Thomas, "Partnership Marriage: The Solution to an Ineffective and Inequitable Law of Support," *Ohio State Law Review* 34 (1974):558; Karl Fleischmann, "Marriage by Contract: Defining the Terms of the Relationship," *Family Law Quarterly* 8 (1974):27; Banks McDowell, "Contracts in the Family," *Boston University Law Review* 45 (1965):43; "Marriage Contracts for Support and Services: Constitutionality Begins at Home," *New York University Law Review* 49 (1974):1161; "Interspousal Contracts: The Potential for Validation in Massachusetts," *Suffolk Law Review* 9 (1974):185; "Marital Contracts Which May Be Put Asunder," *Journal of Family Law* 13 (1974):23; "Marriage as Contract: Toward a Functional

In this essay we view these apparent trends, not with alarm, but with skepticism. We are prepared to accept the view that government's heavy hand has withered substantially in areas of marriage regulation, and perhaps also to some extent in the regulation of the parent-child relationship, especially in the last two decades. Withdrawal of state regulatory control, however, is only a necessary but not sufficient precondition for the emergence of Contract. We believe commentators may have leaped too quickly from the perceived withdrawal of state control to the arrival of freedom of contract for the family.

Our skepticism takes four interrelated forms. First, we attack the philosophical linkage between withdrawal of state control and enhancement of "freedom of contract." Second, we suggest that any actual increase in "freedom of contract for the Family" in the last two decades has come, not from changes made in the traditional legal concept or regulation of Family per se, but rather from more broad-based societal changes with respect to which Family is a third-party beneficiary. Third, we sketch a critique of the perceived trends that depends on analysis of the relationship between "freedom of contract" and "legal enforceability of contracts." And fourth, we suggest the view that the purely legal aspects of the institution of Contract are secondary in importance to the mindsets of the citizens to whom the law relates.

DEREGULATION TRENDS AND FREEDOM OF CONTRACT: A LINKAGE?

Two systems of principles typically are associated with philosophies of individualism that stop short of advocating outright anarchy. The two systems share many common values and many assumptions about human behavior and the role of government. As a result, the natural inclination is to associate these two systems with each other and, indeed, to treat them as inextricably linked to each other.

The first of these systems is associated with laissez faire and the

Redefinition of the Marital Status," *Columbia Journal of Law and Social Problems* 9 (1973):607; Richard Neely, "Marriage Contracts for Better or Worse," *Juris Dr.* 7 (Sept. 1977):38; Jay Folberg, "Book Review," *Family Law Quarterly* 16 (1983):385; Phyllis W. Beck, "Book Review," *Family Law Quarterly* 15 (1982):371. For a somewhat less optimistic view, see Mary Ann Glendon, *The New Family and the New Property* (Toronto: Butterworth & Co., 1981).

minimal state. As political ideology in industrialized and technologically advanced nations, this system is currently allied with movements toward government deregulation across a wide variety of fronts,
and with efforts to enhance individual interests in "liberty," "privacy," or "dignity," usually at the expense of statist ideologies commonly associated with "social utilitarianism." Government's purpose,
the minimal-state theorists assert, is neither to intrude aggressively
to maximize the greatest good for the greatest number of its citizens,
nor to distribute the good (however defined) according to any preset
pattern. Rather, government's purpose is simply to establish an appropriate regime of individual entitlements, then to give that regime
the minimum protection it requires to permit effective utilization of
those entitlements in the "private sector."

The second of these systems is associated with "freedom of contract." In its simplest forms, this system concentrates on "bargained-
for exchange." Two individuals with interests divergent from each
other meet, negotiate for each other's interests, strike a bargain, structure a transaction, and perform in accordance with that transaction.
At transaction's end each participant walks away the proud possessor
of interests formerly possessed by the other participant.

The systems of "minimal state" and "freedom of contract" are
highly compatible with each other. Both systems, no matter how pes-
simistic their protagonists may be with respect to the nature of human
beings, clearly evidence a preference to rely on "the individual" rather
than on government for the appropriate allocation of resources and
responsibilities within a society.

Moreover, the two systems can easily be understood to be complementary of each other. The strategy could be employed of argument from extremes: Here we have thoroughgoing collectivism, in
which a society's everything is bestowed, prohibited, or required by
government according to policies of paternalism and status; there we
have anarchy, a polar opposite, in which all concepts of "society"
disappear and individuals must fend for themselves. Neither extreme,
we soon are led to believe, has much to commend it even as a theoretical matter. Somewhere between these two theoretical extremes
are placed societies with combinations of collectivism and contract:
Collectivism, because societal government necessarily is collectivist;
Contract, because (1) anarchy is ruled out by the existence of government and (2) individuals interrelate in the domains left open to

noncollectivist ordering through contracts and related mechanisms. Every society has at least this collectivist endeavor: the determination of which interests (needs, desires, wants) are entitlements (property) that are available to its citizens. Determination of entitlements entails the definition—the identification—of entitlements. Wherever, within its society's borders, a particular government does no more than define entitlements and does not prohibit or require their redistribution, there government permits its citizens to redistribute (and thus acquire) entitlements on their own. The more government permits—the less it prohibits or requires—the more room government provides for the regime of Contract.

From such a vantage little additional effort is required to transform the two systems of "minimal state" and "freedom of contract" into a single system for societal governance. The argument runs thus: Government is a poorer administrator of entitlements than are individual citizens; the less intrusive the role taken by government with respect to the administration of entitlements, the more liberty individual citizens have to make their own decisions about entitlements; "contract" is an appropriate, and perhaps a highly efficient, methodology by which individual citizens can administer their entitlements in relationship to the entitlements of other individual citizens.

Thus, forms of "minimal state" affiliate, perhaps by definition, with "freedom of contract." The minimal state is the government that, having identified its society's entitlements, gives freedom of contract the maximum leeway—and the minimum protection its processes require—to permit private acquisition and redistribution of those entitlements by the society's citizens. The ambit of "minimum protection" would vary from one minimum state to another (depending, primarily, on the types of entitlements identified and the manner in which they were defined); but legal minds would suppose various devices to insure against nonconsensual takings of entitlements and to insure good faith performance of contract transactions, which then would form the mainstays of minimal-state collectivism.

Having identified the framework for ideal "minimal state plus freedom of contract," the temptation is great to extend the framework into more realistic, explanatory settings. Thus, the thesis is available that the area of "freedom of contract" increases whenever, and to the extent, government deregulation takes place. Apparently following this thesis, many commentators point to trends of deregulation with respect to family and sexual relationships and go on to conclude that the contractarian family is already established on the horizon.[4]

Certainly trends of government deregulation—trends away from status defined and imposed by government—are discernible with respect to these relationships. The modern era of family deregulation in the United States has a substantial constitutional tinge. *Griswold* v. *Connecticut*,[5] decided in 1965 that state laws prohibiting the use of contraceptives by married couples were unconstitutional. *Griswold* became a watershed. Its main principles—constitutionally protected "freedom of association" and "privacy in the marital relationship"— have been extended, at the expense of government, to many other sexual, reproductive, and living-together relationships that formerly had been considered firmly within the ambit of government control.[6]

Parallel deregulation trends have been discerned outside the ambit of explicit constitutional litigation. On a legislative level, the 1970s and 1980s have ushered in dramatic movements toward "no-fault divorce," decriminalization of various extramarital sexual relationships, and the abolition of most distinctions between legitimate and illegitimate children. On the level of civil adjudication, we find widespread disintegration of special rules—intrafamily immunities for tort liability, presumptions of undue influence among family members, family-based testimonial privileges, to mention a few—that formerly served to distinguish state-recognized familial relationships from other relationships in litigative settings.

Given these trends toward the kinds of freedom that come from lifting of governmentally imposed definition and regulation, however, the question still remains unanswered: Do these trends entail—or even

---

4. See especially, Lenore J. Weitzman, *The Marriage Contract: Spouses, Lovers, and the Law* (New York: The Free Press, 1981); Joan M. Krauskopf, ed. *Marital and Non-Marital Contracts: Preventive Law for the Family* (Chicago: American Bar Association, Section of Family Law, 1979); Marjorie Maguire Schultz, "Contractual Ordering of Marriage: A Model for State Policy," *California Law Review* 70 (1982):204; Karl Fleischmann, "Marriage by Contract: Defining the Terms of the Relationship," *Family Law Quarterly* 8 (1974):27; "Interspousal Contracts: The Potential for Validation in Massachusetts," *Suffolk University Law Review* 9 (1974):185; Phyllis W. Beck, "Book Review," *Family Law Quarterly* 15 (1982):371.

5. *Griswold* v. *Connecticut*, 381 U.S. 479 (1965).

6. See, for example, *Eisenstadt* v. *Baird*, 405 U.S. 438 (1972) re the right of single adults to obtain contraceptives; *Carey* v. *Population Services International*, 431 U.S. 678 (1977) re the right of minors to obtain contraceptives; *Roe* v. *Wade*, 410 U.S. 113 (1973) re the right to have abortion in first trimester of pregnancy; *Planned Parenthood of Central Missouri* v. *Danforth*, 428 U.S. 52 (1976) re the right to have abortion without husband's consent; *Bellotti* v. *Baird*, 443 U.S. 622 (1979) re the right to have abortion without parents' consent.

signal—a trend toward freedom of *contract* within the family relationships?

An affirmative answer to this question, today, would be a dishonest answer. Government cessions to individual autonomy do not entail, other than within the definition of the autonomy ceded, freedom to contract with respect to that autonomy; and, in most instances among the discernible cessions, insufficient time has elapsed in which to analyze their definitions from the question's point of view. Consider the questions raised in the following examples, none of which—to our knowledge—has received a definitive answer that counts:

1. Previously, a government had statutes making adultery both a criminal offense and a ground for divorce. Now the government has repealed all this legislation. It may well follow that adultery is now tolerated from this government's point of view; but does it follow that this government now regards adultery as an entitlement within the ambit of freedom of contract? (If government's perspective is not the relevant perspective, then whose is the relevant perspective?) If a husband promises his wife that he will not engage in adultery in exchange for one night a week "out with the boys," do we have a contract here? (What is meant by "contract"?)

2. Previously, married persons were prohibited from using contraceptives. Since the *Griswold* v. *Connecticut* decision, the prohibition is no longer in force. A husband offers: "If you will use the contraceptive, I will buy you a mink coat"; his wife accepts the offer. Do we have a "contract" here, the product of post-*Griswold* "freedom of contract"? (Again, what is meant by "contract"?) Suppose further that the wife fails to use the contraceptive (with obvious results), or the husband refuses to bestow the coat, even though the wife fulfills her part of the bargain. Do we have a "contract" here?

3. Previously, nontherapeutic abortions were outlawed in all states, regardless of the marital status of those seeking them. After *Roe* v. *Wade*[7] in 1973, states must permit those in their first trimester of pregnancy to obtain such abortions if they desire. A post-*Roe* legislature, under the banner of "promoting harmony within the family" and "protecting the entitlements of husbands," enacts

7. *Roe* v. *Wade*, 410 U.S. 113 (1973).

legislation requiring pregnant wives to obtain the consent of their husbands before undergoing an abortion. The statute is held to be unconstitutional—an interference with the wife's unfettered entitlement.[8] Now, suppose the wife executes an agreement with her husband to obtain an abortion if she become pregnant. Is the agreement (for which consideration is given) a "contract"? If so, then will the contract be enforced in the manner of other conceded contracts?

At best, affirmative answers to these hypothetical questions would today be no better than educated guesses, based on (1) a model that presupposes government deregulation is one, but only one, precondition for a contractarian regime, and (2) the historical course of similar trends in past generations and in areas besides government/family relationships. History provides no uniformity for analysis; witness "death of contract" with respect to warranty, unconscionability, implied obligation of good faith—all in the area of business transactions traditionally affiliated with contractarian modes. We are left with a model, a theory that "minimum state entails freedom of contract," that has little besides elegance to support itself.

Or, put yet a little differently, the only honest answer to the question, Do these deregulation trends signal a trend toward freedom of contract within the family relationships? is that only time will tell.

SOCIETAL CHANGES AND INTRAFAMILY CONTRACTING

The premise still seems sound today that family relationships are high-stakes exchange relationships of indefinite duration (hopefully long-term), in which maximization of the happiness and fulfillment of individual members is of great concern. When the observation is accepted that contemporary government is withdrawing from the regulation of family relationships, it seems plausible to argue that family relationships appear to be well suited to a contractarian approach.

In recent years many commentators—running the gamut from legal scholars through social scientists and on to the popular press—have observed an increase in intrafamily contracting. Here we do not dispute the accuracy of their observations, at least so long as "contract" remains undefined. Many of these commentators proceed to advocate the widespread use of intrafamily contracts as a desirable method for

8. *Planned Parenthood of Central Missouri* v. *Danforth*, 428 U.S. 52 (1976).

structuring family relationships. Again, so long as "contract" remains undefined, we express no disagreement with their advocacy.

Our skepticism returns, however, when we hear the position stated that intrafamily contracting is a recent, or even nascent, phenomenon spawned by government's recent withdrawal from the regulation of family relationships. The position to which we refer is epitomized by the following statement of Banks McDowell, made at the beginning of the era with which we are concerned:

> Maine's dictum that progress is from status to contract no longer applies generally to our society as we begin to contract ourselves into new types of status positions, but the statement still holds true for the family which is in the process of moving from essentially status relations to more free contractual or consensual ones. It is time that we admit this as a truth in our law of contract.[9]

The notion expressed here seems to be composed of the following elements: (1) Old contract-and-family law (as in, say, the 1950s) drew a heavy line between intrafamily exchanges and other types of exchanges, with intrafamily exchanges treated as noncontractual while other similar exchanges were treated as contractual. (2) As a matter of fact, family relationships have evolved from status (collectively defined and regulated) to contract (defined and regulated by the relationships' participants). (3) Old law's heavy line will (should) be eliminated as a result of this evolution. (4) New law will (should) accord "freedom of contract"—including full legal contract enforceability—to family relationships.

Our problems with this notion are twofold. First, the notion would have made sense a century ago, but makes little sense when expressed in the last two decades. Second, the notion rests on the assumption that family relationships (and governmental regulation of them) were the basis for nice legal distinctions between contract and no-contract.

The commentators' depictions of the "prior regime" for intrafamily contracts frequently are found to make the mid-nineteenth century seem like only yesterday. Until the mid-nineteenth century, grounds still existed in both common-law and community-property jurisdictions for the bold proposition that intrafamily contracts were legally inconsequential. For marriage, the common-law principle—"husband and wife are one"—effectively ruled out freedom of contract between husband

9. Banks McDowell, "Contacts in the Family," *Boston University Law Review* 45 (1965):43 (p. 62).

and wife (it takes two to contract); a more complex rationale led to the same result in community-property jurisdictions. By the beginning of the twentieth century in the United States, however, nearly every state had passed legislation permitting spouses to contract with each other as well as with third persons. Putting aside an isolated (and erroneous) case here and there, and a very narrow range of topics covered by legislation, most jurisdictions have recognized a freedom-of-contract position for spouses.

The situation has always been different with respect to contracts between parents and their minor children; those have, so far as can be remembered, always been voidable at the child's instance. But little if anything can be found to distinguish this regime from a more general one—the contracts of minors, no matter with whom, were and are voidable at the minor's instance. Contracts between parents and their adult children have always been treated in the manner of other contracts. Parents can now enter into contracts with their 19-year-old sons that, unlike before, their sons cannot avoid; but the reason is the legislative lowering of the age of emancipation from 21 to 18, not special parent-child enabling legislation or the elimination of special child-versus-parent contractual immunities.

It is true that marriage contracts—at least "during marriage" contracts, as opposed to antenuptial contracts or marital termination agreements—have been evaluated by courts according to principles of trusteeship (usually, it turns out, to the husband's detriment). Thus, in terms of the judicial evaluative process, marriage contracts are distinguished from simple sales. But little common sense is required to recognize that exchanges between spouses are different from simple sales exchanges between strangers. The distinction is not between "marriage contracts" on the one hand and "all other contracts" on the other; rather, it is between a wide range of "relational contracts" on the one hand (of which marriage contracts are a subset) and "transactional contracts" on the other.[10]

Indeed, proponents of intrafamily contracts may have overlooked completely—by 180 degrees—the developments that actually have

---

10. Both the terminology and much of the insight in these propositions are attributable to the work of Ian Macneil. See, for example, "The Many Futures of Contracts," *Southern California Law Review* 47 (1974):691; "A Primer of Contract Planning," *Southern California Law Review* 48 (1975):627; "Economic Analysis of Contractual Relations: Its Shortfalls and the Need for a 'Rich Classificatory Apparatus,'" *Northwestern University Law Review* 75 (1981):1018; *The New Social Contract* (New Haven: Yale University Press, 1980).

taken place. We state the proposition boldly, not to insist upon its complete and universal validity but rather to identify it as an honest possibility: The phenomenon is not that intrafamily contracts are beginning to be treated like other contracts; rather, the phenomenon is that whole classes of other contracts—in the realms of employment, insurance, professional services, and so forth—are beginning to be treated as intrafamily contracts have been treated for many years. In other words, it is not unlikely that those who have proclaimed a flow actually have perceived an ebb.

Lawyers, happily, seem more confident today in predicting the legal enforceability of marriage contracts, across a broader range of topics, than they were a few years ago. But again, their confidence need not be traced to any recent revisions in "family law." A California statute, somewhat representative of the law most everywhere in the United States today, has since 1872 provided as follows:

> Either husband or wife may enter into any engagement or transaction with the other, or with any other person, respecting property, which either might if unmarried; subject, in transactions between themselves, to the general rules which control the actions of persons occupying confidential relations with each other. . . .[11]

Although the statute has not changed, the societal concepts of "property" and the societal confidence in the capacity of spouses freely to contract have changed; and these changes lead to a more positive legal-system attitude toward marriage contracts. But, on further reflection, the changes have not been wrought in the field of "marriage." Rather, these changes—primarily in areas of "equal protection," "privacy," and liberty regarding sexual matters—have occurred broadly throughout society, and individuals who are married turn out to be the beneficiaries of these changes along with everyone else.

Eisenstadt v. *Baird*[12] states our point in a slightly different way.

---

11. Cal. Civ. Code § 5103 (formerly § 158) (Deerings Ann.). In 1984, after the draft of this chapter was prepared, California Civil Code § 5103 was amended as follows:

> (a) Subject to subdivision (b), either husband or wife may enter into any transaction with the other, or with any other person, respecting property, which either might if unmarried.
> (b) Except as provided in Sections 143, 144, and 146 of the Probate Code [dealing with limitations on certain "contractual arrangement relating to rights at death"], in transactions between themselves, a husband and wife are subject to the general rules which control the actions of persons occupying confidential relations with each other, as defined by Title 8 (commencing with Section 2215) of Part 4 of Division 3 [dealing with trusts and trustees].

12. *Eisenstadt* v. *Baird,* 405 U.S. 438 (1972).

We have previously discussed *Griswold* v. *Connecticut*, in which a statute prohibiting married persons from using contraceptives was held to be an unconstitutional infringement of the "right to marital privacy." *Griswold* appeared to announce an entitlement that was limited to the marital relationship, but *Eisenstadt* clarified the matter in declaring unconstitutional a Massachussetts law which made illegal the distribution of contraceptives to unmarried persons. The *Eisenstadt* Court observed:

> If under *Griswold* the distribution of contraceptives to married persons cannot be prohibited, a ban on distribution to unmarried persons would be equally impermissible. It is true that in *Griswold* the right of privacy in question inhered in the marital relationship. Yet the marital couple is not an independent entity with a mind and heart of its own, but an association of two individuals each with a separate intellectual and emotional makeup. If the right of privacy means anything, it is the right of the *individual*, married or single, to be free from unwarranted governmental intrusion into matters so fundamentally affecting a person as the decision whether to bear or beget a child.[13]

A byproduct of the post-1970 movement in both consitutional and statutory law toward sexual equality has been a change in the legal view of women's capacity to contract. No longer are women subject to legal incapacities premised upon such "archaic stereotypes" as that they lack business sense or experience, or as that they will be dominated or unduly influenced by their husbands.[14] Such a change of course permits a broader range of legally valid contracts by women within marriage as well as without marriage.

In fact, however, there generally was no difficulty with married women contracting before these recent developments in constitutionalized sexual equality. The principal effect of these legal developments, so far as Marriage is concerned, has been the replacement of statutory "husband as manager of the marital property" regimes with statutory "husband-wife partnership" regimes.[15] Under the former regimes, the husband's status as manager of the marital property was one from which the spouses could opt out by agreement; thus "hus-

---

13. Id. at 453.
14. The idea is from *Stanton* v. *Stanton*, 421 U.S. 7, 14–15 (1975). See also *Reed* v. *Reed*, 404 U.S. 71 (1971); *Weinberger* v. *Weisenfeld*, 420 U.S. 636 (1975).
15. See generally Susan Prager, "Sharing Principles and the Future of Marital Property Law," *U.C.L.A. Law Review* 25 (1977):1; Mary Glendon, "Is There a Future for Separate Property?" *Family Law Quarterly* 8 (1974):315.

band as manager" provided a starting point or presumption for legal analysis and a starting-point entitlement that could be redistributed through bargaining. The analogy here is to the law of intestate succession, in which legislative inferences are made about how a decedent would have left his or her property upon death, but prospective decedents are given the encouraged option of drawing up their own wills to contradict the presumptions of intestate succession statutes.

In summary, then, there have been several recent changes in the legal environment that have opened the door to Contract for family relationships. These changes have been in terms of the scope of government regulation, in terms of the status of women, and in terms of the age definition of adulthood. But these changes, for the most part, have been exogenous to the family relationship itself. Moreover, these changes have coexisted with other exogenous changes that have been pro-Status and anti-Contract.[16] The case for the movement of Family from Status to Contract remains uneasy.

We cannot fail to identify yet another possible reason for confidence in the position that intrafamily contracts are treated more favorably today than before by the legal system. Quite possibly the case could be made that nothing has changed in the realm of intrafamily contracts except (1) the quality of legal draftspersonship and (2) an increase in reliance by family members on attorneys for assistance in contracting. These two changes—without more—could be expected to have a substantial impact on acceptance of intrafamily contracts by the legal system; but they would have little if anything to do with changes in Family, in Family entitlements, or even in judicial attitude toward intrafamily contracts.

THE CONCEPT OF LEGAL ENFORCEABILITY

Thus far we have played as visitors on the turf of those who advocate, or at least who perceive, an increase in intrafamily contracting. Nearly all the lawyer-advocates have included the concept of "legal enforceability" within their definitions of "intrafamily contracts."[17] Their inclusion of this concept has provided much of the basis for our critique.

---

16. See *n.* 2 and *n.* 10 supra. See, also, Richard Epstein, "Unconscionability: A Critical Appraisal," *Journal of Law and Economics* 18 (1975):293; Arthur Leff, "Unconscionability and the Code: The Emperor's New Clause," *University of Pennsylvania Law Review* 115 (1967):485; *Henningsen* v. *Bloomfield Motors, Inc.,* 32 N.J. 358, 161 A. 2d 69 (1960).

17. See especially the commentators, other than Weitzman, collected in *n.* 4.

The equation of "contract" with "legally enforceable contract" comes naturally to lay persons as well as to lawyers. Frequently those who advocate intrafamily contracts are criticized on grounds that a contractual approach to Family will convert into inflexible cement relationships that must necessarily be flexible and continually able to adjust to change. Generally such criticism rests on the assumption that the marriage contract is intended to be legally enforceable. The same may be said for the criticism—from libertarian quarters, no less—that intrafamily contracts would involve the heavy-handed intrusion of government into ongoing family relationships, thus eroding the "privacy" necessary for intimate relationships to flourish.[18] A related criticism is that marriage contracts would place marriage on a sterile, businesslike basis, thus taking "romance" out of the relationship. Again, such criticism appears to rest on the assumption that contracting family members are concerned primarily with the legal enforceability of their agreements.

And now our skepticism turns from considerations of intrafamily contracts to considerations related to "legal enforceability" in contracts. Some commentators—including, perhaps, the most vociferous critics of the intrafamily-contracts advocates—say "legal enforceability" is at least an essential ingredient, if not the essence, of what a legal system means by Contract.[19] Earlier we attacked the view that withdrawal of government regulation entails freedom of contract. Now we turn somewhat to attack the view that Contract entails legal enforceability. We propose here to surround "legal enforceability of contract" in a variety of ways, in an effort to determine the extent to which "legal enforceability" is a meaningful entailment within the concept of Contract.

A. Many good reasons can be adduced in support of more widespread use of intrafamily contracts.

Some of these reasons interface with the deregulation trends we

18. See, for example, Charles Fried, *An Anatomy of Values* (Cambridge: Harvard University Press, 1970), pp. 132–52.

19. A representative statement is John Murray's: "We distinguish those promises which the law enforces from those which it does not by calling the former 'contracts.'" John Murray, *Murray on Contracts* (Indianapolis: Bobbs-Merrill Company, 1974), p. 3. See also Arthur Corbin, I *Corbin on Contracts* (St. Paul; West Publishing Co., 1963), p. 6; Allan Farnsworth, *Contracts* (Boston: Little, Brown and Company, 1962), pp. 3–4; Samuel Williston and George Thompson, *Selections from Williston on Contracts* (New York: Baker, Voorhis & Co., 1938), p. 1; Restatement 2d Contracts §1 (1973); Uniform Commercial Code §1–201 (11).

have discussed previously. Suppose government—and here, for good measure, we may include informal governments like church and neighborhood—has withdrawn from the regulation of intrafamily relationships. The void created by this withdrawal must be filled somehow, by monarchy (patriarchy; matriarchy), by anarchy, or by democracy (including oligarchy, at least among obligarchs). Neither monarchy nor anarchy seems appropriate for various reasons, leaving democracy as the most appropriate alternative. Contract affiliates with democracy. Hence, welcome intrafamily contracts.

Other reasons supporting intrafamily contracts are related to the philosophical and psychological characteristics of Contract. Relationships like marriage entail, typically, a proliferation of exchanges between the relationship's participants. Contract is one important method of exchange between individuals. The employment of contract methodology for exchange permits a measure of planning, negotiation, and structuring to the participants that enhances their individuality, recognizes their dignity within the transaction, and increases the likelihood of fairness and clarity in the exchange. No reasons come immediately to mind that would invalidate these advantages of Contract so far as family relationships are concerned.

The processes of Contract serve valuable communicative functions. The contract's participants are permitted to articulate what they desire from the transaction, to understand each other's position, to exchange information relevant to the exchange and its purposes, and to reach a mutually agreeable compromise in which each participant receives something of benefit. "We aren't communicating with each other any more" is a complaint voiced with increasing frequency by participants in family relationships. Employment of contractarian methodology for intrafamily exchanges would provide at least a partial solution to the problems that are affiliated with such complaints.

Contracts—more so than "resolutions," "precatory utterances," or unilateral position-stating—carry with them the moral force that they will be performed. Contracts serve to enhance the important values that are associated with reliance and fulfillment of expectations. These characteristics of Contract would seem no less applicable, no less desirable, with respect to family relationships than with respect to other relationships in which exchanges are sought and made.

And contracts carry with them the possibility of "legal enforceability" in the event of default by one of the contract's participants. Thus "legal enforceability of exchange"—by an order for specific perfor-

mance, a judgment for damages, a decree of rescission, and so forth—
is one, and only one, of the characteristics of Contract.

Now, having identified some of the main reasons for and characteristics of Contract, we are permited to ask questions like these:

1. If the "contract" in question did not entail a measure of planning,
    negotiation, or structuring for the participants (or for each of the
    participants), then was it a contract? If the "contract" did not
    increase the likelihood of the fairness and clarity of the exchange,
    then was it a contract? If the "contract" served no communicative
    functions, then was it a contract? If the "contract" entailed no
    moral force that it would be performed, or enhanced no reliance
    or expectations of the participants, then was it a contract? If the
    "contract" was not legally enforceable, then was it a contract?
2. How many characteristics of Contract must a "contract" have
    before it is a "real" contract? For example, are *all* the charac-
    teristics—all the *main* characteristics—of Contract required to be
    present in an exchange in order to have a "real contract"? If not
    all, then at least two, or three, or four?
3. Suppose an exchange transaction in which all the main charac-
    teristics of Contract are present except "legal enforceability of
    exchange." Then would it be entirely appropriate to say a "real
    contract" is not present? Suppose, on the other hand, an ex-
    change transaction in which none of the main characteristics of
    Contract are present except "legal enforceability of exchange."
    Then would it be appropriate to say a "real contract" is present?

B. What, exactly, is meant by "legal enforceability of exchange"
so far as Contract is concerned? Suppose that formerly in this jurisdiction, husbands were immunized from criminal prosecution for rap-
ing their wives. Last year the immunity was removed. Within this
new regime, a husband and wife agree to have sexual relations every
other evening. Two weeks later, on an appointed evening, the wife
refuses to comply with the agreement, freely admitting she is in default by refusing. Now, in turn, add each of the following variants:

1. The husband rushes down to court in an effort to obtain an order
    for specific performance of the agreement. The court refuses to
    enter such an order. (The reason could be such an agreement is
    not a "contract." The reason could be that "equity will not com-

pel specific performance of a personal services contract." The reason could be that "contracts for the performance of sexual services are unenforceable." Other reasons—some contractarian, some noncontractarian in character—could be given in refusing specific performance.)

2. The next day the husband rushes down to court and files an action for damages based on contract breach. The wife replies that the complaint states no legally recognized cause of action. The court holds for the wife. (If the doctrine must be accepted that an action for damages is entailed in every contract breach, then either the agreement is not a contract or the court's decision was erroneous.)

3. As part of the consideration for their agreement, the husband had put title to a residence, formerly owned outright by him, into joint tenancy with his wife. After the wife's default, the husband brings an action seeking rescission of the agreement to regain full title to the residence. The action is brought in the same court that previously had denied, or that the husband believes would have denied, his actions for specific performance and for damages. Again, the wife replies that no cause of action is stated.

Now a couple of questions: (a) If the court decides to rescind the agreement, then is the decision inconsistent with refusals to grant specific performance and to entertain an action for damages based on contract breach? (b) If the court refuses to rescind, then it its refusal inconsistent with the view that the agreement for sexual intercourse was a "contract"?

4. After the wife refuses to comply, the husband forces her to have sexual relations with him over her objections. The next day the wife relates the incident to a friend, who urges her to go to the authorities for the purpose of having the husband prosecuted for rape. The wife declines to do so, on grounds she and her husband had an agreement with respect to which she was in default. The friend, well advised in the law, informs her the agreement could not have been enforced against her by her husband. The wife continues to decline to initiate criminal prosecution, on the grounds previously stated. Does the wife's declination, on the grounds stated, still make sense? If so, then does it make sense to say the agreement was a "contract"?

5. After the wife refuses to comply, the husband forces her to have sexual relations with him over her objections. The next day the

wife goes to the authorities, who initiate criminal rape proceedings against the husband in the same court that previously had denied, or would have denied, the husband's actions for specific performance, damages, and rescission. The husband defends on grounds of the agreement with respect to which the wife was in default.

Now we can imagine a regime in which the husband's defense is held to be without consequence, on grounds such agreements are without any legal effect. Such a holding would be consistent with holdings of no specific performance, no damages, no rescission. But we can also imagine a regime in which the husband's defense is held good against the criminal rape prosecution; and such a holding would not be inconsistent with holdings of no specific performance, no damages, no rescission. If the husband's defense is held good, then was the agreement between husband and wife a "contract"—a "legally enforceable contract"—despite no specific performance, no damages, no rescission?

C. Some theorists urge that the essence of Contract is "legal enforceability of exchange." Their theories, we suspect, serve as the primary arsenal for attacks on proponents of contractarian approaches to family relationships. To these theorists, most of whom are trained in the law, a "contract" is a thing—a thing that tends to be equated with a sophisticated set of components, the presence or absence of which implicates the "legal enforceability" of a "bargained-for exchange."

How, according to these theorists, is a thing determined with finality to be a "contract"? The answer seems simple enough: One takes the thing down to a "court," establishes a matrix of components that would permit the court to review the thing in a particular kind of way, engages in protracted pretrial and trial proceedings, and receives a judgment from the court that the thing is, or is not, legally enforceable as a "contract."

Whole courses in law school are devoted to the various components of things called "contracts": "capacity" of the contracting parties; "offer," "acceptance," and "consideration"; the differences among "recitals," "conditions," and "covenants"; differences among "bilateral," "unilateral," and "quasi" contracts; differences between "oral" and "written" contracts; and a host of interpretative problems relating to "default," "termination," "substantial performance," and "fundamental breach." These components typically are examined one by one by means of reading judicial opinions in which issues are posed and resolved with respect to these components.

Indeed, as a thing-based academic exercise, the course called "Contracts" in law school tends to function as an exercise in legal realism. Here we have a dispute over the piece of paper, or over a provision on the piece of paper. The dispute is brought to a court. Will the court accept plaintiff's version of the piece of paper ("There *is* a contract") or defendant's version of the piece of paper ("There is *no* contract")? Will the court accept plaintiff's version of the provision on the piece of paper ("the contract has been breached"), or will it accept defendant's version ("the contract has been substantially performed")? The question whether the court's decision was "right" is answered by examining the internal characteristics of the court's decision, by comparing the court's decision with decisions previously entered by the same court, or by a shrug of the shoulders. The question, "What will happen in court the next time?" is answered by resort to vague rhetoric about "public policy" or by allusion to the intricacies of fact patterns.

It must come as a surprise to many recent law-school graduates that the vast majority of "contracts" never find their way into a court for authoritative pronouncement of their "legal enforceability." Instead the vast majority of contracts are simply performed to the satisfaction of the parties, with little or no concern paid by them to the "legal enforceability" of their respective performances.

It follows that the "legal enforceability" of nearly every contract—including nearly every intrafamily contract—is only a guess, a prediction. Such observations make for interesting academic exercises, but they do not stand in the way of satisfactory performance of the vast majority of "contracts" in the real world. Can it really be said with a straight face that contracts never involved in authoritative judicial proceedings for "legal enforcement," but rather simply performed, are not—were not—"real contracts"?

* * * * * * *

1. "Most intrafamily contracts are not real contracts, because they are not legally enforceable."

We have endeavored to show the superficiality of these sorts of statements in two interrelated ways. First, to the extent these statements are accurate today, their accuracy does not depend on the presence of a family relationship between the contracting participants, but rather depends on statements about "legal enforceability of bargains" that apply generally to all contractarian arrangements. Second, these sorts of statements are superficial—even unrealistic—because they rest on a narrow, "legal enforceability" definition of "contract" that does not comport with the meaning attributed to "contract" in the real world.

2.   Before the fact: "This upcoming exchange will not be a contract, because the exchange is not legally enforceable."

Statements like this one function as moves in a game—a valuable game, to be sure, but nevertheless a game. Such statements, whenever made, are valuable, because they tend to lead to further rethinking about a proposed transaction, continued communication between the transaction's participants, and further clarification and structuring of the transaction. The game is nonetheless a game, because (1) "legal enforceability of exchange" is only a guess before a legal dispute arises and is authoritatively resolved with respect to the transaction, and (2) considerations of "legal enforceability" enter into only a small number of the vast majority of exchange relationships.

3.   After the fact: "This contract was not a real contract, because it was not legally enforceable."

Statements like these, we believe, are very dangerous for the institution of Contract. In the first place, they belittle the institution, relegating Contract to a small corner within the universe of private transactions within a society. In the second place, they turn Contract into an essentially collectivist not private institution, in which a collective determination—a court's declaration of "legal enforceability"—becomes the institution's defining chracteristic.

LAW AND THE FAMILY: ALTERNATIVE SUPPOSITIONS

Family, so we are told, has historically been an institution whose exchanges have been noncontractarian in concept and character. Government today, so we are told, is withdrawing from the external, collectivist regulation of the family relationships. Contract, so we are told, is a legal institution that is compatible with Family.

We have greeted each of these pronouncements with a measure of skepticism. We have worried over contemporary interpretations of Family's history; but history, in any event, cannot be changed. We have worried over proclamations of government withdrawal from the regulation of the family relationships; but, in the end, we have conceded, for argument, that some withdrawal has taken place in recent times. We have worried over assertions that Contract is incompatible with Family; but we have worried as well over contrary assertions that Contract is coming to the family relationship.

Now we turn our attention to a different level of inquiry. For simplicity's sake, our attention will employ childless Marriage as its focal illustration. Then we begin by supposing (1) Government is indeed withdrawing, across a variety of fronts, from the regulation of the marital relationship; and (2) Marriage, a family relationship in which innumerable exchange transactions take place between its participants, is incompatible with Contract.

What would such a view—such suppositions—produce? We have no way of knowing, either because we have not seen a total withdrawal of government from the regulation of Marriage, or because we have not seen truly noncontractarian Marriage, or both. The following, however, would seem to be the basic alternatives:

1. Government withdraws, and the institution of Marriage continues as though nothing had happened.

The notion underlying this alternative is that Marriage is a "natural institution" of humankind that performs a range of essential societal functions regardless of the character of government regulation of the institution.

The notion draws some support from the remarkable resemblance that "Marriage" under one government bears to "Marriage" under another across the world today. If true, the notion suggests that true anarchy is not a possibility; it also suggests that, except at the margins, collectivist regulation of Marriage is inconsequential.

However, we doubt very many would be willing to press for the withdrawal of government regulation on the bet such withdrawal would be without consequence. Anthropologists and cultural relativists dispute the notion of Marriage as a natural, "genetically predestined" institution. Minor manifestations of governmental withdrawal from Marriage regulation—such as the movement from "fault-based" to "no-fault" divorce, or toward increased and formal tolerance of casual living-together and sexual relationships—have been perceived by many to have had a profound effect on the stability of the institution. Advances in birth technologies and work-saving equipment, and societal rethinking of the role of women, would seem to cast grave doubt on the idea that Marriage could survive if government withdrew completely from its regulation.

2. Government withdraws, as a result of which the institution of Marriage is transformed into a relationship whose sole basis is "romantic love."

Without getting involved in the definition of "romantic love," the notion underlying this alternative is that Marriage—rather, particular marriages—ought to last only as long as the participants desire it to last. The "romantic love" concept of Marriage—which became an ideal sometime in the western civilization's nineteenth century and has stuck around ever since—has distinct anarchical overtones.[20]

This notion finds support today along a variety of fronts. Nearly everyone has heard the strain that "unhappy marriages are worse than divorce," that "loveless marriage is empty-shell marriage," that the unattainability of romantic-love idealism is what ruins marriages, and so forth. In the law, the trend toward "irreconcilable differences" divorce can be understood as a partial concession to the "romantic love" ideal; the same understanding may explain a perceived increase, and formalized toleration, of "unmarried cohabitation" as a preferred relationship to the "obligations of legal marriage."

The difficulty with this alternative is not so much in understanding how it would operate, but rather in understanding how its rigorous implementation, without either government regulation or Contract, would lead to anything short of no marriage at all. "Romantic love" takes many forms; its existence and longevity are highly idiosyncratic from relationship to relationship; its qualities would not seem terribly essential for society's perpetuation, at least without resort to speculative indirect effects derived from its presence.

Thus it seems unlikely that anything like an *institution* of Marriage would continue to exist solely on the basis of the "romantic love"

20. Indeed, a major paean to the "romantic love" ideal comes from the pen of Frederick Engels. See Frederick Engels, "The Origin of the Family, Private Property, and the State," in Alice S. Rossi, ed., *The Feminist Papers* (New York: Bantam Books, 1974).

ideal. The more likely result of government's withdrawal of regulation—regulation that would enforce Marriage after "romantic love" had departed one or more of its participants—would be that Marriage would become a vestigial organ in society, and would then disappear.

3. Government withdraws and the institution of Marriage is transformed into anarchy, after which government returns to impose collectivist regulation upon the institution.

The notion underlying this alternative is that Marriage, though not a natural human institution, is important or essential to a society's perpetuation.

This alternative draws some support from history. In 1792, in the midst of the French Revolution, divorce was made easy to obtain in France, and six years later divorces outnumbered marriages in Paris; then, by 1816, the pendulum had swung so dramatically that divorce was outlawed in France. Similar phenomena have been observed in marriage regulation in the Soviet Union and the People's Republic of China, following their early and dramatic revisions of Marriage. Indeed, historical studies of governmental regulation of Marriage tend to support an idea of "progress" that is more pendulumlike—between relative extremes of regulation and nonregulation—than constantly toward deregulation.

However, there is room to doubt that a future government, having once withdrawn from Marriage regulation, would choose to reinstate that institution in anything like its traditional form in order to reestablish control over the societal functions that the institution had previously performed. Recent technological advances (presaged in Huxley's *Brave New World*)—not to mention efficient economic ordering in the "post-Industrial Age"[21]—certainly invite governments to choose something other than "traditional Marriage" as the institution for performance of those functions.

We may assume that, as an institution, Marriage has been serving valuable societal functions during the untold centuries of its existence, almost wherever human society may be found. The accuracy of this assumption today probably can be tested only by complete government withdrawal from Marriage regulation. Of the three postwith-

---

21. Alvin Toffler, *Future Shock* (New York: Bantam Books, 1971), especially chapter 11, "The Fractured Family."

drawal alternatives we have identified, the third seems to be the most realistic. And if complete governmental withdrawal today would likely result in different and more extensive forms of government regulation in the near future, then individualists, at least, have substantial cause for concern.

Our original suppositions, however, have foreclosed a fourth alternative. That alternative, of course, is the replacement of government regulation with Contract regulation in the marriage relationship. We have indicated that nothing stands in the way of this alternative, save perhaps two matters: (1) The supposition that Marriage—and the myriad exchange transactions within Marriage—is compatible with Contract; and (2) the insistence on "legal enforceability of bargain" as the *sine qua non* of Contract.

The first of these two matters seems to rest upon the second. We probably say, "Marriage is incompatible with Contract," because we are thinking about the "legal enforceability" side of Contract. Our thinking goes something like this:

> We can imagine marriage run according to the principles of Contract. Such a regime would entail spouses spending most of their time in courtroom litigation, seeking to enforce their interpretations of bargains across a variety of fronts—sexual relations, nights out with the boys, the doing or not doing of housework, and on down an endless list—against each other. Such a regime is unseemly both for Marriage (which by its nature requires give and take between spouses, attention paid to circumstances that change from day to day, and so forth) and for Contract (the essence of which is legal enforceability of bargain). Therefore, Marriage must be—must be deemed—incompatible with Contract.

Our purpose here is not to return the reader to our previous critique of "legal enforceability as the *sine qua non* of Contract." Rather, we now wish to expose the supposition that "Marriage is incompatible with Contract" for what it is: only a supposition, the presence of which has more to do with mind-set than with law or logic.

First, we observe that many relationships other than Marriage appear to require similar give and take among participants, and attention to day-to-day changes in circumstances. Business partners require such ingredients for their relationship; they typically make allowances for partners' delays, temporary reductions in quality of performance, "off days," and personality quirks. The same ingredients are prerequisites in most long-term employer-employee relationships. Mortgagees typically do not initiate foreclosure proceedings whenever a mortgagor's payment is six days late in arriving.

Grounds for "contract breach" assertions may well be present in these situations. Yet continuance of the relationship generally is preferred to the quest for legal enforcement—because human frailties are accepted; because conflict habituation destroys business reputations; because the relationship's members continue to feel they have a "good deal," all things considered; because legal enforcement proceedings are far more expensive than they are worth; because there is fear that explicit conflict will undermine the core functions of the relationship; and so forth. Yet these sorts of relationships still continue to be characterized as "contractual" in character, not only by their participants but also by the legal system.

Second, within Marriage (and within most other long-term relationships) there are many opportunities for contractlike adjustments between the participants within the boundaries of the relationship. Husband and wife have an "agreement" to have sexual relations three times a week; husband becomes dissatisfied with the burdens of this agreement and takes to working late at the office, putting on weight, forgoing showers, whatever; as a result the "agreement" is adjusted, with wife forbearing sexual relations but compensating for the forbearance by nagging, preparing less imaginative meals, getting a job, going on shopping sprees, whatever. Nothing save supposition stands in the way of treating these adjustments as contractarian in character, in the manner in which partners, employers and employees, mortgagors and mortgagees might, when asked, characterize similar adjustments in their relationships.

Third, the presence of this sort of give and take among participants (and attention to day-to-day changes in circumstances) has more to do with the absence of government regulation than it has to do with the absence of Contract. We could imagine a society in which Contract was completely absent, in which government determined and enforced entitlements among partners, employers and employees, mortgagors and mortgagees, parents and children, and spouses in a highly detailed, collectivist fashion. A government's failure to adopt such a strategy, combined with widespread nonenforcement of relationship details, could be taken to imply a tolerance of anarchy within such relationships.

A more cogent view, however, would be that Contract is intended to encourage just such attention to changes in circumstances and adjustment within these important relationships. This view is strengthened when we recognize that such relationship details may well be legally enforceable, but made very expensive to enforce, by virtue of a government's legal system.

Beyond these observations, the notion today that Marriage—for that matter, all the Family relationships—are incompatible with Contract has some very dangerous side effects. The notion entails the mind-set that the only way to rectify a less than completely desirable relationship is to terminate that relationship. Acceptance of such a mind-set, when coupled with present trends toward government deregulation of the family relationships, would seem necessarily to lead to the perception, on the part of family members, that complete abandonment of the relationship is the only alternative to its unsatisfactory continuance.

If a spouse with such a mind-set is dissatisfied with marriage, his or her alternative is an "easy" divorce, made available by relaxation of divorce laws. If a child or parent with such a mind-set is disenchanted with an unsatisfactory home situation, his or her alternative is to run away from it, or otherwise to obtain a premature emancipation. The costs of such a mind-set would be—are—enormous, both to society and to the participation in such relationships.

The recognition of "freedom of contract" for the family relationships would create the perception of an intermediate ground—and a wide and healthy range of strategies—between these two largely undesirable alternatives. On balance, we believe recognition of "freedom of contract" for the family relationships—whether or not accompanied by the development of mechanisms for "legal enforcement of bargained-for exchange"—would be preferable to a return to collectivist regulation for these relationships akin to that understood to be in effect two or three decades ago.

* * * * * * *

Despite our skepticism, we applaud those who advocate "minimum state plus freedom of contract" for the family relationships. And we go a little farther. We call for revisions in the mind-set that Contract is to be equated with "legal enforceability of bargained-for exchange."

We call, in short, for the recognition that Contract not only is compatible with Family but is also compatible with relationships everywhere in which considerations of legal enforceability of exchange are of secondary importance when compared with the enhancement of the integrity of those relationships and the enhancement of the dignity of the individual participants.

9

THE CHANGING CONCEPT OF CHILD ABUSE AND ITS IMPACT ON THE INTEGRITY OF FAMILY LIFE

John M. Johnson

During the brief span of twenty-five years in the United States, the concept of child abuse has changed dramatically. It has gone from an obscure and hotly contested topic found in arcane medical journals to a position of routine mass-media publicity. Twenty-five years ago most medical doctors, including pediatricians, resisted the legitimacy of the child abuse concept. Today it is widely accepted and discussed by all professionals. It is widely discussed among the citizens as well, and even small schoolchildren talk about child abuse or neglect. Occasionally these children initiate reports to school or police officials, alleging injuries to themselves or others. Clearly these are indices of a massive social change that has occurred over a relatively short period of time.

The social changes concerning child abuse and neglect are intertwined with a "statistical explosion" of officially recognized and officially documented cases. This dramatic increase has led popular and scientific writers to assert a social problem of "epidemic" proportions. The first national study of the incidence of child abuse in the United States was done in 1962 by the American Humane Association. This study documented, for the first eleven months of 1962, a total of 662 cases that were serious enough to warrant some kind of court proceedings. We can thus, by extrapolation, place the 1962 incidence of child abuse at about 720 cases.[1]

The year 1963 marks the beginning of legislative initiative in the field of child abuse. The next decade saw much legislative, governmental, and programmatic action, with the establishment, at the end of the year, of the National Center on Child Abuse and Neglect. Their official statistics for 1973 show an incidence of about 60,000 officially recorded cases of child abuse, a national increase of over 8,300 percent in about ten years. Two years later they produced a national incidence of about 80,000 cases. And the 1976 study by the Department of Health, Education and Welfare put the annual rate at about a million new cases of child abuse and neglect. At the beginning of the 1980s in the United States, estimates of our incidence rate (number of new cases per year) for child abuse and neglect vary between 1 million to 4.5 million cases, and estimates of the prevalence (number of cases at any one time) are commonly two or three times that number. This is the "new math" of family violence in the United States.

Child maltreatment, now the more general term, includes child battering, abuse, neglect, failure to thrive, malnutrition, emotional abuse or neglect, sexual abuses, and a range of other acts or conditions. Child maltreatment is also today a large social movement that includes the activities of many groups: officials, professionals, media personalities, and private citizens. Partisans who promote the causes of the child maltreatment movement want us to think that the officially produced statistics on incidence and prevalence are objective, empirical facts. They wish us to think that a determination of child maltreatment is a scientific assessment made by a trained professional. They wish us to think that assessments of child maltreatment are done without regard to the assessor's values, and that the official statistics are collected without regard for political definitions or realities. But these are the rhetorical promotions of those with partisan interests in this area, those who wish to enlist our support for the political reality they have constructed since the early 1960s. None of these rhetorical claims can be supported by the facts.

Child maltreatment is not an unproblematic, empirical fact. It is a political definition of state legislatures. State officials are the ones mandated by law to respond to and bureaucratically process the child

1. Vincent de Francis, "Parents Who Abuse Children," *PTA Magazine* 58 (Nov. 1963): 16–18.

maltreatment claims brought to their attention. They are the ones who take the immediate, practical action in specific cases. They do so on the basis of their professional, bureaucratic, and personal values, as mitigated by situational constraints and resource practicalities. The national incidence and prevalence statistics on child maltreatment do not make any intelligible sense, because they combine incomparable state political definitions and practical decisions by bureaucratic officials at the local level. To understand the proper context of the present situation, it is important to gain a historical perspective on how children have been treated over the centuries. Such a historical perspective not only produces a sense of the relativity of judgments concerning child maltreatment but—and this is more important—provides a grasp of the essentially political and normative nature of a phenomenon so commonly presented as something else. The beating of children is an old phenomenon, but child maltreatment as a social movement that has mapped out new mandates for state authority and intervention is a relatively new phenomenon.

THE ORIGINS OF CHILDHOOD

Today it is taken for granted that "childhood" is a distinct, and even special, state of life. While the centuries have witnessed relatively little change in the manner by which infants and small children have biologically and physically grown, the social and cultural meanings associated with and imputed to "childhood" have changed greatly over time. For about 90 percent of all human history for which there are some records, societies have condoned and practiced infanticide, the intentional killing of infants. Infanticide was practiced for reasons of birth control, religious ceremony, or social policy. The earliest historical records of infanticide date to 7,000 B.C. in Jericho.[2] Infanticide was practiced for well over 8,000 years, and began to disappear only during the Middle Ages. In ancient Sparta, a public official examined newborns to attest to their health and worthiness to draw upon limited societal resources. The unworthy were thrown into the "Valley of Infants." Roman law forbade the raising of deformed infants. Even in later centuries, when the Christian churches redefined and prohibited infanticide, it was practiced clandestinely, and deaths were attributed to "over-laying," or accidental suffocation by the mother.[3]

---

2. Lloyd de Mause, ed., *The History of Childhood* (New York: Psychohistory Press, 1974).
3. M. Harris, "Why Men Dominate Women," *New York Times Magazine*, 13 Nov. 1977, pp. 46ff.

Recent laws prohibiting infanticide can be found as late as 1843 in Germany, 1870 in Russia, and 1875 in India. Today the practice is largely clandestine and unofficial.

After the Middle Ages, abandonment of infants emerged as a common practice in Western cultures. Harris estimates that by 1820 in France about 40,000 infants per year were being legally abandoned by their parents.[4] In the United States the New York Foundling Asylum was established in 1869 to save abandoned infants, who numbered about 1,400 in 1873.[5]

The growth of Christianity is associated with the emergence and development of many forms of child "discipline." The Puritan concept held that newborns, like adults, were born into a state of sin and depravity; hence strict measures were needed to acquaint the young with the ways of God.[6] Physical punishment, restraint, bodily mutilations, whippings, beatings, and the use of many instruments to bring these about were considered "normal" for members of Western cultures between the 1700s and 1900s. Many of these practices and ideologies thrive today. Radbill observes, "It was always taken for granted that parents and guardians had every right to treat their children as they saw fit."[7] This was additionally emphasized by the following thumb rule from American common law:

> If one beats a child until it bleeds, then it will remember the words of its master. But if one beats it to death, then the law applies.[8]

The fundamental ambiguities of legal applications are illustrated by one of the most famous child maltreatment cases in history. In 1875 the American Society for the Prevention of Cruelty to *Animals* (ASPCA) in New York City was asked to intervene for the purpose of protecting Mary Ellen, a nine-year-old girl who had been neglected, beaten, and even slashed with scissors by her foster parents. Earlier efforts to intervene had failed, because the parental rights to child discipline had been heretofore considered absolute by the law. So the ASPCA was asked to intervene to protect Mary Ellen on the argument that she was a member of the animal kingdom, and thus the legitimate recipient of laws already on the books to protect animals. The case

4. Ibid., p. 120.
5. Samuel X. Radbill, "A History of Child Abuse and Infanticide," in R. Helfer and C. Kempe, eds., *The Battered Child* (Chicago: University of Chicago Press, 1968), p. 10.
6. Ibid., p. 12.
7. Ibid., p. 4.
8. Ibid.

received wide media publicity, and paved the way for the founding of the Society for the Prevention of Cruelty to Children (SPCC) in 1876. In the following years, the SPCC emerged as one important element of the growing social movement to prohibit child labor; their efforts were thus directed more to the abuses by employers of children, and only rarely did they concern themselves with the abuses of natural parents. There would have been relatively little public sentiment for the latter at the time. There were 161 local chapters of the SPCC by the turn of the century. These were later consolidated into the Children's Division of the American Humane Association.

THE MODERN DISCOVERY OF CHILD ABUSE

Historical evidence presents a long record of child victimization. The first medical or scientific studies of parental "abuse," however, can be dated from the 1888 article on acute periosteal swelling by Dr. S. West.[9] Later there was the 1946 study by Dr. John Caffey, analyzing the relationship between long bone fractures and subdural hematoma, the hemorrhaging that follows a head injury.[10] These early studies appeared to produce little publicity or concern.

Two medical studies done during the 1950s gained greater recognition.[11] Both asserted, in effect, that certain patterns of traumatic childhood injuries were caused by parental irresponsibility, neglect, indifference, or immaturity. This was an important departure for the medical profession, which, at an earlier time, had interpreted similar injuries as the result of "unspecified" causes.

A watershed point occurred with the 1962 publication of an article, "The Battered Child Syndrome," by C. Henry Kempe and his colleagues at the University of Colorado Medical School.[12] This research, published in a most prestigious and respected medical journal, was accompanied by an official editorial asserting the seriousness of this new medical problem. The characteristic features of the syndrome

9. T. Solomon, "History and Demography of Child Abuse," *Pediatrics* 51 (1963): 773–76.

10. John Caffey, "Multiple Fractures in the Long Bones of Infants Suffering from Chronic Subdural Hematoma," *American Journal of Roentgenology* 56 (Aug. 1946):163–73.

11. Frederick N. Silverman, "Roentgen Manifestations of Unrecognized Skeletal Trauma in Infants," *American Journal of Roentgenology* 69 (March 1953):413–26; Paul V. Wooley and W. A. Evans, Jr., "Significance of Skeletal Lesions in Infants Resembling Those of Traumatic Origin," *Journal of the American Medical Association* 158 (June 1955):539–43.

12. C. Henry Kempe, et al., "The Battered Child Syndrome," *Journal of the American Medical Association* 181 (July 1962):17–24.

included traumatic injuries to the head and long bones, commonly done to children under three years of age by parents who had themselves been beaten or abused as children. These parents commonly denied the mistreatment of their own children. The publication of this research article was an important step in legitimizing this problem as an appropriate area of medical intervention.[13] An interesting question is why the medical profession's policy and involvement occurred at this time rather than an earlier one. Pfohl[14] argues that the entrepreneurial efforts of the occupational group of pediatric radiologists were important elements of the social movement at this early stage.

EARLY LEGISLATION

One critical social movement organization is the American Humane Association. The AHA has been active in all phases of the child maltreatment movement from the very beginning. They have conducted research, drawn up early "model legislation" for all governmental levels, published and publicized research and program information, provided "expert witnesses" to state legislatures contemplating legislative initiatives, and served important gatekeeping and liaison functions among and between all the professions through their conferences, workshops, and other communications. Most of these activities occurred under the 24-year leadership of Vincent de Francis, a key figure in the child maltreatment movement. He was one of the participants in an important meeting that occurred in January 1962 in Washington, D.C., at the Department of Health, Education and Welfare (HEW). The purpose of this meeting was to begin exploring the possibility of federal and/or state legislation on child abuse. Included in this meeting were Children's Bureau and HEW officials, members of the pediatric section of the American Medical Association, de Francis of the American Humane Association, and some private parties.[15] The main thrust of this meeting was to encourage legislative initiative to protect medical doctors from potential legal action in cases where they made reports of child maltreatment.

13. See Stephen J. Pfohl, "The 'Discovery' of Child Abuse," *Social Problems* 24 (Feb. 1977):310–23; Peter Conrad and Joseph W. Schneider, *Deviance and Medicalization: From Badness to Sickness* (St. Louis: C. V. Mosby Co., 1980), pp. 161–71.

14. Pfohl, *n.* 13.

15. Knowledge of this meeting was gained from personal talks with Vincent de Francis.

An eventual outcome of the 1962 meeting was a draft of "model legislation," which could be taken back to state legislatures, concerning child abuse reporting, liabilities, mandates, and responsibilities. The year 1963 is an important one for child abuse legislation, as eighteen states proposed and eleven states passed enabling bills on child abuse. During the next two years, thirty-six more states followed, and within the first five years fifty of the U.S. states and territories passed some form of child abuse legislation. This is an impressive social change to occur in such a relatively short period of time. It is interesting to contrast the child abuse legislation with the efforts to pass the Equal Rights Amendment (ERA), which failed to gain the needed two-thirds majority required for a constitutional amendment within a period of *ten years*. The contrast shows that, unlike the hotly contested and disputed ERA, child abuse and neglect are "least common denominator social problems" for large numbers of the American public, involving few conflicts and heated confrontations.[16] They are the kinds of problems everyone can be against. The prevailing definitions and realities of child maltreatment and the appropriate policy response are not contested by the major political parties, ideological positions, major churches, or professional and educational institutions.

As legal phenomena, child abuse and neglect are defined at the *state* level of government and, as with most other state definitions, the statutory concepts and mandates differ greatly from one jurisdiction to another. The early legislation generally mandated the *reporting* by physicians of child abuse or neglect. Many states established penalties for failures to report suspected cases. The new laws at first included few changes to existing statutes concerning delinquency, dependency, neglect, and criminal penalties. Since the early legislative period (1963–65), however, all of the state laws have been changed, modified, or revised on these and many other crucial issues.

THE AMBIGUOUS POLITICAL DEFINITIONS OF ABUSE

By 1965, reporting of child abuse and neglect had been mandated by forty-three of the fifty states.[17] By 1967, forty-nine states had the new

---

16. Jack D. Douglas, *Defining America's Social Problems* (Englewood Cliffs, N.J.: Prentice-Hall, 1974).

17. M. G. Paulsen, "The Legal Framework for Child Protection," *Columbia Law Review* 67 (Jan. 1966):1–49.

laws.[18] As a reasonable assumption, one might think that if something is against the law, and hence the subject of potential legal sanction, the phenomenon in question would be clearly defined. How could officials (or professionals) define, identify, or classify something if the law requiring their identifications did not define it? But this is precisely the case for child abuse and neglect. By 1974, only eighteen of the fifty-three states and U.S. territories specifically defined child abuse and neglect in their statutes.[19] The state laws reflect very little consensus on even the most fundamental terms. The 1975 analysis by Sanford Katz observed the following:

> A large majority of the jurisdictions (45) do not have a statutory definition for the term "neglect" and/or "neglected child." Only eight states define "neglect" . . . and less than half of the jurisdictions (22) have a "neglected child" definition. . . . Twenty-three states use some other definition to refer to a "neglected child," such as "deprived child," "dependent or neglected," or "dependent child."[20]

On common sense grounds, it is easy to understand how a perception of "child neglect" might be intertwined with an observer's personal values, since a judgment of "neglect" implies a concept of a "normal home," which is subject to great ambiguity. A physical child battery, however, is hardly less ambiguous or problematic. Western legal traditions have long assessed legal culpability on the basis of determining the *intention* to commit an act. If it can be determined that an individual was fully and legally capable of intending his or her actions, and did in fact do so on a given occasion, then we properly hold that individual accountable for his or her action. If, by contrast, the individual was not capable of intending the action, whether because of reduced capacity, insanity, or mental illness, he or she is held blameless, even for the same action. If the individual is judged capable of forming intentions, but found by a judicial process not to have done so on a specific occasion, then the individual is held blameless. Examples of the latter may be "accidents," that is, events that may indeed produce harmful consequences, even death, but where the judgment is that the act was not a willful or intentional one. The

18. Vincent de Francis, *Child Abuse Legislation in the 1970s* (Denver: American Humane Association, 1970).
19. Vincent de Francis and C. L. Lucht, *Child Abuse and Legislation in the 1970s,* rev. ed. (Denver: American Humane Association, 1974).
20. Sanford Katz, "Child Neglect Laws in America," *Family Law Quarterly* 9 (Spring 1975):295–331.

determination of the caretakers' intention is not just one of many factors to be considered in making an assessment about child battering; it is *definitive*. It is only possible to distinguish a "child battery" from an "accident" by making an assessment of the caretakers' intention to do the act. As an internal mental state of the individual at the time of engaging in an act, intent is not directly observable by an outsider, and is thus inherently problematic (or uncertain). An added complication is that those who are called in to investigate claims about child abuse are invariably called in after the fact, when direct evidence of the actor's internal mental state is impossible, and indirect evidence often ambiguous, contradictory, or uncertain. For these and many other reasons, then, even the assessments of a physical beating are commonly very problematic ones.

It is easier to formulate and operationalize an abstract definition when one is dealing with a more restricted phenomenon, such as a physical battery. New levels of complexity and ambiguity are introduced when the focus is more broad, as in "child neglect." For neglect, again, the issues surrounding definition are of primary importance and logically take precedence over epidemiological or etiological questions. Nevertheless, there is no agreement about the parameters of child neglect. In some respects the definition of neglect is of greater significance than that of battering or abuse, since informed "guesstimates" place the ratio of neglect to abuse cases from three-to-one[21] to ten-to-one.[22] Guesstimates such as these commonly sidestep the logically and empirically prior question of definition by taking as an instance of neglect anything so defined by officials at the local levels, by whatever criteria they may have used.

Those who focus on neglect emphasize either the condition(s) of the parent(s), such as alcoholism, drug abuse, or psychological problems, or some specific harm to the children, such as an identifiable physical or psychological harm. To be neglectful means that the parent has failed in some manner to exercise responsibility over those means within their control. This latter idea about control introduces another level of discretionary judgment into an already complex equation. What about the family that is trying conscientiously and sincerely to provide the basic necessities, but is still unable to do so

21. Saad Z. Nagi, *Child Maltreatment in the United States* (New York: Columbia University Press, 1977).
22. V. Cain, "Concern for Children in Placement," *Analysis of Child Abuse and Neglect* (Washington, D.C.: National Center on Child Abuse and Neglect, 1977).

because of their present condition of poverty, illness, or unemployment? To what extent is their poverty or employment status "within their control"? How does one judge "conscientious" or "sincere" in such a situation? Officials and professionals who routinely make such assessments play an important "gatekeeping" role in the screening of potential child neglect cases.[23] Many studies now show that various kinds of racial, ethnic, social class, and occupational biases creep into such assessments, with the general finding being that official gatekeepers are more likely to "normalize" those persons, behaviors, and situations seen as close to their own lives or circumstances, but are more likely to officially label and bureaucratically process those experienced as more remote from them.[24] This is one of the important factors accounting for the usual overrepresentation of poor and minority persons in official caseloads.[25]

Few states have clear definitions, as we have seen. And there is certainly no agreement between states on definitions. Despite this, however, there have been several important changes to the child abuse and neglect laws since the 1963–65 period of legislative initiative. These changes have occurred in all states. By the 1980s, states have changed, modified, or revised their child abuse and neglect laws two or three times in most cases. One important change concerns the progressive expansion of the mandate to report suspected cases of abuse or neglect. Whereas the early laws commonly required only physicians to report, most laws today require many other professionals as well—any physician (including interns and residents), surgeon, dentist, osteopath, chiropractor, podiatrist, nurse, druggist, pharmacist, laboratory technician, acupuncturist, schoolteacher or school administrator, social worker, and/or "any other person." Another important change involves the increase in the penalties for not reporting. Granting immunity from criminal or civil liability for those who report suspected cases of abuse or neglect is another critical change, now found in all of the state laws. Also, granting doctors and other professionals waivers from the legal or ethical restrictions against revealing confidential communications represents another way by which the law

---

23. Richard J. Gelles, *Family Violence* (Beverly Hills, Calif.: Sage Publications, 1979).

24. See Jeanne M. Giovannoni and Rosina M. Becerra, *Defining Child Abuse* (New York: Free Press, 1979); Gelles, *n.* 22; Alfred Kadushin and John A. Martin, *Child Abuse* (New York: Columbia University Press, 1981).

25. Leroy Pelton, "Child Abuse and Neglect: The Myth of Classlessness," *American Journal of Orthopsychiatry* 48 (Oct. 1978):608–16.

has been changed to encourage reporting to and processing by official, bureaucratic agencies. There have been some other legal changes, too, including revisions of the evidentiary criteria to be used in court cases involving abuse or neglect. These changes have for the most part enhanced and facilitated organizational goals rather than individual or family rights.

Providing incentives as well as sanctions to report abuse and neglect cases, while at the same time ignoring critical matters of defining what it is that is to be reported, has produced many ironic results at local and state levels. After the passage of new laws at the state level, it is common for local and state agencies to experience an initial short-term rate increase of several hundred, even several thousand, percent.[26] This has been observed for crime rates as well, and on many occasions those cities or states with the highest crime rates are those in the process of rationalizing their reporting procedures, or in the process of documenting some "need" for federal or state financial assistance. For child maltreatment, such short-term increases often overwhelm the local bureaucratic resources for responding to or investigating new reports. Such a situation greatly increases the chances of making a "Type II error," that is, failing to diagnose child abuse or neglect when it is in fact present.[27] In given local situations, this may mean that the efforts to stop child maltreatment through enhanced reporting efforts may cause deleterious consequences that may have been otherwise avoided. The bureaucratic welfare state produces many such ironies.

Child maltreatment is not some symptomatic feature of American society, or even of the 1960s and 1970s, but *allegations* of mass maltreatment arose during those two decades. Child maltreatment is thus more usefully seen as a social movement, one that has achieved success at several levels. As such, the current movement is a recent manifestation of the earlier "child saving" movement,[28] a turn-of-the-century moral crusade that asserted the symbolic dominance of middle-class, Christian values. Moral crusades are an indisputable tradition in American history.

The child maltreatment social movement achieved many successes at various state and local levels, as we have seen. The greatest suc-

26. Nagi, *n.* 21.

27. A "Type I Error" would be the labeling and processing of a caretaker as a child abuser who has not in fact abused a child.

28. Anthony M. Platt, *The Child Savers* (Chicago: University of Chicago Press, 1969).

cess, however, and the greatest impetus for the movement, came with the 1974 passage of federal legislation: the Child Abuse Prevention and Treatment Act, also informally known as the "Mondale Bill" after its primary sponsor. This federal law (P.L. 93-247) established a National Center on Child Abuse and Neglect, located within the Department of Health, Education and Welfare. The official mandates of the National Center included changes to conduct research on the causes, incidence, and prevalence of child abuse and neglect, and also to compile and publish a summary of pertinent knowledge in this field.[29] It is additionally important to understand that this bill provided $85 million of resources for the child maltreatment movement over a four-year period. This money was spent for research, publication, and program initiative. The latter typically occurred under the auspices of a "demonstration project," whereby the federal government would provide the "seed money" to get a program started and operational for a specified period, usually two to three years, on the theory that once program effectiveness had been established, local funding sources would then step in to continue the program. This $85 million provided a major resource leading to the institutionalization of the child maltreatment social movement. New programs dealing with child maltreatment were started in hospitals,[30] clinics,[31] volunteer programs,[32] day care centers,[33] and entire communities.[34] Programs such as these greatly enhanced local officials' abilities to gain contact with heretofore undefined abuse or neglect cases, through the mechanisms the practitioners term "case finding." And they also greatly enhanced the gatekeeping role of decision makers in local agencies.

29. Ellen Hoffman, "Policy and Politics: The Child Abuse Prevention and Treatment Act," in Richard Bourne and Eli H. Newberger, eds., *Critical Perspectives on Child Abuse* (Lexington, Mass.: Lexington Books, 1979), pp. 157–70.

30. A. Wolkenstein, "Hospital Acts on Child Abuse," *Journal of the American Hospital Association* 49 (March 1975):103–6.

31. R. Polakow and D. Peabody, "Behavioral Treatment of Child Abuse," *International Journal of Offender Therapy and Comparative Criminology* 19 (1975):100–108.

32. C. Hinton and J. Sterling, "Volunteers Serve as an Adjunct to Treatment for Child-Abusing Families," *Hospital and Community Psychiatry* 26 (March 1975):136–37.

33. Jacobus Ten Broeck, "The Extended Family Center," *Children Today* 3 (April 1974): 2–6.

34. H. Lovens and J. Rako, "A Community Approach to the Prevention of Child Abuse," *Child Welfare* 54 (Feb. 1975):83–87.

AGENCY SCREENING AND CASE FINDING

A somewhat naive view about child abuse and its relationship to community agencies assumes that what is called child abuse or neglect is relatively straightforward and unproblematic. Abuse and neglect are seen to define specific acts, with "abusive" and "neglectful" being considered characteristics of specific individuals who engage in them. Community agencies are assumed to adopt a passive or reactive response to abusive or neglectful acts that precede their interventions in space and time. Community agencies are thought to represent a functional response to the problem, tending to control it.

The available evidence fails to support any of the above assumptions. The formal definitions of abuse and neglect are very ambiguous and problematic. There is very little agreement on the meanings of maltreatment even among the professionals who intervene in such cases. An early study of Viano[35] found dissimilar attitudes and perceptions among the professionals involved. More recently, a very thorough research project found significant differences in the perceptions of child abuse and neglect between the four major occupational groups involved in the investigation, identification, and treatment of maltreatment cases: police, social workers, lawyers, and pediatricians.[36] Some of these differences appeared to be related to the different occupational tasks the professionals commonly performed. This understanding is what led Gelles to propose that "the occupational and organizational mandate of a community agency determines how active it will be in identifying cases of child abuse, how likely the employees of the agency are to label particular cases abuse, and the types of cases which are labeled abuse."[37]

The various occupational groups that find themselves in a situation of receiving, investigating, or otherwise processing child maltreatment cases develop an "occupational ideology" about those cases. This ideology includes a set of perceptions, thoughts, feelings, values, and work experiences that become taken for granted by those in

35. Emilio Viano, "Attitudes Toward Child Abuse Among American Professionals." (Paper presented at the first meeting of the International Society for Research on Aggression, Toronto, Canada, 1974).

36. Giovannoni and Becerra, *n.* 24.

37. Gelles, *n.* 23, p. 61.

a given work setting. The traditional ideology of social workers tends to be supportive and humanitarian, for example, whereas police and prosecutors tend to be more punitive and legalistic in their orientation.[38] Whatever the abstract or ideological values, however, virtually all child abuse screening occurs in some kind of *organizational context*. This commonly involves sets of formal and informal rules that are routinely used to organize work tasks, recipe knowledge of "the way we do things around here," and limited resources to pursue one course of action over another. Such considerations form a practical work context for all decisions, often determining what gets done in specific instances, even independently of other professional or occupational values. Child protective service professionals may investigate a claim of child neglect and determine that the removal of the child is warranted, for example. But perhaps, at that moment, there are no resources available to effect such a decision (such as emergency or regular foster homes). In such a situation, the placement of the child is highly unlikely, unless the case involves an immediate threat to life, which is rare, or the potential for media publicity.

Child maltreatment investigations in public agencies are always made within a context of limited time and resources. Rare exceptions to this involve those "child abuse horror stories" that receive disproportionate mass media publicity.[39] These involve dramatic injuries or circumstances. One example originated from Cleveland, Tennessee, where a father forced his three-year-old daughter to remain awake and walking for three days. When she asked for water, he forced Tabasco sauce down her throat and stomped on her feet. She died of exhaustion. Another case, out of Long Beach, California, involved the discovery of a seven-year-old girl who had been tied to a chair in her room for her entire life. She had been forced to sleep in her own feces; when found, she weighed only 35 pounds and was unable to talk. A third case, from Los Angeles, involved an infant found to have more than 600 cigarette burns over her body. These are the dramatic, horrible child abuse cases. When they occur, there is usually an instantaneous consensus about what should be done to save the child from immediate danger. But these dramatic cases are statisti-

---

38. The research of Giovannoni and Becerra, *n.* 24, suggests that the traditional differences between the more supportive versus the more punitive professions are dissipating.

39. John M. Johnson, "Mass Media Reports and Deviance" (Paper presented at the annual meeting of the Society for the Study of Social Problems, San Francisco, 1982).

cally very rare, and their unrepresentative publication via the mass media presents a distorted picture of the more routinely encountered cases.

The usual child maltreatment cases routinely encountered in the everyday operations of official agencies tend to involve ambiguities, uncertainties, conflicting accounts about what occurred (or why), nonserious injuries, and living conditions that render judgments cloudy. For these kinds of cases, which clearly constitute the overwhelming statistical majority as well as the dominant work tasks of those confronted with them, there is much room for discretion. Police, emergency room physicians, child protective services' social workers, public health nurses, and others who receive allegation of abuse or neglect essentially serve as "gatekeepers," determining which cases will be screened in or out of the system. At all levels the discretion is great, and decisions are essentially free of review. Officials who make these determinations do so on the bases of their occupational ideology, personal values, and immediate practical situation within the bureaucratic organization. In a situation such as this, an uncanny correspondence exists between the official assessments and the resources available at that moment to "do something."

The gatekeeping functions of local agency decisions are illustrated by the concept of "case finding." This refers to the entrepreneurial initiative exercised by officials to recruit new cases, which would not otherwise be there, into the child protective services' caseloads. Case finding is a concept well known to social work professionals. References to the practice can be found throughout the academic and professional literature. Large numbers of social workers and other health services workers openly advocate the discovery and recruitment of new cases through case finding, on the theory that this is a way to bring needed services to those who either would not know to ask about them or who might be mistaken about whether such interventions would serve their best interests. The very concept and practice of case finding, however, disproves the naive view that officials only passively respond to reports that predate their interventions.

One needs hardly to emphasize that large numbers of citizens do not share the naive view about official interventions in child maltreatment cases. Many individuals and families feel a great sense of injustice concerning the official investigations or interventions in their lives. Such feelings have been common in many minority communities for decades now. In such communities a feeling of discrimination and injustice has persisted for years. The available research tends to support this feeling, showing that official decision-making processes recruit disproportionate numbers of poor and minority families into their caseloads. With respect to decisions on specific cases, perhaps there have always been a few instances of officials who make "Type I errors," that is, who incorrectly label someone a child abuser. But in recent years these numbers have grown to the point where aggrieved parties have organized for counteraction. In Phoenix, Arizona, for example, there is a group known as PAPS, or Parents Against Protective Services. The founders of this group claim a membership of about 2,200 parents who have been angered by the treatment they have received at the hands of child protective services. The very existence of such organizations carries important implications. It shows that the steadily increasing power of the state to intervene in family life has reached such a point that organized opposition to it has developed. It also indicates that the state interventions now extend considerably beyond the traditional target groups for official social control: the poor and certain ethnic communities.

THE IMPACT OF THE CHILD MALTREATMENT MOVEMENT ON THE INTEGRITY OF FAMILY LIFE

All persons familiar with the current facts on child abuse and neglect express agreement on this important point: Existing definitions are imprecise and ambiguous, and there is no consensus about their meanings. What remains hotly disputed, however, is whether this state of affairs represents a desirable or undesirable situation. Those who see advantages to the open-ended nature of the definitions, for example, argue that this permits the flexibility needed to "individualize" decision making in specific cases. A respected scholar in the field of family law, Harry Krause, argues as follows:

> Due to the varied nature of the situations to be covered, the neglect and dependency laws are rarely specific. A legal finding of neglect typically is a composite of many factors and requires a highly individualized judgment on all of the circumstances of each specific case. Statutes *need* to be flexible to provide the necessary broad discretion to the courts.[40]

Advocates of the "open definition" consider it advantageous because decision makers can be sensitive to contextual, local, and emer-

---

40. Harry D. Krause, *Family Law in a Nutshell* (St. Paul, Minn.: West Publishing Co., 1977), pp. 236–37.

gent features of the situation. There is an implicit assumption here, however, that officials not only act in good faith, but with the "best interests" of the community foremost in mind at all times. At this stage in our history, such claims are more usefully seen as just ignorant—or as self-interested claims by those who wish to extend the powers and authorities of the welfare state, in what they must presume to be their own best interests.

Opponents of "open definitions" are less sanguine about official good faith and judicial wisdom. They tend to emphasize the potential for injustice that resides in statutory ambiguity and official discretion. Michael Wald, who drafted the child protective model legislation promoted by the American Bar Association, is one who advocates such a stance:

> Most state statutes define neglect in broad, vague language, which would seem to allow virtually unlimited intervention. . . . The definitions of neglect offered by legal scholars are equally broad. . . . The absence of precise standards for state intervention is said to be a necessity, even a virtue. . . . It is both possible and desirable to define neglect in more specific terms and with reference to the types of damage that justify intervention. . . . Vague laws increase the likelihood that decisions to intervene will be made in situations where the child will be harmed by intervention. Because the statutes do not reflect a considered analysis of what types of harm justify the risk of intervention, decision making is left to the ad hoc analysis of social workers and judges. . . . Their decisions often reflect personal values about children which are not supported by scientific evidence and which result in removing children from environments in which they are doing adequately. Only through carefully drawn statutes, drafted in terms of specific harms to the child, can we limit the possibility of intervention in situations where it would do more harm than good.[41]

These continuing disputes about definitions and the proper authority for state intervention have important consequences. They also provide evidence of the critical impact of the child maltreatment movement on American family life. Never before in history has the power of the state expanded so rapidly into the domain of the family. Never before have so many of the traditional rights and obligations of family life eroded so rapidly. Never before have so many families been caught up in the net of official investigation and case processing; our best

---

41. Michael Wald, "State Intervention on Behalf of 'Neglected' Children: A Search for Realistic Standards," *Stanford Law Review* 27 (April 1975):985–1040.

estimates today tell us that about 1 million U.S. families receive an official investigation that results in a *substantiated* claim of abuse or neglect *each year*.[42] Several million others are investigated by official agents, which is in and of itself a great source of anxiety, stress, conflict, and stigma. The legal custody and control of children has been taken away from more and more parents through court proceedings, although there is some evidence that these trends are reversing in more recent years. More and more children are now removed from their homes and "placed" in a foster home or other institution; one needs only the most superficial familiarity with this situation to see that such placement decisions tend to follow resource availability; that is, as new facilities or resources are added to the institutional network, more and more of these placement decisions are seen by officials as "needed," or even "necessary."

We are forever interested in the questions about how our society compares to others, or whether the times we live in are better or worse than before. Is there more or less justice for families today? Is the family stronger or weaker? Are our policies more or less humane? These are often the important questions that animate our academic and research interests. Unfortunately perhaps, the evidence about all of these issues is mixed. A historical perspective tends to produce a complex, mixed judgment. Certainly we no longer practice the forms of infanticide, abandonment, enslavement, bodily mutilation, or severe corporal discipline so common throughout history. Most people would see this as representing an improved, more humane condition. On the question of state authority and intervention in family life, the evidence is again mixed. The United States no longer invests forms of virtually unreviewed discretion as we find in the office of the tithingman in Massachusetts in the 1670s, who was given the mandate to personally inspect local families for their moral rectitude and religious obedience.[43] We no longer condone the removal of children from their families, by private parties, without any due process or legal hearing, to be given or sold to other families. Yet this was a sanctioned policy of U.S. Societies for the Prevention of Pauperism at the turn of the century.[44] When seen in this context, perhaps some

---

42. Gelles, *n.* 23.

43. Peter Conrad and Joseph W. Schneider, *Deviance and Medicalization: From Badness to Sickness* (St. Louis, C. V. Mosby Co., 1980).

44. Radbill, *n.* 5.

of the recent legal cases concerning child maltreatment may be judged more humane.

Historical relativism provides a necessary view, but it should not produce in us a paralysis of perspective or action. There is little doubt that basic family relations are once again caught in the throes of social change, and that the integrity of family life is threatened in new and fundamentally different ways. The recent experience with the Child Maltreatment Movement in the United States forces on us one inescapable conclusion: We must stop thinking that governmental actions merely represent functional responses to family problems, tending to control them. Recent empirical evidence leads us to see that governmental efforts may serve to create and sustain some kinds of problems, and specifically in the case of official interventions into family life, they may make problems worse for the individuals involved. This realization produces a new circumspection and caution about the role of governmental action in resolving family problems, and paves the way for more informed political action.

SELECTED BIBLIOGRAPHY
PART III

Akerlof, George A. "The Market for 'Lemons': Quality Uncertainty and the Market Mechanism." *Quarterly Journal of Economics* 84 (no. 3, August 1970):488–500.

Aries, Philippe. *Centuries of Childhood: A Social History of Family Life.* New York: Random House, 1965.

Bachofen, Johann J. *Das Mutterrecht.* Stuttgart: Krais and Hoffman, 1861.

Becker, Gary S. "A Theory of Marriage: Part 1." *Journal of Political Economy* 81 (no. 4, 1973):813–46.

———. "A Theory of Marriage: Part 2." *Journal of Political Economy* 82 (no. 2, part 2, 1974):S11–26.

———. "A Theory of Social Interactions." *Journal of Political Economy* 82 (no. 6, 1974):1063–93.

———. *The Economic Approach to Human Behavior.* Chicago: University of Chicago Press, 1976.

———. *A Treatise on the Family.* Cambridge: Harvard University Press, 1981.

Bentham, Jeremy. *An Introduction to the Principles of Morals and Legislation.* London: Methuen & Co., 1982.

Bourne, Richard, and Eli H. Newberger, eds. *Critical Perspectives on Child Abuse.* Lexington, Mass.: Lexington Books, 1978.

Briffault, R. *The Mothers.* New York: Macmillan, 1927.

Brodie, Fawn M. *No Man Knows My History: The Life of Joseph Smith, the Mormon Prophet.* New York: Alfred A. Knopf, 1946.

Caffey, John. "Multiple Fractures in the Long Bones of Infants Suffering from Chronic Subdural Hematoma." *American Journal of Roentgenology* 56 (August 1946):163–73.

Cain, V. "Concern for Children in Placement." *Analysis of Child Abuse and Neglect*. Washington, D.C.: National Center on Child Abuse and Neglect, 1977.

Carey, Michael, and Val Nolan, Jr. "Polygyny in Indigo Buntings: A Hypothesis Tested." *Science* 190 (no. 4221, 1975):1296–97.

Coase, Ronald H. "The Problem of Social Cost." *Journal of Law and Economics* 3 (1960):1–44.

Conrad, Peter, and Joseph W. Schneider. *Deviance and Medicalization: From Badness to Sickness*. St. Louis: C. V. Mosby, 1980.

de Francis, Vincent. "Parents Who Abuse Children." *PTA Magazine* 58 (November 1963):16–18.

————. "Child Abuse—The Legislative Response." *Denver Law Journal* 44 (Winter 1967):3–41.

————. *Child Abuse Legislation in the 1970s*. Rev. ed. Denver: American Humane Association, 1974.

de Mause, Lloyd, ed. *The History of Childhood*. New York: Psychohistory Press, 1974.

Douglas, Jack D. *Defining America's Social Problems*. Englewood Cliffs, N.J.: Prentice-Hall, 1974.

Engels, Frederick. *The Origin of the Family, Private Property and the State*. Chicago: Charles H. Kerr, 1910.

Epstein, Richard. "Nonconscionability: A Critical Reappraisal." *Journal of Law and Economics* 18 (no. 2, October 1975):293–315.

Evers, Williamson. "Toward a Reformulation of the Law of Contracts." *Journal of Libertarian Studies* 1 (Winter 1977): 3–13.

Friedman, Lawrence M., and Robert V. Percival. "Who Sues for Divorce? From Fault Through Fiction to Freedom." *Journal of Legal Studies* 5 (no. 1, January 1976):61–82.

Gamble, Charles W. "The Antenuptial Contract." *University of Michigan Law Review* 26 (no. 4, Summer 1972):692–736.

Gelles, Richard. *Family Violence*. Vol. 84 (Sage Library of Social Research). Beverly Hills, Calif.: Sage Publications, 1979.

Giovannoni, Jeanne M., and Rosina M. Becerra. *Defining Child Abuse*. New York: Free Press, 1979.

Gordon, David. "Comment on Hospers." *Journal of Libertarian Studies* 4 (no. 3, Summer 1980):267–72.

Harris, M. "Why Men Dominate Women." *New York Times Magazine* (13 November 1977):46ff.

Herlihy, David. "Deaths, Marriages, Births, and the Tuscan Economy." In R. Lee, ed., *Population Patterns in the Past*. New York: Academic Press, 1977.

————. *Medieval Households*. Cambridge: Harvard University Press, 1985.

Hinton, C., and J. Sterling. "Volunteers Serve as an Adjunct to Treatment for Child-Abusing Families." *Hospital and Community Psychiatry* 26 (March 1975):136–37.

Hoffman, Ellen. "Policy and Politics: The Child Abuse Prevention and Treatment Act." In R. Bourne and E. Newberger, eds., *Critical Perspectives on Child Abuse*, pp. 157–70. Lexington, Mass.: Lexington Books, 1979.

Holzer, Henry Mark. *Sweet Land of Liberty? The Supreme Court and Individual Rights*. New York: Common Sense Press, 1982.

Hospers, John. "Libertarianism and Legal Paternalism." *Journal of Libertarian Studies* 4 (no. 3, Summer 1980):255–65.

Hutt, William H. *The Theory of Collective Bargaining*. Glencoe, Ill.: Free Press, 1954.

Jaffe, A. J. "Differential Fertility in the White Population in Early America." *Journal of Heredity* 31 (no. 9, 1940): 407–11.

Johnson, John M. "Mass Media Reports and Deviance." Paper presented at the annual meeting of the Society for the Study of Social Problems, San Francisco, Calif., 1982.

Kadushin, Alfred, and Judith A. Martin. *Child Abuse: An Interactional Event*. New York: Columbia University Press, 1981.

Katz, Sanford. "Child Neglect Laws in America." *Family Law Quarterly* 9 (Spring 1975):295–331.

Kempe, C. Henry, et al., eds. "The Battered Child Syndrome." *Journal of the American Medical Association* 181 (July 1962):17–24.

Kempe, C. Henry, and Ray E. Helfer, eds. *Battered Child*. 3d ed., rev. and enl. Chicago: University of Chicago Press, 1982.

Krause, Harry D. *Family Law in a Nutshell*. St. Paul: West Publishing, 1977.

Kronman, Anthony T. "Mistake, Disclosure, Information, and the Law of Contracts." *Journal of Legal Studies* 7 (no. 2, January 1978):1–34.

Landes, Elizabeth M. "Economics of Alimony." *Journal of Legal Studies* 11 (no. 2, January 1978):35–63.

Laslett, Peter. *The World We Have Lost*. New York: Charles Scribner's Sons, 1965.

————. *Household and Family in Past Time*. Cambridge: Cambridge University Press, 1972.

Livi-Vacci, Massimo. *A History of Italian Fertility*. Princeton, N.J.: Princeton University Press, 1977.

Locke, John. "An Essay Concerning the True Origin, Extent and End of Civil Government." In P. Laslett, ed., *Two Treatises of Government*. Cambridge: Cambridge University Press, 1960.

Lovens, H., and J. Rako. "A Community Approach to the Prevention of Child Abuse." *Child Welfare* 54 (February 1975):83–87.

McLennan, J. F. *Studies in Ancient History*. New York: Macmillan, 1896.

Murstein, Bernard. *Love, Sex, and Marriage Through the Ages*. New York: Springer, 1974.

Nagi, Saad Z. *Child Maltreatment in the United States: A Challenge to Social Institutions*. New York: Columbia University Press, 1977.

Osmond, M. "Toward Monogamy: A Cross-Cultural Study of Correlates of Types of Marriage." *Social Forces* 44 (1965): 8–16.

Paulsen, M. G. "The Legal Framework for Child Protection." *Columbia Law Review* 67 (January 1966):1–49.

Pelton, Leroy. "Child Abuse and Neglect: The Myth of Classlessness." *American Journal of Orthopsychiatry* 48 (October 1978):608–16.

Pfohl, Stephen J. "The 'Discovery' of Child Abuse." *Social Problems* 24 (February 1977):310–23.

Platt, Anthony M. *The Child Savers*. Chicago: University of Chicago Press, 1969.

Polakow, R., and D. Peabody. "Behavioral Treatment of Child Abuse." *International Journal of Offender Therapy and Comparative Criminology* 19 (1975):100–08.

Posner, Richard. *Economic Analysis of the Law*. Boston: Little, Brown & Co., 1972.

———. "Gratuitous Promises in Economics and Law." *Journal of Legal Studies* 6 (no. 2, June 1977):411–26.

———. "A Theory of Primitive Society, With Special Reference to Law." *Journal of Law and Economics* 23 (no. 2, April 1980):1–53.

Radbill, Samuel X. "A History of Child Abuse and Infanticide." In C. Kempe and R. Helfer, eds., *The Battered Child*. Chicago: University of Chicago Press, 1968.

Rand, Ayn. *The Virtue of Selfishness*. New York: New American Library, 1965.

Rothbard, Murray. *For a New Liberty*. New York: Macmillan, 1978.

———. *The Ethics of Liberty*. Atlantic Highlands, N.J.: Humanities Press, 1982.

———. "Law, Property Rights, and Air Pollution." *Cato Journal* 2 (no. 1, Spring 1982):76–77.

Schoeck, Helmut. *Envy: A Theory of Social Behavior*. New York: Harcourt Brace Jovanovich, 1969.

Silverman, Frederick N. "Roentgen Manifestations of Unrecognized Skeletal Trauma in Infants." *American Journal of Roentgenology* 69 (March 1953):413–26.

Solomon, T. "History and Demography of Child Abuse." *Pediatrics* 51 (1963):773–76.

Temple, Gregg. "Freedom of Contract and Intimate Relationships." *Harvard Journal of Law and Public Policy* 8 (no. 1, Winter 1985): 121–73.

Ten Broeck, Jacobus. "The Extended Family Center." *Children Today* 3 (April 1974):2–6.

Tullock, Gordon. "Public Decisions as Public Goods." *Journal of Political Economy* 79 (July/August 1971):913–18.

Viano, Emilio. "Attitudes Toward Child Abuse Among American Professionals." Paper presented at the first meetings of the International Society for Research on Aggression, Toronto, Canada, 1974.

Weitzman, Lenore. *The Marriage Contract.* New York: Free Press, 1981.

Wolkenstein, A. S. "Hospital Acts on Child Abuse." *Journal of the American Hospital Association* 49 (March 1975):103–06.

Woolley, Paul V., and W. A. Evans, Jr. "Significance of Skeletal Lesions in Infants Resembling Those of Traumatic Origin." *Journal of the American Medical Association* 158 (June 1955):539–43.

Young, Kimball. *Isn't One Wife Enough.* New York: Holt, 1954.

THE IMPACT OF ECONOMIC AND SOCIAL POLICY ON FAMILY LIFE

10

INFLATION, MIGRATION, AND DIVORCE IN CONTEMPORARY AMERICA

Lowell Gallaway and Richard Vedder

The decline in the stability of the American family in recent decades roughly coincided with another purely economic trend, namely the rise in the rate of inflation. Were these two seemingly disparate phenomena in fact related? In this chapter we will suggest that the answer to that question is yes.

Specifically, we will argue that inappropriate and ineffective macroeconomic policies caused an increase in the rate of inflation, which, in turn, caused economic stress in families. When inflation is unanticipated, family income falls below expectations, causing financial problems and interpersonal tensions. Even when inflation becomes anticipated, the rise in money interest rates serves to reduce family mobility, removing an important "safety valve" that can alleviate family tensions associated with location.

We are not claiming that inflationary macroeconomic policies are the *only* cause of rising divorce. Indeed, we will present results that show that rising public-assistance payments also contributed to the surge in divorce rates in modern times, as did the rise in female labor-force participation. By contrast, we find no relationship between unemployment and divorce. Our findings clearly suggest that macroeconomic policies aimed at income stabilization and redistribution have had some unanticipated and socially costly consequences.

WHY DO PEOPLE MARRY AND DIVORCE?

Marriage is a contractual arrangement, a "trade." Like all noncoercive exchanges, parties to a marriage expect mutual benefits—both expect to be better off. As Ricardo demonstrated almost two centuries ago, traders will specialize in areas in which they have a comparative advantage (in which the opportunity costs of the activity are lower than they are for the trade partner).

Marriage partners jointly produce a product, children, but more generally trade goods and services with their spouses. In the traditional family arrangement that dominated American life until a generation or two ago, the male typically specialized in selling some good or service in outside markets. He was the breadwinner, the provider of the pecuniary means needed by the family. He also provided certain household services (e.g., mowing the grass, making household repairs, etc.). He provided the wife with income for food, clothing, shelter, leisure time activities, etc. The wife, in turn, was the general manager of the household, responsible for maintaining the house, serving as the household purchasing agent, cook, maid, babysitter, and provider of sexual services. In a sense, the husband provided income, affection, and some household maintenance services to the wife in exchange for other household maintenance services, domestic services, affection, and sexual favors.

Divorce rationally occurs when some or all the basis for exchange breaks down, so that the trading arrangement is no longer mutually advantageous. For example, if the wife becomes employed and cuts down on housework, she no longer has the same need of the income the husband previously provided, and the husband no longer has as many household services to "buy" from her. Divorce is a rational response to the breakdown in the exchange for which one of the marriage partners initially had a comparative advantage.[1]

INFLATION AND DIVORCE: SOME EVIDENCE

Table 10–1 shows that the average rate of divorce per thousand population in the United States has risen over the six decades for which

---

1. The whole economic approach to the analysis of marriage, divorce, and other so-called noneconomic forms of human behavior was pioneered by Gary S. Becker of the University of Chicago. Two representative and relevant studies by Becker are his *Economic Approach to Human Behavior* (Chicago: University of Chicago Press, 1976) and his *Treatise on the Family* (Cambridge: Harvard University Press, 1981).

Table 10–1.   Divorce and Inflation Rates by Decades, 1920–1980.

Decade	Mean Divorce Rate[a]	Increase in Prices[b] (%)
1920s	1.56	−16.7
1930s	1.65	−16.0
1940s	2.78	+71.7
1950s	2.36	23.0
1960s	2.66	31.2
1970s	4.57	112.2

SOURCES: U.S. Department of Commerce, *Historical Statistics of the U.S., Colonial Times to 1970; Statistical Abstract of the United States,* various years.

[a]Per 1,000 population; mean is the average of the 10 years comprising the decade.
[b]As measured by the consumer price index.

data are available. Note that the divorce rate was relatively low in the 1920s, rose very slightly in the thirties, climbed sharply in the forties, declined somewhat in the 1950s, only to increase a bit in the sixties and rise explosively in the 1970s.

It is also interesting to observe that the low divorce rate in the 1920s and 1930s coincided with a period of moderate deflation, with prices falling an average of less than 2 percent a year. The era since 1940, characterized by higher divorce rates, has also been a period of continuous and very significant inflation.

Table 10–2 reveals that the association between changes in the mean

Table 10–2.   Changes in Divorce Rates and Inflation, 1930–1980.

Decade	Change in Divorce Rate[a]	Change in the Inflation Rate[b] (%)
1930s	+0.09	+0.7
1940s	+1.13	+87.7
1950s	−0.42	−48.7
1960s	+0.30	+8.2
1970s	+1.91	+81.0

SOURCES: Authors' calculations, based on figures in Table 10–1.

[a]Mean annual number of divorces per 1,000 population in decade minus the mean annual number of divorces per 1,000 population in the previous decade.
[b]Increase in the consumer price index in the decade minus the increase in the consumer price index in the previous decade.

divorce rate and changes in the rate of inflation is very striking. The two decades of sharp increases in the divorce rate, the 1940s and 1970s, were also periods of rapidly rising prices. The periods of stability or decline in the divorce rate, the 1930s and 1950s, were periods of disinflation or continued deflation. The 1960s was a period of moderate increase in the divorce rate associated with moderately high rates of inflation relative to past periods. The correlation between changing divorce rates and changing inflation rates is striking, with the Spearman rank order correlation coefficient being $+0.90$; the periods of rapid increases in divorce rates correspond very closely to periods of increases in the amount of inflation.

UNANTICIPATED INFLATION AND THE FAMILY

Before presenting more detailed evidence of an inflation-divorce relationship, why is there any reason to believe that inflation might have an impact on divorce?

Let us first make the important distinction between unanticipated and anticipated inflation. Unanticipated inflation is a general increase in prices that catches people off guard. A persuasive argument can be made that much twentieth century inflation, at least until recently, has been unanticipated. Between 1800 and 1940, the general level of prices remained roughly constant, even though there were shorter periods of pronounced instability.[2] Since 1940, there have been no significant episodes of price declines, and for thirty consecutive years there has been growth annually in the consumer price index.[3] Only well into this inflationary episode, however, did people come to realize that the "natural" tendency for prices to remain constant no longer holds.

A very crude measure of unanticipated inflation is presented in Ta-

2. Splicing together the Bureau of Labor Statistics wholesale price index since 1890 with the Warren-Pearson index before that date, the index falls from 129 in 1800 to 115 in 1940 (1910–14 = 100), a decline of more than 11 percent. Prices, however, were inflated in 1800 compared with earlier periods, and were also deflated in 1940 because of the Great Depression. Comparing 1789 (the first year of George Washington's tenure as President) with 1929, the index rises from 86 to 139, still a compounded increase of less than 0.4 percent a year. See U.S. Department of Commerce, Bureau of the Census, *Historical Statistics of the United States, Colonial Times to 1970* (Washington, D.C.: Government Printing Office, 1975), Series E-40 and E-52 (hereafter referred to as *Historical Statistics*).

3. That may be an underestimate; there have been thirty-six consecutive years of increase in the GNP price deflator. For modern price history data, see any recent issue of the *Economic Report of the President* (e.g., p. 236 of the 1982 report).

ble 10–2. One might argue that the price experience of the previous decade very roughly determines the expectations of people about inflation in the current decade. To the extent that the inflation rate in the current decade exceeds that in the past decade, people are caught "off guard." As Table 10–2 indicates, in four of the past five decades inflation rose from the previous decade, and in two cases, the 1940s and the 1970s, it rose very substantially. Thus episodes of substantial unanticipated inflation have been commonplace in modern times.

At first blush, it might appear that unanticipated inflation should *reduce* marital discord arising out of financial stress, since inflation reduces the real burden of debt. Since loans are paid back in dollars of lower purchasing power than the dollars borrowed, this reduces debt financing pressures on families.

While this is true, it is more than offset by several other factors. First, intangible assets in the form of stocks, bonds, cash, life insurance, etc., have historically amounted to far more than the financial liabilities of households. For example, in 1972, financial assets of individuals and households were estimated to be $1,998.2 billion, 2.47 times the financial liabilities of $808.5 billion.[4] Cash (including bank accounts) and bond holdings *alone* exceed total liabilities.

Inflation, other things equal, serves to lower the current market value of financial assets with a fixed return and redemption value. With continued increases in the general price level, the real value of the income earned from those assets falls over time. The market value of those assets thus declines, so that inflation lowers the real wealth balances of families below expected levels. This, in turn, leads to increased perceptions within households of financial inadequacy and failure.

While the devastating impact of inflation is most obvious with regards to fixed income assets such as bonds or certificates of deposits, a portfolio effect drives prices of other financial assets down as well. Long-term bond prices *in nominal terms* fell dramatically (around 50 percent) from 1965 to 1980, an era of rising and increasingly anticipated inflation.[5] This, however, increased the nominal yield (interest

4. See James D. Smith and Stephen D. Franklin, "The Concentration of Personal Wealth, 1922–1969," *American Economic Review* 64 (May 1974): 162–67, or U.S. Bureau of the Census, *Statistical Abstract of the United States: 1982–83*, 103rd edition (Washington, D.C.: Government Printing Office, 1983), p. 449.

5. *Statistical Abstract, n.* 4, p. 518. Standard and Poor's Corporate AAA bond index fell from 93.9 in 1965 to 41.4 in 1980, a decline of 55.9 percent.

rates) earned on bonds, and some owners of stocks sold their assets to "lock in" on high bond yields. This depressed stock prices. It is not surprising, then, that stock prices in real terms fell sharply as well. Standard and Poor's 500 stock index expressed in 1967 dollars (as measured by the consumer price index) fell from 107.14 in 1965 to 48.10 in 1980, a decline exceeding 55 percent, at a time when the economy was exhibiting positive (if modest) economic growth.[6]

To be sure, families that invested in tangible assets like real estate, gems, or fine oil paintings fared far better, even making real gains. This disparity itself, however, no doubt contributed to marital discord. As a family's hard-earned real assets declined sharply, the conservative spouse who invested in supposedly "safe" bonds or stocks might very well have been increasingly berated by the other spouse for "not protecting us from inflation by putting money into real estate like the Joneses did."

Wealth effects aside, inflation, other things equal, served to lower real wages below expected levels. The decline in purchasing power that resulted can give rise to family tensions. The husband may increasingly criticize the wife for spending too much, while the wife may feel increasingly resentful of the inability of the husband to provide a higher standard of living.

The impact of inflation in lowering income was exacerbated by federal income tax laws. Inflation raised effective tax rates by pushing persons into higher tax brackets, the well-known phenomenon of "bracket creep." For example, a married couple with two dependents whose income in 1980 dollars was $35,000 paid 16.1 percent of income in federal income taxes in 1960 but 18.8 percent by 1980; more strikingly, the *marginal* rate of taxation rose from 26 percent to 37 percent.[7] Thus inflation-created tax increases lowered the disposable income associated with any level of total income, aggravating the household financial pressures associated with inflation.

The decrease in expected wealth and income caused by unanticipated inflation increases the pressure for housewives to enter the labor force in an effort to reach targeted (but not achieved) income and

6. Authors' calculations from *Statistical Abstract, n.* 4, pp. 518, 461.

7. Ibid., p. 258. Interestingly, between 1952 and 1972 the more skilled occupations became increasingly divorce-prone, consistent with the notion that inflation-induced "bracket creep" increases family tensions and divorce, particularly among the middle and upper middle class. See Kenneth S. Thompson, *The Divorce Profile: Differential Social Correlates in 1952 and 1972* (San Francisco: R and E Research Associates, 1978).

wealth standards. It is a common complaint that "my wife is working because we cannot keep up with inflation on my income." The entrance of the wife into the labor force may increase male insecurity (since the husband no longer fills the role of the sole breadwinner), reduce female dependence on the marital relationship, cause a reduction in time spent on family concerns, and so forth. In short, the gains from marital "trade" diminish, increasing the probability of divorce.[8]

The evidence strongly supports the contention that female labor-force involvement has been enhanced by inflationary pressures. Between 1890 and 1940, a relatively noninflationary era, the proportion of all females in the labor force rose from 18.9 to 25.8 percent, an increase of 6.9 points or about .14 percent point per year.[9] From 1940 to 1980, an era of high inflation, the female labor-force participation rate almost doubled, going to 51.6 percent, an increase of almost 0.60 percentage points a year, or four times the growth observed in the less inflationary period.[10] Moreover, the proportion of married women working rose from 36 percent in 1940 to nearly 60 percent in 1980.[11] The proportion of women with children under 6 years old who were working grew even more dramatically, going from 11.9 percent in 1950 to 41.6 percent in 1978.[12]

The relationship between inflation and female labor-force participation is more strikingly illustrated in Table 10–3. While the participation rate has risen constantly over time, the period of greatest increase in prices, the 1970s, was the period of greatest increase in female labor-force participation, while the decades of modest deflation, the 1920s and 1930s, were periods of modest growth in female labor-force participation. The Spearman rank order correlation coefficient between the variables is an impressive +0.89.

The above discussion and evidence is all very consistent with the

8. On this point, see W. H. Greene and A. O. Quester, "Divorce Risk and Wives' Labor Supply Behavior," *Social Science Quarterly* 63 (March 1982): 16–27.

9. See *Historical Statistics, n.* 2, p. 133.

10. *Statistical Abstract, n.* 4, p. 383.

11. Ibid.

12. U.S. Bureau of the Census, *American Families and Living Arrangements, Current Population Reports,* Special Studies, Series P-23, No. 104, May 1980. The female labor-force particiption rate varies enormously according to marital status. In 1981, the rate for married women with a husband and children under 6 present was 47.8 percent, while for divorced women with children under 6 the participation rate was 65.4 percent. See U.S. Bureau of Labor Statistics, *Special Labor Force Reports,* No. 13, and the *Statistical Abstract, n.* 4, p. 382.

Table 10–3.   Inflation and Female Labor-Force Participation, 1920–1980.

Decade	Change in Prices[a] (%)	Change in Female Labor-Force Participation Rates[b] (%)
1920s	−16.7	+1.1
1930s	−16.0	+1.0
1940s	+71.7	+4.0
1950s	+23.0	+3.4
1960s	+31.2	+7.8
1970s	+112.2	+9.0

SOURCE: Authors' calculation from U.S. Department of Commerce data.

[a]From first year of decade to first year of next decade, based on the consumer price index.
[b]The absolute change in the mean average percentage of the female population that was in the labor force from the mean average percentage of the female population in the labor force in the previous decade.

theorizing of Becker, Landes, and Michael (hereafter BLM) in their pathbreaking analysis of marital instability:[13]

1. An increase in the expected value of variables positively sorted in the optimal sorting of mates, such as the earnings of men . . . lowers the probability of dissolution. On the other hand, an increase in the expected values of variables negatively sorted in the optimal sorting of males, such as the earnings of women relative to those of men, raises the probability of dissolution. . . .
2. A large deviation between actual and expected values, such as actual and expected earnings . . . raises the probability of dissolution. . . .[14]

BLM's theorizing seems to be consistent with the following three propositions: (1) A fall in real male earnings (because of inflation) will increase divorce; (2) the entrance of females into the labor force (a move that increases their earnings relative to males) will increase the rate of divorce; and (3) since unanticipated inflation will tend to lower actual real earnings below expected levels, an increase in divorce is expected. In other words, the various effects of inflation serve

13. Gary S. Becker, E. M. Landes, and R. T. Michael, "An Economic Analysis of Marital Instability," *Journal of Political Economy* 85 (Dec. 1977): 1141–87.
14. Ibid., p. 1156.

to increase the incidence of divorce.[15] The evidence to this point, while crude, is nonetheless consistent with all three of the above propositions.

MORE EMPIRICAL EVIDENCE

The major evidence to this point, presented in Tables 10–1 and 10–2, can be criticized as superficial, based on largely casual (noneconometric) observation of only five or six cases. Accordingly, a somewhat more formal test of the inflation-divorce relationship was performed. Data were gathered for sixteen 4-year time periods, beginning with 1920–23 and ending with 1980–83 on mean divorce rates and the change in prices. A four-year period was used instead of annual data for several reasons, most important of which is that the onset of inflation would not reasonably be expected to induce immediate divorce. Rising inflation most likely would typically lead to an increase in family tension, followed perhaps by separation and then divorce, a process that could take several years. Unanticipated inflation in 1980 may result in divorce in 1982 or 1983, but most probably not in 1980 itself. By defining a time period of several years, problems associated with estimating the lagged relationships are very substantially reduced.

Also, we stated that increases in inflation from the previous time period might be viewed as a measure of the amount of unanticipated inflation, assuming that expectations largely derive from previous period experiences. That would seem to be a reasonably realistic assumption if the previous period is fairly long (e.g., several years), but it is not realistic to assume that expectations derive solely from a single year's (e.g., last year's) experience.

---

15. An extension of the Becker et al. hypothesis is found in J. Huber and G. Spitze, "Considering Divorce: An Expansion of Becker's Theory of Marital Instability," *American Journal of Sociology* 86 (July 1980): 75–89.

Becker and associates, of course, are not the only persons to state or imply this line of reasoning, but their model is perhaps the best known of those that utilize an economic approach. An interesting sociological study that discusses the impact of economic pressures on marriage (and also other forms of "couples") is Philip Blumstein and Pepper Schwartz, *American Couples* (New York: William Morrow, 1983).

In analyzing the effect of income on divorce, some sociologists distinguish between an "income" and an "independence" effect, an approach roughly compatible with that of Becker. See, for example, Michael T. Hannan, Nancy Brandon Tuma, and Lyle P. Groeneveld, "Income and Independence Effects on Marital Dissolution: Results from the Seattle and Denver Income-Maintenance Experiments," *American Journal of Sociology* 84 (Nov. 1978): 611–33.

In Table 10–4, the observed values for the divorce rate and the inflation rate are indicated for the sixteen periods in question. The four periods with the highest divorce rate (1976–79, 1980–83, 1972–75, and 1944–47) were also the four most inflationary periods. The mean divorce rate for the eight periods of greatest inflation was 3.64 per thousand population, over 90 percent higher than the 1.88 per thousand average divorce rate observed in the eight least inflationary periods.

Somewhat more sophisticated and precise analysis is possible, however. Ordinary least squares regression procedures that regress the divorce rate against the inflation rate for the same time period were accordingly used. The statistical results are as follows:

$$D_t = 2.01 + .0581 \ \%\Delta P_t, \ \bar{R}^2 = .75, D\text{-}W = 1.28,$$
$$(6.73)$$

where D is the average annual number of divorces per thousand population during the t th period of four years, and $\%\Delta P$ denotes the

Table 10–4.   Divorce and Inflation, 1920–1980.

Period	Mean Divorce Rate[a]	% Change in Prices[b]	Unemployment Rate (Avg.)
1920–23	1.5	−14.67	6.5
1924–27	1.6	+0.20	3.3
1928–31	1.6	−20.27	8.0
1932–35	1.5	+1.47	22.6
1936–39	1.9	+ 1.20	16.9
1940–43	2.3	+25.48	7.8
1944–47	3.5	+36.81	2.7
1948–51	2.7	+13.87	4.6
1952–55	2.4	+2.39	4.0
1956–59	2.2	+8.97	5.2
1960–63	2.3	+4.74	5.9
1964–67	2.5	+12.16	4.3
1968–71	3.3	+20.25	4.5
1972–75	4.5	+36.07	6.2
1976–79	5.2	+44.75	6.5
1980–83	5.1	+31.83	8.5

SOURCE: U.S. Department of Commerce, Bureau of the Census, authors' calculations

[a]Per 1,000 population.

[b]Percentage increase in consumer price index from first year in period to first year of next period.

percentage increase in the consumer price index from the first year of the *t* th time period to the corresponding year of the next time period, and the number in parentheses is a *t*-value.

The results suggest the following:

1. Three-fourths of the considerable variation (from 1.5 to 5.2) in the divorce rate over time is explainable by variation in the rate of inflation.
2. The positive relationship between inflation and divorce rates is statistically significant at the 1 percent level, and there is no proof of autocorrelation (the hypothesis that autocorrelation exists is not accepted at the 95 percent level).
3. In the period 1976–79, had stable prices existed instead of an average annual inflation rate of about 10 percent, the predicted divorce rate would have been under 2.0 instead of 5.2; in other words, most of the secular rise in the divorce rate from the low prewar levels is explainable by inflation. Alternatively put, roughly 700,000 divorces more a year are estimated to have been granted in the late 1970s because of the existence of substantial inflation.
4. The social costs of inflation-induced divorce are accordingly enormous. If, for example, one were to estimate the average cost of a divorce in terms of legal costs, plus the "pain and suffering" involved, at $25,000, the annual social cost of divorces created by 10 percent continued annual inflation is in excess of $18 billion a year; to the extent $25,000 understates the true cost of a typical divorce, the estimate of $18 billion is conservative.
5. The natural rate of divorce—that is, the annual divorce rate that would exist in a stable price environment—is about two per thousand population. More about that later.

These results are exceedingly robust and are highly consistent with both the BLM analysis and our own earlier hypothesizing. At the same time, however, the findings are far less consistent with the studies of some other social scientists writing about divorce.[16]

The basic positive relationship between inflation and divorce exists if one uses alternative model specifications. For example, a model

---

16. Some of the other studies emphasize noneconomic factors, such as changes in the divorce laws (e.g., the institution of "no fault" divorce). We know of no other study that concentrates on inflation as an important causal factor.

that regressed changes in the divorce rate with changes in the inflation rate was estimated. The positive relationship between changes in the inflation rate and the change in the divorce rate was statistically significant at the 5 percent level, with the model explaining about 30 percent of the variation in the change in the divorce rate over time.

OTHER POSSIBLE DETERMINANTS OF DIVORCES

There is some suggestion in the literature that a major economic determinant of social unrest is unemployment.[17] There is also the vast Phillips curve literature that suggests that high inflation is associated with low unemployment.[18] Could it be that the observed inflation-divorce relationship is in fact spurious, and that the true relationship is between unemployment and divorce?

Certainly, it is understandable that unemployment can raise tensions within a family, increasing frustrations and friction between spouses. Also, casual observation of the last decade or so reveals that unemployment has been generally higher than its normal or natural rate, as has divorce.[19] On the other hand, some of the tensions associated with unemployment have been ameliorated by income maintenance programs, so much so that those programs almost certainly

17. In regard to family relationships, a recent representative study that suggests that unemployment increases tensions is Phyllis Moen, "Unemployment, Public Policy and Families: Forecasts for the 1980s," *Journal of Marriage and the Family* 45 (Nov. 1983): 751–60.

18. As expounded by A. W. Phillips, "The Relation Between Unemployment and the Rate of Change in Money Wage Rates in the United Kingdon, 1861–1957," *Economica,* N.S. 25 (Nov. 1958): 283–99; extended by Richard G. Lipsey, "The Relation Between Unemployment and the Rate of Change in Money Wage Rates in the United Kingdom, 1862–1957: A Further Analysis," *Economica,* N.S. 27 (Feb. 1960): 1–31; and popularized in the United States by Paul A. Samuelson and Robert M. Solow, "Analytical Aspects of Anti-Inflationary Policy," *American Economic Review* 50 (May 1960): 177–94, the Phillips curve notion might suggest that inflation would reduce family economic tensions by reducing unemployment.

19. The secular rise in the equilibrium or "natural" rate of unemployment during the 1970s is described in Lowell E. Gallaway and Richard K. Vedder, *The "Natural" Rate of Unemployment,* Staff Study, Subcommittee on Monetary and Fiscal Policy, Joint Economic Committee of the Congress (Washington, D.C.: U.S. Government Printing Office, 1982). At the heart of the increase in the "natural" rate of unemployment is the expansion of the "safety net" of government programs that ameliorate the impact of unemployment on individual workers. Especially important is the extension of coverage under the unemployment compensation program. For discussions of the impact of unemployment compensation on the unemployment rate, see the early work done by Gene Chapin, "Unemployment Insurance, Job Search and the Demand for Leisure," *Western Economic Journal* 9 (March 1971): 102–7, and, later, Martin Feldstein, "Unemployment Compensation: Adverse Incentives and Distributional Anomalies," *National Tax Journal* 27 (June 1974): 231–44.

have caused a significant increase in unemployment.[20] Unemployment insurance cushions the family against substantial earnings loss, and federal income tax laws have served to narrow further the loss in income associated with unemployment. Also, the increased leisure of the unemployed person presumably means he or she spends more time on family concerns, reducing any sense of neglect that might otherwise be present. Finally, if the unemployed is the female, the male-female earnings differential widens and, following BLM, this might reduce the husband's resentment over the decrease in his importance as the family's primary income provider. On balance, it is not clear to us, a priori, what the relationship between unemployment and divorce is expected to be.

In addition to unemployment (U in the regression equations we will report), there has been much written recently that suggests that the increased public assistance programs growing out of the War on Poverty in the 1960s have served to promote the disintegration of American families; the work of George Gilder and Charles Murray is particularly persuasive in that regard.[21] In the Gilder-Murray view, the principle of comparative advantage leading to marital trading arrangements has been undermined by governmental financial payments to households without a married couple present. Accordingly, in our analysis we have introduced as a variable federal public assistance payments per capita (A), measured in constant 1980 dollars.[22] The hypothesis is, the greater such public assistance payments, other things equal, the greater the rate of divorce.

Our earlier discussion of inflation suggested that one way that inflation encouraged divorce was through its positive impact on female

20. For specific quantitative estimates, see Chapin, *n*. 19 and Feldstein, *n*. 19.

21. George Gilder, *Wealth and Poverty* (New York: Basic Books, 1980) and Charles Murray, *Losing Ground: American Social Policy, 1950–1980* (New York: Basic Books, 1984). Some interesting confirmation of the thesis that welfare benefits and income maintenance programs encourage marital instability is provided by the Negative Income Tax (NIT) experiment. While there may be some ambiguity with respect to the Gary, Indiana, results, on the whole the evidence strongly supports the view that negative income tax payments stimulated marital dissolution. See, for example, John H. Bishop, "Jobs, Cash Transfers and Marital Instability: A Review and Synthesis of the Evidence," *Journal of Human Resources* 15 (Summer 1980): 301–34, and Lyle P. Groeneveld, Nancy Brandon Tuma, and Michael T. Hannan, "The Effects of Negative Income Tax Programs on Marital Dissolution," *Journal of Human Resources* 15 (Fall 1980): 654–74.

22. Most of the data were derived from Murray, *n*. 21, p. 242, supplemented by various editions of the *Statistical Abstract of the United States* and, for recent years, the *Social Security Bulletin*. Annual population estimates were obtained from the *Statistical Abstract*.

labor-force participation, which in turn reduced the advantages of a marital trading arrangement. We do have direct evidence on female labor-force participation rates; accordingly, we can enter a labor force participation variable (L_f) into our model, seeing if inflation has an impact *independent* of that related to rising female labor-force participation.

Unfortunately, consistent annual data on public aid and labor force participation are not available since 1920; accordingly, we confined our analysis to the ten 4-year periods beginning in 1944. The results of the augmented regression are as follows

$$D = 2.235 + .0424\,\Delta P + .0950\,U - .0237\,L_f + .0080\,A,$$
$$\quad\;\;(1.16)\quad (3.71)\qquad (0.82)\qquad (0.42)\qquad (1.43)$$
$$\bar{R}^2 = .95, D - W = 1.99.$$

The inflation-divorce relationship remains robust (although the coefficient is a bit smaller), even after other variables are introduced. The model as a whole now explains over 95 percent of the variation in divorce rates, and there is no evidence whatsoever of autocorrelation. The results with respect to the other variables, however, are somewhat disappointing. The labor force participation variable has the wrong sign. The unemployment variable has a positive coefficient, but is clearly not significant in any statistical sense. The public assistance variable behaves as expected and more robustly, but even it is of somewhat dubious statistical significance.

As indicated earlier, the inflation and labor force participation rate variables are highly correlated with one another, and an examination of the correlation matrix with respect to other variables in the augmented equation suggests that massive multicolinearity exists. Accordingly, we estimated alternative models omitting one or more of the four independent variables included above. With all the models tried, the unemployment variable was not significant at any level (and, indeed, often had a negative sign). Excluding unemployment, the statistical relationship between the public assistance and divorce variables becomes significant at the 5 percent level, although the labor force participation variable is still not significant.

A model incorporating only the inflation and public assistance variables is particularly robust:

$$D = 1.836 + .039\,\Delta P + .008\,A, \bar{R}^2 = .96, D - W = 1.62.$$
$$\quad\;(13.76)\quad (5.138)\qquad (5.786)$$

We would conclude from this regression that the Gilder-Murray hypothesis on the debilitating effects of public assistance on family life is confirmed. At the same time, the inflation-divorce relationship remains quite robust.

In the twelve years between the periods 1964–67 and 1976–79, the divorce rate more than doubled, going from 2.5 to 5.2 per thousand population. The amount of public assistance and inflation also increased substantially. Applying the coefficients from the equation immediately above to the increases in inflation and public assistance actually observed, we can calculate an estimate of the proportion of the great growth in divorce attributable to each of these phenomena. Doing so, we observe that 1.36 (50 percent) of the 2.70 point growth in the divorce rate is explainable by the welfare growth, while 1.27 points (47 percent) is explainable by increasing inflation. These factors are thus roughly equal in importance and together explain almost all of the more than doubling in the divorce rate observed in this period.

The results suggest that rising welfare expenditures have imposed very significant social costs not contemplated when statutory enactment of the spending programs occurred. The numbers also suggest that the post–Great Society welfare buildup increased the number of divorces by the late seventies by over 300,000 annually, about an $8 billion annual loss if one places the social cost of a divorce at $25,000.

The tragedy is that these costs are borne disproportionately by the poor and minorities. Moreover, the divorce rate is merely an imperfect proxy for generalized breakdown in nuclear family arrangements. In many cases, marriage never occurs in the first place. Daniel Moynihan's explosive report on the role that welfare played in the destruction of black families first appeared in 1965, but the results above suggest that the problem has grown extraordinarily since.[23] It appears that the Great Society has succeeded in doing what slavery, the Civil War, Reconstruction, Jim Crow laws and the Ku Klux Klan were unable to do—substantially destroy the black family in the United States.[24]

The female labor-force participation variable is highly correlated with other variables in the model. A simple model including only the

---

23. See Daniel P. Moynihan, *The Negro Family: The Case for National Action* (Washington, D.C.: U.S. Department of Labor, March 1965).

24. We are indebted to our colleague Professor Jan Palmer for this historical insight.

inflation and labor force participation variables as explanatory forces shows a robust relationship between the rise in female labor-force participation and divorce:

$$D = -0.946 + .081 L_f + .049 \Delta P, \bar{R}^2 = .94, D - W = 1.57.$$
$$(1.402) \quad (4.333) \quad (5.962)$$

Obviously, the multicolinearity problem is significant. It is fairly clear from the alternative model formulations, however, that the results are highly consistent with the hypotheses that enhanced inflation, public assistance, and female labor-force participation have increased the divorce rate; unemployment, by contrast, seems to have had no significant role in explaining variations in divorce over time, contrary to the feelings of some economists and others, for example, Barbara Bergmann.[25]

MIGRATION AND DIVORCE

The impact of inflation on divorce partly relates to direct causes, such as the impact on family finances of price increases and the associated decline in real wages. Yet it is possible that inflation has far more extensive and indirect effects on the marital relationship as well. We will speculate about one such indirect impact here. Specifically, we argue that inflation restricts labor mobility and that this restriction, in turn, increases the risk of divorce, since migration has traditionally acted as a "safety valve" in reducing various forms of discontent. This argument, then, is a variant on a theme developed by followers of Frederick Jackson Turner's "frontier thesis" and others, who claim that migration (particularly to the West) largely explains the general stability of American society and, indeed, the American character.[26]

It is generally conceded that "one of the most obvious facts of recent monetary history is that inflation is associated with high nom-

---

25. In a *Los Angeles Times* syndicated article that appeared, among other places, in the *Cleveland Plain Dealer,* 28 June 1983, Bergmann approvingly cites research suggesting that "broken marriages" can be "traced to the prolonged hard times."

26. For the complete statement of Turner's views on the role of the frontier, see Frederick Jackson Turner, *The Frontier in American History* (New York: Henry Holt, 1920). Actually, the "safety valve" notion is not explicitly stated in Turner. See, however, Joseph Schafer, "Was the West a Safety Valve for Labor?" *Mississippi Valley Historical Review* 24 (Dec. 1937): 299–314. For an alternative view, see Clarence H. Danhof, "Farm-Making Costs and the Safety Valve: 1850–1860," *Journal of Political Economy* 49 (June 1941): 317–59.

inal interest rates."[27] How does an inflation-induced rise in interest rates influence human migration? We would argue that rising interest rates mean rising movement costs, which in turn reduce the gains from migration and thus the quantity of migration flows.

The impact of inflation on moving costs can take several forms. One of the most important in recent years relates to the fact that unanticipated inflation often provides a windfall addition to wealth that is location-specific, that is, a windfall that cannot be realized in another geographic locale. Specifically, lots of Americans borrowed money for homes in the 1960s and 1970s at single-digit interest rates. Since prevailing interest rates after inflation became more fully anticipated were in the double digits, the true market value of those earlier mortgages was far less than the stated balance of the mortgage due. Put differently, the net worth of the borrower was enhanced by long-term borrowing at fixed interest rates below prevailing market levels.

In some cases, this windfall has been transferable, that is to say the mortgage holder can transfer the low-interest debt when the house is sold, but increasingly the ability to make such mortgages "assumable" has been restricted, so that a person contemplating moving faces losing much, if not all, the wealth windfall associated with a low-interest loan. This reduces the willingness to move. A person with a $50,000 mortgage at 8 percent who must pay 14 percent to borrow that amount in a new location faces interest rate increases of $250 a month, or $3,000 a year. Inflation, then, imposes an "exit tax" of considerable magnitude on any such movers.

Empirical tests performed several years ago confirm the hypothesis that the volume of migration varies inversely with interest rates.[28] Using migration data for the 1948–71 period, a statistically significant negative relationship was observed between nominal interest rates regressed against the volume of migration. Indeed, a significant negative relationship was observed between real interest rates and migration as well.[29] The relationship has probably, if anything, strength-

27. This is the opening sentence of Joel Fried and Peter Howitt, "The Effects of Inflation on Real Interest Rates," *American Economic Review* 73 (Dec. 1983): 968.

28. Richard K. Vedder, "Migration and Permanent Income" (Paper presented at the 1973 annual meetings of the Western Economic Association, Claremont, Calif. Available as Research Paper No. 165, Ohio University, Athens, OH 45701).

29. Significant at the 10 percent level in a regression that includes nominal interest rates as well. The nominal interest rate variable is significant at the 5 percent level.

Table 10–5.   Migration and Interest Rates, 1950–1980.

Year[a]	% of Pop. Moving in Year[b] (%)	Int. Rates, Home Mortgages[c] (%)
1950–51	21.0	4.55
1960–61	20.6	6.16
1970–71	18.7	9.03
1980–81	17.2	13.44

SOURCE: U.S. Department of Commerce, Bureau of the Census.
[a]From March of the first year indicated to March of the following year.
[b]The proportion of those one year of age or over at the end of the year living in a different house from the one lived in at the beginning of the year.
[c]FHA insured mortgages.

ened over time because of sharp increases in nominal interest rates. Table 10–5 shows how rising interest rates on home mortgages coincide with a decline in migration over the past thirty years.

The decline in migration, which was at least partially the consequence of inflation-induced increases in interest rates, reduced the potency of one means of dealing with family dissension, namely geographic movement. Some of the causes of marital discord are location-specific in nature, relating to job-oriented problems, disagreement over how to handle family members' relationships with undesirable friends, etc. Movement allows a fresh start and encourages the family to maintain a closeness, at least until new extrafamilial relationships form in the new locale. The migration safety-valve was rendered less effective by the moving costs associated with enhanced rates of inflation.

We have argued that declining migration is related to rising divorce, but have not presented direct evidence. This is done in Figure 10–1, which shows a striking negative association between migration and divorce. Incidentally, this relationship is all the more significant since the act of divorce itself induces a certain amount of migration, as spouses physically separate.[30]

30. One study shows that almost 50 percent of a sample of divorced persons made an interstate move as a result of the divorce. See Shirley J. Asher and Bernard L. Bloom, "Geographic Mobility as a Factor in Adjustment to Divorce," *Journal of Divorce* 6 (Summer 1983): 69–84.

A study that suggests that migration contributes to raising the divorce rate is W. R. Freundenburg, "Women and Men in an Energy Boom Town: Adjustment, Alienation and Adaption," *Rural Sociology* 7 (Summer 1981): 220–24. A study that argues that migration has little impact on the divorce rate is Kenneth P. Wilkson, Robert R. Reynolds, James G. Thompson and Lawrence M. Ostresh, "Divorce and Recent Net Migration into the Old West," *Journal of Marriage and the Family* 45 (May 1983): 437–45.

Figure 10–1.   Migration and Divorce, 1960–1980.

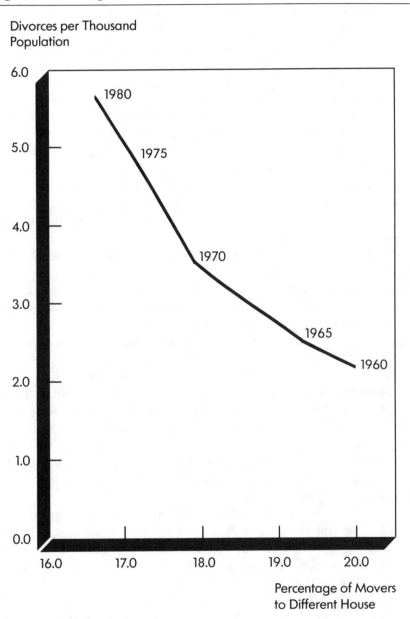

Divorces per Thousand
Population

Percentage of Movers
to Different House

THE RISING NATURAL RATE OF DIVORCE

The positive relationship between inflation and divorce ought to disappear in the very long run as people develop strategies to guard against the impact of price changes on household finances and marital relationships. As inflation becomes better anticipated, the inflation-divorce relationship should eventually, resemble the analogous long-run vertical Phillips curve, as illustrated in Figure 10–2. The short-run curve is positively sloped but shifts with changing inflationary expectations. As inflation rates have come down from the elevated levels of the late seventies, one might expect divorce rates to fall because of the fact that the disinflation was initially largely unanticipated. In time, as people better anticipate inflation (or learn to protect themselves from unanticipated inflation through such devices as indexed contracts), we would expect the divorce rate to fall. This has already occurred to some extent.

At the same time, the historical experience makes it doubtful that the divorce rate will fall dramatically (to, say, 2.0 or less per thousand) in a short time period. Institutional and structural changes, including rising public assistance payments, have reduced the advantages of marital trading arrangements, raising the natural rate of divorce; the natural rate has risen about 50 percent since the mid-sixties from rising public assistance payments alone.

Of course, in the very long run the impact of factors like public assistance payments on the divorce rate will probably change. In the short run, higher public assistance payments mean more divorce. In the long run, they may lead to fewer marriages and, as a consequence of a smaller pool of married persons, a lower crude divorce rate (divorces as related to the total population). In other words, the divorce rate might "naturally" tend to drift downward somewhat in time, in the absence of other changes.

Certainly some changes in our institutional setting almost definitely would lower the natural rate of divorce—lower welfare incentives to having single-parent households, stricter laws permitting divorce, and lower interest rates enhancing geographic mobility, are a few examples. The decline in inflation alone will probably only partly return us to the days of low divorce observed in the interwar period. Still, improvement in family life is a consideration in evaluating the benefits of noninflationary macroeconomic policies.

Figure 10–2.   The Inflation-Divorce Relationship.

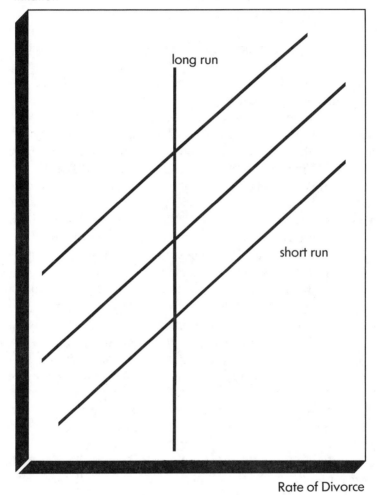

Rate of
Inflation

long run

short run

Rate of Divorce

POLICY IMPLICATIONS

Macroeconomic policies that lead to increases in prices can be justified only if the benefits from such policies exceed the costs. This study suggests that a byproduct of inflation (which itself results from macroeconomic policy) is a substantial cost associated with marital discord. Accordingly, recognition of that cost reduces the likelihood that any inflationary policy will be socially desirable.

There is, of course, real doubt among many economists as to whether the inflationary policies of modern times have any of the claimed benefits attributed to them. Those doubts are especially pronounced regarding reducing the rate of unemployment. We share these doubts and, accordingly, can think of no good reason to permit a debasement in the value of the currency unit over time.[31] The findings here reinforce the view that inflationary macroeconomic policies are, on balance, a burden to our society.

At the same time, however, many economists still believe (despite the overwhelming evidence of the 1970s) that one can "buy" lower unemployment through monetary and fiscal policies that are basically inflationary.[32] Even if this were true, it is possible that the cost to society in terms of social conflict may well exceed the benefits as measured in reduced unemployment.

For example, if a 10 percent inflation rate lowers unemployment by 2 million but creates 500,000 divorces, the $12 billion social cost of the divorces (putting a $25,000 cost on the average divorce) would exceed the benefits if the creation of a job for a year were valued at less than $6,000. Thus even if the Phillips curve is a valid policy tool, expansionary (i.e., inflationary) macroeconomic policies to alleviate unemployment may well be inappropriate.

It is possible, of course, that the inflation-divorce relationship observed historically may be changing, in part because the public now more correctly anticipates future inflation. Nonetheless, the evidence presented lends strong support for those who advocate policies that would prevent inflation, such as a slowing in the growth in monetary aggregates, a reduction or elimination of the monetizing of new federal debt, etc.

We must keep in mind that every time the Federal Reserve permits an expansion in the money stock of, say, a billion dollars, it not only

31. See Gallaway and Vedder, *n.* 19. Unemployment variation, in our view, is best explained by a model incorporating wages, prices, and labor productivity variables. See also Lowell Gallaway and Richard Vedder, "Wages Prices and Employment: Von Mises and the 'Progressives,'" *The Austrian Economic Review,* forthcoming.

32. In a study for the Center for National Policy, Otto Eckstein, Robert Gordon, and Joel Popkin recently reaffirmed their belief that the Phillips curve is a valid policy tool. One popular textbok writer, Bradley R. Schiller, in a letter to academic economists on November 14, 1983, said that "the Phillips Curve . . . is surprisingly accurate. . . . Unemployment increases before prices fall."

has an impact on prices, interest rates, and possibly unemployment, but it also creates thousands of divorces. Every time the Federal Reserve System buys bonds to stimulate money expansion, it is probably creating divorces as well as money. In 1940, when the Fed held less than $2.5 billion in federal debt, the divorce rate was two per thousand population; more recently, the Fed has held about $150 billion in federal debt, and the divorce rate exceeds five per thousand.[33] The evidence, then, provides support for those who want to constrain the ability of the monetary authorities to create money, be it in the form of a legislated constitutional amendment mandating a monetary growth rule, a move to a gold or other commodity-based standard, or some other indirect means (e.g., a balanced budget amendment). The American family is too important an institution to be left, in part at least, to the mercy of the Federal Reserve Board and the makers of fiscal policy.

Beyond stabilization policy, the federal government's well-intentioned program to alleviate poverty and enhance redistributive justice seems to have some very significant social costs. Again, these costs need to be taken into account in assessing the efficacy of those social policies. Our findings are consistent with Charles Murray's view that welfare programs have imposed a debilitating burden on the black family.[34] Reform of our system of entitlements should address the alleviation of this burden, restoring the basis for marital trading arrangements, thereby reducing the natural rate of divorce.

Finally, we find it worth noting that after 1981, the incidence of divorce declined somewhat in the United States. This is quite consistent with our analysis. The rate of inflation fell from the double-digit level in 1979 and 1980, and became much more fully anticipated. Similarly, real per capita federal public-aid expenditures declined by about 9 percent between 1980 and 1983. Thus, strains on the traditional marital trading relationships imposed by inflation and public assistance payments eased somewhat. To the extent these trends continue, there may well be some additional reduction in the rate of divorce in the United States.

---

33. See *Historical Statistics, n.* 2, and *Statistical Abstract, n.* 4, for statistics on Fed ownership of debt and on divorce rates.

34. Murray, *n.* 21.

11

GOVERNMENT POLICY AND THE DISTORTIONS IN FAMILY HOUSING

Dwight R. Lee

A stated objective of U.S. government policy is that of making adequate housing available to all. According to the Housing and Urban Development Act of 1968, a goal of the federal government is "a decent home and a suitable living environment for every American family."[1] An important prong in this commitment has been government policies designed to bring homeownership within reach of most, if not all, family units.[2] The goal of adequate housing and widespread homeownership is no doubt a worthy one, although there are reasons to question whether it is an appropriate goal for government policy. But leaving aside the question of appropriateness, which will be discussed in our concluding remarks, the main purpose of this paper is to consider how successful, in a broad sense, government housing policy has been.

It would appear, at least superficially, that government has been very successful at encouraging homeownership. Soon after the end of

---

1. Cited in Roger Pilon, "Property Rights and a Free Society," in M. B. Johnson, ed., *Resolving the Housing Crisis: Government Policy, Decontrol, and the Public Interest* (San Francisco: Pacific Institute for Public Policy Research, 1982), p. 369.

2. For example, the federal government has a program that in 1977 provided mortgages at interest rates as low as 5 percent to families who qualified by earning less than 95 percent of the median income in the area where they lived. See *U. S. News and World Report*, 14, March 1977, p. 42.

World War II, a little less than half of the nation's houses were owner occupied. By the late 1970s almost two-thirds of the housing stock was owner occupied. Of course, many things would have to be taken into consideration to explain the increased percentage of homeownership since World War II, not the least of which is increasing per capita income. Strong evidence exists, however, in support of the view that government policy has been the reason for much of the growth in homeownership. Rosen and Rosen have estimated that 25 percent of the growth in the proportion of homeowners during the post–World War II period is explained by the fact that U.S. tax policy favors homeownership.[3]

Unfortunately, however, for government policy aimed at specific objectives like encouraging homeownership, there is a well-known, but underappreciated, economic phenomenon that is summed up in the saying, "You can never do only one thing." There are always unintended consequences arising from attempts to achieve particular economic results with policy manipulation. And it is typically the case that these unintended consequences have long-run implications that are unfortunate, not only from a general perspective, but from the perspective of the policy objective as well. Examples here are too numerous to itemize, ranging from minimum wage legislation (for helping the working poor) to energy policy (for reducing our dependency on foreign oil).

Policy designed to encourage homeownership has been no exception to the general perversity of government policy. The effect of artificially encouraging homeownership has worked, at least over the short run, by creating what might be considered relatively mild distortions in the allocation of resources. Over the longer run, however, housing policy has combined with undisciplined macroeconomic policy to generate economic dislocations of major significance. The result has been an undermining of the productive potential of the economy, which has not only been disastrous to economic performance in general, but has also frustrated the very objectives housing policy was supposed to accomplish.

The housing slump that began in earnest in 1980 was in many respects the result of delayed perversities in policies designed to stimulate demand for housing. The prevailing opinion seens to be that

---

3. Harvey S. Rosen and Kenneth T. Rosen, "Federal Taxes and Homeownership: Evidence from Time Series," *Journal of Political Economy* 88 (Feb. 1980): 59–75.

housing suffered from high interest rates and depressed economic activity, and once interest rates dropped and the economy picked up again, the housing industry was on the road to recovery. It is also widely believed that a revitalized housing industry was a crucial ingredient in a recovery of the economy in general. It is no doubt true that lower interest rates and a pickup in business activity were of some help to housing. But if we are to have any hope for a sustained improvement in economic performance, it is important that many of the effects of past government housing policy be reversed and that the housing industry not experience too much of a boom, at least in the short run.

The unprecedented housing boom of the 1970s was not a realistic benchmark against which to judge performance in this industry. That boom was instead the result of a combination of government policies that are largely responsible for the slow economic growth we have experienced on average during the past decade and a half. Any attempt to return the housing industry to its former health by following these policies will lead to failure. The housing industry cannot be sustained at past levels, and any attempt to do so will ultimately result in economic stagnation.

The option of encouraging homeownership with those policies that appeared to work in the past is no longer a viable one. On the other hand, a move back to responsible economic policy, one designed to improve economic performance by motivating productive investment rather than by stimulating current consumption, will require readjustments that will in some ways make it difficult for young families to become homeowners. Past policy, which did encourage homeownership in previous decades, has left us the legacy of an economic environment that actually *discourages* homeownership. In order for us to develop these points more systematically, it will be helpful to consider first some of the policies that were specifically designed to promote homeownership.

THE POLICY SETTING

Federal encouragement of homeownership goes at least as far back as the Homestead Act. For our purpose, however, the relevant history begins about fifty years ago. During the Great Depression the federal government began a series of policies with the expressed intention of stimulating housing demand. The first major move in this direction was to direct more of the country's saving to home buyers. This was done by providing significant tax advantages to the savings and loan industry in return for channeling their funds almost exclusively into long-term mortgages to be made available at low fixed rates. This policy was eventually followed by Regulation Q, which further assisted the savings and loan industry to carry out its appointed task by reducing intraindustry competition for funds. Additional government assistance was offered through the Federal Savings and Loan Insurance Corporation, which was established to insure deposits; the Federal Housing Administration and the Veterans Administration, which were created to further insure and subsidize home mortgages; the Federal National Mortgage Association (Ginnie Mae), which was brought forth to increase the liquidity of mortgages, and so on.

For purposes of our discussion, the most important policy stimulus to homeownership comes through tax incentives. Homeowners can receive a significant tax break because the law allows them to deduct mortgage interest payments from their taxable income. One might argue that this is entirely appropriate, as it puts mortgage interest payments on equal footing with interest payments on business capital, which are also deductible. Such is not the case, however. The difference arises from the fact that the return to business capital is subject to tax whereas the return to homeownership is effectively untaxed. The major return to homeownership is the implicit rental value received by homeowners, and this is never taxed. The capital gains realized when an owner-occupied house is sold may be taxed, but this tax is easily avoided and therefore seldom imposed. The important point to note here is that tax deductibility of mortgage interest artificially increases the private return to investment in homeownership relative to investment in business capital.

Although policies giving differential advantages to homeowners are all "justified" on the grounds that they help families afford their own home, it is interesting to ask where the effective political support for these policies is found. Housing costs represent a major portion of most family budgets, but even so it is unlikely that homeowners and potential homeowners ever found it individually rational to join a political movement for the purpose of influencing housing legislation at the national level. The gain any individual could expect from attempting to influence such legislation is small relative to the personal benefits to be realized from concentrating on private endeavors in which personal efforts are more likely to be decisive. Homeowners make up a group of such size and of such diverse interests that it would be almost impossible to organize them for effective political action. This is not the case for those whose primary source of income is tied to the profitability of, say, the savings and loan industry. The members of this group share a common interest of overriding importance to each, and they will be in communication with each other through professional associations, both formal and informal. This group will find it relatively easy to coalesce around political objectives—and will often find compelling reasons for doing so. One such compelling reason was the opportunity to obtain legislation favorable to the savings and loan industry (e.g., Regulation Q) through an organized lobbying effort. We can be sure that it was the savings and loan lobby, not the nation's homeowners, that exerted the political influence needed to enact laws favorable to homeowners—albeit only as a byproduct.[4]

Once these laws have been passed, however, and homeowners have made decisions appropriate to the environment that has been created, there will be political resistance to the elimination of these laws. Even the radical tax overhaul plan drafted in 1986 by the Senate Finance Committee did not touch the deductibility of mortgage interest payments. Eliminating their deductibility would impose losses on existing homeowners because it could decrease the resale value of the existing stock of houses. This loss would be visible enough, significant enough, and widespread enough that the politician who seriously proposed eliminating the mortgage interest deduction would face spontaneous retribution from unorganized homeowners.[5]

It is true that policies favoring housing create resource misallocations that cost more than any benefits provided. But this cost is widely diffused, difficult to trace back to any particular set of policies, and therefore politically invisible. Even those who acknowledge the economic distortions generated by preferential treatment given homeowners will typically argue that such distortions are a small price to pay for the social advantages derived by putting homeownership within

4. The 1981 legislation establishing the All Savers certificates is a recent example. It was the savings and loan industry, not homeowners, that pushed hard for this legislation. Of course, according to the political rhetoric, All Savers certificates were desirable because they would help young families afford homes by increasing the availability of mortgage money. There was certainly some truth in this rhetoric, but the effective push for the certificates was motivated by the benefits they promised the savings and loan associations, not young homeowners.

5. Jimmy Carter proposed the elimination of the mortgage interest deduction early in his presidential bid. The reaction was quick and unmistakable, and the proposal was immediately dropped.

reach of more Americans. An economist might accept this argument and turn his attention to more serious problems in an otherwise un-distorted economic environment. Unfortunately, in periods when the distortions of inflation begin interacting with the distortions of housing policy, the economic costs reach magnitudes that are not easily ignored.

NEGATIVE INTEREST RATES

The mortgage interest rate deduction creates the most significant housing policy distortion during periods of inflation. The key to understanding this distortion is the recognition that it is the nominal rather than the real interest rate that determines the size of the deduction. During periods of inflation, the nominal rate of interest increases (assuming that the inflation is fully anticipated) enough to provide lenders a real rate of return equal to the rate that would have existed in the absence of inflation, that is, the normal rate. Thus the nominal interest rate is approximately equal to the inflation rate plus the normal rate.[6] So while the real interest rate remains constant at the normal rate, the amount that the home buyer can deduct from taxable income increases as inflation increases. In addition, inflation boosts nominal incomes and has historically moved families up the progressive income tax structure into higher marginal tax brackets. Once state income taxes are considered, an American family needed little more than an average income in the late 1970s to find itself facing a marginal tax rate of 40 percent or more. The combined effect of mortgage interest deductibility, inflation, and a progressive income tax structure can mean dramatic reductions in the after-tax real interest payment required to buy a house.

An illustrative example will be useful here. Assume that the normal interest rate is 3 percent (which probably is not far off), the inflation rate is zero, and the prospective home buyer is in the 30 percent marginal tax bracket. In this case the nominal interest rate will equal the 3 percent normal rate and, after taxes, the home buyer will face a 2.1 percent real annual interest charge. Let us now assume a 13 percent

---

6. Three qualifications have to be made here. First, inflation creates additional uncertainty that will be reflected as a risk premium in the nominal interest rate. Secondly, ignoring the risk premium, the nominal interest rate, i, is actually equal to $\dot{p} + r + \dot{p}r$, where $\dot{p}$ is the inflation rate and r is the normal interest rate. The interaction term will be ignored for purposes of exposition. Finally, after-tax considerations are important in determining what nominal interest rate translates into a given after-tax real rate. After-tax real rates are important to the upcoming discussion, but will be ignored as a qualification to the rough equality $i = \dot{p} + r$.

rate of inflation with the prospective home buyer having been elevated into the 40 percent marginal tax bracket. The nominal interest rate will be 16 percent which will be 9.6 percent after taxes. But this is 3.4 percent less than the inflation rate and thus translates in a negative 3.4 percent after-tax real interest rate.

As is easily determined, the higher the inflation and nominal interest rates the lower (more negative) the after-tax real interest rate becomes. One might argue that by picking a relatively high inflation rate of 13 percent, we have chosen an example that dramatizes the point being made.[7] True enough, but an important consideration has been ignored in these examples that adds further downward pressure on after-tax real interest rates. In the beginning of an inflationary period, the inflation is seldom fully anticipated, and the inflationary premium will lag the inflation rate. The consequence is low real interest rates (possibly negative) even before the marginal tax rate effect is considered. During much of the 1970s real interest rates before taxes were negative and after-tax real rates were decidedly so.

Lagging expectations add something of a complication, which needs to be mentioned, to this analysis. If home buyers were paying negative real rates after taxes, then it was also generally true that lenders were receiving negative real rates after taxes. It cannot be argued that borrowers were able to anticipate inflation more accurately than were lenders, since there is no reason for believing this to be the case. So why were lenders willing to make loans for a negative return? There are two responses to this question. First, much of the lending during the seventies was financed by small savers who, because of such banking controls as Regulation Q, had little opportunity to receive competitive rates of return. While the supply of saving is interest-elastic, in the short run this elasticity is surely not large. Second, lenders were willing to finance the housing boom at a negative return only for a relatively short period of time. After-tax real interest rates turned sharply positive during the early 1980s. But during the seventies home buyers received enormous subsidies in the form of negative after-tax real interest rates; this was certainly an important contributing factor to the boom in housing.

SUBSTITUTING LIVING SPACE FOR PRODUCTIVITY

Inflation and high marginal tax rates not only made homeownership more attractive, it made investment in business enterprise less attrac-

---

7. The inflation rate approached 13 percent during 1974 and 1980.

tive. The tax burden on the return to business capital is increased by inflation in two distinct ways. First, the tax on capital gains is applied to increases in the nominal value of capital stock, not the real value. During periods of inflation the increase in nominal value is always greater than the increase in real value. Second, business capital is usually carried on the books at its historical cost for purposes of tax accounting. Inflation, therefore, causes allowable depreciation expense to be understated relative to real replacement cost and thus results in taxable profits being overstated.[8] Operating together, these two factors reduced the after-tax real return on investment in business capital. From 1970 through 1977 inflation increased the tax burden on corporate sector capital income by a total of over $180 billion. In each of the years 1973 through 1977, inflation increased the taxes paid on corporate capital income by at least 50 percent above what would have been required in the absence of inflation. In 1974 inflation nearly doubled the total tax burden on corporate capital by increasing this burden 95.1 percent.[9]

With people finding it difficult to obtain positive, much less attractive, real returns on their savings, it should come as no suprise that savings declined during the 1970s. As indicated earlier, the interest elasticity of saving, at least in the short run, is not large, but it is certainly not zero. The nation's total net saving rate was 15.2 percent in the 1960s, but only 11.7 percent in the 1970s, a 23 percent decline. This decline is explained primarily by a reduction in the rate of household savings out of disposable income. If the rate of household savings had not changed between the sixties and seventies, for example, the nation's saving rate would have fallen to only 14.8 percent during the seventies.[10]

The unfortunate consequences of the reduction in the saving rate accentuated the policy distortions we have been discussing. By in-

8. It might seem that these two biases in the tax law have been offset, at least somewhat, by the ability of businesses to deduct nominal interest charges from taxable profits. But for business in general this advantage has been negated by the fact that the interest paid by one business is generally received by another business; the deduction against taxable profits for one is an addition to taxable profits for another. For empirical support for the view that these two effects have, in fact, approximately offset each other, see Martin Feldstein and Lawrence Summers, "Inflation and the Taxation of Capital Income in the Corporate Section," *National Tax Journal* 32 (Dec. 1979): 445–70.

9. These figures result from the empirical work of Feldstein and Summers. n. 8.

10. See the *Economic Report of the President* (Washington, D.C.: U.S. Government Printing Office, January 1982), pp. 116–17.

creasing the private return on housing investment while lowering the private return on investment in business capital, government policy caused a smaller percentage of the savings that were available to be directed into productive capital. The ratio of net investment in housing construction to net investment in business plant and equipment was 52 percent during the last half of the 1960s. This ratio had increased to 76 percent by the last half of the 1970s. Some of this shift can be explained by the maturation of the post–World War II baby boom. But that this is only part of the explanation is easily established by the fact that much of the increased investment in housing went into additional quality rather than additional numbers of units.

The average size of a newly constructed house, measured in square feet, increased every year during the 1970s, with the exception of 1975 when it remained constant. In 1970 the newly constructed house averaged 1,510 square feet. By 1979 the size of the newly constructed house had increased over 16 percent to 1,760 square feet.[11] The percentage of new homes containing one or more fireplaces, air conditioning, and two or more baths all rose between 1975 and 1979.[12] The quality of the average housing start was more than 10 percent higher during the period 1977–79 than it would have been in the absence of the distortions caused by inflation and tax policy.[13] Measured in terms of dollars, the quality of the housing stock in 1979 was approximately $66 billion greater (in 1979 prices) because of these distortions.[14]

The significance of the distortions in the housing market caused by government policy is best appreciated by recognizing that in a distortion-free environment the size of housing would have almost surely fallen, not increased, during the decade. Houses would have become smaller for much the same reasons that automobiles became smaller. Let us first consider energy cost. The cost of space heating increased dramatically during the seventies. While consumer prices in general increased by a factor of 1.98 between 1970 and the end of 1979,[15] the price of household fuels was increasing by a factor of 2.89 over

11. U.S. Bureau of the Census, *Construction Reports*.
12. See page 425 of Patric H. Hendershott, "Real User Costs and the Demand for Single-Family Housing," *Brookings Papers on Economic Activity* 2 (1980): 401–44.
13. Ibid., p. 441.
14. Ibid., p. 444.
15. *Economic Report of the President* (Washington, D.C.: U.S. Government Printing Office, January 1981), p. 289.

the same interval.[16] Also, the number of members per household declined steadily during the 1970s. The average household contained 3.14 members in 1970 but only 2.78 members in 1979.[17] Finally, consider that after the effects of inflation and federal taxes are accounted for, the median family income declined from $8,412 in 1970 to $7,976 in 1980.[18]

The policy-induced distortions that undermined the motivation to save and misdirected an increased percentage of our saving into residential capital obviously served to encourage homeownership in the short run. These distortions have had longer-run consequences, however, that are unfortunate for the economy in general and very probably for the hope of widespread homeownership in particular. Savings that were devoted to increasing the size of houses—to be occupied by smaller families and heated by more expensive energy—would have provided much more long-run benefits in the form of general economic productivity had they been used to maintain and expand our capital base. The 1970s will not be known as a period of economic growth and vitality for the United States. Rather, lagging capital formation and stagnating productivity characterized U.S. economic performance during that decade. From 1973 through 1979, for example, the annual increase in labor productivity was only 0.1 percent in the U.S. As Table 11–1 shows, this was the smallest annual increase of any major industrial economy in the free world. The route to genuine economic growth and prosperity is through business investment in plant, equipment, and innovation, not through investment in oversized houses. It is not surprising that the housing boom of the 1970s coincided with stagnating economic performance.

FAILING ON ITS OWN TERMS

One can question whether it has ever been desirable for government to institute polices having the narrow objective of making homeownership a viable option for the widest possible segment of the population. It is true that empirical studies have indicated that the current

16. Ibid., p. 290.

17. U.S. Bureau of the Census, *Current Population Reports*, series p-20.

18. These figures were cited in James T. Bennett and Thomas J. DiLorenzo, "How the Government Evades Taxes," *Policy Review* 19 (Winter 1982): 71–89. According to Bennett and DiLorenzo, these figures understate the actual decline in real after-tax income because they do not include state and local taxes, which increased more rapidly than did inflation during the 1970s.

Table 11-1. Increase in Labor Productivity, 1973-1979.

Country	Annual Increase in Labor Productivity (%)
Japan	3.4
Germany	3.2
France	2.7
Italy	1.6
Canada	0.4
United Kingdom	0.3
United States	0.1

SOURCE: *Economic Report of the President*, January 1980, p. 85.

homeownership rate is higher than it would have been in the absence of government policies encouraging homeownership.[19] What these studies do not consider, however, is the negative impact that housing policies have also had on national income. Given that government policies designed to promote homeownership have hampered the growth in real income and that homeownership is an increasing function of income,[20] it is certainly possible that government housing policy has been counterproductive, even when judged from a narrow perspective.

In addition to the negative impact on real income exerted by government housing policies, much of the subsidy these policies supposedly provided to new home buyers was dissipated by rapidly escalating housing prices. In the absence of restrictions on competition, this would have been much less of a problem, since the supply of housing space would have been highly price elastic. But building codes, zoning ordinances, and growth controls have all served to artificially restrict housing supply from responding to the policy-induced increase in the demand for housing. It has been estimated, for example, that over 27 percent of the increase in the real price of housing over the period 1974 through 1979 in Santa Barbara County, California, is explained by government restrictions on supply.[21] Rather

19. See Rosen and Rosen, *n*. 3, and Hendershott, *n*. 12.

20. Harvey Rosen has found, not surprisingly, that higher income families are more likely to own their home. See Harvey S. Rosen, "Housing Decisions and the U.S. Income Tax: An Econometric Analysis," *Journal of Public Economics* 11 (Feb. 1979): 15.

21. See Lloyd J. Mercer and W. Douglas Morgan, "An Estimate of Residential Growth Controls' Impact on House Prices," in Johnson, *n*. 1, pp. 189-215. Many of the chapters in

than helping new home buyers, much of the benefit derived from federal policies supposedly designed to aid home buyers was captured by existing homeowners, building contractors, and local governments in the form of higher housing prices and municipally imposed development fees.

The effect of this was to price new home buyers out of the market. The percentage of families able to afford a medium-priced new house declined from 46.2 percent in 1970 to 27.0 percent in 1976.[22] By 1981 this percentage had further dropped (plummeted) to 10 percent.[23] More geographically specific evidence comes from the city of Los Angeles, where it was found that 54 percent of the city's renters could have afforded to purchase a house in 1970. The city's Community Development Department found in 1979 that only 16 percent of the renters could afford to buy their own house.[24] Obviously, it is the low-income purchaser who is hurt most by rapidly escalating housing prices. Despite the stated intention of government policy to bring homeownership within reach of the widest possible segment of the population, it is clear that the percentage of middle- and low-income families who could afford their own home declined between the 1960s and 1970s. In 1965–66, for example, 17 percent of all new house purchases were made by families in the bottom third of the income distribution. By 1975–76 this percentage had declined to 4 percent.[25]

What is the appropriate government response to the housing problems that past government policies have created? Depressingly, but not surprisingly, the prevailing sentiment seems to be more of the same. In the realm of government policy, nothing succeeds so well as failure. In discussing what they refer to as the "housing deprivation" resulting from "people paying excessive housing costs," Frieden and Solomon have stated, "Public policy has not yet come to grips

---

this excellent volume deal with the problems in housing that can be traced back to government restrictions on supply. As is often the case, what government gives with one hand it takes back with the other.

It should be noted that some of the increase in the size of new houses can be explained by supply restrictions of the type discussed in the Johnson volume.

22. Bernard J. Frieden and Arthur P. Solomon, *The Nation's Housing: 1975–1985* (Cambridge: Joint Center for Urban Studies of the Massachusetts Institute of Technology and Harvard University, April 1977), p. 124.

23. See "Downsizing the American Dream," *Time*, 5 Oct. 1981, p. 95.

24. See Johnson, *n.* 1, p. 4.

25. This information comes from Frieden and Solomon, *n.* 22, p. 130.

with this growing type of housing deprivation. The most effective approach would be some form of income assistance. . . ."[26] Adding to and expanding the housing subsidies that already exist can only dig us deeper into the productivity hole in which we still find ourselves. Little thought seems to be given to eliminating some of the government policies that have led us to our existing problems.[27] The typical response to the problems brought on by government intrusion into the economy is to suggest more government intrusion into the economy. It is as if the economic boat were sinking because the water level is rising through a hole that the policy makers drilled in the bottom, and the policy makers all agree that the best response is to drill some more holes in the bottom in the hope that the water will run out.

It is probably true that some temporary improvement in the ability of people to purchase their own home could be realized through an expansion of government subsidies. But the long-run effect of bailing out mistaken government policy is clear. Attempting to maintain the high housing demand of the seventies with a continuation of that decade's policies can only further weaken the productive capacity of the economy—productive capacity upon which all demand, including the demand for housing, ultimately depends. Unfortunately, the political time horizon is a very truncated one. It is the short-run consequence of policy that guides political decisions, not the long-run consequences. And this does not bode well for a reversal of the past government policies that have created many of our continuing housing problems. The undeniable benefits from such a reversal will be reached only in the politically irrelevant long-run. In the politically relevant short-run, the impact of a genuine improvement in government policy will be painful, and, in fact, will aggravate our housing problems before it can, in time, alleviate them.

SUPPLY-SIDE ECONOMICS AND HOUSING

Government policy that has stimulated housing demand in the short run has undermined economic productivity and, very likely, housing

---

26. Ibid., p. 133.

27. Frieden and Solomon are aware of the harmful effect of at least some government policies. They state, "Where these [restrictive land development] controls are in force, home builders have a narrower choice of locations where they can operate, and landowners are able to raise prices for those sites where building remains feasible." See Frieden and Solomon, *n.* 22, p. 139. Also, see Bernard Frieden, "The Exclusionary Effect of Growth Controls," in Johnson, *n.* 1, pp. 19–34.

demand in the longer run. Government policy genuinely oriented toward increasing long-run economic productivity will undermine housing demand in the short run, but in the longer run it is the only way of efficiently promoting further expansions in home ownership.

The stagnation in economic productivity experienced during the 1970s prompted a renewed emphasis on the supply side of the economy. The important point made by supply-side economists is that the difficult economic problem lies in expanding our productive capacity, not in encouraging consumption. If we are able to increase the goods and services produced, we can rest assured that demand will keep pace. But if we do not increase productivity, the old adage, "You can't consume what hasn't been produced," remains as true today as it was before Keynesian economists started worrying about demand management.

It is easy to get the impression from the political pundits and the popular press that supply-side economics is nothing more than a passing fad based on a combination of political rhetoric and economic snake oil. Quite the contrary. Supply-side economics is soundly rooted in a body of economic analysis that has been developing for over 200 years.[28] Once it is stripped to its fundamentals, supply-side economics is a restatement of the most basic of all economic principles—increase the relative return of engaging in an activity and there will be an increase in that activity. Of primary concern to supply-side economics is the return to leisure and consumption relative to the return to production and investing. If the relative return to leisure and consumption is increased, people will produce less and attempt to consume more—an attempt that can be successful only in the short run. On the other hand, if the relative return to productive activity is increased, people will substitute production for consumption—a substitution that in the long run will result in more consumption than otherwise.

While supply-side economics is concerned with the entire spectrum of economic policy and the effect this policy has on productive incentives, it concentrates attention primarily on the incentive effects of taxation. From the supply-side perspective, the importance of a change in taxes arises from the impact this change has on relative

28. See David G. Raboy, "The Theoretical Heritage of Supply Side Economics," in D. Raboy, ed., *Essays in Supply Side Economics* (Washington, D.C.: The Institute for Research on the Economics of Taxation, 1982).

prices.[29] The advantage a supply-side economist sees in reducing the marginal tax applied to interest income, for example, is that the increased incentive to save will translate into more savings and increased potential for investment and long-run economic growth. Similar advantages are seen for reductions in the marginal tax rate on income (the return to labor) and capital gains (the return to investment). In each case the tax reduction may increase take-home income immediately and, by doing so, motivate more spending.[30] This short-run effect is not, however, of primary concern to supply-side economists. The focus of supply-siders is on long-run increases in productivity.

Supply-side economics is also concerned with the problem of inflation and the disruptive effect it has on productivity. To the extent that long-run increases in economic productivity are achieved through tax reductions, inflation will be held down as a consequence of an increase in the growth of available goods and services relative to the growth in the money supply. A necessary complement to supply-side economics in this regard is restraint on monetary growth. A program of supply-side incentives and monetary restraint will, in the long-run, restore the productivity of the economy and restrain inflation. But as an important side effect of supply-side economic policy and improved economic performance, the attractiveness of housing as an investment will be diminished, at least in the short run.

In an expectational environment created by a history of profligate government policy, an environment in which people believe that tax cuts and reductions in inflation are temporary detours from the long-term trend, the short-run effect of a partial return to responsible government policy during the 1980s was unpleasant. In the absence of significant government spending restraint, tax cuts can be said to have contributed to the federal deficit in the short run.[31] This deficit re-

29. In this regard it is changes in marginal tax rates that are crucial. For more on this point see Robert E. Keleher, "Supply-Side Tax Policy: Reviewing the Evidence," in T. Hailstones, ed., *Viewpoints on Supply-Side Economics* (Richmond: Robert F. Dame, 1982).

30. Marginal tax rates can be reduced, of course, without lowering the average tax rate. So a reduction in marginal tax rates may have no effect on spendable income. Even if a tax cut does reduce total tax payments, it does not follow that there will be a positive income effect when the value of politically provided services are taken into consideration.

31. This is true even if we were on the upper half of the celebrated Laffer curve, where tax rates have been increased to the point of actually reducing the tax revenue the government receives. In this situation the long-run effect of a *permanent* tax cut is to motivate an expansion in investment and the tax base sufficient to result in an increase in government revenue. A tax cut does not result in a quick or complete investment response, however, if investors believe that the cut will soon be rescinded by continued inflation or overt policy.

quired increased government borrowing, which meant increased demand for loanable funds and higher real interest rates.[32] Also, bringing inflation under control depressed economic activity temporarily, because it required time for the expectations of economic decision-makers to adjust to actual economic conditions. This meant that the decline in nominal interest rates lagged the decline in inflation rate, and real interest rates were temporarily very high as inflation was reduced.[33] These transitional impacts of supply-side economic policy go far in explaining the sharp downturn experienced by the housing industry in the early 1980s.

But what about the long-run effects? The application of supply-side policy did eventually moderate the squeeze on financial markets and bring a decline in both real and nominal interest rates. The mechanism here operated through lower inflation and restored incentives for production activity, both of which led to a larger tax base, increased tax revenues, and, eventually, a smaller deficit. (Eventual reductions in the growth of defense spending played a role as well.) A smaller deficit helped ease the upward pressure on real interest rates as government demand for loanable funds was reduced. The eventual result by 1986 was an economic environment characterized by a more stable price level, lower nominal interest rates, lower marginal tax rates on personal and business income,[34] and expanding business investment. But strengthening on already-improved economic climate will not necessarily provide the type of recovery those who want to stimulate homeownership and the housing industry are looking for. Establishing the conditions that will be necessary for a genuine re-

---

This provided the rationale for the Reagan administration's insistence that Congress commit itself to a multiyear tax cut. For more on this point see James M. Buchanan and Dwight R. Lee, "Politics, Time and The Laffer Curve," *Journal of Political Economy* 90 (Aug. 1982): 816–19, and, by the same authors, "Tax Rates and Tax Revenues in Political Equilibrium: Some Simple Analytics," *Economic Inquiry* 20 (July 1982): 344–54.

32. Since a tax cut on personal incomes will result in some increase in savings, and a tax cut on corporate profits will allow for more internal financing, it is, however, possible for there not to be any increased pressure on the market for loanable funds.

33. This is an example of the price that ultimately has to be paid for earlier indulgences that gave the temporary illusion of a free lunch. As inflation escalated during the 1970s, the inflationary premium lagged behind the inflation rate, since it took time for inflation to become incorporated into people's expectation. The result was real interest rates that were very low, and often negative, during the seventies. The price for this is paid, in terms of high real rates, as inflation is being brought under control.

34. Under the tax reform bill drafted by the Senate Finance Committee in 1986, marginal tax rates were reduced even further without affecting average tax rates.

vitalization of the economy, a revitalization based on supply-side rather than demand-side considerations, will ensure that the housing industry will not soon recover to the boom levels it experienced during the 1970s. Strange as it may sound, genuine economic recovery depends in part on keeping the housing industry mildly depressed.

A decline in the nominal interest rate, given a constant real rate, increases the interest cost on a mortgage because the interest tax write-off declines. This increase in the cost of carrying a mortgage is further increased by tax reductions that drop people into lower marginal tax brackets—the interest write-off that does remain is worth less. While these considerations are making housing a less attractive investment, they are making other investments more attractive. For the same reasons that high taxes and inflation reduced the incentive for people to invest in business capital, lower taxes and a stable price level increase the return to business investment.

A depressed housing market is often cited as evidence that the economy is in bad shape and that policy corrections aimed at stimulating housing demand are called for. Exactly the opposite is closer to the truth. If a strict supply-side economic policy is put in place, a shift of investment funds out of residential construction (or a failure of investment funds to shift back into residential construction to the extent necessary to restore the boom of the seventies) would constitute solid evidence that the policy is working as it should. This is not to say that housing is an unimportant good or that the objective of adequate housing for the American people is not a worthy one. It has to be remembered, however, that housing is only one of many desirable goods that people want, and policies that subsidize the consumption of one good do so at the expense of a disproportionate reduction in the consumption of other goods. There is little to be said in favor of a policy that undermines the productive capacity of the economy in order to encourage people to spend more on housing. It can only fail in the long run.

CONCLUDING REMARKS

This paper has been concerned with some specific problems that have arisen out of government attempts to encourage homeownership. What one finds is that the benefits from government policy designed to achieve a particular result (more homeownership) have been realized in the short run only at the expense of long-run consequences that undermine many worthwhile objectives, including the objective of widespread homeownership. Criticizing such a policy is, of course, an easy task *ex post*. In concluding, however, it is worthwhile to point out that all political attempts to accomplish specific outcomes are flawed from the beginning in ways that have been exemplified by government policy to encourage homeownership.

An important reason why the United States is a wealthy country today derives from the fact that the framers of the Constitution had little confidence in the ability of the government to promote social well-being through the exercise of government power to achieve particular ends. In their view the best that government can hope to accomplish is to establish a social setting where individuals are free, within the limits of general laws, to pursue their own objectives. By protecting private property and enforcing contracts voluntarily entered into, the government can encourage a system of specialization and exchange that promotes economic efficiency and allows individuals to solve their problems in cooperation with each other. Fundamentally, the founding fathers had a negative view of government. Government was to have a limited role, with little expectation that it was capable of solving specific problems.

This negative view of government contrasts sharply with the orthodoxy which developed in the sixties and seventies. The restrictions on government that the founders placed in the Constitution were seriously eroded by the view that unfettered discretion in the use of government power was a force for social good. Government was seen as the problem-solver of last resort, with the obligation to provide a solution to any problem not instantly eliminated by the private sector. Unfortunately, this "positive" view of government was less conducive to positive consequences than the negative view of the founding fathers. In the words of Friedrich A. Hayek, winner of the Nobel Memorial Prize in Economic Science:

> The first [view] gives us a sense of unlimited power to realize our wishes, while the second [view] leads to the insight that there are limitations to what we can deliberately bring about, and to the recognition that some of our present hopes are delusions. Yet the effect of allowing ourselves to be deluded by the first view has always been that man has actually limited the scope of what he can achieve. For it has always been the recognition of the limits of the possible which has enabled man to make full use of his powers.[35]

35. Friedrich A. Hayek, *Law, Legislation and Liberty*, vol. 1, *Rules and Order* (Chicago: University of Chicago Press, 1973), p. 8.

In the real world of resource scarcity there will always be specific problems. No matter how well the free market economy is performing, people will always face troublesome choices and will perceive ways of solving their particular problems, or of realizing their particular objectives, through the selective use of government power. Yet, as Hayek points out, it is a delusion to believe that genuine social progress can be promoted by calling upon government to do more than can be done. The use of government to solve specific problems cannot reduce the always-present (to some degree) scarcity that is the fundamental cause of these problems. The effect of extending the role of government to force particular solutions to particular problems is to reduce the flow of information and the discipline that are provided by free market exchange and that are needed if we are to respond intelligently to the challenges we face. It is for this reason that government housing policies, along with a multitude of other policies, are seriously flawed.

12

THE STATE AND ADOLESCENT SEXUAL BEHAVIOR

Jacqueline R. Kasun

The modern theory of public choice may have no better illustrations than can be found in the case of government attempts to influence adolescent sexual behavior. These efforts began rather quietly in the mid-1960s as part of the "War on Poverty," when the Office of Economic Opportunity began to make family planning grants to community action agencies.[1] In 1967 Congress amended the Social Security Act to provide funds for family planning in maternal and child health programs, and in 1970 Congress passed the Family Planning Services and Population Research Act, amending Title X of the Public Health Services Act to make it the vehicle for the largest continuing federal funding of birth control. Thus an expanding array of federal programs was gradually made available to persons of reproductive age, "including," the law stated, "minors who can be considered to be sexually active."[2]

---

1. Population Reference Bureau, *World Population Growth and Response: 1965–1975— A Decade of Global Action* (Washington, D.C.: The Population Reference Bureau, April 1976), p. 184.

2. 42 U.S. Code, sec. 602(a).

THE GROWTH OF PROGRAMS TO CONTROL
TEENAGE PREGNANCY

Nevertheless, in the classic manner of public programs, the agenda as well as the funding not only grew far beyond the domain originally provided but, even so, came to be seen as woefully inadequate. Although fertility among women under 20 had declined precipitately since the late 1950s, as shown in Figure 12–1, along with the declines in fertility for all groups of American women, groups concerned with "excessive" population growth expressed increasing worries over "teenage" pregnancy and child-bearing. In 1969 President Nixon's Commission on Population Growth and the American Future, appointed in response to pressures exerted by the Population Crisis Committee and like-minded groups,[3] sponsored several *Research Reports* on the topic.[4] Though written on a note of alarm regarding such topics as "illegitimacy," "unwanted" pregnancies, and "genetic implications," the *Reports* failed to document any special problems for young parenthood that could not be explained by low income. They also noted that comprehensive birth control programs do not reduce illegitimacy.[5]

The *Reports*, however, made clear their real concern by stating that *the size of the population could be significantly reduced* by eliminating all births to teenage mothers.[6] Accordingly, the Commission "deplore [d] the various consequences of teenage pregnancy" and recommended that "birth control information and services" and sex education be provided to teenagers,[7] as was, in fact, already being widely done. With the same object in view, the Commission also recommended that all restrictions on voluntary sterilization be eliminated[8] and that "abortions . . . be performed on request" at public expense.[9] Thus the groups whose special interests were represented by the pub-

---

3. Elizabeth Moore, "How American Big Busines Sold Us the Population Bomb," *The Uncertified Human* (August 1978): 3–6.
    4. Commission on Population Growth and the American Future, *Research Reports*, vol. 1 (Washington, D.C.: Government Printing Office, 1972).
    5. Ibid., pp. 349–50, 419–21.
    6. Ibid., p. 350.
    7. *Population and the American Future: The Report of the Commission on Population Growth and the American Future* (New York: New American Library, 1972), pp. 189–90.
    8. Ibid., p. 171.
    9. Ibid., p. 178.

Figure 12–1.   Pregnancies, Births, and Abortions per 1,000 Women Aged 15–19, 1950–1982.

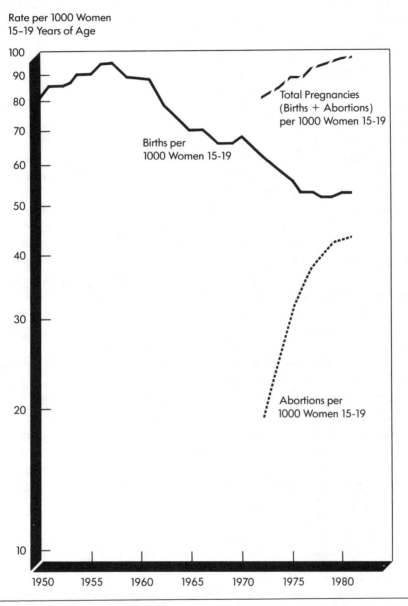

SOURCE: Birth data from National Center for Health Statistics; abortion data from Alan Guttmacher Institute.

Note: Plotted using a semi-log scale.

lic birth-control programs exerted their continuing pressures for the expansion of those programs.

These pressures mounted throughout the 1970s despite continued declines in adolescent fertility. In 1974 the Population Council published a study of "Parental Age as a Factor in Pregnancy Outcome and Child Development,"[10] which again failed to show any marked disadvantages of youthful parenthood but which concluded that the elimination of births to women under 20 and over 34 "would . . . bring relief to a world coping with growth rates that retard economic development and threaten nature's ecological balance."[11] Though the paper had offered no evidence whatever of these last-named problems—indeed, had not even discussed them—this was no more of an obstacle to its publication and warm reception in population circles than its failure to demonstrate the bad effects of youthful childbearing.

These promotional efforts, however, were as nothing compared to what was to come. In 1976 Planned Parenthood, an organization explicitly committed to stopping population growth,[12] and its subsidiary, the Alan Guttmacher Institute, launched their media campaign against the so-called "teenage pregnancy epidemic" with the publication of *11 Million Teenagers: What Can Be Done About the Epidemic of Adolescent Pregnancies in the United States.* This pamphlet was distributed, largely at government expense, to officials of the Carter administration, members of Congress, television broadcasters, newspaper publishers, parent-teacher organizations, churches, youth organizations, and other creators of public opinion. It was presented to the House Select Committee on Population and reproduced in its *Hearings* of 1978, which, in the course of illuminating the crisis of "excessive" population growth, concentrated especially heavily on the problems presumed to be created by youthful childbearing.[13] Many of the assertions and colorful headlines of *11 Million Teenagers* appeared in a blitz of press releases, letters to the editor, and reports to community groups throughout the country.

10. Dorothy Nortman, "Parental Age As a Factor in Pregnancy Outcome and Child Development," *Reports on Population/Family Planning,* no. 16 (New York: The Population Council, Aug. 1974).

11. Ibid., p. 49.

12. *A Five Year Plan, 1976–1980, for the Planned Parenthood Federation of America, Inc.,* approved by the PPFA membership, Oct. 22, 1975, Seattle, pp. 3, 4.

13. *Hearings* before the House Select Committee on Population, "Fertility and Contraception in America: Adolescent and Pre-Adolescent Pregnancy," 95th Congress, 2nd Session, vol. 2 (Washington, D.C.: Government Printing Office, 1978).

With its headlined messages that "U.S. Teenage Childbearing Rates Are Among the World's Highest," "11 Million Teenagers are Sexually Active," and "One Million Teenagers Become Pregnant Each Year," *11 Million Teenagers* not only swept the media up in a wave of astonished concern but is said to have "dazzled" the Secretary of Health, Education, and Welfare.[14] Reinforced by assurances on the part of Frederick Jaffe, late president of the Guttmacher Institute, that Planned Parenthood and other providers of birth control services, could, if suitably provided with increased public financing, manage the newly created crisis of adolescent pregnancy, the campaign also clearly dazzled Congress.[15]

National opinion- and policy-makers were still reeling from the news of the "epidemic" when, in the following year, the Guttmacher Institute published Planned Parenthood's plan for dealing with the crisis described in *11 Million Teenagers*. Sponsored by Planned Parenthood itself, together with Zero Population Growth, the American Public Health Association, and other "family planning" organizations, the document *Planned Births, the Future of the Family and the Quality of American Life: Towards a Comprehensive National Policy and Program* was, as its name implied, a comprehensive plan for public action. It called for the creation of a "national network for early detection of pregnancy," "school-based education programs," "community information and outreach programs," and programs to "encourage hospitals to provide abortion services,"[16] with special efforts "to reduce . . . the number of unintended pregnancies and births among teenagers."[17] It demanded "immediate attention from the Administration and Congressional leadership"[18] for its stated requirements of some $800 million to be provided annually by 1981 for domestic "family planning."

This "immediate attention" was indeed forthcoming. In the following year not only did Congress greatly increase appropriations for existing programs of birth control but also enacted special legislation, the Adolescent Pregnancy Act of 1978, to deal with the so-called "epidemic of teenage pregnancy."

14. Gilbert Steiner, *The Futility of Family Policy* (Washington: The Brookings Institution, 1981), p. 80.

15. Ibid., pp. 80–85.

16. *Planned Births, the Future of the Family and the Quality of American Life* (Planned Parenthood, et al., June 1977), Table 1, pp. 18–19.

17. Ibid., p. 3.

18. Ibid., p. 30.

Thus the special interest groups whose goals were represented in the legislation and whose incomes flowed from the appropriations labored to accomplish their purposes in the fashion described by the modern theory of public choice. They labored virtually without opposition, since the programs and funds they sought had only marginal apparent significance to the average citizen. Their federally financed, professionally prepared plans and documents impressed and persuaded congressional committees and molders of public opinion throughout the country. They were the acknowledged "experts," whose opinions were sought and whose very words appeared in presidential messages and statements by high officials.

ASSERTIONS VS. FACTS IN TEENAGE PREGNANCY

By ordinary standards of objectivity, however, their claims and promises were another matter. Though Congress found in the Adolescent Pregnancy Act of 1978 that "pregnancy and childbirth among adolescents . . . often results in severe adverse health, social, and economic consequences" and that therefore pregnancy testing, "referral services," and "educational services in sexuality" should be provided to them, the evidence was markedly at odds with these assertions and prescriptions. There was, first, the very large decline (unmentioned by Congress or the adolescent-pregnancy alarmists) in fertility among this age group, as shown in Figure 12–1. The decline of 46 percent in teenage fertility during the 1957–1983 period was actually the same as the decline among women of all ages. The decline occurred among both blacks and whites, although black fertility remained higher than that for whites. Nor was this decrease confined to older girls within the 15–19 age group, as has been so often claimed by adolescent-pregnancy alarmists. While it is true, as Table 12–1 shows, that the largest declines have occurred among women 18 to 19 years of age, where most of the births to young mothers are concentrated, there were declines also among girls 15 to 17 years of age. Fertility is very low among these younger girls—fewer than four out of a hundred girls aged 15 to 17 and about one out of a thousand girls under 15 give birth in a typical year. The table also shows that not only birthrates but numbers of births to women under 20 have been falling, with a decline of more than 155,000 births to women of this age group between 1970 and 1983.

Though frequently described with alarm by adolescent-pregnancy

Table 12–1.   Birthrates By Age of Mother and Numbers of Births To Women Aged 15–19, 1966, 1970, and 1983.

Year	Births per 1000 Women 15–19	Number of Births to Women 15–19	Births per 1000 Women 18–19	Births per 1000 Girls 15–17	Births per 1000 Girls Under 15
1966	70.6	621,426	121.2	35.8	0.9
1970	68.3	644,708	114.7	38.8	1.2
1983	51.7	489,286	78.1	32.0	1.1
Percent change, 1966–83	−26.8%	−21.3%	−35.6%	−10.6%	+22.2%
Percent change 1970–83	−24.3%	−24.1%	−31.9%	−17.5%	−8.3%

SOURCES: Derived from the following: U.S. Department of Health, Education, and Welfare, Public Health Service, National Center for Health Statistics, *Monthly Vital Statistics Report* for September 8, 1977, and March 29, 1978; *Vital Statistics of the United States,* annual; and *Monthly Vital Statistics Report,* Advance Report of Final Natality Statistics, 1983, (PHS) 85–1120, Vol. 34, No. 6, Supplement, Sept. 20, 1985.

controllers, the statistics on out-of-wedlock births are somewhat ambiguous. In contrast to the large decline in fertility for all teenage women, the birthrate among *unmarried* teenagers has risen since 1970, as Table 12–2 shows. Still, fewer than three young women out of a hundred in the unmarried 15–19 age group give birth each year, suggesting something less than the much decried "epidemic." But it is the increase in the *proportion* of births to teenagers that occur out of wedlock that is startling indeed. Thus although young mothers are having fewer babies—more than 155,000 fewer in 1983 than in 1970—they are having a markedly larger proportion of them outside of marriage. If illegitimacy is a social problem, as most people believe, it is one that has grown *worse*—notably worse by one indicator—as government birth-control programs have expanded.

A fact related to illegitimacy is that marriage is occurring at later ages and rising proportions of both sexes have never married. In 1960, for example, 76 percent of all 18-year-old females had never been married; by 1983 this proportion had risen to 91 percent.[19]

19. U.S. Bureau of the Census, *Statistical Abstract of the United States: 1985* (Washington: U.S. Government Printing Office, 1984), p. 39.

Table 12–2.   Estimated Live Births Out of Wedlock per 1,000 Unmarried Women 15–19 and as a Proportion of All Births to Women 15–19, 1970 and 1983.

	1970	1983
Estimated live births out of wedlock per 1,000 unmarried women, 15–19	22.4	29.7
Estimated live births out of wedlock as a percentage of all births to women, 15–19	29.5%	53.4%

SOURCE: Derived from U.S. Department of Health, Education, and Welfare, Public Health Service, National Center for Health Statistics, *Monthly Vital Statistics Reports*, Sept. 8, 1977, and Advance Report of Final Natality Statistics, 1983 (PHS) 85-1120, vol. 34, no. 6, Supplement, Sept. 20, 1985.

Much of the discussion of adolescent pregnancy has reported in painful detail on the pregnancy problems of girls 11 to 15 years old without stating that less than 2 percent of all births to women under 20 occur in this younger age group.[20] In fact, most young mothers are 18 years of age or over, and before the government birth-control programs were introduced, the great majority were married, although now the majority are unmarried. A generation or so ago a young married woman of 17, 18, or 19 starting her family was not regarded as a cause for public consternation. In the modern bureaucratic state, however, such events are matters of concern to the highest organs of the government.

Most of the alleged causes of alarm regarding teenage pregnancy tend to disappear under examination. For example, *11 Million Teenagers* began its recitation of problems with the claim that "U.S. Teenage Childbearing Rates Are Among the World's Highest," based on a graph[21] comparing births to women under 20 in several countries, most of which had higher rates of teenage childbearing than the United States. In making the comparison, however, the Planned Parenthood

20. See Dorothy Reycroft Hollingsworth and A. Karen Kessler Kreutner, "Teenage Pregnancy: Solutions Are Evolving," *New England Journal of Medicine* 303 (no. 9, Aug. 28, 1980): 516–18, and compare U.S. Department of Health, Education, and Welfare, National Center for Health Statistics, *Monthly Vital Statistics Report: Natality Statistics*, (HRA) 77-1120, vol. 26, no. 5, Supplement, Sept. 8, 1977, "Teenage Childbearing: United States, 1966–75."

21. Alan Guttmacher Institute, *11 Million Teenagers*, reproduced in *Hearings*, n. 13, p. 556.

statisticians simply left all but three of the more than thirty countries with rates higher than the United States off the graph, thus concealing the fact that on a scale of all adolescent births for which United Nations estimates are available, the United States stands in the lowest one-third.[22]

The effort to portray fertility among young American women as the highest in the world has continued without abatement, despite its lack of factual basis. In the spring of 1985, as federal family planning appropriations were coming up for consideration, the Guttmacher Institute published another of its comparisons of the United States with other countries.[23] This time the study even stated that the five other countries—England, Sweden, the Netherlands, France, Canada—had been selected for their low fertility. The press, nevertheless, reported the study as evidence of the teenage pregnancy epidemic raging uniquely in the United States.[24] Not only is teenage fertility low in the countries selected for comparison, but fertility among women older than 20 is also very low by world standards, so low that three of the five—Sweden, England, and the Netherlands—face absolute declines in population in the near future.[25] Why countries whose populations are dying off should be held up as models for the United States is a question not addressed by the Guttmacher Institute.

Nor does the Institute tell us how low our fertility should be in order to satisfy its requirements. This essential standardlessness of the government-financed family planning movement is one of its most baffling and foreboding aspects, as William Ball has pointed out.[26] In this case, however, though there is no answer to a nonargument, certain facts can be pointed out. The United States is not like Sweden. The United States not only has a large black and other nonwhite population, but even the white population includes millions of people of Latin American and southern and eastern European origin. All of these subcultures have traditionally high fertility. White teenage fertility in

22. Jacqueline Kasun, Testimony, the House Select Committee on Population, *Hearings,* n. 13, p. 310, based on United Nations *Demographic Yearbook,* 1975.

23. Elise F. Jones, et al., "Teenage Pregnancy in Developed Countries: Determinants and Policy Implications," *Family Planning Perspectives* (published by the Alan Guttmacher Institute) 17 (no. 2, March/April 1985): 53–63.

24. "A Teen-Pregnancy Epidemic," *Newsweek* 105 (no. 12, March 25, 1985): 90.

25. Population Reference Bureau, *1985 World Population Data Sheet.*

26. William B. Ball, *Population Control* (Export, Pa.: U.S. Coalition for Life), reprinted from Donald A. Grannella, ed., *Religion and the Public Order,* No. 4 (Ithaca: Cornell University Press, 1968).

the United States stands at the midpoint of the scale for Europe, half-way between the rate of 9 for the Netherlands and 81 for Bulgaria,[27] which is hardly astonishing in view of the diverse origins of our people. When one then makes allowance for the 6 percent of our people who are Latin American, the 12 percent who are black, and the 5 percent who are "other nonwhite," the resulting estimate of what U.S. teenage fertility "should" be is in fact a bit higher than we observe it to be.[28]

Further limiting the validity of comparisons between teenage pregnancy rates in the United States and Europe, it is not clear that the European reporting of abortions is comparable to that of the United States. In the United States abortionists are paid on a fee-for-service, cost-plus basis, giving them an incentive to maximize the number of procedures performed and reported. In Europe, on the other hand, national health service physicians are largely on salary, receiving no extra income from the government for larger numbers of procedures. In Sweden the government is troubled by a "shortage" of physicians in the national health service, but national health physicians work part-time in private practice on a fee-for-service basis. Since the government frowns on these part-time activities in the private sector and since physicians can add significantly to their incomes this way, they have an incentive to perform abortions privately without reporting to the government.

Rates of teenage pregnancy, abortion, and fertility vary widely among the American states. Several states have rates of white teenage abortion plus out-of-wedlock births similar to those reported for northern Europe. All of these restrict teenage access to abortion and spend relatively small amounts on publicly funded sex-education and birth control. Several other states that also restrict youngsters' access to birth control have rates only slightly higher. States that provide easy access to publicly funded birth control tend to have higher rates. For example, California, which provides free access to contraception and abortion without parental knowledge and spends more than any other state for public birth control—three times as much as Texas and almost twice as much as New York—has the highest rate of white teen-

27. *United Nations Demographic Yearbook 1981.*
28. Based on midpoint teenage fertility in Europe and teenage fertility in Mexico and other Latin American countries and among American blacks and other nonwhites, weighted in accordance with their estimated proportions in the U.S. teenage population. The resulting expected rate is 55 compared with the actual rate of 53 for 1982.

age abortion—four times as high as Utah's—and the second highest rate of pregnancy.[29]

Similarly, though it is often claimed that maternal mortality is higher among younger mothers,[30] the United States official vital statistics in Table 12–3 (the latest available in 1986) show that maternal mortality is actually lower among teenagers than among women of all ages and that it advances steeply with increases in the mother's age. Nor is it the case that the babies of teenage mothers are clearly less healthy than the babies of older mothers. Studies have found no clear relationship between infant mortality and the mother's age. In some populations the babies of younger mothers have lower rates of infant mortality than babies of older mothers, while in other groups the opposite has been the case.[31] It appears that differences in income and access to health care account for much of the observed differences in rates. Similarly, it has been shown that teenage mothers have a lower proportion of low-birth-weight infants than mothers over age 20 when women of the same income are compared.[32] National data, however, which are not corrected for income differences, show that mothers of age 15–19 have a somewhat higher proportion of babies weighing less than 5-1/2 pounds than do older mothers.[33] In 1983, 9 percent of all babies born to women of age 15–19 fell within this definition of low birth weight, as compared with 7 percent for babies of mothers aged 20–24.[34]

Low birth weight is associated with prematurity, which is turn is associated with various developmental difficulties; numerous studies, however, have found little observable difference between the physical, mental, and social development of the children of teenage moth-

29. Based on data for teenage pregnancy, abortion, and married and unmarried fertility by states and race, 1980 and 1981, published by the U.S. National Center for Health Statistics, the U.S. Center for Disease Control, and the Alan Guttmacher Institute; and expenditures for contraceptives, sterilizations, and abortions, by states, 1980 and 1981, published by the Alan Guttmacher Institute.

30. California State Department of Education, *Education for Human Sexuality: A Resource Book and Instructional Guide to Sex Education for Kindergarten Through Grade Twelve,* 1979, p. 1.

31. Nortman, *n.* 10, p. 33.

32. Jane A. Menken, "Teenage Childbearing: Its Medical Aspects and Implications for the United States Population," Commission on Population Growth and the American Future, *Research Reports,* vol. 1 (Washington: Government Printing Office, 1972), p. 349.

33. National Center for Health Statistics, *Monthly Vital Statistics Report, Advance Report, Final Natality Statistics, 1983,* vol. 34, no. 6, Supplement, Sept. 20, 1985.

34. Ibid.

Table 12–3.   Maternal Mortality Rates by Age, 1977, 1979, and 1980.

Age Group	1977 Rate	1979 Rate	1980 Rate
Total	11.2	9.6	9.2
Under 20	7.0	6.2	7.6
20–24	7.9	7.5	5.8
25–29	9.2	7.6	7.7
30–34	18.8	12.8	13.6
35–39	38.9	33.3	31.3
40–44	66.3	65.2	60.6
45 and over[a]	148.7	414.9	166.7

SOURCE: National Center for Health Statistics, *Vital Statistics of the United States.*

Note: Maternal death rates per 100,000 live births in specified group.

[a]Rate computed by relating deaths to women 45 years and over to live births to women 45–49 years.

ers and the children of older mothers.[35] A recent major study of 11,000 teenage mothers and 28,000 older mothers found that ". . . teenage mothers tend to be of small stature and weight. . . . The small size of their infants is in proportion to their smaller size and not to their early age at conception."[36]

Moreover, by the age of 7 the children of teenage mothers were no smaller than the children of older mothers.[37] In addition,

. . . undesirable pregnancy outcomes are not necessarily more common in teenage pregnancies or in the younger teenage pregnancies. . . . Some undesirable pregnancy outcomes are actually less frequent in the progeny of teenage mothers.[38]

The physicians Semmens and Lamers, who studied a large number of teenage pregnancies, found that "complications are rare" and that the incidence of prenatal death of the baby was only a fraction as high as in the general population.[39] The Rochester Adolescent Maternity

35. See Wendy Baldwin and Virginia S. Cain, "The Children of Teenage Parents," in F. Furstenberg, Jr., ed., *Teenage Sexuality, Pregnancy, and Childbearing* (Philadelphia: University of Pennsylvania Press, 1981), pp. 265–79.

36. Stanley M. Garn and Audrey S. Petzold, "Characteristics of the Mother and Child in Teenage Pregnancy," *American Journal of Diseases of Children* 137 (April 1983): 365–68.

37. Ibid.

38. Ibid.

39. James P. Semmens and William M. Lamers, Jr., *Teen-Age Pregnancy* (Springfield, Ill.: Charles C. Thomas, 1968), pp. 86, 93.

Project studied predominantly black, inner-city teenagers with an average age at delivery of 16 years—that is, a group that would be expected to have multiple problems at a high rate, according to the new teaching. In fact, however, the Rochester investigators found no greater obstetric or neonatal risks among this group than among women in their twenties.[40] A Johns Hopkins study found that "with optimal care, the outcome of an adolescent pregnancy can be as successful as the outcome of a nonadolescent pregnancy."[41]

Contrary to claims by adolescent pregnancy alarmists, studies of the mental and social development of the children of teenage mothers have failed to discover significant differences between them and other children. A major study of 375,000 children in the United States found that the children of teenage parents showed somewhat less academic aptitude in high school than did other children but that this difference tended to disappear when children of similar family background— that is, matched as to whether they were living with both parents or in some other situation—were compared. This study followed the same children up to the age of 30 and found that, by that age, although those born to teenage parents had had less formal education, *they were earning as much income as those who had been born to older parents.*[42] The author concluded by commenting that she had found "much smaller consequences for the future lives of the children involved" than previous studies that claimed to discover an "enormous impact" of teenage childbearing.[43]

While it has been shown that women who begin childbearing while under the age of 20 obtain fewer total years of formal education than do other women, this is hardly an astonishing or necessarily regrettable fact. It points up again, however, the standardlessness of the population control effort. How much formal education should a young woman have (whether she wants it or not)? Similarly, it should be asked, by what standard has it been determined that teenage pregnancy is "too high," is indeed an "epidemic?" The would-be controllers have provided no indication of what they mean by "high"

40. Elizabeth R. McAnarney, et al., "Obstetric, Neonatal and Psychosocial Outcome of Pregnant Adolescents" (Paper presented at the American Public Health Association meetings, Miami, Fla., Oct. 21, 1976).

41. "Pregnant Teens Needn't Bear Low-Birth-Weight Infants," *Ob. Gyn. News* 14 (no. 14, Dec. 15, 1979).

42. Josefina J. Card, "Long-Term Consequences for Children of Teenage Parents," *Demography* 18 (no. 2, May 1981): 137–56.

43. Ibid., p. 154.

adolescent fertility other than to tell us that ours is "too high." Obviously, without any definition of what "high" means, it will be impossible ever to decide a priori when determined national action has brought these rates of childbearing to levels that are no longer "too high." Without objective standards, society can only continue to rely, as it is now being told to do, on the allegedly superior judgment of the public family-planning advocates.

As shown above, however, rather than comparisons with agreed-upon objective standards, the advocates of government family planning offer a catalog of calamities alleged to be caused by adolescent pregnancy. Continuing the examples, the House Select Committee on Population, in common with many discussions of adolescent pregnancy, asserted that "there are indications that child abuse is more prevalent among young mothers than among older mothers,"[44] but in 689 pages of testimony by twenty-four expert witnesses over a period of three days, no evidence was submitted that this is so.

One of the most melodramatic assertions concerning teenage pregnancy is made by the California Department of Education in its introduction to an explicit new sex-education curriculum proposed for the management of the so-called epidemic: "Adolescent mothers have a suicide rate many times higher than the general population."[45] This much-repeated claim stems from two articles. One is a study of 105 pregnant teenagers admitted to the Yale-New Haven Hospital during 1959 and 1960;[46] there were no suicides in the group but fourteen of the young women "were known to have made subsequently one or more self-destructive attempts or threats serious enough to require care or to be reported to a physician at the hospital."[47] The investigators made no attempt to determine whether their very small sample resembled or differed from the national population of expectant mothers under the age of 20. The other study referred to in numerous articles was conducted in Sweden in 1955–59. It found that less than 5 percent of a group of women under the age of 21 who had attempted suicide were pregnant.[48] This was about the same proportion as would

44. *Hearings*, *n*. 13, p. 65.

45. California State Department of Education, *n*. 30, p. 1.

46. Ira W. Gabrielson, et al., "Suicide Attempts in a Population Pregnant as Teenagers," *American Journal of Public Health* 60 (no. 12, Dec. 1970): 2289–2301.

47. Ibid., p. 2289.

48. U. Otto, "Suicidal Attempts Made by Pregnant Women under 21 Years," *Acta Paedopsychiatrica* 32 (1965): 276–88.

be expected to be pregnant in the general Swedish population of this age.[49]

WELFARE COSTS: EXAGGERATIONS VS. REALITY

Advocates of government family planning frequently belabor the "soaring welfare costs" of youthful childbearing. Thus the House Select Committee on Population reported with alarm that "in 1975 the Federal Government disbursed nearly half ($4.65 billion) of the total AFDC appropriation to households with women who were teenagers when they first gave birth."[50] The claim stems from an Urban Institute estimate based on data for 1975.[51] What the estimate, if accurate, actually suggested was that the women receiving AFDC were not very different from the female population at large, because at that time about a third of all first births to American women (and about half of all black first births) were occurring to women under the age of 20.[52] And the same study found no direct connection between early childbearing and the probability of receiving public assistance. It suggested that an "indirect role" might exist, however.[53]

Though much decried by adolescent-pregnancy alarmists, the AFDC program is one of the smaller public transfer programs, accounting directly for only 2 percent of all public expenditures, and for no more than a probable 4 percent when allowance is made for the addition of food stamps, health care, and housing allowances.[54] Two-thirds to three-quarters of teenage mothers do not become welfare clients.[55] One study of low-income adolescent mothers found that five years after delivery only 15 percent were totally dependent on public as-

49. Based on Swedish births by age, 1958, appearing in *Demographic Yearbook of the United Nations*, 1960.

50. *Hearings, n.* 13, p. 63.

51. Kristin A. Moore, Testimony, House Select Committee on Population, "Fertility and Contraception in America: Adolescent and Pre-Adolescent Pregnancy," 95th Congress, 2nd Session, vol. 2, pp. 284–304.

52. U.S. Bureau of the Census, *Current Population Reports*, Series P-20, No. 358, "Fertility of American Women: June 1979," Table 17, p. 62.

53. Moore, *n.* 51, p. 289.

54. Based on *Economic Report of the President, 1978* (Washington: Government Printing Office, 1978), p. 222, and *Statistical Abstract of the United States*, various issues.

55. Derived from the 1979 number of AFDC mothers under 20 (see *note* 60) divided by the number of women under 20 who had had a first birth, derived from birth data for 1974–1979; see also *Teenage Pregnancy: The Problem That Hasn't Gone Away* (New York: The Alan Guttmacher Institute, 1981), p. 32.

sistance and only half of those on welfare had received it for more than 12 months.[56] In 1982, almost a third of AFDC recipients had received aid for less than a year and another 30 percent had received it for one to three years.[57] Only a minority of AFDC recipients are totally dependent on it as their sole source of support.[58] Recent research indicates that the children whose mothers become dependent on public assistance for a time have little higher than average probability of becoming themselves dependent as adults.[59]

About 7 percent of the mothers on AFDC are teenagers.[60] Despite the increasing proportion of births out of wedlock to both teenagers and women over 20, there were actually fewer people dependent on AFDC in 1983 than in 1975; more family units were dependent in the latter year but these families had fewer children than in 1975. And money outlays, amounting to less than $13 billion in 1982, were smaller in real terms and amounted to a smaller share of government expenditures than they had in 1975.[61] During the decade of the 1980s the number of young women in the 15–19 age group will fall by about 20 percent, a fact that promises a decline in their contribution to fertility and welfare dependency.

In the meantime, the exaggerated reports of the "soaring welfare costs" caused by adolescent childbearing have poured from the publicly funded population research establishment. John C. Robbins prepared one of the most widely reported and creative of these in 1979 for SRI International,[62] a research agency often reported as belonging to Stanford Institute[63] but which in fact had been separated from the

56. Frank F. Furstenberg, Jr., "The Social Consequences of Teenage Parenthood," in C. Chilman, ed., *Adolescent Pregnancy and Childbearing: Findings from Research*, U.S. Department of Health and Human Services, NIH Publication No. 81-2077, Dec. 1980, p. 294.

57. U.S. Bureau of the Census, *Statistical Abstract of the United States: 1985* (Washington: U.S. Government Printing Office, 1984), p. 382.

58. Greg J. Duncan, et al., *Years of Poverty, Years of Plenty* (Ann Arbor: Institute for Social Research, University of Michigan, 1984), pp. 90–91.

59. Martha S. Hill, et al., "Motivation and Economic Mobility of the Poor," (Ann Arbor: University of Michigan Survey Research Center, Aug. 3, 1983).

60. Social Security Administration, *Aid to Families with Dependent Children, 1979 Recipient Characteristics Study*, Part 1: Demographic & Program Statistics, pp. 2, 50.

61. Based on figures appearing in *Statistical Abstract of the United States, 1985*, Table No. 637, p. 378, and Table No. 638, p. 379; and *Economic Report of the President, 1984*, Table B-52, p. 279, and Table B-75, p. 308.

62. SRI International, *An Analysis of Government Expenditures Consequent on Teenage Childbirth* (Menlo Park: SRI International, April 1979).

63. See, for example, Paul Crosbie, "Sex Education: Another Look," *The Public Interest*, No. 58, Winter 1980, p. 124.

University some years ago. Robbins's report estimated that the present discounted value of the twenty-year public costs associated with births to teenage mothers in 1979 amounted to $8.3 billion. This staggering estimate is interesting mainly for the insight it provides into the methods used by publicly funded special-interest groups to justify increasing appropriations for their programs. Robbins arrived at this estimate as the combined result of exaggerations in several components of costs: He assumed unrealistically high and prolonged per capita assistance payments, extraordinary medical costs and social service expenditures, and high welfare payments for long periods of time not only to these mothers and children but also to the husbands and subsequent children of the mothers. The results were not only reported by the population network, that group of several score organizations dedicated to population stabilization and supported by the United States government,[64] but were also widely reported in the popular press. In 1986 the Center for Population Options, in support of its campaign to establish birth control clinics in public junior and senior high schools, issued to the media yet another colossal estimate of the "costs" of teenage pregnancy. The methodology was similar to that of the other reports, but the numbers were even higher.

The concentrated attention given by the population network to the alleged welfare burdens created by youthful childbearing is thus highly biased. No account is taken of the fact that eventually these children grow up as other children do and make their contributions to society as workers, taxpayers, and parents themselves. It is characteristic of the population establishment to report the costs but never the benefits of childbearing and to see all people, the self-supporting as well as those dependent on public assistance, solely as users of resources and polluters of the environment and never as creators of wealth and guardians of the nation's security. The adolescent pregnancy "epidemic" is but one aspect of this generally myopic view.

In fact, however, the average baby born in the United States in 1983 will spend about forty-seven years in the labor force, will earn more than two-thirds of a million dollars over his lifetime and will pay more than a quarter of a million dollars in taxes. As shown above,

---

64. For a listing of these organizations and their receipts of government funds see The Population Crisis Committee, "Private Organizations in the Population Field," *Population,* No. 10, Sept. 1979; see also Population Reference Bureau, *Directory of The Population-Related Community of the Washington, D.C. Area,* 4th ed. (Washington, D.C.: The Population Reference Bureau, October 1981).

Table 12–4. Public Benefit-Cost Calculation for a Baby of a Teenage AFDC Mother, 1983.

Expected Public Benefits		*Expected Public Costs*	
Expected average annual tax payment during adulthood	$5,394	Cost of delivery	$2,174[b]
Total expected taxes to be paid during lifetime	$253,518	Annual public assistance costs, 1983, for mother and child[c]	
Present discounted value[a] in 1983 of total taxes	$56,031	AFDC cash payment	$2,567
		Food stamps	971
		Medical costs	906
		School lunch	200
		Housing assistance	834
		Total annual costs	$5,478
		Present discounted value[a] of costs of delivery and annual public assistance for 2-1/2 years	$15,451

$$\frac{\text{Benefit}}{\text{Cost}} = \text{Ratio} = \frac{\text{Present value of taxes to be paid}}{\text{Present value of public assistance costs}} = \frac{\$56,031}{\$15,451} = 3.6$$

[a] Discounted at 4 percent real rate

[b] Estimated from actual Medicaid costs in California, 1980; correct by 1983 medical care price index.

[c] Estimated from actual payments and numbers of recipients reported in *Statistical Abstract of the U.S., 1984* and *Social Security Bulletin*.

the children of teenage mothers will grow up and become income producers and taxpayers, with no greater probability of becoming welfare dependent than other children and with the same expected income as other children. The value of the tax payments to be made by these children during their adult lives will greatly exceed the cost of public assistance even for those very rare children (no more than two out of a hundred)[65] who spend their entire childhood on public assistance. For the baby of a typical teenage welfare mother who will spend less than three years on public assistance before marrying or becoming otherwise self-supporting, the present value of the expected tax payments to be made by that child during his adult lifetime is several times as great as the present value of the public assistance costs incurred on his behalf, as Table 12–4 shows.

This does not mean, of course, that human beings can really be assigned an economic value, or that it would not be preferable for all families to be self-supporting, but that the much publicized figures on the "costs of children" represent only part of the economic facts. The fact is that parents in modern societies bear the economic costs of their children but experience few of the economic benefits; the economic incentives, therefore, lie on the side of low fertility. This is true for both higher and lower income groups. In addition, among families where the wife is a high-salaried worker, the earnings she must sacrifice to bear and raise children discourage fertility. And public policy is now attempting to establish this pattern of low fertility as the norm for all groups.

A number of specific public policies have made it increasingly difficult for young people to marry and support their families in the traditional ways. Economists have shown in numerous studies that minimum wage laws discourage employers from hiring inexperienced young workers and that increases in the height and coverage of minimum wages are correlated with rising levels of youth unemployment.[66] These developments may be in part, perhaps in large part, responsible for the fact that a larger proportion of the declining number of births to young mothers are now occurring out of wedlock. Official public policy has prevented young people from entering the

65. Duncan, et al., *n.* 58, p. 75.

66. Charles Brown, Curtis Gilroy, and Andrew Kohen, "The Effect of the Minimum Wage on Employment and Unemployment," *Journal of Economic Literature* 20 (no. 2, June 1982): 487–528.

labor force and acquiring the experience and earning power they need to support families. It is therefore hardly surprising to find that young people are delaying marriage and that rising numbers are becoming "single parents."

The public assistance system itself also encourages these choices: (1) Its payments to single mothers are more generous and more easily obtainable than its payments to intact families and (2) it provides more money and benefits than low-income fathers are able to give their families. Though these policies may encourage the unmarried pregnant woman to remain unmarried, at least until the large maternity expenses have been met, they probably discourage further childbearing on her part, because federal law requires that all AFDC and Medicaid recipients be offered a full range of family planning services, penalizing states that fail to do so (Social Security Amendments of 1967 and 1972); and these offers are likely to be accompanied by considerable pressure on the part of the welfare authorities, as will shortly be shown.

High and rising taxes on earned incomes and a declining real value of dependents' exemptions also contribute to the economic difficulties experienced by today's young families who try to be self-supporting, thus tipping the incentives toward illegitimacy and welfare dependence.

Given the powerful forces operating to discourage childbearing in the modern developed economy and the fact that fertility has been below replacement levels in the United States since 1972, it is strange that so many public policies and programs should create still more pressures to restrict family formation and fertility. Americans of the twenty-first century, struggling to care for an increasing proportion of the aged, may look back in mystification at our generation's frenetic efforts to stamp out births.

In view of the counterindicative nature of the evidence, the success with which the creators of the adolescent pregnancy "epidemic" have promoted their beliefs is remarkable. One of their own has, in fact, stated what had long been common knowledge among obstetricians: "By age 18 or 19, the human female may be at or close to her prime physical condition for reproduction."[67] It has long been known that, as shown in Table 12–3, maternal mortality rises rapidly with the age

---

67. Nortman, *n.* 10, p. 4.

of the mother,[68] and that other risks to mother and child also rise with the age of the mother.[69]

Spokesmen for the epidemic, however, have a counterargument to these facts. They maintain that since a high proportion of adolescent pregnancies are "unwanted" or "unintended," the government has the duty to improve teenagers' access to contraception, sterilization, and abortion. In fact, however, most births to all age groups probably result from unintended pregnancies,[70] and investigators have failed to find significantly adverse effects from supposedly "unwanted" or "unintended" pregnancies.[71] There is also a troubling problem of definitions. What is an "unwanted" or "unintended" pregnancy? An initially "unwanted" pregnancy may subsequently become very much wanted. The fact that small percentages of babies are relinquished for adoption suggests that the large percentages that family planning advocates claim are "unwanted" may be the result of unjustifiably inclusive definitions. Throughout the population discussions, the words "unwanted," "unplanned," "unintended," "born out of wedlock," and even "conceived out of wedlock" have for years been used interchangeably without definition and in the face of repeated protests.[72] Once again the standardlessness of the government family-planning movement leaps into view.

Probably of more immediate significance than these problems, however, is the question whether government family planning can improve adolescent behavior and/or the outcomes of that behavior. To answer this question it is not necessary to define the difficult term "improvement." It is sufficient to describe the programs proposed and implemented by the government family planners and to trace the changes

68. Louis M. Hellman, et al., *Williams Obstetrics,* 14th ed. (New York: Appleton-Century-Crofts, 1971), p. 5.

69. James P. Semmens and William M. Lamers, Jr., *Teen-Age Pregnancy* (Springfield: Charles C. Thomas, 1968), pp. 93, 86; Hellman, et al., *n.* 68, p. 1073; W. P. D. Logan, "Cancer of the Female Breast—International Mortality Trends," *World Health Statistics Report* 28: 232–51, World Health Organization, 1975.

70. James Ford, Testimony Before United States Senate Committee on Labor and Human Resources, March 31, 1981, Part II, p. 5.

71. Ford, *n.* 70; E. H. Pohlman, *Psychology of Birth Planning* (Cambridge, Mass.: Schenkman Publishing, 1969), p. 332.

72. Juan Ryan, Statement, Hearing before the Subcommittee on Public Health and Welfare of the Committee on Interstate and Foreign Commerce, "Family Planning Services," 91st Congress, House of Representatives, 2nd Session, Serial No. 91–70 (Washington: U.S. Government Printing Office, 1970), pp. 448–53.

in adolescent behavior that have followed upon the implementation of those programs. The reader can then judge whether these changes constitute "improvement" and whether they are the result of the government programs or some other cause.

The promoters of the adolescent pregnancy epidemic have proposed and, to a large extent, implemented a comprehensive public program of school-based sex education together with publicly financed, universal access to contraception, abortion, and sterilization. These "services" have been provided through the public school system, county health departments, publicly financed hospitals and research institutes in universities, and the publicly supported national network of some 5,000[73] family planning clinics. The bulk of the available financing has been provided under the Social Security Act and Title X of the Public Health Services Act, as previously described, augmented by other federal, as well as state and local, grants.

SEX EDUCATION AND BIRTH CONTROL FOR TEENAGERS

The school-based sex education programs have constituted the first line of government defense against adolescent pregnancy. One recent survey, based on questionnaires, estimated that 40 percent of all teenagers have received sex education in school; another found that the proportion was over three-quarters.[74] Apart from illustrating the large margins of error involved in surveys based on questionnaires, the studies in question indicated the high prevalence of sex education in contemporary American schools. The "model" programs begin in preschool or kindergarten with a description and explanation of the genital organs of the two sexes and a description of human sexual intercourse.[75] In addition, the programs instruct children in "alternative" family forms and life-styles, encouraging them to discuss their family affairs and

73. According to *Family Planning Perspectives* (no. 3, May/June 1981): 132.

74. Both estimates are reported in Melvin Zelnik and Young J. Kim, "Sex Education and Its Association With Teenage Sexual Activity, Pregnancy and Contraceptive Use," *Family Planning Perspectives* 14 (no. 3, May/June 1982): 118.

75. California State Department of Education, *Education for Human Sexuality: A Resource Book and Instructional Guide to Sex Education for Kindergarten Through Grade Twelve* (Sacramento, 1979), pp. 93, 94, 99.

problems openly in their sex classes.[76] One program, for example, asks children of age six whether their parents "molest" them.[77]

This instruction continues with increasing intensity throughout elementary school, stressing not only the personal physiological and psychological aspects of sex but the full implications of the so-called "population explosion" as well.[78] Junior high school students review ovulation, intercourse, fertilization, erection, ejaculation, orgasm, genetics, and childbirth,[79] and in addition learn how they can avoid pregnancy by means of masturbation, homosexuality, contraception, sterilization, and abortion.[80]

High school students again review this same material, reinforced with increasingly intense exercises in "values clarification." At this stage, for example, students "role play" the parts of young people who have been having intercourse with each other "for a long time."[81] They work as boy-girl pairs on "physiology definition sheets" in which they define "foreplay," "erection," "ejaculation," and similar terms.[82] Under the guidance of their sex teachers, they discuss and choose among the various "options" available in the event of an "unplanned" pregnancy,[83] deciding whether it is better to have an abortion or to give birth to an "unwanted" child.[84] They learn Sol Gordon's com-

76. Ibid., pp. 20, 22, 26, 146, *Teacher Resource Kit,* Goal 6, Concept 6.

77. Ibid., pp. 138–39.

78. See, for example, John J. Burt and Linda Brower Meeks, *Education for Sexuality: Concepts and Programs for Teaching* (Philadelphia: W. B. Saunders Company, 1975), pp. 408–9; also Oscar Harkavy, *Implementing DHEW Policy on Family Planning and Population* (Washington, D.C.: Department of Health, Education, and Welfare, 1967), p. 16a, attachments B; a typical local example is the *Arcata School District Family Life/Sex Education Curriculum Guide* (Arcata, Calif., 1976).

79. *Arcata School District Family Life/Sex Education, n.* 78; Burt and Meeks, *n.* 78, pp. 337–403.

80. Ibid. See also California State Department of Education, *n.* 75; Planned Parenthood of Santa Cruz, *Family Life Education* (Santa Cruz, Calif., 1979).

81. Planned Parenthood of Santa Cruz, *Sex Education: Teacher's Guide and Resource Manual* (Santa Cruz, Calif., 1979), p. 256.

82. Ferndale Elementary School District and Ferndale Union High School District, *Family Life/Sex Education Curriculum Guide: Kindergarten-Twelfth Grade* (Ferndale, Calif., July 1978), p. 303.

83. California State Department of Education, *n.* 75, p. 143.

84. Kathy McCoy and Charles Wibbelsman, *The Teenage Body Book* (New York: Simon & Schuster, 1978), p. 190–96, recommended in California State Department of Education, *n.* 75, p. 77.

mandment that "no one has the right to bring an unwanted child into the world."[85]

Increasing numbers of schools now have "comprehensive" health clinics that provide contraceptives, pregnancy testing, and abortion referrals "confidentially"—that is, without notifying parents.[86] Where these do not yet exist, children learn the bus routes to the birth control and abortion clinics in their neighborhoods;[87] they listen to visiting speakers from Planned Parenthood; they take "field trips" to birth control clinics, filling out a patient form,[88] and, on occasion, take part in a group examination of each other's genital organs in order to demonstrate the insertion of a diaphragm.[89]

The school-based sex education programs thus play an essential role in recruiting young people for the guidance and services of the groups and businesses dedicated to the control of adolescent pregnancy. This recruitment advances the groups' ideological interests and increases the net incomes of their clinics. It is therefore little wonder that Planned Parenthood and like-minded groups have devoted so much effort and expense to the promotion of school-based sex education. Where the school programs are not yet fully developed, however, other means of recruitment exist. Youth groups, such as the YWCA, Girl Scouts, Girls Clubs of America, Camp Fire, and Four-H Clubs also provide sex education;[90] and the PTA and the March of Dimes promote it,[91] as do the Episcopal Church, the United Methodist Church, the United Presbyterian Church, and the Salvation Army.[92] In addi-

85. Sol Gordon, *You* (New York: Times Books, 1978), p. 79, quoted in California State Department of Education, *n.* 75, p. 80.

86. Joy Dryfoos, "School-Based Health Clinics: A New Approach to Preventing Adolescent Pregnancy?" *Family Planning Perspectives* 17 (no. 2, March/April 1985): 70–75.

87. California State Department of Education, *n.* 75, pp. 125, 135.

88. Ibid., p. 133, 135.

89. Ruth Bell, et al., *Changing Bodies, Changing Lives* (New York: Random House, 1980), p. 175. This is an account of such a school field trip to the Feminist Women's Health Center in Los Angeles.

90. "Program to Expand Sexuality Education in Cooperation with Youth Service Agencies," *Network Report* (Fall 1981): 8–9; "Camp Fire Support," *The California Family Life Educator*, Preview Issue, May 1982, p. 12; *Adolescent Reproductive Health: Organizational and Policy Statements* (Washington, D.C.: Center for Population Options, October 1982), compiled for conference on "Preventing Adolescent Pregnancy: The Role of the Youth Serving Agency."

91. "National PTA: Listening to the Young," *California Family Life Education Network Report*, Spring 1981, pp. 9–10.

92. See *note* 90.

tion, county health departments and the federally supported national network of "nonprofit" family planning clinics vigorously recruit youthful customers by various ingenious means. Some agencies, for example, employ teenage "peer counselors" to seek out other young people in "parks, pools and recreational centers" for instruction in birth control.[93]

Numerous articles have described the activities of publicly supported agencies that provide "confidential" sex and pregnancy services to minors. In San Bernardino, California, for example, the health department has provided "one-to-one, in-school counseling sessions for adolescent women who come to the health department for pregnancy tests;"[94] these sessions exemplify what Hollingsworth and Kreutner call "active worker involvement" and "easy access to abortion,"[95] that is, "within one week of their health department visit, students are contacted at their school by what appears to classmates to be a routine call to visit the nurse or guidance personnel." The social workers make an average of "three to four visits per student" and almost none of the girls so "contacted" have refused to "participate." In St. Paul, federally funded family-planning and abortion referral clinics have operated within the schools. In this program, "students who miss appointments are called to the clinic." It is reported to have achieved remarkable reductions in teenage fertility.[96]

It should be noted that proponents of these programs do not claim that they reduce sexual activity or pregnancy among the affected young people but that they reduce fertility by means of "intensive, one-to-one, 'find-them-where-they-are'" pregnancy counseling and "easy access to abortion."[97] For example, a federally funded adolescent pregnancy program that combined the efforts of the schools, the health

---

93. The Center for Population and Family Health, Columbia University, "Reaching Out to a Teenager in Washington Heights," reprinted from the *Journal* of the College of Physicians and Surgeons, undated, distributed in 1981; see also Ling Chin and Marjorie B. Dahlin, *Peer Education Programs: Sexuality Education Strategy and Resource Guide* (Washington, D.C.: Center for Population Options, 1983).

94. Edward A. Brann, et al., "Strategies for the Prevention of Pregnancy in Adolescents," reprinted by the U.S. Department of Health, Education, and Welfare, Public Health Service, from *Advances in Planned Parenthood*, 14 (no. 2, 1979).

95. Hollingsworth and Kreutner, *n.* 20.

96. Brann, et al., *n.* 94.

97. Hollingsworth and Kreutner, *n.* 20; also Jacqueline Darroch Forest, *Exploration of the Effects of Organized Family Programs in the United States on Adolescent Fertility,* Final Report (New York: The Alan Guttmacher Institute, October 1980).

department, Planned Parenthood, and other family planning and abortion providers in Hackensack, New Jersey, achieved a 74 percent rate of abortions on pregnant teenagers.[98] Similar programs now operate in most communities in the United States. According to the Guttmacher Institute, the enrollment of teenagers in family planning clinics "grew by seven times, between 1970 and 1979."[99] Frederick Jaffe, president of the Institute, estimated in 1978 that of 11 million nonvirgin teenagers in the United States only 2 million, or less than one-fifth, lacked "access" to family planning services.[100] Given that federal family planning expenditures had expanded nineteenfold from an estimated $13.5 million in 1968 to $279.0 million in 1978[101] and that contraceptives were by this time widely available in drugstores, markets, and public restrooms, it is hard to imagine that any teenager lacked "access" at the time Jaffe spoke. And by 1983 federal and state government spending on domestic contraceptives, sterilizations, and abortions had climbed to $482 million[102] (additional hundreds of millions went for supplies to foreigners), rendering it still less likely that any "access" problems might remain.

HOW THE PROGRAMS AFFECT ADOLESCENT SEXUAL BEHAVIOR

The most notable change in adolescent behavior that has occurred since the onset of the government programs is the increasing resort to abortion, as shown in Figure 12–1. Abortions have increased explosively in numbers, rates, and as a proportion of total pregnancies, as shown in the figure and in Table 12–5. By 1981, 45 percent of all pregnancies among women 15–19 years of age were ended by induced abortion, as compared with 24 percent in 1972. Since statistical associations do not prove causation, it is not, of course, justifiable on the basis of the statistics alone to attribute this tremendous increase in abortions to the government adolescent pregnancy pro-

98. Brann, et al., *n*. 94, p. 75.

99. *Family Planning Perspectives* 13 (no. 3, May/June 1981): 108.

100. Frederick S. Jaffe, Testimony in *Hearings* before the House Select Committee on Population, "Fertility and Contraception in America," *n*. 13, pp. 537–50.

101. The Alan Guttmacher Institute, *Informing Social Change* (New York: The Alan Guttmacher Institute, 1980), p. 7.

102. Rachel Benson Gold and Barry Nestor, "Public Funding of Contraceptive, Sterilization and Abortion Services, 1983," *Family Planning Perspectives* 17 (no. 1, Jan./Feb. 1985): 25–30.

Table 12–5.   Federal Expenditures on Family Planning; Births and Abortions to Women 15–19; Pregnancies, Births, and Abortions per 1,000 Women 15–19, 1970–1981.

Year	Federal Expenditures on Family Planning ($ thousands)	Births to Women 15–19	Abortions to Women 15–19	Pregnancies per 1,000 Women 15–19	Births per 1,000 Women 15–19	Abortions per 1,000 Women 15–19
1970	—	644,708	—	68.32	68.32	—
1971	80,000	628,000	—	64.66	64.66	—
1972	99,420	616,280	191,000	81.22	62.01	19.22
1973	137,280	604,096	231,890	82.61	59.69	22.91
1974	142,780	595,466	279,700	85.36	58.08	27.28
1975	148,220	582,238	325,780	87.77	56.28	31.49
1976	157,140	558,744	362,680	88.26	53.52	34.74
1977	184,620	559,154	397,720	91.87	53.69	38.19
1978	217,771	543,407	418,790	92.82	52.42	40.40
1979	233,031	549,472	444,600	94.7	52.3	42.4
1980	298,572	552,161	444,800	95.9	53.0	42.7
1981	324,977	527,392	433,000	96.0	52.7	43.3

SOURCE: Figures for 1970–1978 from Susan Roylance testimony before U.S. Senate Committee on Labor and Human Resources, March 31, 1981, based on data from National Center for Health Statistics, U.S. Department of Health and Human Services, U.S. Bureau of the Census, and the Alan Guttmacher Institute; figures for 1979–1981 from National Center for Health Statistics and the Alan Guttmacher Institute. The figures for family planning expenditures are estimates of certain categories of spending only. While they apear to be internally consistent, they are substantially smaller than other estimates of the same kinds of spending.

grams. It is possible that the increase would have occurred whether or not the government programs had been implemented, given the changes in the temper of the times and the legalization of abortion-on-demand under the Supreme Court decisions of January 1973. It should be noted, however, that the statistical association between annual federal family planning expenditures and the adolescent pregnancy rate, calculated as the sum of the fertility rate and the abortion rate for this age group, is very high and positive, yielding an R of .882 for the cross-lag correlation during the decade of the 1970s, as shown by Susan Roylance.[103] What these figures mean is that in the late 1970s for every additional million dollars being given to the fam-

103. Susan Roylance, Testimony Before the U.S. Senate Committee on Labor and Human Resources, March 31, 1981.

ily planners by the federal government, another 2,000 adolescent pregnancies were occurring two years later.

Even more damaging to the case for public adolescent pregnancy programs is Roylance's demonstration that in fifteen states with similar social-demographic characteristics and similar rates of teenage pregnancy in 1970, those with the highest expenditures on family planning showed the largest increases in the abortion rate and the rate of births out of wedlock among teenagers between 1970 and 1979.[104]

Moreover, as shown in Table 12–5 and Figure 12–1, adolescent pregnancy—the sum of the fertility rate and the abortion rate among teenage women—abruptly reversed its downward trend in 1971 at the same time that the government programs commenced in earnest, and since then has climbed steeply without interruption. And *after 1976 the mounting increases in adolescent pregnancy swamped even the explosive rise in abortions, so there were no further declines in teenage fertility,* even though government spending for the purpose continued to spiral upward.

Numerous studies, many of them financed by government, have undertaken to evaluate the public adolescent sexuality programs. A principal feature of the government-funded evaluations is that they use criteria that are markedly different from the justifications originally proffered for the introduction of the programs. Rather than studying the effect on adolescent pregnancy, which was the stated concern of the programs, the investigations have focused on changes in attitudes. Thus a major study conducted by MathTech, Inc., and financed by the federal government found that school sex instruction programs "tend to make students more tolerant of the sexual practices of others, but they do not change the students' personal values that guide their own behavior."[105] Similarly, a review of thirty-three studies of sex education found the most notable effect to be "gains in sexual knowledge and shifts toward more tolerant and liberal sexual attitudes."[106] A study conducted in Humboldt County found that increased levels of sexual activity followed upon classroom sex instruc-

104. Ibid.

105. Douglas Kirby, Judith Alter, and Peter Scales, "An Analysis of U.S. Sex Education Programs and Evaluation Methods," MathTech, Inc., for the U.S. DHEW, July 1979, Report #CDC-2021-79-DK-FR, Executive Summary, p. 1.

106. Review of Peter R. Kilmann, et al., "Sex Education: A Review of Its Effects," (*Archives of Sexual Behavior* 10 [no. 2, 1981]: 177–205) appearing in *Family Life Educator*, Preview Issue, May 1982, p. 27.

tion.[107] Enrollment in family planning clinic programs has been shown to be associated with higher planned frequencies of sex activity among teenagers.[108] A Falls Church study found that students who had received sex education claimed to have "a greater understanding of sexuality-related issues."[109] They were also significantly more likely than other students to regard premarital intercourse as "easy."[110] And teachers of other subjects reported that sex was a topic of discussion at this school more frequently than at others where they had taught.[111]

Other authorities have given quite different evaluations of the programs. Dr. Myre Sim, Professor of Psychiatry at the University of Ottawa, has described them as "bad education."[112] Dr. Rhoda L. Lorand, New York psychoanalyst, has said they promote "unhealthy self-absorption" and "primitive behavior."[113] Bruno Bettelheim has called them "a danger . . . implicated in the increase in teenage sex and teenage pregnancies."[114]

In 1982, in time for several government budget struggles, Planned Parenthood disseminated a study purporting to demonstrate the benefits of public sex instruction for young people.[115] The study was one of a series of reports on adolescent sexual behavior by the investigators Zelnik, Kantner, and others. It shows, as others have shown, that teenage sex activity and pregnancy have increased along with the increases in sex instruction and public family planning services to teenagers. Another study in the series reports a greater increase in the

107. Humboldt–Del Norte County Information/Education Project, *Research Component Report* (unpublished), 1978, cited in Planned Parenthood of Santa Cruz, *Family Life Education Curriculum Guide*, 1979, pp. 15, 18.

108. Laurie Schwab Zabin and Samuel D. Clark, Jr., "Why They Delay: A Study of Teenage Family Planning Clinic Patients," *Family Planning Perspectives* 13 (no. 5, Sept./Oct. 1981): 205–17.

109. Susan Gustavus Philliber and Mary Lee Tatum, "The Impact of Sex Education on Students, Parents, and Faculty: A Report from Falls Church" (Paper presented at annual meetings, American Public Health Association, November 1979), p. 11.

110. Ibid.

111. Ibid., p. 5.

112. Quoted in Sean O'Reilly, *Sex Education in the Schools* (Thaxton, Va.: Sun Life, 1978).

113. Rhoda L. Lorand, Letter to Mrs. Charlotte Loftus, dated April 10, 1976.

114. Bruno Bettelheim interviewed by Elizabeth Hall, "'Our Children Are Treated Like Idiots,'" *Psychology Today* 15 (no. 7, July 1981): 28–44.

115. Melvin Zelnik and Young J. Kim, "Sex Education and Its Association with Teenage Sexual Activity, Pregnancy and Contraceptive Use," *Family Planning Perspectives* 14 (no. 3, May/June 1982): 117–26. This article is the most recent of several reporting on the same survey. *Note* 116 cites another.

rate of premarital pregnancy among teenagers than in sex activity and an increase in premarital pregnancy among those reporting that they always use contraceptives, suggesting that government-funded contraceptive programs are not solving the problem.[116] In comparing young people who say they have had sex education, however, with those who say they have not, the study reports that such instruction does not affect teenage sex activity but does reduce pregnancy among those who are sexually active. These conclusions are based not on national data but on questionnaires answered by small numbers of young people; for example, only 57 unmarried white women of age 18–19 in the 1976 sample said they had not had sex education. There were only 18 young women in this demographic group who said they had ever been pregnant. In a 1981 report on their work the authors of the series had themselves written about "the almost total absence of evidence" of any benefits of sex education.[117] In 1982, however, with the results of a 1979 questionnaire added to their previous material, Zelnik and Kim reported evidence of benefits from public sex instruction. The 1979 sample was also small, with only 66 young unmarried white women of age 18–19 reporting that they had not had sex education. Adding to the statistical errors introduced by the small sample are the errors known to affect questionnaire responses, especially to intimate questions. The respondents to the 1976 survey, for example, reported 44 percent fewer abortions than national data indicate that women in their age group have had.[118] Both kinds of errors may have accounted for the fact that some of the results were logically impossible—for example, for the fact that some teenagers apparently received *negative* amounts of sex education between 1976 and 1979 (based on their percentages for the two years). The study's value for establishing the benefits of the government sex programs for teenagers therefore remains doubtful.

In November of 1985 Laurie Schwab Zabin, a leader of Planned Parenthood, distributed a description of her "Johns Hopkins Pregnancy Prevention Program," which claimed to have achieved a large reduction in teenage pregnancy among students patronizing confiden-

---

116. Melvin Zelnik and John F. Kantner, "Sexual Activity, Contraceptive Use and Pregnancy Among Metropolitan-Area Teenagers: 1971–1979," *Family Planning Perspectives* 12 (no. 5, Sept./Oct. 1980): 230–37.

117. Melvin Zelnik, John F. Kantner, and Kathleen Ford, *Sex and Pregnancy in Adolescence* (Beverly Hills: Sage Publications, 1981), p. 179.

118. Ibid., p. 222.

tial birth control clinics in two schools, one a junior high school, in Baltimore. The claim was widely heralded in the press, but Baltimore's superintendent of public instruction informed this author, in a letter dated February 13, 1986, that the questionnaire on which Dr. Zabin claimed to have based her conclusions had "not even been administered in the schools." Moreover, stated the superintendent, a "committee of some thirty community leaders" was currently investigating the project "because of conflicting views."

Widely circulated press accounts in 1985 were also reporting that the school birth control clinics in St. Paul had reduced teenage pregnancy, but the official statement issued by the Saint Paul Public Schools Health Program claimed only that fertility has declined (as it has done throughout the nation as rising levels of abortion have counteracted rising pregnancy rates). What the school programs have clearly shown is that when birth control and pregnancy counselors can summon young people out of class for their "confidential" services, abortion can be elevated to any level necessary to achieve desired low levels of fertility.

Schwartz, Ford,[119] Luker,[120] and others have analyzed the effects of the government sex programs for young people in terms familiar to economists. As these authors have pointed out, unwanted pregnancy has traditionally been perceived as one of the principal costs of sexual activity, especially among the unmarried. By offering free contraceptives with the "backup" of free abortion, reinforced by values education stressing that these constitute the essence of "sexual responsibility," the government programs have enormously reduced the cost of sexual activity among the unmarried young. It would be surprising indeed if sexual activity did not increase under these circumstances, as by all available measurements it has. By analogous reasoning, the availability of free abortion reduces the risk of sex without contraceptives, thus leading to the expectation of another observed event, increasing rates of pregnancy terminated by rising rates of abortion.

As has been shown, the government programs for teenagers have typically placed heavy reliance on abortion. In its publicly funded model school sex curriculum, Planned Parenthood of Santa Cruz sums

119. Michael Schwartz and James H. Ford, "Family Planning Clinics: Cure or Cause of Teenage Pregnancy," *Linacre Quarterly* (May 1982): 143–64.

120. Kristin Luker, "Contraceptive Risk Taking and Abortion: Results and Implications of a San Francisco Bay Study," *Studies in Family Planning* 8 (no. 8, Aug. 1977).

up the prevailing teaching: "Legal abortion is a relatively safe, un-complicated procedure . . . teenagers may be eligible for [government-funded abortions] without their parents' income (or consent) taken into consideration."[121] Childbirth, on the other hand, according to the same manual, entails the "risk of death," the risk of bearing a mentally retarded child or one with cerebral palsy or epilepsy, and an assortment of other dire consequences. The practice of dismissing girls from school without their parents' knowledge to obtain government-funded abortions was growing during the late 1970s and early 1980s.[122]

Government promotion of abortion as the "solution" to adolescent pregnancy raises obvious moral and political questions in a society dedicated to official neutrality regarding ideology. It also raises questions as to the physical consequences for the patients involved. On this point the federally funded population-research establishment has been adamant: Abortion is safer than childbirth.[123] Safer for whom? ask the antiabortionists with unanswerable logic. Even for the young mothers, however, the supposed safety of abortion may be questioned. In the first place, the studies purporting to demonstrate the low mortality rate of abortion suffer from the fact that there is no standardized reporting requirement or procedure for abortions, abortion complications, or resulting deaths. There are large discrepancies in these figures as estimated by various agencies. On the other hand, all fatal complications of delivery, such as hemorrhage and toxemia, are separately listed in annual reports that have been collected and published for years by the National Center for Health Statistics in accordance with standards established in the International Classification of Diseases. Moreover, the persons and agencies reporting on the supposed safety of abortion and dangers of childbirth have selected their data to give this impression; Willard Cates of the Center for Disease Control, for example, used a figure for maternal mortality among women under 20 that was 40 percent higher than the rate reported for 1976.[124] Such manipulations to the contrary, Thomas Hil-

---

121. Planned Parenthood of Santa Cruz, n. 81, p. 163.

122. See Hearings of the California Assembly Education Committee, May 4, 1982, on AB 3766, which would have made it unlawful for public schools to dismiss students for abortions.

123. See, for example, Willard Cates's speech to adolescent pregnancy conference sponsored by Johns Hopkins University School of Medicine, reported in *Family Practice News* 10 (no. 2); also Christopher Tietze and Marjorie Cooper Murstein, *Induced Abortion: 1975 Factbook* (New York: Population Council, 1975), p. 61.

124. Reported in *Family Practice News* 10 (no. 2).

gers and Dennis O'Hare compared mortality among women having abortions at various stages of pregnancy and women continuing their pregnancies and delivering babies, and found that natural pregnancy is safer than abortion in both the early and late stages of pregnancy.[125]

Abortion practitioners have spoken frankly about the dangers of abortion and its consequences for subsequent childbearing.[126] Several large studies have substantiated these beliefs.[127] One of the largest investigations of the effects of induced abortion, a six-year follow-up study of 20,000 New York women who underwent abortion in 1970–71, found that these women subsequently delivered a significantly higher percentage of premature infants than did a matched control group of women whose first pregnancies resulted in live births. Rates of complications during subsequent pregnancies for women who had had abortions were several times as high as for women who had not aborted.[128] There was a 53 percent greater incidence of fetal death within the group who had had abortions.[129] There was a 25 percent higher incidence of neonatal mortality among their babies and a 26 percent higher incidence of congenital malformations, although the authors did not regard these results as statistically significant. The significance of the study's findings, though based on a very large investigation and agreeing with a good deal of other research on the topic, has been minimized by the population establishment.[130]

There is no disagreement, however, on one point, and that is that abortion reduces fertility, both immediately and apparently also subsequently among the women who experience it. The Guttmacher Institute reported in 1981 that 10 percent of teenagers whose first

125. Thomas W. Hilgers and Dennis O'Hare, "Abortion Related Maternal Mortality: An In-Depth Analysis," in Thomas W. Hilgers, et al., eds., *New Perspectives on Human Abortion* (Frederick, Md.: University Publications, 1981), pp. 69–91.

126. Kenneth Wright, Testimony, Official Transcript of Public Hearing on Regulations, California State Department of Health Services, March 25, 1980, pp. 31–35.

127. For a review of a large number of these studies, see Leslie Iffy, et al., "Perinatal Statistics: The Effect Internationally of Liberalized Abortion," in Thomas W. Hilgers, et al., eds., *New Perspectives on Human Abortion* (Frederick, Md.: University Publications 1981), pp. 92–127.

128. Vito M. Logrillo, et al., *Effect of Induced Abortion on Subsequent Reproductive Function, Final Report*, New York State Department of Health, Office of Biostatistics, April 18, 1980, Contract No. N01-HD-6-2802, National Institute of Child Health and Human Development, Table 49.

129. Ibid, Table 58.

130. See, for example, Christopher Tietze, *Induced Abortion: A World Review, 1981* (New York: Population Council, 1981), pp. 83–89.

pregnancies ended in induced abortion were pregnant again within a year; this compared with 17.5 percent of those whose first pregnancies resulted in a live birth.[131] Investigators in many countries have for years reported lower levels of fertility among women who have had abortions.[132] It has been found that, of women being treated for infertility, several times as high a proportion have had induced abortions as is true of all women.[133] The large New York study previously mentioned found that the women who had abortions had 37 percent fewer pregnancies and less than half as many live births in the six following years than did the women who did not have abortions.[134] The women who had abortions also subsequently had 71 percent more abortions than did the control group.

Though less emphasized than contraception and abortion, sterilization is also a part of the government porgrams for young people. The new sex education programs begin their instruction regarding the benefits of sterilization in elementary school.[135] Free public vasectomy services are widely advertised and promoted in communities having high concentrations of young people.[136] Federal Medicaid funding is available for sterilization in cases where the patient is at least 21 years of age, has low income, and has given informed consent. State laws permit the sterilization of teenagers and provide for compulsory sterilization in some cases.[137] An audit of federally funded sterilizations performed in nine states in 1979–80 found numerous cases where patients under the age of 21 had been sterilized and where the operation had been performed without the patient's informed consent. The nine states in question were asked to return nearly $1 million to the federal treasury.[138]

131. The Alan Guttmacher Institute, *Teenage Pregnancy: The Problem That Hasn't Gone Away, n.* 55, p. 21.

132. Tietze and Murstein, *n.* 123, p. 50.

133. D. Trichopoulos, et al., "Induced Abortion and Secondary Infertility," *British Journal of Obstetrics and Gynecology* 83 (Aug. 1976): 645–50.

134. Logrillo, et al., *n.* 128, p. 10.

135. *Arcata School District Family Life/Sex Education Curriculum Guide, n.* 78.

136. "How Men Can Help With Birth Control," informational brochure distributed by Everyman's Center to students at Humboldt State University; "Humboldt Open Door Clinic Presents Everyman's Center," distributed to students at Humboldt State University; "Vasectomies," in *Humboldt Life and Times,* November 12, 1980, distributed free to all residents of Arcata, home of Humboldt State University.

137. Christian S. White, IV, *Situation Report: Sterilization in the United States* (Stafford, Va.: The American Life Lobby, 1981).

138. *MCCL News,* March 1981; Department of Health and Human Services, State Assessment Audits of sterilization and hysterectomy claims for 1979.

CONCLUSIONS

The story of government efforts to influence adolescent sexual behavior is clearly one of ever widening interventions and ever increasing expenditures, with each new attempt at a "solution" leading to still further perceptions of problems and corresponding interventions. By the adroit manipulation and selective presentation of statistical facts, a special interest group has turned the public perception of "adolescent pregnancy" from a natural but declining fact of young womanhood into a plague. To combat the newly delineated plague, the groups in question have received rapidly mounting grants from the public treasury. Hard on the heels of these developments have come accelerating changes in the real events: adolescent pregnancy, which was the original focus of official concern and which had been rapidly declining before the public programs began, has greatly increased since the programs began; abortion has increased explosively since the initiation of the government programs, and teenage fertility, which had been sharply declining before the programs began, has ceased falling. The proportion of out-of-wedlock births among women under 20 has increased markedly. It is difficult indeed to discern in these events any indication that government-funded birth control programs benefit young people or anyone except those who are paid to operate the programs.

And perhaps the most significant development is that a huge new publicly financed bureaucracy has sprung up, extending from the federally supported population groups through the public health and educational establishments, to take charge of the psychological and moral development of the young in its most intimately human aspects. Committed to the proposition that standards of truth and goodness are not constant but must instead, in the words of a leader of the movement, be continually revised by those (i.e., themselves) who are "up-to-date on important facts science has discovered,"[139] the new bureaucracy has arrogated awesome rights and duties to itself—nothing less than the duty to reevaluate and redesign all human standards and the human material itself, in accordance with its own perceptions of the requirements of "science."[140] By declaring all preexisting standards

139. Mary S. Calderone and Eric W. Johnson, *The Family Book About Sexuality* (New York: Harper & Row, 1981), p. 1.

140. Mary S. Calderone, "Sex Education and the Roles of School and Church," *The Annals of the American Academy of Political and Social Science* 376, (March 1968): 57–59.

to be "out of date" and therefore irrelevant, the new public sex authorities render themselves exempt from all traditional judgments and, thus, from all limits that might be imposed on their behavior. The movement is thus inherently authoritarian. With all traditional values swept away by the new subjectivism and authoritarianism, the public no longer has a standard of the reasonable exercise of authority; no one, therefore, can call the new tyrants tyrannical.

The progression has been sudden and swift. The original public grants to special interest groups have been used to lobby for more grants, more programs and more power. The billions of tax dollars poured into the effort have purchased not only projects, jobs, offices, professional organization, publications, and power, but credibility as well. The opposition—though widespread[141]—without public funds and forced to provide the tax funds that support its antagonists, lacks all of these.

Government control—which is, by its nature, special interest control—of adolescent pregnancy has become a national commitment. Further developments seem assured. Only slight adaptations of the same rationalizations used to justify government attempts to control adolescent pregnancy, reinforced by the logic of public bureaucratic growth, would serve to justify government control of all pregnancy.

141. "The Frontiers of Controversy: Sex Education and Public Action in America," *California Family Life Education Network Report*, Spring 1981, p. 5.

13

ON THE LIMITS OF THE WELFARE STATE: THE CASE OF FOSTER CARE

Brigitte Berger

In a book dedicated to the exploration of the relationship between the family and the state, the theory and practice of foster care deserve special attention. Foster care—the state-initiated, -monitored, and -financed practice of caring for children in homes other than their own—is significant as an example of a massive intervention by the state into the family. As it has become increasingly evident in recent years that the commitment of the modern welfare state to meet the basic needs of its people has produced a series of policies, programs, and services that are often contradictory and counterproductive, questions as to the nature of this relationship have once again arisen.

The claim can be made that in no other area have well-intentioned policies and programs performed as poorly as in this. Indeed, we may speak today of a foster care crisis, if not of a foster care scandal. And all this in spite of public commitment and in spite of—or as some would claim, because of—massive intervention by the state and immense sums spent from public coffers. No other area is better suited to explore the dimensions of liberal assumptions underlying the relationship between individuals and the state, and the unexpected, baneful consequences of those assumptions.

At the same time, foster care illustrates in a particularly illuminating way the central issues intrinsic to all family-state relationships. As a general disillusionment with the modern welfare state is now beginning to challenge Americans to rethink the relationship, the case of foster care may be paradigmatic for public policy questions on the family in general.

And finally, foster care as it has come to be practiced today brings into sharp focus the discrepancy between "official" perceptions of individual needs and rights on the one hand and the very different social practices, values, and hopes of the majority of Americans on the other. This latter dimension makes it clear that a mere tinkering with the shortcomings and deficiencies of a good number of welfare state programs will not suffice. At issue are the basic assumptions upon which the welfare state rests. At the same time, deeply rooted values and commitments of Americans to assist those in need, and help those who cannot help themselves, make it imperative that a new vision come to the fore—one that can either supplement, modify, or, if necessary, replace the liberal vision that has arrived at an impasse. In the final analysis, then, the paramount tasks in the organization of American domestic life revolve around such questions as what lessons can be learned from the past and how can we arrive at a public stance toward the family that is able to respond adequately and compassionately to the very different needs and values of the many distinctive social groupings that make up and are the strength of our pluralistic society.

This paper seeks to address these questions, not in a global or comprehensive way, but more in the form of a general exploration of the theory and practice of foster care that brings into focus those constitutive features in the relationship between the family and the state that tend to be overlooked in other more general analyses and that have to be addressed with a modicum of urgency.

THE EVOLUTION OF THE FOSTER CARE CRISIS

Of the roughly 2 million American children under the age of 18, who, for a variety of reasons, are separated from their biological parents temporarily or for extended periods, only a fraction (current estimates run between 350,000 and 600,000) become wards of the state. Only a small number of these dependent, neglected, and handicapped children are placed in institutions or quasi-institutional settings. By far the majority are placed in foster care. It is their life and their fate— and by extension that of their families—that is of concern to us here.

In the course of the past hundred years, and more pronouncedly so since the New Deal, governmental involvement in the lives of children was found to be necessary in cases of sudden crisis, severe neglect, and abuse—as well as in the absence of other "viable" alternatives. At the same time, this new public consciousness was accompanied by two significant perceptual shifts: On the one hand, we see a trend whereby increasingly "public" (i.e., state) agencies are called upon to replace prior voluntary, ethnic, and religious ones in the management and care of needy chilaren—thus giving rise to a "public"/"private" controversy. On the other hand, we see a redefinition of the type and nature of state intervention designed to meet the needs of dependent children.

This is not the place to embark upon a history of foster care in the United States. For our purposes, it is important to keep in mind, that out-of-home care for children—be this now institutional, group, or foster care—was designed for temporary periods and conceived to be only of a surrogate nature, with the primary goal being to return children to their own families as soon as possible. In other words, in seeking to protect children who cannot fend for themselves and secure the most propitious environment for their development and growth, public intervention was originally understood as a stopgap measure. In this sense, state intervention into the family was thought of as a form of relief and support.

In the past two decades there has been a significant shift in the conceptualization of foster care: Instead of providing relief, we now speak of "rehabilitation;" instead of giving support, we now supply "services." At the same time, the concept of "rehabilitation" is an amorphous and vaguely defined one, leaving itself open to built-in accusations of ethnic and racial bias, while the "service delivery" approach has led to the development of foster care as a permanent way of life with service professionals as permanent fixtures.

The consequences of this shift in foster care theory, as well as practice, are reflected in a number of novel features, the most prominent of which will be discussed below.

THE EXPLOSION OF FOSTER CARE

There are today an unprecedented number of children in foster care. Estimates, usually arrived at by extrapolation, range between 350,000 and 502,000.[1] Regardless of which numbers are accepted as being

---

1. Considerable discrepancy exists in the estimates of the number of children in foster care, since these estimates are arrived at by extrapolation. Thus, for instance, Joseph Califano,

more realistic, the fact remains that the largest number of children in the history of the United States, are recorded to be in foster care today. In 1963, 37 in 10,000 children were placed in foster care; in 1969, 45 in 10,000; and in 1977, 77 in 10,000. (There seems to have been no significant change in number since 1977.) In view of the legal changes that have occurred during this same period, the astounding increase in the number of children placed in foster care may well be directly related to the changing definitions of child abuse and neglect. It was not until the early 1960s that dramatic references to the "battered child" began to draw professional and public awareness on a national level. What followed is well known. The Children's Bureau formulated a model child-abuse reporting law; by 1967 all of the states had their own laws, most of which were mandatory; and in 1974 federal legislation was passed creating the National Center on Child Abuse and Neglect.

This is not the place to explore the mechanisms that have turned a stopgap measure into an accepted alternative way of life. Arguments abound with contradictions and ironies. The Children's Defense Fund, for instance, denounces foster care as intrusive and unnecessary, while at the same time charging that children in need are denied access to foster care. Accusations of coercive state intervention are typically countered by arguments on behalf of children who have to be "saved" from their disorganized, damaged, and abusing families. However, unless one is willing to argue that American parents have overnight developed antichild attitudes and practices leading to abuse and neglect—and precise data on this are hard to come by—the question of whether increased government involvement has led to an explosion in the number of children in foster care is a legitimate one.

FOSTER CARE AS A "WAY OF LIFE"

Aside from the pressing inquiry into the reasons underlying changes in definitions and laws that allow professionals, public agencies, and

---

Secretary of the Department of Health, Education, and Welfare under the Carter administration, reported 350,000 children in foster care. See Hearings before the Subcommittee on Public Assistance of the Senate Finance Committee, 95th Congress, 1st Sess., "Public Assistance Amendments of 1977" (Washington, D.C.: Government Printing Office, 1977), p. 58. However, the *National Study of Social Services to Children and Their Families,* prepared for the National Center for Child Advocacy, Administration for Children, Youth, and Families, DHEW 1978 (OHDS 78-3015), reports the number of children to be 502,000. Since then, the higher number is generally accepted.

courts increasingly to intervene in the affairs of the family, another set of questions has emerged as well. It has become dramatically evident in recent years that once children have been placed in foster care, they tend to stay there for a considerable length of time, often to be released only when graduating into legal adulthood. At this point, the national average for years spent in "temporary foster care" is five years, and in some places up to ten. Frequently shunted from one foster care home to the next, this revolving-door system of foster care has in the past two decades developed into an unconscionable failure for many of the children trapped in a system that sucks the child deeper and deeper into its recesses, where the child can be neglected, misplaced, or lost track of altogether. Generally speaking, children placed in foster care grow up in foster care. Children adrift in foster care are thus not only cut off from their natural parents but also from the officials responsible for them. In the meanwhile, maintenance payments continue to flow from government coffers to foster parents or institutions and, above all, to the various agencies handling them.[2]

At the same time, the foster care system is marked by a curious financial paradox. While the costs of children in out-of-home care have risen phenomenally in recent decades (the federal government alone spends more than $1 billion under a variety of provisions, and states and local sources come up with roughly another billion), only a fraction of these sums go to the actual care of children. Clearly, administration and services swallow up a considerable portion of the moneys allocated. In one well-documented case, that of the City of New York, the annual average cost per child paid to foster homes amounted to $4,964 in 1977, while the average cost to the city went as high as $12,754.[3] Hence, whether open-ended funding gives rise to and perpetuates services—services of a questionable nature, to boot— is a real issue.

Regardless of wishes and claims of "doing good" on behalf of those who are weak and cannot speak for themselves, the "do-gooders" themselves seem to benefit in a measurable degree from their hu-

---

2. A summary of arguments and evidence along these lines may be found in the following: (a) Gilbert Y. Steiner, *The Futility of Family Policy* (Washington, D.C.: The Brookings Institution, 1981), esp. ch. 5, "Abuse and Neglect"; (b) Robert Woodson and Ruth Erikson, "Doing Good Well: Benevolent Injury to Foster Children," position report (Washington, D.C.: National Center for Neighborhood Revitalization, 1983); (c) New York City Council President Report, 1981.

3. Office of the Comptroller, City of New York, "Audit Report on Foster Care Agencies' Achievement of Permanent Homes for Children in Their Care," 1977.

manitarian interventionist activities. Recent criticisms that the creation and maintenance of a growing "dependency class," whose primary purpose seems to be to serve the interests of those who are to serve them, cannot be shrugged off easily. The case of foster care certainly provides ammunition for such claims.

And again, this is not the place to adjudicate in the financial paradox controversy; neither is this the place to cast aspersions upon well-intentioned, dedicated, and overworked social workers laboring under a good variety of pressures. Rather, what is at issue here is the therapeutic ethos of the liberal state and its growing tendency to focus on the solitary individual and not the family as the basic administrative and legal unit. And, to put it mildly, this ethos has led to rather unexpected—and as we shall continue to show, devastating—consequences for the individuals involved.

THE CALVARY OF CHILDREN IN FOSTER CARE

Not only has foster care become a way of life to many children, its particular effects are far from beneficial. As evidence begins to mount, it becomes apparent that, more often than not, adverse results have been produced by government involvement in the lives of minor children thought to be in danger. A large proportion of children in foster care (40 to 50 percent) show symptoms of poor adjustment and emotional distress; their proneness to deviance (truancy, delinquency, alcoholism, drug addiction, etc.) is pronounced; their death rate is twice that of the national average. In other words, foster care as practiced today costs more than money.

If children were seen to benefit from foster care, the size of the taxpayers' bill that accrues from these intervention measures would be of little concern. Yet, as documented by the above established evidence, along with recent supplementations, a frightening number of confused identities and emotional maladjustments—all increasing with length of stay in the foster care system—demonstrate that there is virtually no assurance that a child's removal from his natural family is indeed in his best interest. Thus the state may take children from "abusing" parents only to put them into alternative situations where they may be abused as well—a fact that has begun to haunt many concerned individuals.[4]

4. New York City Committee for Children, "Report on the State of Foster Care," 1980; Woodson and Erikson, *n.* 2(b); New York City Council President Report, 1981.

Let me repeat once more: These unanticipated consequences flowing from well-intentioned and seemingly humane intervention practices are due neither to malfeasance on the part of anyone involved in the foster care complex nor to failures in the delivery systems or the government's willingness to release adequate moneys. Professionals, government representatives, child advocates, as well as the general public are equally perplexed and perturbed.

THE REGULATORY JUNGLE

The sorry state of the current foster care system, its poor performance, and the persistence, if not magnification, of seemingly intractable problems have led to the typical response of the welfare state in such situations, namely, the introduction of provisions, regulations, and legislation to protect the rights of individual children. Yet these legal and administrative measures have in the main served to complicate further an already untenable situation. Ill-defined rationales for the removal of children from their families, for giving preference to one particular placement over another, for the rendering of supplementary services, for placement in institutional settings, for moving children out of institutional settings, for adoption, for return to their natural families, etc., have turned the foster care complex into an administrative jungle. Moreover, the Adoption Assistance and Child Welfare Act of 1980 (Public Law 96-272) has brought to light all sorts of controversies and very little change.[5]

Since then there have been major efforts in three distinct areas: The first center around a redefinition of children's rights; the second center around the removal of legal, administrative, and financial barriers in order to facilitate placement and adoption; and the third center around public versus private childcare management. All these efforts aim to overcome the crisis in foster care and to improve the scandalous situation of an all too large number of children trapped in it.

TOWARD A NEW DEFINITION OF CHILDREN'S RIGHTS?

For some time now there has been a strong movement toward a legal conceptualization of children's rights vis-à-vis the rights of parents.

5. Peter Skerry, "Foster Care and Mediating Structures," unpublished report for the Mediating Structures Project (Washington, D.C.: American Enterprise Institute, 1980); Woodson and Erikson, *n.* 2(b).

In recent years the child liberation crusade has received new impetus with the presentation of the concept of "psychological parents," as formulated by Joseph Goldstein, Anna Freud, and Albert Solnit in their much heralded *Beyond the Best Interest of the Child.*[6] The "beyond the best interest of the child" argument has, of course, broader implications. It is, however, of considerable significance to the cases of foster care as well, for it is relevant to efforts that seek a new definition of the legal standard courts have to rely upon in making child placement decisions. Taking issue with the customary emphasis upon the "physical" needs of a child at the expense of his psychological ones, the authors charge that existing standards sacrifice a child's primary needs to those of adults claiming to act on his behalf. In the establishment of criteria that give preference to "psychological parents" over natural ones, the children's rights movement has now received a psychiatric cloak as well.

This policy proposition brings to light once more the fundamentally antifamily bias that characterizes so many liberal efforts. In the case of foster care, it leads national policy down the slippery slope of terminating parental rights in the absence of any parental wrongdoing. In this the "beyond the best interest of the child" formulation embraces the worst features of the traditional "best interest" philosophy and the "emotional neglect" standards. Not only does it rely in an extremely subjectivistic manner upon questionable predictions of a child's future emotional adjustment, it is also the most extreme case yet made on behalf of the supremacy of the state. In the words of Rena K. Uviller, a civil court judge in New York, "Whether rationalized by the 'best interest' argument or because the foster parent has become the 'psychological parent,' the cumulative effect of agency and court decision and indecision is to sever the parental relationship. The state's own dilatory tactics, combined with an invidious comparison between the natural parent (typically poor or in strained emotional circumstances) and the foster parent, combine to deprive a non-abusive parent of her own children. The state becomes the *de facto* judge of who may be a parent."[7]

---

6. Joseph Goldstein, Anna Freud, and Albert J. Solnit, *Beyond the Best Interest of the Child* (New York: Free Press, 1973).

7. Rena K. Uviller, "Save Them From Their Saviors: The Constitutional Rights of the Family," in George Gerbner, Catherine J. Ross, and Edward Zigler, eds., *Child Abuse: An Agenda for Action* (New York: Oxford University Press, 1980).

In sum, in the "beyond the best interest of the child" argument we have perhaps one of the most dramatic illustrations of the fundamentally antifamily animus, carried to its logical conclusion, that is inherent in the liberal vision. At the same time it provides a devastating illustration of the class and ethnic-racial bias built into the liberationist ideology informing the liberal approach to the family in general. Juxtaposed here are the rights of children and the rights of parents. But this is essentially a sham issue. In arguing for the emancipation of children from their parents, poor, ethnic, and racial families receive little confidence. Whereas it is possible for strong middle-class parents to resist professional and state interference in their family life, the poorer classes, lacking the protection of money, status, and verbal know-how, are thus particularly vulnerable to outside interference. More than anyone else, they become the powerless victims of "friendly intruders," as they and their children come under the tutelage of experts, agencies, and institutions. To argue that minor children have individual rights independent of adults is illusory and ultimately deceptive. Either parents care and are responsible for them, or the state cares and is responsible for them. Advocates can opt to support either. In arguing in the foster care issue on behalf of "psychological" parents, child liberationists superimpose a highly questionable standard that by definition is prejudiced against lower class families. They also overlook the fact that a very large number of foster care children—as we have tried to show above—move within the foster care system from one foster family to the next, thus being put into precisely the kind of "abusive" emotional situation from which child advocates had set out to rescue them. In the face of this paradox, the above quoted judge Rena Uviller thus calls for "saving them from their saviors."

REMOVAL OF BARRIERS TO PLACEMENT AND ADOPTION

Of the various attempts to ameliorate the foster care crisis, efforts concerned with changes in regulations that act as barriers to permanent placements and adoption are the most promising ones yet. In the past, procedures and regulations served to exclude a potentially large pool of foster parents and adopting parents from qualifying for foster care and adoption. This is particularly true for the black community with its time-honored tradition of self-help to take care of children in need. With changes in placement and adoption regulations, we should see an improvement in the lot of the disproportionate number of black children who have accumulated in foster care. Just by revising and simplifying procedures with adoptive parents, Homes for Black Children in Detroit, in its first year of operation, was able to place more children in permanent homes than all thirteen other Detroit child service agencies combined.

Along these lines, we observe today among a new breed of black leaders a growing emphasis upon ethnic institutions in the management of foster care. This constitutes a significant departure from their previous reliance upon integrated public institutions. At this time, the new black leadership is about to rise to the challenge posed by the foster care crisis, which particularly endangers the lives of black children: They have established an "adoption hot-line" that seeks, through established grass-roots networks,[8] to match children in need of a home with homes in need of children. This shift augurs well for allegedly "unplaceable" black children. It may not be incidental that this hopeful shift constitutes also a significant divergence from the liberal vision of foster care.

THE "PUBLIC VERSUS PRIVATE" CONTROVERSY

By the same token, the "public versus private" issue in the delivery of services to minor children deemed to be in need of saving is a sham issue. On the one hand, the same arguments that can be made against the practice of foster care in general apply to the private delivery sector as well; both public and private agencies are susceptible to similar problems and malfeasance, such as ambiguous standards for separation, slowness in assessment, placement, monitoring, adoption, etc. On the other hand, basic costs are not greatly dissimilar in either system, and in any case, both depend equally upon public funding. To be sure, private agencies tend to be somewhat less expensive to run, for a variety of reasons (private matching of funds, availability of well-established physical plants, etc.), and perhaps it can be argued as well that the astronomical rise in all service costs in foster care was initiated and accelerated by public agencies, with private ones quick to follow.

The history of foster care in the United States has traditionally been marked by regional differences, with voluntary forms (typically ethnic, church, and sectarian) dominating in the East, a mixture of public

8. Woodson and Erikson, *n.* 2(b).

and voluntary in the Middle West, and public arrangements being the preferred ones in the West. As indicated earlier, there has been a significant shift in favor of public service delivery in recent decades. This shift was carried by a number of thrusts directed against voluntary agencies. One particularly well-publicized one, the case of *Wilder* versus *Sugarman* in the City of New York, based its brief on the alleged inability of sectarian agencies to locate foster homes for the growing number of black children in the foster care system, thus dooming these children to be warehoused in infamous public shelters for an indefinite length of time. Voluntary child care agencies, supposedly enjoined by their particularistic ethos to give preference in terms of religious backgrounds, were charged with discriminating against black children, and the unconstitutionality of such practices was argued. At closer look, however, evidence demonstrates that these allegations cannot be substantiated. Such discriminatory practices may, perhaps, have existed in the past; they certainly are no longer practiced by the majority of voluntary agencies today. Although a religious ethos may be still alive in many sectarian agencies, there is at the same time a general pattern of increasing out-of-religion placements, especially in difficult cases. So for instance, one careful statistical study of New York City practices shows that in 1973, 26 percent of the children in Catholic agencies were black, 29 percent in Jewish agencies, and 86 percent in Protestant agencies.[9]

Others—like Peter Skerry, formerly of the Mediating Structures Project and currently with the Department of Government at Harvard—have researched and assessed with great skill the various claims made in the public/private controversy in foster care.[10] And again, others—like Robert Woodson of the National Center for Neighborhood Enterprise, who spearheads the above-mentioned thrust against existing regulations that act as barriers to placement and adoption— seek to tackle a seemingly intractable problem with new methods. However, what both these different assessments of the foster care crisis, and in the latter case, the proposal of a new approach, demonstrate is that the public/private controversy is a sham issue. The real issue, once more, rests with the liberal conceptualization of family-state relationships.

9. An excellent summary on voluntary agencies and foster care can be found in Skerry, *n.* 5.

10. Skerry, *n.* 5.

And here the anchorage of the voluntary sector in ethnic and religious communities—the very point that incites liberal wrath—deserves special attention. In addition to their claims that they are able to save the taxpayers some money and their pride in having a larger pool of dedicated personnel—a by no means insignificant feature in the delivery of human services—they possess other noteworthy advantages. In the case of foster care, the argument can be made—as Peter Skerry, for instance, has done—that since voluntary agencies are distinct from government, they are able to respond in different ways to different needs: They are more easily able to establish different programs based on different philosophies, and hence provide choices to their users. Individuals, parents and children alike, involved in foster care can more easily escape the welfare stigma. Voluntaristic agencies, moreover, have well-developed roots in ethnic and religious communities and are hence better able to attract foster care families. At the same time, they offer families in distress some assurance that their own values and preferences are made available and passed on to their children. To disorganized families, who for whatever reasons have no other options but to surrender their children into temporary foster care, the placement in specific foster homes by agencies embodying the natural families' own values, preferences, and hopes—however vaguely expressed—may well provide a sense of parental responsibility to which they can continue to relate. This lasting component, moreover, can serve as a link between natural family and foster home, a link that ultimately should prove to be of considerable benefit to the children in foster care.

In light of the foregoing description of the current state of the foster care crisis—albeit fragmentary and general—it can well be argued that the case of foster care is of great significance to any consideration of the relationship between family and state. In recent years we have witnessed several oscillations in the public perception of this relationship. After a massive assault against the family in the 1960s and early 1970s, its staying power was rediscovered in the late 1970s. Left behind is a battlefield strewn with assumptions about that relationship, all of which are begging for reassessment. Yet, when all is said and done, by far the majority of recent policy proposals—such as those of K. Kenniston and the Carnegie Council on Children; those of the failed White House Conference on Families in 1980; the Goldstein, Freud, and Solnit reasoning in *Beyond the Best Interest of the Child;* and even the otherwise sober and careful expositions that grace the policy proposals of Gilbert Steiner—continue to be informed by the same liberal assumptions that have dominated for so long. The limits of the liberal vision have become woefully apparent in the foster care crisis. The only promising avenues that have opened up so far break distinctly out of the liberal tradition. And although the futility of past policy efforts in relation to American families is widely recognized, the childcare establishment continues along the same liberal path that has produced such dire consequences and confusion. The question that springs to mind is, Why is this so?

LIMITS OF THE LIBERAL VISION OF THE RELATIONSHIP BETWEEN FAMILY AND STATE

That there is an antifamily bias built into the liberal conception of the welfare state is nothing new. Some years ago, Jacques Maritain in his *Man and the State* noted that strains of eighteenth century rationalism still active in the twentieth century produce diametrically opposing tendencies: individualism and statism. In the course of the past decades, these tendencies have become increasingly evident in the development of the relationship between the family and the state. On the one hand, an ever more pronounced individualism along with an abstract notion of justice feeds increasingly into a preoccupation with individual rights—those of women, children, gays, etc. On the other hand, an all-encompassing reliance upon the state, legally, financially, and prescriptively, dominates the public discourse.

In the United States—the quintessentially liberal state—the discussion of the relationship between state and family has been carried on between the representatives of the individualistic and the statist camps respectively, that is to say, between the public interest lawyers representing the interests of particular individuals, and the representatives of state agencies, programs, and policies attempting to respond to the pressures brought upon them by the first. Typically ignored in this debate are those institutions in which individuals have always been and continue to be embedded: religious, ethnic, and voluntaristic groupings, and, above all, the family. This relationship is apprehended, if at all, only in a negative way. Both partners to the public discourse perceive such traditional ties as bascially anachronistic and fundamentally ancillary to the individual-state relationship. After all, the chief prophet of modern individualism, Jean-Jacques Rousseau, denounced these traditional ties of the modern individual as "shackles" to his individualism and social progress. Above all, the family was declared to be the chief obstacle to the emancipation of individuals and society alike. Since these early formulations, there have not been any fundamental changes in the perception of the relationship between individuals and the state. That is to say, the perception has always been a basically liberal one with minor oscillations veering in either direction.

This is not to say, however, that there has been or that there exists today a conscious design to obliterate or penalize structures like the family, the religious, ethnic, and voluntaristic groupings that stand between the individual and the state and mediate between the two. But the endeavors of both—the champions of individual rights as well as the agents of the state apparatus—conveniently start with a quite innocent assumption of total government responsibility and supremacy. In this sense, the two adversaries to the public debate are united by a common enlightenment philosophy that is basially hostile to any challenge to its primacy. Needless to say, there are public servants and jurists who are benevolently predisposed toward the primacy of the family, just as there are professionals and groupings, both within government and without, that directly oppose family interests. But the diametrically opposed tendencies of individualism and statism inherent in the liberal vision is resolved in the taken-for-granted assumption common to both: that only the state and/or professional experts can solve any and all social and individual problems. The case of foster care clearly shows that this is a fallacious assumption.

There is yet another dimension that deserves our attention. Most families, especially those of the lower strata, are embedded in larger communities—of ethnic or racial subcultures, neighborhood, church, and voluntary association. All of these, taken together, constitute a network of mediating structures—as Peter Berger and Richard Neuhaus have termed them in their *To Empower People*[11]—a network that is of crucial importance both in giving meaning to private life and in providing linkage with the large public institutions of the economy and polity. Many of the problems of the modern welfare state would be greatly mitigated, if not eliminated, if public policy would favor and even utilize these mediating structures to a greater extent, instead of ignoring or even running over them, as has been the tendency of the liberal state. This is particularly important for family policy.

---

11. Peter Berger and Richard Neuhaus, *To Empower People* (Washington, D.C.: American Enterprise Institute, 1976).

A general direction of public policy should be to turn to *other* mediating structures if individual families are no longer able to cope, *before* there is a recourse to professional or bureaucratic agencies of "service delivery," who more often than not are the direct agents of the abstract, anonymous state. Clearly, this cannot be done in all cases, but it can and should be done in many cases. There are two reasons for this, in addition to reasons of cost effectiveness and expediency. One, where an individual family is still extant and able to take responsibility for its needy members, these communal institutions are much closer and much more likely to respond to the values and desires of the family. Two, where such a family is no longer "available," experience has shown that the most effective institutions in many areas of social services are those that resemble natural families as much as possible. These considerations—and details cannot be spelled out within the context of this essay—have far-reaching implications for policies of childcare, for the treatment of troubled adolescents, for the care of the aged, and above all, they are of considerable significance for the rethinking of foster care.

14

WELFARE, FAMILY COHESIVENESS, AND OUT-OF-WEDLOCK BIRTHS

Gregory B. Christainsen and Walter E. Williams

INTRODUCTION

The main point of this paper is not simply that government has foolishly pursued certain policies and that we would be better served by other policies. It is rather that we should question the *institutions* through which policies are formed. Our argument is that given a democracy upon which there are relatively few constitutional restrictions, one set of outcomes can be expected. Under other institutional arrangements—e.g., centrally planned socialism, fascism, anarchism, or a democracy with more severe constitutional restrictions—other sets of outcomes could be expected. From this perspective, then, the important question is not so much which policies would be optimal, but which of the possible institutional arrangements would tend to produce the best results—keeping in mind the likelihood that there are no institutional arrangements that will unambiguously tend to produce "Pareto optimality" (or whatever definition of nirvana is used).

This paper applies the above perspective to the issue of government welfare expenditures and their alleged effects on family cohesiveness and out-of-wedlock births. Ever since the formation of programs like Aid to Families with Dependent Children (AFDC), critics have charged that government efforts to reduce poverty have had the unintended side-effect of undermining family formation, thereby increasing the likelihood that children will be born and raised without a father who is present on a regular basis. Given the inherent difficulties of earning income while at the same time caring for one's children, it is then only a short step to the claim that programs like AFDC foster a dependence by husband-less mothers on state support and result in the "feminization of poverty." The case of single teenage mothers has been especially worrisome in this regard.

The second section looks more closely at the question of what is at stake in debates over family cohesiveness and out-of-wedlock births. The following section presents the essential data on female-headed households, the number of out-of-wedlock births occurring, the amounts spent on welfare programs, and the key changes in program regulations that have occurred over the years. The relationship between welfare programs and the number of female-headed households is examined in the fourth section, which is followed by an examination of some recent proposals for welfare reform. The sixth section of the paper asks the reader to compare the range of plausible outcomes under existing institutional arrangements with that under a radical alternative whereby all governmental measures to redistribute income would be prohibited. The final section offers a summary of the arguments presented and a conclusion.

WHY SHOULD WE CARE ABOUT FAMILY COHESIVENESS AND OUT-OF-WEDLOCK BIRTHS?

People would certainly prefer to live in families characterized by harmony and mutual love and respect as opposed to families ravaged by conflict, but it is not obvious on the surface why an increase in single-parent families should be cause for alarm. It might be argued that single-parent families should be viewed simply as another life-style to be accorded a measure of tolerance. It would be nice if the parties to a relationship loved each other and wanted to be married to each other, but what if they do not? Putting these questions in a more manageable perspective, an economist would ask, "Taking personal preferences as given, is there optimization?"

Many people will today say that if there are no children involved, the marriage decision should be left to the parties to resolve. In conventional economists' jargon, let the free market work as long as there are no significant externalities. The rest of us can hope that the parties love each other and want to be together. We can point out that most conflicts are temporary and should not deter the parties from reaping the benefits of a long-term relationship; but if the parties honestly believe that the cost of the relationship exceeds its benefits, most people would today say that the parties have the right to terminate it.

It is when children are involved that the thorniest issues arise. What are the responsibilities of parents to their children? Even if they would otherwise prefer to separate, do the parties to a relationship have an obligation to stay together for the sake of the children? That answer has to be weighed against the costs to the children from being in a household characterized by continual conflict. In the case of unwed mothers, are the remedies offered by paternity suits sufficient? In cases of divorce, are child support requirements sufficient?

These questions are, of course, extremely difficult to answer. The important point here is that the very resolution of these issues involves conflicts and enormous costs. If government welfare programs serve to increase the number and scope of these conflicts, it is indeed cause for major concern, especially if a sizable portion of these costs in terms of court time and additional welfare payments will be under-written by taxpayers.

A complete discussion of the importance of encouraging and main-taining intact families requires an analysis of the effects of the mar-riage decision on all three of the groups involved: children, women, and last but not least, men. It must be said that the understandable aforementioned focus on children and the much discussed "femini-zation of poverty" have diverted attention from the effects the mar-riage decision generally has on men.

One of the little-noticed facts in the discussion of pay differences between men and women, or between whites and nonwhites, is the incredible disparity in the earnings of married men and unmarried men. Adjusting for differences in age and credentials, bachelors earn less than 60 percent of what married men do.[1] This reflects two im-portant factors: the amount of time spent at work and the effort put forth while working (and probably the contribution of a wife to a man's productivity). On an unadjusted basis, single men work about 20 percent fewer hours than do married men.[2] Even if we restrict our attention to full-time workers, the median earnings of married men in 1980 were 31 percent higher than those of unmarried men.[3]

1. This result can be computed from U.S. Census Bureau data. See also the more formal analysis by Jacob Mincer and Solomon Polachek of the National Longitudinal Survey: U.S. Department of Labor, *Economic Problems of Women*, Hearings before the Joint Economic Committee, 93rd Congress, 1st Session, Part 1, July 10, 11, 12 (Washington, D.C.: U.S. Government Printing Office, 1973).

2. See Irwin Garfinkel and Robert Haveman (with the assistance of David Betson), *Earnings Capacity, Poverty, and Inequality* (New York: Academic Press, 1977), pp. 32–33.

3. U.S. Bureau of the Census, *Statistical Abstract of the United States, 1982* (Washington, D.C.: U.S. Government Printing Office), computed from information on pp. 404 and 38.

For more sophisticated evidence, consider the "earnings capacity utilization rates" developed by researchers at the University of Wisconsin's Institute for Research on Poverty. After controlling for age, education and other credentials, and after correcting for employment opportunities, disability, and presumed discrimination, one can estimate the degree to which various demographic groups make use of their labor market opportunities. The eye-opening finding is that based on this "earnings capacity utilization rate," married men work about twice as hard as comparable single men.[4] Furthermore, a married man's hours worked annually increase with the number of children. Reflecting the traditional practice of sharing the man's income in return for childcare and household services, a married woman's hours—and earnings—decrease with the number of children.[5]

It might be objected that the above discussion blurs cause and effect. It may not be the case that marriage and family responsibilities encourage a man to work more. Rather, it might be the case that those who are harder working from the very beginning are more likely to become married. In this view, it is not "singleness" that causes a man to become less ambitious. The fact that he is less ambitious may be the cause of his singleness.

One can try to test this hypothesis by dividing up the category "single men" into those who have never married, and those who have married and have subsequently become divorced, widowed, or separated from their wives. Those who were formerly married were presumably not viewed as "losers" at the time their spouses agreed to a formal relationship. Yet, divorcees, widowers, and separated men show many of the same kinds of work patterns as never-marrieds. This lends support to the view that singleness does cause lower earnings; note, too, that for whatever reason, there are proportionately twice as many single black as single white men. In short, marriage is a powerful motivating force for men, and the economic well-being of children very much depends on it.

Assuming that a shattered relationship involving children will result in a household headed by a single female, a child's chances of experiencing poverty increase dramatically. Whether the reason is childcare responsibilities, lack of training, or sex discrimination, female

4. Garfinkel and Haveman, *n*. 2.
5. See Shirley J. Smith, "Estimating Annual Hours of Labor Force Activity," *Monthly Labor Review* 106 (Feb. 1983):19.

family heads typically have a lower earnings capacity than do married men. And even if one adjusts for childcare responsibilities and presumed sex discrimination, the earnings capacity utilization rate of female family heads appears to be only about half that of married men—about the same as that of single men.[6]

Gordon Green and Edward Welniak, analysts at the U.S. Bureau of the Census, examined the effects on poverty levels of trends in the numbers of households headed by single females. They looked at 1980 poverty levels as compared to the levels one would have expected had the composition of families in 1980 been the same as in 1970. They concluded that changes in family composition (the growth in single-female-headed households) accounted for over 2 million additional poor families in 1980 versus what would have otherwise occurred. This accounted for almost *one third* of the number of poor families reported in 1980.[7]

Beyond strictly economic concerns, there are serious questions about the impact of single-parent-induced poverty on child development—language and other educational skills. As with other studies in these areas, it is difficult to sort out the lines of causality. The best we can do is say that parents with high incomes tend to have more successful children. This may in part be due to the fact that such parents tend to have higher IQs, but they are also more likely to provide their children with a good education, a supportive home environment, and some inheritance of financial and professional assets. In addition, there may be difficult-to-quantify effects associated with the stigma attached to children, especially illegitimate ones, from fatherless homes.[8]

The disproportionate increase in *teenage*, single-parent families suggests another source of concern. There is a link between the age of a mother and low-birth-weight babies (less than 2500 grams). Low birth weight is in turn associated with numerous physical and mental handicaps. To be sure, the period from 1950 to 1980 saw great advances in the technology of prenatal and infant care, and indeed the

6. Garfinkel and Havemen, *n.* 2.

7. See Gordon Green and Edward Welniak, *Changing Family Composition and Income Differentials,* Special Demographic Analyses CDS-80-7 (Washington, D.C.: U.S. Government Printing Office, 1982).

8. For a more complete analysis of the possible lines of causality, see the following: Zena Smith Blau, *Black Children/White Children* (New York: Free Press, 1981); Christopher Jencks, *Inequality: A Reassessment of the Effect of Family and Schooling in America* (New York: Basic Books, 1972); and Arlene Leibowitz, "Home Investments in Children," *Journal of Political Economy* 82 (March/April 1974):S111–S131.

percentage of low-weight newborns among whites fell from 7.2 to 5.7 during this time, but it rose from 10.4 to 11.5 among blacks.[9]

If it is true that government policies are causal factors in increased marital instability, decreases in hours worked, higher-than-otherwise levels of poverty, stunted child development, higher birthrates among unmarried teenagers, and higher-than-otherwise percentages of low-weight babies, who could fail to be concerned? The fact that these problems have been more prevalent among blacks than whites only adds to the controversy. But testing for the possible impact of government policies requires a more careful examination of the stylized facts and the other possible explanations for the observed problems.

THE STYLIZED FACTS

Data on Female-headed Households

Table 14–1 presents statistics on the percentage of all family members living in a household headed by a single woman.

The percentage of all family members living in households headed by a single woman grew by *63* percent from 1960 to 1980. Table 14–2 presents figures that contrast the growth in family members living in households headed by a single woman by broad income class. From 1960 to 1980 there was a 115 percent increase among the poor in the percentage of family members living in a household headed by a single woman. If we break the figures down further, the statistics by race are the most dramatic of all.

Across all income classes, Table 14–3 shows that the percentages of nonwhites living in female-headed households were higher to begin with in 1960. And between 1960 and 1980, the percentages of poor and low-income nonwhites living in female-headed households grew by a remarkable 135 and 268 percent, respectively.

---

9. See Charles Murray, *Losing Ground: American Social Policy 1950–1980* (New York: Basic Books, 1984), p. 129. A note of caution should be issued on the relationship between births to teenage women and child development. Despite the data on low-birth-weight babies, the child development literature has not established that young mothers per se tend to have less-healthy children. It is the interaction of teenage motherhood with *poverty* that appears to be decisive.

Table 14–1. Percentage of All Family Members Living in Households Headed by a Single Woman.

Year	Percentage
1960	8.8
1965	9.2
1970	10.6
1975	12.4
1980	14.3

SOURCE: U.S. Census Bureau, *Characteristics of the Population Below the Poverty Level: 1980* (Washington, D.C.: U.S. Government Printing Office), Tables 1 and 2.

Table 14–2. Percentage of All Family Members Living in Households Headed by a Single Woman, by Income Class.

Year	Poor	Low Income	Middle & Upper Income
1960	20.8	8.1	5.4
1965	26.5	11.4	5.4
1970	36.9	18.2	6.7
1975	42.6	22.3	7.9
1980	44.8	24.5	9.2

SOURCE: U.S. Census Bureau, *Characteristics of the Population Below the Poverty Level:1980* (Washington, D.C.: U.S. Government Printing Office), Tables 1 and 2.

Note: "Poor" means living below the official poverty line. "Low Income" means living between the poverty line and 125 percent of it.

Table 14–3. Percentage of All Family Members Living in Households Headed by a Single Woman, by Income and Race.

Year	Poor Nonwhite	Poor White	Low-Inc. Nonwhite	Low-Inc. White	Upper Inc. Nonwhite	Upper Inc. White
1960	27.5	17.7	11.6	7.6	10.1	5.1
1965	34.8	22.1	16.2	10.3	11.9	5.0
1970	53.4	28.2	27.2	15.4	16.8	5.8
1975	61.1	33.2	38.5	17.2	18.5	6.8
1980	64.6	33.9	43.5	18.7	21.0	7.8

SOURCE: U.S. Census Bureau, *Characteristics of the Population Below the Poverty Level:1980* (Washington, D.C.: U.S. Government Printing Office), Tables 1 and 2.

Data on Out-of-Wedlock Births

Table 14–4 shows that overall U.S. illegitimacy increased by 247 percent from 1960 to 1980. Both whites and nonwhites showed marked increases.

Table 14–5 indicates that although the illegitimacy rate for nonwhites skyrocketed, it went up even faster among whites.

The data for teenagers shown in Table 14–6 are the most provocative yet. Over *80* percent of all nonwhite babies born to teenagers were illegitimate as of 1980. By 1980, there were two-thirds of a million illegitimate births annually, more than half of them to nonwhites. More than 40 percent of the illegitimate births were to teenage mothers.

While the *proportion* of babies born out of wedlock has increased, the fertility rate has dropped, with the notable exception of unmarried teenagers. Women in general are having children at a much slower rate. Combining the data on the illegitimacy proportion with the data on fertility, 2.2 percent of all single women gave birth to a child in 1960, and 2.9 percent in 1980.[10] This is a significant increase, but less shocking than the data presented in the tables.

Data on Welfare Expenditures and Program Rules

In presenting some of the stylized facts on welfare expenditures, we begin with an interesting table showing Aid to Families with Dependent Children (AFDC) benefits for various states. If anything, Table 14–7 appears to show an *inverse* correlation between the level of welfare benefits and social problems. Minnesota, for example, has a relatively high level of AFDC benefits, but has significantly lower rates of female-headship, divorce, and fertility than does Mississippi, a low benefit state. Of course, other benefit programs—food stamps, Medicaid, etc.—must be considered as well to get a full picture, and this story is very complex, depending on the precise circumstances of individuals in each state.

The data on social welfare expenditures *over time* are dramatic. It may be helpful to note that if someone had spent $1,000 a day from the birth of Christ to the present day, he would not yet have spent a

10. Murray, *n.* 9, p. 125.

Table 14–4.   Percentage of Newborn Children Born out of Wedlock.

Year	Percentage
1960	5.3
1965	7.7
1970	10.7
1975	14.2
1980	18.4

SOURCE: National Center for Health Statistics, *Vital Statistics of the United States, 1980,* vol. 1, Natality Table 1–73 (and comparable tables in earlier editions); DHHS Pub. No. (PHS) 85–1100, Public Health Service (Washington, D.C.: U.S. Government Printing Office, 1984).

Table 14–5.   Percentage of Newborn Children Born out of Wedlock, by Race.

Year	Nonwhite	White
1960	21.6	2.3
1965	26.3	4.0
1970	34.9	5.7
1975	44.2	7.3
1980	48.4	11.0

SOURCE: National Center for Health Statistics, *Vital Statistics of the United States, 1980,* vol. 1, Natality Table 1–73 (and comparable tables in earlier editions); DHHS Pub. No. (PHS) 85-1100, Public Health Service (Washington, D.C.: U.S. Government Printing Office, 1984).

Table 14–6.   Percentage of Newborn Children of Mothers Aged 15–19 Born out of Wedlock, by Race.

Year	Nonwhite	White
1960	42.2	7.2
1965	49.2	11.5
1970	61.3	17.1
1975	74.3	22.8
1980	82.1	33.0

SOURCE: National Center for Health Statistics, *Vital Statistics of the United States, 1980,* vol. 1, Natality Table 1–73 (and comparable tables in earlier editions); DHHS Pub. No. (PHS) 85-1100, Public Health Service (Washington, D.C.: U.S. Government Printing Office, 1984).

Table 14–7.   Maximum AFDC Benefits and Selected Family Structure Measures, Selected States, 1970 and 1975.

State	Maximum Monthly AFDC Benefits (1975)[a]	Female Heads As a % of All Women (1970)[b]	Divorce Rate Per 1000 Married Women (1975)	Birthrate Per 1000 Unmarried Women (1975)
Alaska	$400	4.2	39	19
Michigan	399	3.9	19	13
Minnesota	385	2.7	14	8
Mississippi	60	4.6	23	27
Texas	140	3.9	26	14
Utah	360	3.4	22	7

SOURCE: David J. Ellwood and Mary Jo Bane, "The Impact of AFDC on Family Structure and Living Arrangements," (Washington, D.C.: U.S. Department of Health and Human Services, 1984), p. 2

[a]Maximum benefits for a family of four as of July 1975.
[b]Female heads with children. This variable is not available for 1975.

billion dollars! According to Table 14–8, social welfare spending by the federal government grew by *338* percent in constant dollars from 1960 to 1980. In per capita terms, it grew *248* percent. As a percentage of gross national product, it went from 4.8 to 10.4, a *117* percent increase.

What matters for the present paper are not the aggregate amounts per se, but how the benefits available to each individual affected his or her life. In this regard, one must consider program eligibility rules as well as the dollar amounts available to each eligible person. As far as AFDC was concerned, the key decision points on eligibility were as follows:

1966—The U.S. Department of Health, Education and Welfare issued guidelines forbidding at-home eligibility checks of women on AFDC (e.g., Was she living with a man?).

1967—Women on AFDC were permitted to keep one-third of labor market earnings. Previously, earnings reduced benefits dollar for dollar.

1968—The Supreme Court struck down man-in-the-house eligibility restrictions.

Table 14–8. Federal Social Welfare Expenditures (billions of 1980 dollars).

Year	Social Insurance	Public Aid	Health & Medical	Other	Total
1960	39.7	5.9	4.8	18.9	69.3
1965	56.8	9.4	7.3	24.8	98.3
1970	95.8	20.4	10.1	37.5	163.8
1975	152.5	41.6	13.0	49.0	256.1
1980	191.2	48.7	12.9	49.9	302.8

SOURCE: U.S. Bureau of the Census, *Statistical Abstract of the United States, 1985*, Table 589 and comparable tables in earlier editions. (Washington, D.C.: U.S. Government Printing Office.)

Notes: Nominal dollar amounts adjusted using the Consumer Price Index. "Other" includes spending for veterans' programs, education, and housing.

1969—The Supreme Court struck down one-year state residency requirements for welfare eligibility.

1974—Stricter child support enforcement provisions were enacted. (It should also be noted that, by the mid-1970s, real AFDC benefits had started to fall.)

THE RELATIONSHIP BETWEEN WELFARE AND THE INCREASE IN THE NUMBER OF SINGLE MOTHERS

As we have seen in the previous section, welfare expenditures shot up from 1960 to 1980, and eligibility rules were liberalized greatly from 1966 to at least 1974. Single-parent families and illegitimacy increased at the same time. But was it a case of cause and effect? Perhaps single-parent families and illegitimacy arose for reasons *besides* programs like AFDC.

The Argument for a Direct Cause-and-Effect Relationship

The claim that welfare programs, particularly AFDC, promote marital dissolution and out-of-wedlock births has been put most forcefully by Charles Murray in his book *Losing Ground*.[11] Looking at the increase in out-of-wedlock births and female-headed households during the 1970s, Murray argues that there is a simple explanation for people's

11. Murray, *n.* 9.

behavior that we can try to deny or downplay, but from which there is no escape: People were paid to behave that way. This is not, says Murray, to deny that there are other factors that may have contributed to these problems, nor is it to claim that most poor people sit on the corner with calculators and all the needed information to determine the economically most advantageous course of action. But at the margin, where we ask simply whether economic incentives affect human behavior, the answer is an unambiguous "yes." The undeniable fact of economic life is that if the cost of a particular form of behavior is lowered, or if the benefits of the particular form of behavior are increased, we can expect to observe more of it. These incentives may then interact in complex ways with people's capacities for rationalizing what they do as being independent of economic incentives. Whole new cultural norms can then emerge. Or the change in cultural norms that brought about controversial changes in AFDC can be reinforced.

Consider a young unmarried couple living in 1970 where the woman has become pregnant and suppose the man's only possible source of income is working 40 hours a week at a minimum-wage job. Making all calculations in terms of what a dollar was worth in 1980, the man could earn $136 a week. If they stay unmarried and the woman has the child, she will be eligible for $106 a week in AFDC payments in a typical northern state like Pennsylvania, plus $23 in food stamps. She might also be eligible for rent subsidies and Medicaid; to be conservative, add just $5 more per week in benefits. Her benefits thus add up to $134 a week. So if they stay together, but in an unmarried state, the couple's income will be $270 a week. If they marry, she loses her benefits and they end up with just $136 a week.[12]

Contrast this case with the case of a similar couple in 1960. In 1960, a single mother with a child would have been eligible (in terms of what a dollar was worth in 1980) for only $63 a week in benefits. A full-time minimum-wage job was worth $111 a week. Furthermore, 1960 law prohibited benefits from being paid to an unmarried woman if there were a man in the house. Is it any wonder, asks Murray, that couples in 1960 were more likely to get married and/or take sterner precautions to avoid the pregnancy in the first place?[13]

---

12. Ibid. pp. 157–162.

13. Ibid. It should be emphasized that, while Murray believes monetary factors to be important, he does not regard the relationship between cause and effect to be quite as straightforward as the above discussion suggests. Nor does he think that AFDC is the only program at issue. See, e.g., Murray, *n.* 9, pp. 175–76 and chap. 14.

The above examples involved unmarried couples. What about married couples? Are they going to file for divorce and have an illegitimate child in order to collect the additional $134 a week they could get in 1970? The answer again would be that most couples might not think in such crass terms, but that at the margin, where a marriage is teetering, such incentives could tip the balance.

Evidence From Regression Studies

The argument presented above is a powerful one and certainly has validity. As with any attempt to establish causal relationships, however, one must be careful to consider alternative explanations for the observed phenomena. There certainly were changes in welfare benefits and eligibility rules in the late 1960s and early 1970s, and there was an undeniable increase in marital instability, out-of-wedlock births, and single-parent families during the late 1960s and 1970s. Nonetheless, it is possible that there are other explanations for decreasing family cohesiveness and increasing illegitimacy. The 1970s was a decade of a higher average unemployment rate than the 1960s. Higher unemployment may have contributed to increased marital instability. Social mores have likewise undergone large changes, including changes in attitudes toward marriage and illegitimacy. At least some of these changes in social mores may have been independent of the structure of welfare programs.

The most formal attempts to control for the effects of the various factors involve elaborate statistical (regression) models. The models can try to analyze the behavior of disparate groups of people at a single point in time—a cross-sectional analysis—or try to analyze the behavior of a single group over a period of time—a time-series analysis. Most of the studies done have been cross-sectional in nature, the question being whether areas with high AFDC benefit levels experience higher rates of marital instability and illegitimacy after controlling for other possible explanations for these problems.

Honig[14] found a significant effect of AFDC on marital instability in both blacks and whites. Curiously, however, the effect was larger in 1960. Honig estimated that a doubling of the 1970 AFDC payment would increase the proportion of families headed by single mothers

14. Marjorie Honig, "AFDC Income, Recipient Rates, and Family Dissolution," *Journal of Human Resources* 9 (Summer 1974):303–22.

by only 6 percent. Ross and Sawhill's study[15] of low-income neighborhoods of forty-one cities found an effect on blacks more than twice that estimated by Honig for all races for 1970. Ross and Sawhill also obtained an estimate that suggested AFDC *increased* marital stability among whites. Two other investigations[16] using data collected for the Panel Study of Income Dynamics did not find *any* significant effect of AFDC on marital instability.

The most recent thorough study[17] of the effects of AFDC performed for the U.S. Department of Health and Human Services (DHHS) concluded that differences in welfare payments do not appear to be the *primary* cause of variations in family structures across states, *or* over time; largely unmeasurable differences in culture or attitudes or expectations seem to account for a large portion of differences in birthrates among unmarried women, and divorce and separation patterns among families with children.

At the same time, the authors of the DHHS study concluded that there is relatively strong evidence that benefit levels influence divorce and separation rates to some degree. The impact is not particularly large among middle-aged and older women, but among very young married mothers, the impact is sizable. A woman with a child who married before age 20 was estimated to have about an 8 percent chance of being divorced or separated by age 20 if she is white, and a 15 percent chance if she is nonwhite. If AFDC benefits were $100 per month higher in every state, it was estimated that the chances of being divorced or separated jump to 12 percent for whites and 25 percent for nonwhites.

Furthermore, a $100 increase in AFDC was estimated to increase the number of female-headed households by 15 percent. About one-third of this 15 percent was attributed to an increase in the number

15. Heather L. Ross and Isabel Sawhill, *Time of Transition: The Growth of Families Headed by Women* (Washington, D.C.: The Urban Institute, 1975).

16. See Isabel Sawhill, et al., *Income Transfers and Family Structures* (Washington, D.C.: The Urban Institute, 1975); and Douglas A. Wolf, "Income in Labor Supply and Family Stability: An Empirical Analysis of Marital Dissolution" (Ph.D. dissertation, University of Pennsylvania, 1977).

17. David J. Ellwood and Mary Jo Bane, "The Impact of AFDC on Family Structure and Living Arrangements" (Washington, D.C.: U.S. Department of Health and Human Services, 1984). For Charles Murray's comments on this study and related work, see Charles Murray, "Have the Poor Been 'Losing Ground'?" *Political Science Quarterly* 100 (Fall 1985):427–45. See also Charles Murray, "How to Lie with Statistics," *National Review*, 28 February 1986:39–41.

of single mothers; roughly two-thirds was attributed to the fact that AFDC may induce a person who would have been a single mother in any case to live independently rather than with relatives.

The authors found almost no impact of welfare on fertility, regardless of the alternative acceptable research methods employed. The study thus supports the view that welfare does not, in general, lead women to have babies, but it does not necessarily negate the claim that welfare encourages single women who are *already* pregnant to remain unmarried and keep their babies.

Whether AFDC provides a significant, direct economic incentive to terminate a relationship must also be regarded as a clouded issue. Prior to the DHHS study, when the regression evidence was weaker, regression studies were, in general, criticized for not adequately capturing "esteem effects" or what are sometimes called "independence effects" from welfare programs. The point was not that couples could live better unmarried with AFDC than married without AFDC, but that the very existence of welfare, however structured, weakened the attractions of marriage and the marriage bond. It was argued that statistical studies were not adequately measuring this impact. In particular, some have argued that welfare undermines the traditional male role of provider, thereby, for whatever cultural or biological reasons, lowering the esteem of the man in the eyes of both parties to the relationship.[18] In any event, it has been argued that the fact that welfare to some extent makes the parties less dependent on each other increases tensions and marital instability.[19]

Lending some limited support for this view have been studies of programs sometimes referred to as *AFDC-U*. Under these programs, more than half of all states made AFDC payments available to *intact* families as well as those headed by a single parent, thereby eliminating to some degree the direct economic incentive for marital dissolution. Ross and Sawhill and Minarik and Goldfarb,[20] and also Honig, failed to find that AFDC-U significantly decreases the likelihood of

18. This argument was forcefully made by George Gilder in *Wealth and Poverty* (New York: Basic Books, 1981).

19. Discussions of an independence effect often speak of the woman gaining independence from the man. As with other portions of this paper, the issue is tied to questions about traditional sex roles. In other words, note that an independence effect could also involve a man gaining independence from a woman.

20. Joseph J. Minarik and Robert S. Goldfarb, "AFDC Income, Recipient Rates, and Family Dissolution: A Comment," *Journal of Human Resources* 11 (Spring 1976):243–50.

marital dissolution, and one of Honig's results and a study by Silverman and Wiseman[21] suggested that marital dissolution was *increased* as more people were brought on to the "new and improved" AFDC program.

Thus, a determined effort could be made to interpret the statistical evidence in either one of two ways. One could argue that the traditional AFDC program has not been consistently shown to have significant effects on marital dissolution or illegitimacy, and that one should therefore not be surprised that AFDC-U could not be shown to have a consistent effect either. Alternatively, one could argue that, on the whole, it is clear that AFDC has had some effect on marital dissolution—through independence, esteem, or other nonpecuniary effects, if not a direct economic effect—and that AFDC-U has if anything, exacerbated these effects.

RECENT PROPOSALS FOR WELFARE REFORM

Irrespective of the competing views on the link between welfare and family cohesiveness, there have been repeated calls for welfare reform during the past twenty years. This section discusses some of the most prominent proposals, particularly as they affect the family.

The Rise and Fall of the Negaive Income Tax

The idea of a "negative income tax" (NIT) was the darling of economists concerned with welfare policy during the 1970s. From Milton Friedman and George Stigler to Paul Samuelson and James Tobin—four Nobel Prize winners—the idea of a negative income tax gained acceptance. Administratively simple, it would replace the current grabbag of welfare programs—AFDC, food stamps, Supplemental Security Income, Disability Insurance, etc.—with a cash grant to people who were poor for whatever reason, married or unmarried. In other words, the incentives for marital dissolution would, it seemed, be lessened.[22] As a person worked and earned income, the amount re-

---

21. Gerald Silverman and Michael Wiseman, "Family Fragmentation in the Aid to Dependent Children" (Paper presented at the 1979 meetings of the Western Economic Association, Las Vegas, June 17–21).

22. It can be shown that, even under most negative income tax schemes, there will exist cases in which couples will have monetary incentives to be unmarried. See Michael C. Keeley, "The Effects of Negative Income Tax Programs on Marital Dissolution" (Unpublished paper, November 1983).

ceived from the government would gradually taper off and eventually, at some reasonable income level, fall to zero. In no case could a person be financially worse off by working, and by assuring some minimum level of income to all, the NIT would provide security.

During the Nixon administration, and again during the Ford and Carter administrations, welfare programs were proposed involving major shifts toward the concept of an NIT. On each occasion, the proposals became viewed, not as substitutes for existing programs, but as additions. Rather than improving incentives for work, as most supporters had envisioned, it was demonstrable that incentives would be worsened. Indeed, Milton Friedman testified *against* Nixon's Family Assistance Plan.[23]

As former Reagan adviser Martin Anderson has put it, under current institutional arrangements "there is no way to achieve all the politically necessary conditions for radical welfare reform at the same time."[24] To be politically feasible welfare reform must provide a "decent" level of support, it must contain strong incentives to work, and it must have a reasonable cost. And it must do all three at the same time. If from a political perspective, however, a "decent" level of support requires that few if any current recipients are to receive less from the reformed program than they now do, then it is impossible to achieve all politically necessary objectives simultaneously, given the benefits many people currently receive. At the same time that Martin Anderson was writing in 1978, some families of four were receiving payments of as much as $12,000 a year.[25]

Concerns about the NIT program during most of the 1970s were relatively minor. Relatively small experiments with negative income taxes for groups in New Jersey and Pennsylvania, and also in Iowa and North Carolina, had produced some results showing larger-than-forecast disincentives for labor supply and marital stability, but a final assessment would have to await an experiment in Gary, Indiana, and in by far the most extravagant studies, experiments conducted in Seattle and Denver from 1971 to 1978.

---

23. For a discussion of the early fight for a negative income tax, see Walter E. Williams, "The Continuing Struggle for a Negative Income Tax: A Review Article," *Journal of Human Resources* 10 (Fall 1975):427–44.

24. See Martin Anderson, *Welfare: The Political Economy of Welfare Reform in the United States* (Stanford, Calif.: Hoover Institution Press, 1978), p. 135.

25. Ibid.

The results from these experiments were shocking. The experimental programs had no work or job search requirements, and payments made were based only on a person's current income; previously accumulated wealth was considered irrelevant. In Seattle and Denver, transfer payments to able-bodied persons that would have, other things equal, raised participants' incomes[26] above what they could otherwise attain under AFDC and food stamps, resulted in income gains of less than 20 percent of the value of the payments![27] In other words, to the extent that the monetary value of the NIT was more generous than existing programs, able-bodied participants consumed more than 80 percent of this value as leisure. After their first year, husbands reduced their hours worked by an estimated 12.7 percent as compared to the behavior of comparable individuals in the existing welfare system. Women reduced their labor supply by roughly 25 percent.[28]

With respect to family cohesiveness, groups participating in the various experiments generally experienced a *much* higher rate of marital instability than did control groups eligible for the traditional AFDC and food stamp programs under the existing system.[29] It can be argued that there was no effort to collect child support payments from divorced or separated fathers in the experimental groups—there is at least some attempt made in the existing welfare system—but if the goal of the experiments was to find a government welfare system with

26. If the NIT payments had been based on pre-experimental labor supply, the average payment would have been $1,039–$1,046 per month for two-parent families and $925 for female-headed families. See Philip Robins, Richard West, and Michael Keeley, "A Structural Model of the Labor Supply Response to the Seattle-Denver Income Maintenance Experiments." Menlo Park, Calif.: SRI International, August 1980, p. B1. Actual payments made were not reported.

27. See Philip Robins and Richard West, "Labor Supply Response to the Seattle-Denver Income Maintenance Experiments on Alternative Estimates of a Structural Model," Menlo Park, Calif.: SRI International, January 1980 (draft).

28. See John Bishop, "The Labor Supply Response to the Seattle-Denver Income Maintenance Experiment: A Reinterpretation" (Paper presented at the 1981 meetings of the Western Economics Association, San Francisco, July 2–6), p. 2.

29. See John Bishop, "Jobs, Cash Transfers and Marital Instability," *Journal of Human Resources* 15 (Summer 1980):301–34. White family dissolution was 36 percent higher in Seattle/Denver. It was 42 percent higher among blacks. In New Jersey there was no measured effect on whites but a 66 percent increase for blacks and an 84 percent increase among Spanish-speaking individuals. In Gary, there were no measured effects, but note that families were told that "any one-person unit formed as a result of marital dissolution would not be eligible for the NIT"! See Lyle P. Groeneveld, Nancy Brandon Tuma, and Michael T. Hannan, "The Effects of Negative Income Tax Programs on Marital Dissolution," *Journal of Human Resources* 15 (Fall 1980):654–74, especially p. 671.

insignificant effects on labor supply and family composition, it must be said frankly that the experimental programs were a colossal failure. A negative income tax with eligibility limited to those below a certain wealth level might still hold some appeal. In light of evidence linking marital instability to unemployment, such a reform could be combined with job search and work requirements, including "workfare." Employment subsidies to be granted to firms that hire certain categories of disadvantaged citizens might also be considered. The political obstacles to fine-tuning such policies, however, would most probably be insurmountable.

Child Support Requirements and Child Allowances

A modest approach to welfare reform would be to simply tinker with the current system by trying to remove direct incentives for marital dissolution and illegitimacy while at the same time watching for independence, esteem, or other nonpecuniary effects. Aside from modest AFDC-U programs, tougher child-support rules have been proposed as an equitable way by which direct incentives for marital dissolution and illegitimacy might be weakened. Along with work requirements and strict eligibility rules for welfare recipients, enforcement of child support rules was a focal point of the welfare reforms initiated by Ronald Reagan as governor of California. AFDC might create incentives for marital dissolution and illegitimacy, but these could perhaps be offset by stiff child-support requirements. The father would know that if he left the family, he would still have heavy responsibilities.

It has been argued that the system of child support could be strengthened by utilizing the withholding systems for state income tax payments. At present it is very difficult to hunt down delinquent fathers in order to enforce child support obligations. As an alternative, one might advocate that state tax authorities be notified of fathers' child-support obligations, and that the appropriate amounts be withheld from fathers' paychecks. Single mothers would then receive child support from the funds collected.[30]

While the above system might be a more efficient way of enforcing child support requirements, its effects on marital stability and ille-

---

30. For a full discussion, see Irwin Garfinkel and Elizabeth Uhr, "A New Approach to Child Support," *The Public Interest* 75 (Spring 1984):111–22.

gitimacy are open to question. To the extent that AFDC creates direct incentives for marital dissolution and illegitimacy, stiffer child support obligations would, from the father's perspective, offset them to some degree.

From the mother's perspective, however, stiff child-support obligations *further weaken* the attractions of marriage. Under a nonexistent or poorly enforced system of child support, the woman has an incentive to try to maintain the relationship; she can have little confidence that she will receive support from the man if they separate. Under a strongly enforced system of child support, however, the incentives for her to separate are stronger because she can have greater confidence that the man will still provide some support.

As a substitute or a complement to stricter rules for child support, some have proposed a system of child allowances. Under such a system, intact families with children would be given monthly allowances, a policy that it is hoped would promote such families. As an alternative or supplement, one could raise the value of tax deductions for children; the real value of these deductions fell sharply during the 1960s and 1970s. David Stockman was an advocate of child allowances while in the Congress, and Daniel Patrick Moynihan supported them prior to becoming a member of the U.S. Senate. Most other industrial nations have them, though especially in Sweden, the incentives created by child allowances have been swamped by countervailing incentives from other programs.

The New Federalism of Charles Murray

Charles Murray has made one of the few recent challenges to the entire institutional structure of the modern welfare state. Convinced of a cause-and-effect relationship between federal welfare programs and marital dissolution, out-of-wedlock births, and workforce withdrawal, Murray has advocated the elimination of the federal role in the welfare system. AFDC, food stamps, Medicaid, Worker's Compensation, subsidized housing, and disability insurance would be eliminated; he would retain Social Security and unemployment insurance.

Murray argues, first, that a large proportion of the population would be unaffected. "A surprising number of the huge American middle and working classes go from birth to grave without using any social welfare benefits until they receive their first Social Security check."[31] Others would be affected, but only trivially so. A third group would be significantly affected and would have to adjust to the new reality, but in many cases this would be a desirable development, according to Murray. Young single mothers might have to move in with friends or relatives, who would then pressure them to become self-supporting; a reluctance to face such pressure would deter some from acting irresponsibly in the first place. Young workers tempted to quit menial jobs might now realize that they should continue; some would indeed acquire new skills or land a new position that they otherwise would not have gotten.

But would there not be some who fall through the cracks? Of course, says Murray. State and local governments and other agencies would have to deal with such cases. It is not denied that people in some areas would get more and better help than people in other areas. It is argued, however, that there would be much more flexibility to experiment with different eligibility rules, with—as a last resort—people being able to move from one place to another if conditions are unsatisfactory.

One might well complain that we cannot be *sure* that everyone will be taken care of in the degree to which we would wish. "But this observation," says Murray, "by no means settles the question":

> If one may point in objection to the child now fed by Food Stamps who would go hungry, one may also point with satisfaction to the child who would have an entirely different and better future. Hungry children should be fed; there is no argument about that. It is no less urgent that children be allowed to grow up in a system free of the forces that encourage them to be poor and dependent. If a strategy reasonably promises to remove those forces, after so many attempts to "help the poor" have failed, it is worth thinking about.[32]

Murray concludes by saying that there is simply a dilemma we must face: We want to help people, but an overreliance on "help" creates more problems than it solves. It is understood that life is dif-

---

31. Murray, *n*. 9, p. 228. This claim appears dubious if one considers subsidized school lunches, farm subsidies, loan guarantees and the many other ways by which income is redistributed.

32. Ibid. p. 233.

ficult for many people and many things happen for which they are not to be blamed, but in striking the balance, we must give weight to the importance of encouraging individuals and their families to be responsible for their respective fates. We must always ask what is the effect of our helping an individual on his incentives to help himself.

BACK TO BASICS: WHY DO WE HAVE GOVERNMENT WELFARE PROGRAMS?

In 1792 the great German political philosopher Wilhelm von Humboldt, who was later to have a profound effect on John Stuart Mill, wrote an extraordinary essay in which he argued that the only legitimate function of government was the articulation and enforcement of laws protecting individuals' rights to private property and freedom of contract.[33] Within this framework of law with respect to property (and torts), and contracts (and fraud), individuals would be free to do as they pleased, with their fates being determined by their respective efforts and the operation of market forces. Such a view of government provides for no public sector services such as welfare programs.

We have by now become so accustomed to government welfare programs that few people question their basic legitimacy. Yet, it is only during the last half-century or so that they have emerged as a major source of support. It may, therefore, be useful to compare existing institutional arrangements with a radical alternative such as Humboldt's in order to clarify what the appropriate role of government is with respect to charitable support.

The Public Goods Argument

Putting to one side the question how much the nonpoor *should* want to give to those who are poor, what are the best institutional arrangements for the exercise of existing inclinations to help disadvantaged citizens? What objections might one have to arrangements whereby there were strict constitutional prohibitions on *any* level of govern-

---

33. Wilhelm von Humboldt, *The Limits of State Action* (London: Cambridge University Press, 1969). The words Mill put in front of his essay *On Liberty* were Humboldt's "The grand, the leading principle, towards which every argument in these pages directly converges, is the absolute and essential importance of human development in its richest diversity."

ment undertaking *any* service activities outside of articulating and enforcing the laws of property and contract?

Taking people's preferences as given, and ignoring questions of justice for the time being, most economists argue that the markets that will evolve on the basis of the institutions of private property and freedom of contract are generally the best means of allocating resources that are scarce relative to people's desires for them. The conventional neoclassical view, however, is that the outcomes of free markets are less than optimal if there are tendencies toward monopoly, or if a transaction throws onto third parties costs or benefits that are not accounted for.

A special case involving third-party effects (externalities) is that of public goods. A pure public good is one that has, to an infinite degree, two properties: nonexclusion and nonrivalness. Nonexclusion is said to exist if it is prohibitively costly to prevent those who do not pay for a good from nevertheless consuming it. Nonrivalness is said to exist if one person's consumption of a good does not diminish the possibilities for others to consume the same amount of the good. National defense is an example of a good with both these properties. Thus, if a private producer provided a public good, people could consume it even if they did not pay the producer for it; they could be free-riders. No one, it is thus argued, has any incentive to pay for a public good since, once it is provided, he cannot be deprived of its benefits. If no one will make payment, however, no private producer will find it worthwhile to provide such a good; private producers operating in free markets, it is argued, will fail to provide public goods.

Looking at the provision of charitable support, we see such public good problems. If a person gets satisfaction from seeing disadvantaged people helped, he may have a latent willingness to pay to alleviate their poverty. If someone else pays to alleviate their poverty, he cannot be excluded from satisfaction. So people like him may be free-riders; they want to see others helped, but they hope that others will pay. If this attitude were widespread, however, a regime in which government was prohibited from providing services might result in a "suboptimal" level of charitable support. The institutional arrangements advocated by Humboldt appear, according to the public goods argument, to be undesirable—even if we simply take people's latent preferences as given. If we question the adequacy of people's underlying preferences to help others as well, it might be argued that the situation is even worse.

The Implications of Public Choice Theory

The fact that one set of institutional arrangements cannot be expected to achieve some standard of perfection does not necessarily indicate that there exist other institutional arrangements which can. We could of course think of ways that an optimum *might* be achieved under alternative arrangements—*if* X, Y, and Z were to occur. But what if under these alternative arrangements undesirables like A, B, and C could be expected instead? Should we continue to support the alternative arrangements and hope that X, Y, and Z will occur?

Consider a representative democracy with few constitutional restrictions as an alternative to Humboldt's institutional arrangements. In analyzing this alternative, let us ask not what we should *hope* for, but what types of outcomes can be reasonably expected. In particular, what sort of income redistribution patterns can we expect? How are these likely to be financed? How do the results compare with the neoclassical optimum? How do they compare with Humboldt's arrangements?

In the absence of constitutional restrictions, one can expect the passage of various sorts of programs. These programs will be financed largely by taxation. In other words, representatives will vote that some citizens have portions of their incomes (or other assets) seized. If citizens are caught trying to evade or resist seizure, they will be punished—even if they have no interest in the program for which their incomes are being seized.

It should be clear that the expected outcome under such institutional arrangements will be replete with third-party effects and will, therefore, be inefficient from a neoclassical perspective; people will have all sorts of costs (taxes) and benefits (subsidies) thrown onto them by government actions. Some people will be forced to pay for goods in amounts that (at the margin) exceed their subjective valuations of those goods. Other people will (at the margin) pay *less* than their subjective valuations, suggesting (from a neoclassical perspective) that they are paying too little, or that they have not received enough of the good. Even for public goods, where taxation appears to offer a way of thwarting the free-rider problem, it will be mere happenstance if efficiency is served.[34]

34. More formally, public choice theorists have argued that from the standpoint of a neoclassical optimum, a representative democracy with a few constitutional restrictions has the following weaknesses:

Perhaps the most important consideration for efficiency involves the acquisition and use of information. With respect to the question of how to provide charitable support, the "knowledge problem," as we may call it, involves, first, the issue of who ought to be given help. Just the poor? Just the severely disabled poor? The elderly? The elderly poor? Farmers? Poor farmers? Inner-city residents? Poor inner-city residents? The blind? The blind who are poor? For any or all of the aforementioned, what type of help should be given? Cash, housing, food, special facilities for the handicapped, medical care? How much? Will person *P* want to work as much if he can get support? Will an unwed, pregnant woman be more likely to marry if support is denied? Is it appropriate to request that someone work in return for charitable support? Attend religious activities? There are literally thousands and thousands of particulars that might be consid-

----

1. *Voter ignorance and imperfect information.* Because good information is costly in terms of time and effort (if not money), and because voters cannot capture the full benefits of being well-informed, it is rational for many voters to be ignorant about many public issues. As a result, the political process has a tendency to concentrate benefits and diffuse costs, allowing political entrepreneurs to serve constituency groups through regulations, quotas, and subsidies that promote economic inefficiency.

2. *Special-interest effects.* With benefits concentrated and costs diffused, well-informed and articulate interest groups dominate the policy arena, contributing to campaigns and receiving political favors. Again, there is no check on economic efficiency.

3. *Shortsightedness effect.* Politicians who must face the electorate every few years may have little interest in policies that take many years to produce beneficial effects, although even after considering the time value of money, such policies are economically efficient.

4. *Little entrepreneurial incentive for internal efficiency.* Politicians and bureaucrats are not rewarded for efficiency per se. Politicians gain votes by serving organized interests in their constituency, and administrators obtain benefits by enlarging the size of their bureaucracy. Efficiency is not a necessary byproduct of either. In other words, even if a large number of dollars is earmarked in a certain direction ("education," "the poor"), one cannot assume the supposed beneficiaries are receiving much in comparison to the sizes of the budgets involved; there may not be much "bang per buck."

5. *Imprecise reflection of consumer preferences and the bundle purchase effect.* Voters cannot effectively shop around for specific policies. They must compare a *bundle* of political goods offered by one candidate with the bundles offered by opposing candidates. The policies that result may tend to reflect the preferences of a coalition of special interests rather than the wishes of typical voters.

Given these characteristics, the economics of public choice suggest that the information and incentive structure associated with a relatively unconstrained representative democracy is likely to generate government failure (from a neoclassical perspective) in the production and distribution of *whatever* good or service is being considered.

ered. Who, if anyone, has the requisite information about these particulars?

The essential point is that whatever knowledge exists—and it will always be incomplete—will not be located centrally, but dispersed among all the members of society. Moreover, the knowledge problem and the dispersion of knowledge among society's members are not one-time affairs. Under existing institutions, for example, about one-third of the poor move out of poverty each year, if only temporarily, and are replaced to some degree by others. Changes in family composition—births, deaths, etc.—are the most important cause of these shifts.[35] So the problem cannot be addressed by a large research project that assembles all of the information once and for all and for all time. Somehow, the man on the spot with a relevant bit of knowledge must be induced to act spontaneously on it (because the problems and the available information about them change rapidly), and there must be a mechanism for coordinating his actions with those of everyone else, each of whom has fragmentary knowledge.

Public sector agencies that are granted near-monopoly status to grapple with issues will not provide efficient solutions even if they establish offices in the various localities to get "closer" to the problems; moving geographically closer to a problem is not the same as making spontaneous use of dispersed knowledge to provide effective responses. Unfortunately, a public monopoly, in contrast to any one of several private agencies, is unlikely to know the precise nature of various problems, and by the time it finds out (and assuming there are incentives to do the right thing), the problem is likely to have changed. Conceivably, ever larger amounts of public welfare could eliminate poverty, but, as with other activities, one runs into diminishing returns that make the worthwhileness of the whole enterprise more and more suspect. In the case of *some* unwed mothers, for example (the question of *which* unwed mothers is part of the knowledge problem), the returns from public welfare spending may already be negative.

---

35. For a fuller discussion, including a discussion of what is here called the "knowledge problem," see Greg Duncan, *Years of Poverty, Years of Plenty,* Ann Arbor: Institute for Social Research, University of Michigan, 1984. The degree to which free markets and government planners, respectively, may be expected to be able to cope with the knowledge problem was first given prominence in the famous article by F. A. Hayek, "The Use of Knowledge in Society," *American Economic Review* 35 (Sept. 1945):519–30.

The Private Production of Public Goods

The public goods argument suggests that institutional arrangements whereby government is constitutionally prohibited from undertaking service activities (aside from articulating and enforcing rights to private property and freedom of contract) will result in a suboptimal level of charitable services (from a conventional, neoclassical perspective). The public choice and "knowledge problem" arguments presented in the previous section suggest, however, that a democracy upon which there are relatively few constitutional restrictions is *also* likely to result in substantial inefficiency (as judged by conventional, neoclassical criteria)—irrespective of the way we might *hope* such a government would exercise its powers. This section is devoted to a reexamination of public goods objections to Humboldt's proposed institutional arrangements.

Why do purely private charities have *any* revenues? According to a strict interpretation of a simple public goods argument, they will not indeed have any. People have a latent willingness to pay to have poor people helped, but they will free-ride; the actual willingness to pay, according to the strict version of the argument, will be zero. Why isn't the real world number equal to zero?[36] Listed below are some of the possibilities:

1. Samaritanism, guilt. A person may not only wish that poor people be helped; he may receive satisfaction only if it is he who does the helping.
2. Reputation, public relations. People may think better of a person (or his firm) if they know he is helping others.
3. A tie-in sale. A person may purchase a good (e.g., a cupcake at a charity bake sale) from which he would be excluded if he did not pay; a charity gets some of the proceeds.

The important point to be made here is that the revenues that charities derive from each of the above can be said to be the result of purchases of *private* goods. That is, each of the above involves a good

---

36. Why does anyone vote, given that his single ballot is extremely unlikely to sway the outcome?

from which the person will be excluded if he does not pay. Furthermore, the good in question cannot be simultaneously consumed by others. If, for example, a person will suffer from a guilty conscience if he does not make a charitable donation, his problem will not disappear if he abstains from contributing while someone else makes a donation.

Private charities may thus provide a public good, but it is a *public* good only to the extent that people's desires to have others helped can be satisfied by the contributions of third parties. To the extent that people's desires to have others helped can be satisfied only if they themselves make a payment, charity is a *private* good, and there is no significant market failure from a conventional, neoclassical perspective. As with other private goods, one can expect firms to try to stimulate and/or accommodate demand so long as the costs of doing so are less than the revenues firms can expect from such measures.[37] In the case of charities, this implies attempts to play upon people's consciences and reputations. It also implies looking for economies of joint production (e.g., those for a charity softball game) involving tie-in sales, where each activity taken separately (e.g., the softball game versus the separate act of raising funds for the poor) might not be worthwhile; together, however (i.e., raising funds for the poor through the medium of a softball game), *both* activities (the softball game *and* the charitable activity) might now be worthwhile. What percentage of people's desires to have others helped can be effectively satisfied in free markets is thus an empirical issue to which more discussion will be devoted shortly.

To the extent that a partial public good is involved, it is by no means clear that there will be a suboptimal level of production. Remember first that a pure public good has two properties, the nonexclusion property and the nonrivalness property. Suppose people could be excluded from a good's benefits if they did not make payment, but that the consumption of benefits by one person would not reduce the possibility of someone else consuming the same good. In other words, suppose the nonrivalness condition existed, but not the nonexclusion condition. Suppose also that several producers vie for the attention of consumers, but that with respect to any single producer,

---

37. This is essentially true whether one considers for-profit or nonprofit firms. Nonprofit firms can be treated as profit-maximizers who simultaneously make charitable donations.

consumers regard the goods of the other producers as imperfect substitutes. Suppose, finally, that firms can charge different prices to different consumers (price discrimination). In contrast to the usual view that nonrivalness and imperfect competition would lead private firms to underproduce the good, it is indeed quite possible for there to be *over*production from a neoclassical point of view.[38] As far as the reader's intuition is concerned, the key is that price-discriminating firms can capture more revenue than nondiscriminators, and they may find it worthwhile to produce more output than would otherwise be the case.

Charities obviously engage in large-scale price discrimination; if the good being produced is "help for others," different people pay differing amounts to have similar amounts of "help" produced. As we have seen, however, private charity markets clearly contain an element of nonexclusion as well as nonrivalness, making overproduction much less likely.

So how is the overall revealed willingness to pay for "help" in private charity markets likely to compare with that which would occur in a hypothetical state of neoclassical bliss? No one knows for sure, but the empirical research done to date suggests outcomes that may surprise the reader. Many experiments on the extent of free-riding behavior to be expected under conditions of nonexclusion (and nonrivalness) have now been conducted.[39] The results appear to be quite sensitive to the way the participants are induced to take part in the experiments. If it is suggested that participants can benefit themselves

---

38. See the exchange between Earl Thompson and Harold Demsetz in the following: Earl A. Thompson, "The Perfectly Competitive Production of Collective Goods," *The Review of Economics and Statistics* 50 (Feb. 1968):1–12, and "The Private Production of Public Goods: A Comment," *The Journal of Law and Economics* 16 (Oct. 1973):407–12; Harold Demsetz, "The Private Production of Public Goods," *The Journal of Law and Economics* 13 (Oct. 1970):293–306, and "Joint Supply and Price Discrimination," *The Journal of Law and Economics* 16 (Oct. 1973):413–15. See also Stephen Shmanske, "The Relationship of Competitive Public Goods Models and Monopolistic Competition," California State University, Hayward, School of Business and Economics Faculty Working Paper #17, 1985.

39. See, for example, the following: Earl R. Brubaker, "Demand Disclosures and Conditions on Exclusion," *Economic Journal* 94 (Sept. 1984):536–53; Friedrich Schneider and Werner Pommerehne, "Free Riding and Collective Action: An Experiment in Public Microeconomics," *Quarterly Journal of Economics* 91 (Nov. 1981):668–704; and R. Mark Isaac, James M. Walker and Susan H. Thomas, "Divergent Evidence on Free Riding: An Experimental Examination of Possible Explanations," *Public Choice* 43 (no. 2, 1984): 113–49.

by free-riding, then indeed much free-riding occurs.[40] But if the experimenter—or in the real world, a private charity—does not bias the outcome, or biases it in another way, then the result is very much different, even without making a serious attempt to play upon people's feelings of guilt, their reputations, or utilizing tie-in sales (e.g., rock concerts and aid to Ethiopia). On the basis of the research to date, it appears that for *one-time* fund-raising events, private mechanisms are capable of generating revenues of 65%–85% of the amount that could have been raised under (almost) perfect price discrimination.[41] It should also be mentioned that payments have not been tax-deductible in these experiments. Percentages such as those noted above are all the more likely if the experimenter (fund-raiser) sets an overall target for the group of potential donors and offers to return all donations if they do not add up to an amount that equals or exceeds the targeted amount—a sort of "joint contract" arrangement.

For fund-raising that is continuous through time, however, the above percentage appears to drop. As people learn that others besides themselves are willing to contribute to the cause in question, and that the good will be provided or not provided almost independently of what they themselves do, free-riding incentives increase. Furthermore, joint contracting now appears to hold little advantage over simply asking for donations on a person-by-person basis. Nevertheless, the evidence to date is that even without tax-deductibility, donations can be collected equal to almost half of the amount that could have been raised under (almost) perfect price discrimination.[42] Again, this is also before elaborate attempts to play upon people's feelings of guilt or their reputations, or to utilize tie-in sales.

Let us assume for the sake of argument, however, that the amounts private charities can expect to collect are not only far short of the amount that would be collected under perfect price discrimination, but also below the amount required to achieve the neoclassical optimum. A conventional neoclassical economist would thus argue that

40. This is an explanation for results reported by Charles Plott. See the discussion and other Plott papers referenced in Charles Plott, "The Application of Laboratory Experimental Methods to Public Choice," in Clifford Russell, ed., *Application of Social Choice Theory* (Washington, D.C.: Resources for the Future, 1980).

41. Perfect price discrimination refers to a situation where the firm charges a different (market-clearing) price for each successive unit of the good produced. Under such discrimination the firm captures as much revenue as is possible from a given level of output.

42. See Brubaker, *n.* 39.

there is a market failure here on the demand or "willingness to pay" side of the charity market.

What about the supply side? On the production (supply) side of the market, there is only the problem of fraud—and this problem exists with respect to almost any activity. That is, the producer (charity) might do something with his revenues other than what he promised to consumers (donors). He may divert funds to personal uses. But this problem refers not to a market failure in the sense of monopoly or third-party/public goods problems, but simply the enforcement of rights required by Humboldt. Promises should be kept, and we know that people in both the private and public sectors often break them.

Apart from questions of fraud, however, the important point here is that private producers have incentives for cost-minimization. Furthermore, they most effectively make use of the bits of knowledge scattered among all the members of society. As discussed in the previous section, there isn't just one big problem—help the needy—which is to be solved by mobilizing an army of funds under central control. Rather, there are demands for many different kinds of help, each to be tailored to local circumstances. What is required is a mechanism that provides incentives for spontaneous action and that effectively spreads the knowledge that a certain demand exists to others who might not have been aware of it. Putting free-riding issues aside, private institutions accomplish this better than any real-world alternative. People still have imperfect information and will make mistakes, of course, but note how rapidly they can withdraw their patronage from a firm that is not so proficient in meeting their demands and then turn around and contribute revenues to a new firm that offers a better product at a lower price. Note how ineffective firms will have to adapt or go into decline, and how the successes of some will foster imitation by others. Note the incentives for seeking out economies of scale and any economies associated with the joint production of technologically related goods (e.g., charity and golf tournaments).

Thinking the Unthinkable

Is it really obvious that income redistribution is done more effectively by a democracy with relatively few constitutional restrictions than would be done under Humboldt's proposed arrangements? The primary objective here is not to gain the reader's endorsement of the writings of Wilhelm von Humboldt—this paper does not endorse them—but to have the reader ponder what we can realistically expect from the various institutional possibilities.

Seriously consider what Humboldt's arrangements would require. Strictly speaking, they would require almost a complete dismantling of government—spending cuts of about a trillion dollars according to 1984 budget figures.[43] Everything from streets and roads to the production of money would have to be done privately, subject, of course, to the laws of property, torts, contracts, and fraud.

If we just focus attention on redistributive activities, consider what would happen if all government transfers were eliminated. In 1984, these *officially* amounted to $407.1 billion,[44] a sum that exceeded the gross national product of the United Kingdom, a country of 60 million people. What we have done so far amounts to over $4,000 per U.S. household.

In addition, suppose we auction off the now-idle assets of the various agencies involved. We would also completely deregulate all licensed occupations. Anyone could go into any occupation he chose, subject to laws against fraud. Allow anyone to deliver first-class mail. Eliminate minimum wage laws and other restrictive labor legislation that prices lesser skilled workers out of the market—legislation that empowers unions to represent workers who do not want to join them, the Davis-Bacon Act, etc. Open up schools, especially in inner-city areas, to competition. All of these actions could begin after, say, a two-year public relations campaign to alert people to what was about to happen.

What would happen? Millions of nonpoor people would see their disposable incomes rise and millions of (very angry) nonpoor people would see their disposable incomes fall. Assuming away questions about the appropriate monetary institutions to cope with business cycle possibilities, the economy as a whole would clearly benefit from the

43. *Economic Report of the President* (Washington, D.C.: U.S. Government Printing Office, 1985), p. 321.

44. Ibid. As this book is being published, transfers are surpassing one-half trillion dollars per year. Programs like Old Age and Survivors Insurance (OASI) and Medicare are difficult to discuss here, because they involve intergenerational transfers and insurance. If one were to honor government commitments made under such programs, a shift to Humboldtian institutions would have to be accomplished, first, by abolishing the Social Security payroll tax. Then, each person would receive (tradable) bonds equal to the net present value of his accumulated entitlements under these programs. Revenues of some sort would still have to be collected until all outstanding government liabilities had been met. There would, of course, be numerous transitional problems with other programs as well.

decline in marginal tax rates and/or the reduction in the budget deficit made feasible. Employment and capital formation would clearly show net gains. On average, there would be a higher overall standard of living.

Many people would, of course, be shocked and outraged that such an idea was being enacted. There would be tremendous debates in the media about whether some sort of holocaust was about to occur with respect to the poor. Many people would take action; many would not be free-riders. Many would, of course, want to repeal the new Humboldt constitution, but suppose they were unsuccessful. To what activities would they turn?

There is no claim here that private institutions would end up providing offsetting transfers anywhere close in magnitude to the government spending cuts. What the reader is being asked to do is evaluate the likely outcome here with what actually occurs under unconstrained representative democracies. Before considering in more detail what would happen under the Humboldt constitution, consider further what actually happens under unconstrained representative democracies.

Consider first the poverty deficit. The poverty deficit refers to the number of dollars that, in principle, would be required to lift all poor persons above the official poverty line. Column 1 of Table 14–9 lists estimates for 1980–83 on the poverty deficit that would have existed *if no one changed his or her behavior* and government transfer payments had simply been discontinued. This column is followed by statistics on the impact of government transfers on the poverty deficit.

Why was not poverty easily wiped out by several hundred billion dollars worth of government redistributive activity?[45] A principal reason is that, aside from program inefficiencies and the effects of government transfers on behavior—effects that made the pretransfer poverty deficit higher than it otherwise would have been—an unconstrained representative democracy will result in government diversion of large flows of resources toward middle- and upper-income people. These people include not only administrators and consultants, but others who possess most of the political power. Many of the (costly) programs

---

45. For recent estimates of the respective roles played by government transfers and economic growth in combating poverty, see Peter Gottschalk and Sheldon Danziger, "A Framework for Evaluating the Effects of Economic Growth and Transfers on Poverty," *American Economic Review* 75 (March 1985):153–61.

Table 14–9.   Transfers and the Poverty Deficit (billions of current dollars).

Year	(1) Pretransfer Poverty Deficit	(2) Prewelfare Poverty Deficit	(3) Posttransfer Deficit Excl. In-Kind Transfers	(4) Posttransfer Deficit Incl. In-Kind Transfers
1980	87.5	42.6	30.3	20.2
1981	102.3	51.4	37.8	25.2
1982	113.2	58.5	43.9	29.2
1983	119.9	63.0	47.1	31.4

SOURCE: University of Wisconsin–Madison, Institute for Research on Poverty; computed from the U.S. Census Bureau's Current Population Survey.

Notes: Column 1 does not reflect the impact of programs like farm price supports, which raise the market incomes reported by survey respondents. Column 2 reflects Column 1 adjusted for the impact of non-means-tested programs such as Social Security, Workers' Compensation, and Unemployment Insurance. Column 4 was added by the authors of the present paper; it assumes, based on other Census Bureau data, that in-kind transfers reduce poverty by one-third of what it otherwise would be. In-kind transfers include food stamps, Medicaid, and housing subsidies.

involved are understandable government responses to middle- and upper-class desires for social insurance. Whole communities of poor people may nevertheless be worse off than if there were no government redistributive activity and the taxes to support it. A provocative study done for the Institute for Policy Studies found, for example, that despite an estimated $45.7 million of transfers to Washington, D.C.'s Shaw-Cardozo ghetto in the year under study, there was an outflow of taxes of *$50.0 million* in that year from the same area.[46]

Who over the years have been the primary beneficiaries from airport subsidies, zoning, postal subsidies, FHA-subsidized mortgages, the Export-Import bank, federal loan guarantees, subsidies for synthetic fuels, aid to higher education, subsidies for Amtrak, maritime subsidies, etc.? Who have been the primary beneficiaries from tax expenditures? Only a fraction of all government activities to redistribute income results in income trickling down to the poor.

46. Earl F. Mellor, "Public Goods and Services: Costs and Benefits, A Study of the Shaw-Cardozo Area of Washington, D.C." (Washington, D.C.: Institute for Policy Studies, 1969); cited in Murray R. Rothbard, *For a New Liberty* (New York: Macmillan, 1973).

Consider activities where little budgetary outlay is involved. Who lobbies most vigorously for restrictions on unlicensed taxicabs? Existing taxi interests, not groups representing the poor. The number of taxis in Washington, D.C., is fifteen times the number in Los Angeles, even though Los Angeles has about five times as many people and seven times as much area.[47] If there were just four times as many taxis in Los Angeles as there presently are under restrictive licensing, that would instantly mean lower fares for poor riders and thousands of additional jobs for which low-income and minority citizens would be eligible. When one considers that there are about 3,000 licensed occupations, the impact of government restrictions looms very large.[48]

The point of this discussion is not necessarily to lobby for ever larger redistributive activities targeted on the poor. On balance, the poor as a class may receive more in (explicit) transfers than they pay in (explicit) taxes, but this is not the same thing as saying that present institutional arrangements are in their best interest. An unrestricted representative democracy is likely to engage in all sorts of redistributive activity (both explicit and hidden—e.g., zoning), with a substantial amount being targeted on the poor, and much that is not. Beyond this, there are significant losses for the economy as a whole in terms of tax-and-transfer disincentives for work, saving, and investment and many other resource misallocations that impair almost everyone's long-run standard of living.[49] When it has majority control, one political party may generate bundles of outcomes that some of us would prefer to the bundles generated by another party but the whole tug-of-war is promoted by institutional arrangements with obvious flaws.

How would Humboldt's arrangements fare in the face of pretransfer poverty deficits such as those shown in Table 14–9? First, it is unlikely that the deficits would be as high, because of regulatory bar-

47. This example is taken from Thomas Sowell, *Markets and Minorities* (New York: Basic Books, 1981).

48. For a fuller discussion of the impact of government licensing on blacks, see Walter E. Williams, *The State Against Blacks* (New York: McGraw-Hill, 1982).

49. For estimates of the impact of major transfer programs, see the survey article by Sheldon Danziger, Robert Haveman, and Robert Plotnick, "How Income Transfers Affect Work, Savings, and the Income Distribution," *Journal of Economic Literature* 19 (Sept. 1981):975–1028. The authors conclude (ignoring the effects of private transfers) that major government transfer programs reduce labor supply by about 5 percent and savings anywhere from 0 to 20 percent. The authors did not consider the many other ways by which government redistributes income in addition to the major (explicit) transfer programs.

riers and disincentives present under existing welfare programs and because of the general diminution in wealth resulting from the burden of taxation entailed by a redistributive state. Second, even if the general level of wealth were not higher, one could expect a sizeable amount of private transfer activity to take place—probably not the neoclassical optimum but a sizable amount, nonetheless—private insurance schemes, charities, etc. In 1983, despite having to devote 39 percent of their incomes to government in the forms of taxes and fees,[50] and despite the fact that government is now viewed as the primary instrument for philanthropy, Americans gave $64.9 billion to charity.[51] Finally, private transfer institutions have greater incentives for internal efficiency and are better able to deal with the "knowledge problem" outlined earlier. More so than public institutions, they fill the interstices of society and change spontaneously as new conditions arise and as new information is acquired. Disincentive effects on labor supply and family composition are lessened. In other words, private institutions provide more "bang per buck." *Ignoring* labor supply and other disincentives for earning pretransfer income, existing government redistributive activity reduces the poverty deficit by less than $100 billion at present; it reduces the poverty deficit by even less when one considers disincentive effects. To repeat: Is it obvious that income redistribution would be done less effectively under Humboldt's constitution? Perhaps, but the answer is not clear.

We can, of course, examine the history of private charity prior to large government welfare programs, but different people will have different interpretations of that history. To be sure, perhaps 80 percent of the U.S. population in 1900 was, by today's standards, living in poverty. This does not necessarily mean, however, that the institutional arrangements in effect were not superior in many ways to a variety of possible alternatives. Even if the reader could instantly install his preferred institutions in Ethiopia, a large percentage of its population would be mired in poverty for many years to come. In fact, late nineteenth century America was a place of rapid economic growth, which attracted millions of penniless immigrants. It is worth noting that by 1929, state surveys indicated that more than *90* percent

---

50. *Economic Report of the President, n.* 43. Computed from pages 321 and 254.
51. U.S. Bureau of the Census, *Statistical Abstract of the United States, 1985* (Washington, D.C.: U.S. Government Printing Office), p. 385.

of the elderly were self-supporting.[52] Along with rapid economic growth, there was a large surge in eleemosynary activity. Consistent with the experimental evidence on the private production of public goods, nonprofit private hospitals, orphanages, and the Salvation Army sprang up. There were the YMCA, the YWCA, the Indian Rights Association, and hundreds of other organizations. The St. Vincent De Paul Society and Goodwill Industries instituted sheltered workshops for the disabled. During the early years of the Great Depression, there were still no large government welfare programs, yet there was no sort of general starvation as there is in Ethiopia (under very different institutional arrangements). This is not to deny that Roosevelt's New Deal improved the lives of many poor people, at least in the short run.[53]

The fact that, under a single Constitution, the United States originally operated with a reliance on private charities, then went to the New Deal, and then to the Great Society programs of the 1960s, might appear to offer support for the claim that it is not institutions after all that are of vital concern here. It might be argued that this history provides support for the claim that activists can shape policy, and that what we need at the present time is not constitutional reform, but activism that will push existing institutions to move in the "right" direction.

Aside from the fact that, independently of the information spontaneously and continually communicated to us through market processes, we do not really know—and could not reach agreement on—what the "right" direction is, and that, in an unconstrained democracy, the successes of some interest groups in removing inequities can be overturned by others at a later date, the activist argument does not give proper appreciation to the economic and institutional—indeed constitutional—changes that have occurred since the late nineteenth century. The main economic change is the increase in wealth that has

52. See Carolyn L. Weaver, *The Crisis in Social Security: Economic and Political Origins* (Durham, N.C.: Duke University Press, 1982), pp. 41–44.

53. Whether Humboldt's arrangements, including private production of competing monies, would avoid Great Depressions altogether would make for a fascinating discussion, but this issue goes beyond the scope of the present paper. For a discussion of the workability of competing monies, see Lawrence H. White, "Competitive Money, Inside and Out," *The Cato Journal* 3 (Spring 1983):281–99. For the relationship between public and private transfer payments during the Depression, see Russell D. Roberts, "A Positive Model of Private Charity and Public Transfers," *Journal of Political Economy* 92 (Feb. 1984): 136–48.

occurred, a change that has increased the affordability of transfers (private or public) and increased our sensitivity to the remaining poverty. The institutional change involves the very nature of the U.S. Constitution. Though nominally a single document throughout its existence, it has in fact been subject to great changes, most of which resulted from judicial actions rather than explicit amendments to the document. The key changes, the questioning of which would today be quickly dismissed by most courts and law schools, involved the Ninth and Tenth Amendments. The Tenth Amendment reserved to the states all powers not *expressly* granted to the federal government.[54] The Ninth Amendment was intended to underline a commitment to uphold individual rights to private property and freedom of contract under the Rule of Law; it was intended to preclude discriminatory legislation, as was the Constitution's "due process" clause.[55] A series of court decisions from the 1930s to the 1960s has greatly weakened the import of these and other sections of the Constitution. The upshot of all of this is that democracy is much less constrained now than it was before the 1930s, and it is far from clear that these institutional changes have benefited the economy as a whole or the poor as a class on a long-run basis.

Questions of Justice

It may well be objected that the discussion up until now has concentrated too much on economics and neoclassical theory, and not enough on simple questions of fairness. Regardless of "donor preferences" and "economic efficiency," are not government welfare programs a matter of justice? It should be mentioned first that, according to the powerful arguments of Richard Posner, a prominent jurist, economic

54. In *Federalist* 45, James Madison wrote that the powers of the national government are "few and defined," while those of the state governments are "numerous and indefinite." "The former will be exercised principally on external objects, as war, peace, negotiation, and foreign commerce . . . . The powers reserved to the several States will extend to all the objects, which, in the ordinary course of affairs, concern the lives, liberties, and properties of the people; and the internal order, improvement, and prosperity of the State." After his retirement as president, Madison wrote that the Constitution's clause giving responsibility to the federal government for the "general welfare" was inserted by accident: "inattention to the phraseology occasioned doubtless by its identity with the harmless character attached to it . . . . " See Max Farrand, ed., *Records of the Federal Convention*, vol. 3 (New Haven: Yale University Press, 1937), p. 486.

55. For a discussion of the now-neglected Ninth Amendment and its origins, see F. A. Hayek, *The Constitution of Liberty* (Chicago: University of Chicago Press, 1960), pp. 185–86.

efficiency and justice are virtually synonymous.[56] If one compares the alternative institutional arrangements, not with an unattainable ideal, but with each other, it is not obvious that Humboldt's constitution should be ruled out.

If Posner's perspective on justice is discarded in favor of that of the Harvard philosopher Robert Nozick,[57] the case for Humboldt's constitution becomes even stronger. Indeed, Nozick's view of the state as first and foremost a guarantor of individual rights to property and contract is very similar to Humboldt's.

If one regards the view of Nobel Laureate F. A. Hayek[58] as the correct one, the Humboldt position again comes off well in comparison with unconstrained representative democracy. Like Humboldt and Nozick, Hayek regards the state's primary duty to be the protection of individual rights under the Rule of Law, but with the ultimate objective being the rather utilitarian one of improving the chances that any randomly selected citizen will be as well off as possible. The articulation of individual rights compatible with economic efficiency is thus paramount again.

Finally, we come to the view of justice most discussed over the last fifteen years, that of John Rawls.[59] This provides the most severe challenge to the Humboldt position, placed in competition with unconstrained representative democracy, but even here one cannot *confidently* conclude that Humboldt loses, especially from a long-run vantage point. Rawls asks the reader to imagine he is in an "original position" behind a "veil of ignorance," where he does not know who he is or what his life will be like. Placed in such a situation, what institutional arrangements would a self-interested individual prefer? Rawls argues that the individual would prefer arrangements that guarantee the most extensive liberty for each compatible with the most extensive liberty for all. Secondarily, Rawls argues that given a natural inclination to risk-aversion, he would prefer arrangements whereby the least well-off members of society are as well-off as possible. Rawls

56. For a defense of the "efficiency theory" of justice, see Richard Posner, *The Economics of Justice* (Cambridge: Harvard University Press, 1981).

57. Robert Nozick, *Anarchy, State, and Utopia* (New York: Basic Books, 1974). For a slightly more moderate position, see Richard A. Epstein, *Takings: Private Property and the Power of Eminent Domain* (Cambridge: Harvard University Press, 1985).

58. See F. A. Hayek, *Law, Legislation, and Liberty*, vol. 2, *The Mirage of Social Justice* (London: Routledge and Kegan Paul, 1982).

59. John Rawls, *A Theory of Justice* (Cambridge: Harvard University Press, 1971).

assumes that this requires the existence of government transfer agencies.[60] He notes, however, that institutional arrangements that at first appear to violate his principles might turn out to be the most preferred.[61] Institutional arrangements that generate inequality might be justified by the fact that they nevertheless promote the interests of the least fortunate more so than the alternatives.

Is Humboldt consistent with Rawls? When one considers the priority both give to liberty, one is tempted to say yes. In considering the least fortunate members of society, the reader (and Rawls) may say no. But nobody really knows. Especially when one considers the dynamic capacities of unfettered market economies, the answer from a long-run perspective is not obvious.

One overriding point should be made with respect to justice and the distribution of income. The term "distribution" refers to an ordering of outcomes and is a useful scientific concept. Applied to the ordering of income, the term has useful descriptive value. However, when an income distribution is characterized as "unjust" or "just" or "unfair" or "fair," it leads to confusion and demagoguery over the *sources* of income. It carries the insidious suggestion that there is a *distributor* of dollars, or as it were, a dealer of dollars. Such a line of reasoning suggests that the reason why some people have much more income than others is because the dealer is unfair, a sexist, a racist, an imperialist, etc.

The policy suggested by this line of reasoning is quite simple: Fairness and justice require a redealing of income, or income redistribution. The person who was dealt too many dollars must forcibly be made to give up his ill-gotten gain for the sake of the person who was dealt too little. A slight variation of the theme is the expropriation hypothesis, namely, that one person or country is poor *because* another person or country is rich. Again, simply justice mandates relieving the rich of their ill-gotten gain for the sake of the poor.

The fact of life, particularly in free societies, is that income is nearly

60. Ibid. p. 276.

61. "In practice we must usually choose between several unjust, or second best, arrangements; and then we look to nonideal theory to find the least unjust scheme. Sometimes this scheme will include measures and policies that a perfectly just scheme would reject. Two wrongs can make a right in the sense that the best available arrangement may contain a balance of imperfections, an adjustment of compensating injustices." Rawls observes that, practically speaking, "these are questions of political judgment and not part of a theory of justice." Ibid. p. 279. There exist, of course, many critiques of Rawls's basic theory. See, for example, Nozick, *n.* 46, chap. 7.

always the result of productive activity by individuals, or collections of individuals in the form of partnerships and corporations. In short, income is primarily produced by resource owners pleasing others. Henry Ford amassed millions by the fact that consumers were better satisfied with his product than with their next best alternative.

Massive income redistribution programs raise important moral questions about the legitimate role of government in a free society. How income is distributed, or who gets what, is not simply an issue of one set of statistical outcomes compared with another, as believed by those who offer as evidence of injustice this lament, "The lowest income quintile had 5 percent of the national income in 1940 and they still have 5 percent today."

Who gets what is largely determined by the decisions of millions of people making millions of independent decisions. Popular singer Michael Jackson has a higher income than opera singer Luciano Pavarotti as a result of millions of people deciding with their dollars. Less direct determinations apply when we compare the income of a janitor with that of a manager. The income determination process is the same—millions of people making independent decisions. The communication of their decision is through their agent, the entrepreneur. If he pays too little to the janitor, he loses that resource to another entrepreneur. If he pays too much, he fails to earn the going rate of return on equity and risks going out of business.

When people say that the income distribution is fundamentally unfair, they are really saying that millions of people made the wrong decisions. Income redistribution thus boils down to a battle of one set of decision makers forcibly ruling out the results of another set of decision makers on the question of who gets how much of the national income. The operative question is then *not* what is the best income distribution, but *who* will decide what is best? Through what institutions?

SUMMARY AND CONCLUSION

This paper has made the following major points:

1. The rise of single-parent households and out-of wedlock births is a serious problem. Because of its effects on children, it cannot be dismissed as "just another life-style." These include higher poverty rates and probable impairment of child development.

2. The rise of single-parent households and out-of-wedlock births coincided with an explosion in federal social welfare expenditures. Data on AFDC payments by state, however, suggest an almost *inverse* correlation between benefit levels and a culture of single-parent households with illegitimate children. On the other hand, this inverse correlation appears to be less pronounced when other transfer programs—food stamps, Medicaid, etc.—are considered in addition to AFDC.[62]

3. The most powerful argument for a direct cause-and-effect relationship between welfare and such a culture is that, financially speaking, it has often been much more advantageous for a couple expecting a child to live in an unmarried state.

4. The evidence from elaborate statistical studies is that there is some validity to the direct cause-and-effect argument, but other factors such as independent cultural changes and unemployment problems, particularly among blacks, may have been quantitatively more important than programs like AFDC.

5. The most prominent welfare reform proposal of the 1970s was the "negative income tax" (NIT), which would provide a guaranteed income for poor citizens, but which had been presumed to provide stronger work incentives than existing programs. Extravagant experiments with NITs, especially in Seattle and Denver, proved extremely disappointing. Work disincentives proved to be strong, and even more surprising, marital dissolution occurred at a very high rate.

6. Public choice theory suggests that constructive welfare reform is not something that will occur simply by getting academics and other citizens to support it. There are *inherent* political reasons why it is so difficult. The debate should therefore concern the possible alternative *constitutional* arrangements rather than policies that, as Martin Anderson has so forcefully argued, are nearly impossible to expect under existing arrangements—even assuming we could know and agree on what those policies would be. We have already passed through a period when there was a consensus in favor of a negative income tax.

62. See General Accounting Office, "Public Assistance Benefits Vary Widely from State to State, But Generally Exceed the Poverty Line," Washington, D.C.: U.S. Government Printing Office, November 1980.

7. The institutional arrangements proposed by Charles Murray—
    welfare provided primarily by state and local governments and
    private agencies—are largely consistent with the intentions of the
    framers of the Constitution. Court decisions have, however,
    brought about a relaxation of the limits the Constitution was in-
    tended to put on a representative democracy.

8. Policies that are not cost-effective in helping the poor, and pol-
    icies that *target* benefits on the middle class and the rich, cannot,
    in this context, be dismissed as mistakes we can reasonably hope
    to rectify by urging our representatives to act differently. Such
    outcomes are the *expected* results of present institutional
    arrangements.

9. Institutional arrangements whereby *no* level of government was
    permitted to redistribute income to *anybody* ("Humboldt arrange-
    ments") would be unlikely to achieve optimal results from the
    perspective of neoclassical economic theory, but they would come
    closer than is commonly assumed. Compared to the operation of
    other institutional arrangements in the real political world, it is
    not obvious that they would be less efficient or less in accordance
    with various conceptions of justice.

There are, of course, other possible institutional arrangements besides those of the original American Constitution, the relatively unconstrained representative democracy of recent times, and those
suggested by Humboldt. Anarchists despair of any government living
within constitutional constraints and would do away with the public
sector altogether, relying on private enforcement of rights. Hayek, a
classical liberal, has proposed[63] that one chamber of the Congress be
given exclusive control over specific spending and tax issues regarding public goods, but subject to nondiscriminatory rules laid down by
Congress's other chamber, which would not be given any power to
grant favors to special-interest groups.

Whatever one's desired institutional arrangements, it might be objected that any transition from present institutions would face the same
kinds of special-interest pressures that unconstrained representative
democracies presently face. There is validity to this charge, but note

63. Hayek, *Law, Legislation, and Liberty*, vol. 3, *The Political Order of a Free People*,
n. 58.

that in contrast to the *continual* Hobbesian interest-group war that characterizes current arrangements, such a struggle to alter our institutions fundamentally would, at least from the standpoint of the foreseeable future, presumably be a one-time affair. Few people would have more at stake in the outcome than the children of poor young couples agonizing over unexpected pregnancies.

15

THE FAMILY: FEDERAL POLICY AND PRIVATE ALTERNATIVES

J. Craig Peery

FAMILY STRUCTURES

The desire to marry and to raise a family remains virtually universal in the United States. About 95 percent of our population aged 40 or more have married at least once. Dr. George Gallup, citing data from a national survey, has said that a "good family life" is the number-one social value for Americans, ranking above physical health, self-respect, and freedom of choice in our national hierarchy of values.[1] More than being just a national value, marriage and family life are an integral ingredient in civilization as we know it. In testimony before the Senate "family" subcommittee, Dr. Wesley Burr, then president of the National Council on Family Relations, said:

> [The family] is an absolutely *essential* component of a society that is based on freedom and democratic processes . . . In fact, it is one of the most basic foundation stones upon which organized and civilized society rests; and . . . it cannot be eliminated.[2]

At the beginning of the Reagan presidency, there were 82.4 million

1. George Gallup, "Americans Believe Personal Goals More Vital Than Material Gain," *Salt Lake Tribune*, 28 Jan. 1982.
2. Wesley Burr, Testimony in Hearing Before the U.S. Senate Subcommittee on Aging, Family and Human Services, "Work Ethic: Materialism and the American Family," March 2, 1982.

households in the United States.[3] About 27 percent of these were considered by the Census Bureau to be "nonfamily" households. The majority of nonfamily households were headed by individuals who were living alone. The median age for female heads of nonfamily households was 64 years, while for males who headed nonfamily households, the median age was about 36 years. A very high proportion of nonfamily households thus consisted of individuals who were either beginning the family life cycle, and were very likely to be moving into family household status, or individuals who were at the end of the family life cycle, after having participated in family households in earlier periods of their life.

There are a number of social and economic forces that have fostered changes in the structure of families. Despite an increase of 17 million in the number of families in the United States between 1970 and 1981, the number of married couples with their own children aged 18 or under actually declined by 0.6 million during the same period.[4] Married-couple families comprise about 82 percent of all families.

Perhaps the most dramatic influence for change in family structure during the last two decades was the dramatic rise in divorce. Between 1965 and 1979, divorce rates increased 115 percent! This amounts to a virtual epidemic of divorce and is, in my judgment, the most significant social phenomenon that has occurred in our country during this century. For the cohort of couples married in 1950, fully 28 percent are now divorced. Projections for the more recently married cohorts are no more encouraging. Approximately 30 percent of the couples married between 1960 and 1970 have already divorced, and the National Center for Health Statistics is projecting that 50 percent of the couples who have married since 1970 will eventually be divorced.[5] Considerably over 1 million children per year are now involved in divorce. The cumulative number of children who are affected by divorce is alarming, particularly given research findings that divorce has a substantial and long-lasting negative effect on children.[6]

3. Family demographic data were taken from U.S. Bureau of the Census, *Household and Family Characteristics, March 1981, Current Population Reports: Population Characteristics,* Series P-20, No. 371 (Washington, D.C.: U.S. Department of Commerce).

4. James Weed, "Status of Families," Population Division, U.S. Bureau of the Census, June 15, 1982. (Unpublished.)

5. Ibid.

6. Judith S. Wallerstein and Joan B. Kelly, *Surviving the Breakup: How Children and Parents Cope with Divorce* (New York: Basic Books, 1980); Mavis Heatherington, "Divorce: A Child's Perspective," *American Psychologist* 34 (1979):851–58.

Unprecedented divorce rates do not mean that our national commitment to marriage is decreasing. In recent years there have been more marriages performed in the United States than ever before. A higher proportion of these marriages were remarriages for one or both of the spouses. Never-married single women tend to be putting marriage off, marrying later than in the past, but marriage and child-rearing are still considered an essential part of life-planning for almost all Americans.

Single-Parent Families

One of the byproducts of burgeoning divorce rates (and to a lesser but growing extent the tendency among never-married women to have children) is an increase in the number of single-parent families. In recent years, there have been more than 6.6 million single-parent families in the United States. About 6 million of these are maintained by women; this is about 19 percent of all families with children under 18. About one-half of the black families with children are one-parent families. Of the roughly 11.5 million families with children under 6 years of age, approximately 2 million (17 percent) are headed by a single woman.

HOUSEHOLD ECONOMICS

Economic concerns are at the top of the priority list for most families. Presidents and political parties obtain popular support during eras when the economic well-being of the family is improving. Economic stagnation, loss of family purchasing power, and unemployment are frequently more important to families than are other domestic or international developments.

Declining Growth in Family Income at the Dawn of the Eighties

Even though median family income increased every year during the 1970s, family income, adjusted for inflation, remained approximately constant for ten years. Table 15–1 shows that the decade of the seventies brought the smallest increase in real family income since the end of World War II. In fact, between 1979 and 1980 there was a 5 percent *decline* in real family income, the largest decline recorded in

Table 15–1.   Median Family Income (in constant 1980 dollars).

1947	$11,182
1950	11,361
1960	15,637
1970	20,939
1979	22,236
1980	21,023[a]

SOURCE: U.S. Bureau of the Census. Money Income and Poverty Status of Families and Persons in the United States: 1980. *Current Population Reports,* Series P-60, No. 127, Table 4, p. 14.

[a]$84 increase from 1970 to 1980

the post–World War II era, as a result of a 14.2 percent increase in consumer prices.[7]

Americans had become used to having an ever increasing standard of living during the fifties and sixties. A constant climb up the ladder of economic prosperity had become an integral part of the American dream. To experience a steady rate of economic development and then to experience real decreases in living standards was a source of great disillusionment for many Americans. The Reagan "revolution" of 1980 can perhaps be partially interpreted by understanding the attempt of members of American families to regain some economic stability, if not restored prosperity.

Increase in Women Working Outside the Home

Political reaction was not the only family response to waning prosperity. One of the most dramatic changes for both the family and the civilian work force was the entrance of women into the labor market in unprecedented numbers. Labor force participation by women has doubled since 1930. Currently 52 percent of all working-age women are employed. Women now comprise 43 percent of the entire labor force. By 1981, 60 percent of intact families reported having both spouses working. By comparison only 46 percent of intact families in 1969 reported husband and wife as both working. If husband and wife both work, the economic component of the American dream is still attainable. Family income where both spouses work is 36 percent higher than that of married couples where only one person is employed.[8]

7. Weed, *n.* 4.
8. Weed, *n.* 4.

Other factors have contributed to the increased number of women participating in the labor force. The recent tendency of young unmarried women to postpone marriage has influenced the labor force participation rate among women in two ways. Not only have women had to find a source of income outside of marriage; they have also in many cases formed commitments to careers that endure even after marriage. Finally, with female-headed households growing rapidly as a result of divorce (or illegitimacy), many women have faced constant economic stress. Women have an initial 29 percent loss of income after the divorce, and after one year their income has dropped 73 percent.[9] Such stress has provided yet another reason for many women to participate in the labor force.

GOVERNMENT SPENDING PATTERNS

During the past twenty-five years, growth in government spending has become a major factor in the American economy. Not only the economic health of the nation but the economic health of the American family is (for better or worse) now intricately intertwined with government taxing and spending.

Growth in Social Spending

Though President John Kennedy had been a social activist, he had experienced considerable difficulty in obtaining passage of his legislative programs dealing with social issues. In the wake of the emotional outrage and sympathy that followed President Kennedy's assassination, President Johnson was able to convince Congress to take action on many of the projects that had been of interest to Kennedy. Johnson also developed his "Great Society" concept, and the 1960s saw an outpouring of legislation designed to use the instrument of government to try to eliminate the perceived ills of society. Armies of technocrats with some expertise in social science began churning out social programs. They seemed to share a naive view of mankind as almost infinitely plastic, and an equally naive view that enlightened professional service-providers (with enormous budgets) could direct the less fortunate (and less enlightened) in solving many of society's problems. By providing those enormous budgets, for the first time in

9. Lenore Weitzman, "The Economics of Divorce: Social and Economic Consequences of Property, Alimony and Child Support Awards," *UCLA Law Review* 28 (1981).

Table 15–2. Federal Budget Outlays (in billions of constant 1972 dollars).

Type of Spending	FY 1951	FY 1961	FY 1971	FY 1981
National Defense	48.7	74.8	81.5	76.6
Social Welfare	16.6	37.2	81.8	163.6
State & Local Grants	2.3	7.4	18.1	27.1
Net Interest	8.2	9.6	15.5	35.5
All Other	17.9	20.6	25.6	27.8
Total outlays	93.7	149.6	222.5	330.6

SOURCE: Office of Management and Budget, *Federal Government Finances: 1983 Budget Data* (Washington, D.C.: Office of Management and Budget, February 1982).

a peacetime economy the federal government began consuming major proportions of the national income. "The Great Society, in contrast to the New Deal, led to a far greater emphasis on public expenditure as the basic mode of government action."[10] Table 15–2 shows the outpouring of federal dollars during the three decades from 1951 to 1981.

By 1983 federal government budget outlays were about $800 billion, or approximately $3,500 for every man, woman, and child in the United States. In 1986 President Reagan submitted a proposed budget for fiscal 1987 which, for the first time, called for spending of approximately $1 *trillion*. The federal government now spends over 33 percent of national income (see Figure 15–1); total government spending at the federal, state, and local levels adds up to about 45 percent of our national income!

Even though the federal government spends an ever increasing proportion of our national income (up about 10 percent in the last thirty years), the most dramatic changes in federal spending have been in the actual allocations of that spending.

Forty-six percent of President Kennedy's federal budget for fiscal 1962 was allotted for national defense, and about 25 percent was allotted for human services programs. In comparison, President Reagan's federal budget outlays in fiscal 1983 (twenty-one years later) showed about 28 percent of the budget for defense and 55 percent for human services programs.

10. Samuel Beer, Foreword, in J. Ellwood, ed., *Reductions in U.S. Domestic Spending* (New Brunswick, N.J.: Transaction Books, 1982).

Currently just over 40 percent of federal spending goes for the constitutionally mandated functions of defense and paying interest on the national debt (28 percent and 13 percent of the federal budget respectively). Substantially over half the budget goes for human services and public charity programs, including over $400 billion in income

Figure 15–1. Federal Spending as a Percentage of National Income.

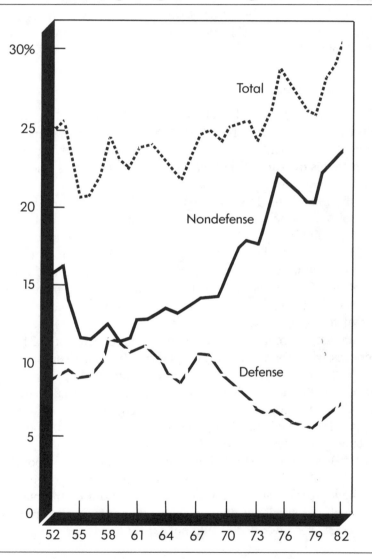

Source: Milton Friedman, "High Taxes, Low Security," *Newsweek* (18 April 1983).

transfer payments in order to redistribute income from one economic group to another.

This remarkable increase in human-service and income-transfer programs has been primarily responsible for the marked rise in nondefense spending as a percentage of national income (see Figure 15–1). Any attempt to curb the growth in federal spending must therefore be concerned with nondefense as well as defense spending. This will be particularly true if the trend toward $200 billion deficits is to be halted. Otherwise the vastly increased amounts of interest on the national debt will be crippling.

Paying the Federal Bill

Before any attempt is made to look at federal programs, for spending, another question needs to be asked. Who pays the federal spending?[11] Although never identified directly as a "federal family policy," the answer to this question identifies, in unmistakable terms, the previous federal attitude toward families.

On the eve of the 1981 tax changes, there were about 83 million households in America, about one-third of 1 percent making more than $150,000 per year. Those families paid an average of about $100,000 in taxes, thus accounting for only 7 percent of total government spending and about 12 percent of the taxes. Since 1981, the percentage of all taxes paid by the rich has, in fact, increased, but the fact remains that the rich do not, and simply cannot, help pay for much of total federal spending.

Again just before the 1981 tax changes, there were about 31 million Americans who reported earnings less than $10,000. Even though they comprised about 35 percent of all wage earners, they paid only about 2 percent of the taxes. They also received a substantial share of the $400 billion in income transfer payments. The poor do not—and cannot—pay for federal spending, and several tax reform proposals recommended that they pay no federal income taxes at all.

In 1980–81, after-tax corporate income accounted for about 3 percent of the national income. Though some members of Congress sound as if they expect giant corporations to bear more of the burden for public welfare, simple arithmetic shows that even if all corporate income were taxed away, one could not expect to pay for a large portion

11. Thanks to Tracy Collins Bank and J. S. Peery for the initial idea for this analysis.

of the 33 percent federal share of national income with taxes collected from corporations. Besides, taxes assessed on corporations are paid by shareholders (including pension and retirement funds, which hold large blocks of corporate stocks) in lower dividends, by employees in lower wages, or by consumers in higher prices. As the saying goes, corporations don't pay taxes—people pay taxes.

Since we could not pay for federal spending by taxing the rich, the poor, or the corporations, who was then left to foot the federal tab? *The middle-income American family*. Even though it may seem surprising that we asked the family of four earning $15,000 to buy food stamps for the family of four earning $12,000, it has nevertheless been federal policy to demand that middle-income Americans give up ever increasing proportions of their earnings in order to pay for the spiraling costs of government bureaucracy and social spending.

There are more than 35 million American households that earn between $20,000 and $72,000. They earn more than 60 percent of the income, and they pay more than 60 percent of the federal taxes.

When we ask Washington for increases in housing subsidies, food stamps, Social Security benefits, and health care support, we should always remember that we are forcing the families of America to pay the bill. The federal government has forced the middle-class American family to pay for runaway human-services bureaucracies and programs with an ever growing proportion of household income. Although never articulated as such, this has been the most salient "family policy" developed in Washington during the past twenty years.

Well-intentioned motivations notwithstanding, the success of the "Great Society" has been spotty. From the perspective of the American family (with rising divorce rates and a marked increase in single-parent families), one is hard pressed to find evidence that the quality of life was markedly better in 1981 than it was in 1951. The number of middle-class families, coerced into paying for the explosion of social spending, who feel 1,000 percent happier or better as a result of the 1,000 percent increase in federal social spending from 1951 to 1981 seems remarkably small indeed.

THE FEDERAL ROLE

During this century the federal government has moved from a position of governing best by governing least, to a position of trying to be all things to all people. In terms of dollar amounts spent, by far the most ambitious government activity has been in the area of social insurance and retirement programs. Medical insurance and unemployment compensation have also become a part of our thinking about government-as-insurance-agent. The other, much more minor, social functions the federal government has assumed deal directly with providing money, food, and housing for certain individuals.

Table 15–3 shows the breakdown in a typical recent year of major expenditures for social programs (rounded to the nearest $10 billion). *All* other federal expenditures for social purposes round to less than $10 billion on a program-by-program basis, so Table 15–3 accounts for the overwhelming majority of social spending.

There are more appropriate roles for the federal government than acting as a direct supplier of retirement programs, health insurance, and alternative income. Running pilot and demonstration programs, doing research and development, acting as information clearing houses, and evaluating existing programs are not only necessary but probably best accomplished at the national level. It is unlikely that any state or organization would be willing to set up the equivalent of the National Institutes of Health, for example. Yet the cost of these approaches would be only a tiny fraction of current expenditures for social programs, and the mechanism for accomplishing most of these functions is already in place.

It is interesting that the majority of working Americans between

---

Table 15–3. Major Federal Social Welfare Expenditures, Fiscal 1982 (rounded to the nearest $10 billion).

OASI (basic Social Security)	$140 billion
Railroad retirement	10
Military retirement	20
Civil Service retirement	20
Total Retirement	$190
Disability insurance	20
Unemployment compensation	20
Health Insurance	
Medicare	50
Medicaid	20
Direct Income Delivery (poverty income-level required)	
Food stamps	10
Supplemental Security Income	10
Housing assistance	20
AFDC (Aid to Families with Dependent Children)	10

SOURCE: Congressional Budget Office.

20 and 40 never expect to realize any return from their investment in Social Security. They have, most realistically, accepted Social Security as a tax, rather than as a contribution to a retirement program. One challenge for the next decade is to make adjustments in the Social Security program and to develop private sector alternatives that will decrease the burden of that tax for the American family. During this transition, we must still provide for the older Americans who have been lured into the false hope of thinking of Social Security as a retirement program and who have no alternatives.

The other major expense category is health care, costs of which have been increasing at an astronomical rate. We now spend about 11 percent of our gross national product on health care, compared with an average of 9 percent in western Europe countries with socialized medicine. Continued government growth (or even spending at current levels) is clearly not acceptable. What is needed is a transition out of the reliance we have developed on Washington and a movement toward exploring nongovernmental alternatives, if the economic quality of family life is not to deteriorate further. Getting the government off the family's back has been one of Ronald Reagan's favorite phrases. In terms of actual reductions in government spending, however, not much happened during the first term of the Reagan administration.

THE "FAMILY" COMES TO CONGRESS

In January 1981, at the beginning of the 97th Congress, for the first time in over two decades the Republican Party took control of the Senate. In the process of reorganizing the Senate committee structure, something occurred—almost unnoticed in the media—that had great potential significance for those interested in the family and its relationship to the federal government. For the first time in the history of the United States, the word "family" was used in the title of a subcommittee of Congress, and the Subcommittee for Family and Human Services came into being.[12] The creation of the family subcommittee was the joint product of two senators, Orrin Hatch (R–Utah) and Jeremiah Denton (R–Alabama).

12. The original name in the 97th Congress was "Subcommittee for Aging, Family and Human Services." In 1983, at the beginning of the 98th Congress, the Aging Subcommittee of the Senate Labor and Human Resources Committee was restored, and the "family" subcommittee was renamed, "Family and Human Services."

Hatch, then in his fifth year as a U.S. senator, had joined the select group of sixteen influential senators who chair the standing committees, becoming the chairman of the Senate Committee on Labor and Human Resources. As a father of six and a senator representing the state with a prominent national reputation for being "family centered,"[13] it was no surprise that Hatch should be interested in drawing the attention of the Senate to the concerns of the family. Denton, an admiral in the Navy and a national hero who was a prisoner of war for seven years in Vietnam, was serving his first year in the Senate. Concerned about the erosion of moral fiber in America (brought into sharp focus by the before-and-after contrast his lengthy absence enabled him to make), Denton had sought a place on the Labor and Human Resources Committee primarily because of his desire to promote a climate that would encourage healthy family life. Creation of a subcommittee that would focus on the family was a natural outcome of the joint work of these two senators.

Part of the jurisdiction of the Subcommittee on Family and Human Services, prior to 1981, had been vested in the Subcommittee on Child and Human Development. After Robert Kennedy's tragic assassination, Walter Mondale took his place on the Labor and Human Resources Committee and created the Child and Human Development Subcommittee. When Mondale left the Senate, Alan Cranston took his place as subcommittee chairman.

Typical of the differences between conservative and liberal approaches, the liberal Democrats Mondale and Cranston had pursued issues that applied to a particular constituency (children and service providers who deal with children), while the more conservative Republicans Hatch and Denton tended to see the family as a cornerstone of society; they were concerned with protecting that societal foundation from undue government taxation, interference, and intrusion.[14]

It soon became clear that the conservative political influences had

13. President Carter made his only trip to Utah to present a "family" award to the Church of Jesus Christ of Latter-Day Saints and to speak in the Salt Lake Mormon Tabernacle about the importance of families.

14. The concern with monitoring the effect of government policy on families had also begun to take root during the Carter presidency. Mondale's former subcommittee staff director, A. Sydney Joynson III, had begun an organization called the Family Impact Seminar. Carter had developed a White House Conference on Families, under Mondale's direct supervision, but it became fractured by special-interest groups (e.g., women's activists, gay rights activists, pro- and antiabortion groups, children's providers lobbyists), who wanted to use the "family" rubric to pursue their standard political agenda.

identified the importance of family life and family preservation—and the need to protect the family from government invasion—as a powerful political issue. As a result, toward the end of the 97th Congress in 1982, Representative George Miller (D–California) proposed a House Select Committee on Children, Youth and Families. Mr. Miller's proposal was accepted by the House, and in 1982, for the second time in America's history, a committee of the Congress was created to deal with family issues specifically.[15]

By using the name of the agency within the Department of Health and Human Services that deals with several leftovers of the Great Society programs from the Lyndon Johnson era (the Administration for Children, Youth and Families), Miller—almost certainly by intention—attracted some of the most liberal House Democrats to his committee's membership and began to rally the special-interest groups and lobbying forces who has used "children" as their key word in the past. Most of these groups and individuals are both conceptually and politically opposed to the kinds of government reforms proposed by the Reagan administration. As an example of using children as a vehicle for pushing a liberal social agenda, in the summer of 1983 Mr. Miller's committee held hearings on child reactions to the nuclear threat. This hearing prompted Dr. Edward Zigler, a nationally prominent expert in children and public policy, to comment, "I cannot for the life of me imagine what constructive purpose such hearings could serve."[16] It remains to be seen whether the Miller committee will take a genuine look at family issues, or will merely use the family as an anti-Republican whipping boy and as a referendum on Reaganomics.

The Democrats are now using the "family" in their campaign rhetoric. As recently as winter 1986, Congressman James Wright (D–Texas), in responding to President Reagan's State of the Union address, argued that a runaway national deficit posed a major threat to the economic well-being of the American family. It will be interesting to see if either Republicans or Democrats translate concern for the deficit into reductions in social spending (as we are advocating needs to be done) or if they decide that the way to help the family will be to add further to the tax burden the middle-class family is already bearing.

---

15. In 1983 the House voted to renew this committee. (Select committees in the House typically have a life that lasts only for one Congress.)

16. Letter from Dr. Zigler to Congressman Dan Marriott.

PRIVATE SECTOR INITIATIVES AND ALTERNATIVES

In the summer of 1981 Senator Hatch began to look into private sector programs and activities beneficial to family life. As the child and family specialist on the committee staff, I was assigned to do the investigating. The Library of Congress responded to my question with a blank stare. No one had ever before inquired about private sector contributions to family life. They had answers to inquiries about *government* programs for children and adolescents, for education, for the elderly, or for single women who head households. But no one, it seems, had ever conceptualized the services available to individuals *as members of a family;* and further, no one had ever expressed an interest in what was being done in the nongovernmental domain.

Suggestions were made that we contact the national office of the chambers of commerce and some national business organizations. But the response was not much better. Policies that were helpful to families were not represented—by name, at any rate—on the agenda of organizations that lobbied Congress as representatives of business.

After Senator Hatch and I discussed the disappointing results of our search, we decided to go directly to the businesses themselves to generate information. Accordingly, for the next several months the committee contacted several hundred major businesses throughout the country with the question, "What policies or procedures have you adopted in your corporation that are designed to be helpful—directly or indirectly—to families?" The responses we received were most instructive. Some did not respond at all. More often substantial information was received, sometimes with a cover letter from the chairman of the board that would say something like, "When we first received your letter, our immediate reaction was, 'We don't have any *family* policies,' but as we began thinking about it, we have decided that we have a number of approaches that have a positive impact on families." Many responded that as a part of their role as good citizens, they felt they should be concerned about the families whose lives were affected by their business—not just the families of employees, but frequently families in the communities where they were doing business.

In all, responses were received from approximately 300 major corporations. The richness of the ideas they shared was certainly unexpected, particularly in light of our previous failure to identify any private-sector family policies. There was a continuing expression of support for the notion that reliance on the federal government for the solution to society's problems was a blind alley. For example, one executive wrote: "Implicit in your open invitation for comments is a recognition that our society is at a turning point in which reliance on leadership from the federal government needs to be replaced by local initiative." There were also many expressions that much of the activity supportive of families was largely ignored by government and by society as a whole. One business leader put it this way: "A lot of good work occurs because of private support, but many times goes unrecognized by society at large."

For many, developing programs that were helpful to families was just good business: "We do not consider that any of our programs are unique or in any way represent the solution to all of the problems of our society. To us, they are good business and are a positive influence on our employees, their families, and communities." Far from being concerned exclusively with bottom-line profit motives, several felt that firms had a responsibility "to honor our obligation to society by being an economic, intellectual and social asset to each nation and each community in which we operate." Nearly all who responded agreed that maintaining a climate in which family life can flourish is a major national priority.

The family-oriented programs already commonplace in the private sector can be divided into six categories: (1) health and education; (2) alcohol and drug rehabilitation; (3) alternative work arrangements (flextime, job-sharing, etc.); (4) special development programs for the young, minorities, and the elderly; (5) insurance, income support, mobility, and childcare assistance; (6) counseling and community support services. Not all firms surveyed mentioned all, or even a majority of, these programs. Some are appropriate for a particular business or community circumstance but would not apply elsewhere. In total, however, these ideas represent a surprisingly broad range of approaches and activities that American business sees as helpful in pursuing its goals. A detailed list of private sector initiatives is given in an Appendix to this chapter. The composition and organization of the list reflect both the frequency with which the various issues were mentioned and the conceptual grouping of the issues developed by the Labor and Human Resources Committee. In November 1983, the committee held hearings on Private Sector Initiatives, which documented these findings.

As with the federal approach, most of the programs described by the businesses surveyed were not designed primarily to be an aid to families. However, each has a positive impact on one or more family members and thus contributes to a better quality of family life. The spectrum of the ideas and approaches is *broader than that in the public sector*.

When we asked why many of the policies in the private sector were developed, a frequent response was, "Everyone else in our industry is providing these benefits, and we must do it in order to obtain the best people." Frequently health promotion programs were put in place because the firm had concluded that it would be cost-effective in the long run. Many firms are convinced, for example, that alcoholism treatment programs are successful in curing the problem and are cost-effective compared to the expense of retraining a new employee. With health care costs comprising a major proportion of a business's benefit package, steps to foster a healthier life-style not only lead to an improved quality of life for the employee, but can be cost-effective when they also reduce health care insurance costs.

Of course, the direct payment for food stamps and housing subsidies is never a part of private sector programs; that is what wages are for. As Chrysler Corporation's Lee Iacocca said when responding to our questions, "Quite frankly, we believe the greatest contribution we have made in the last couple of years is to maintain employment for approximately half a million American workers." Ultimately the most beneficial program for families is to enable them to provide for their needs and manage their own affairs.

SUMMARY AND CONCLUSIONS

The federal government is caught in a painful squeeze—between trying to fulfill impossible promises and trying to pay the piper. The problem of skyrocketing government expense is now a major factor in the American economy. There seems to be widespread agreement that 45 percent of the national income is enough to spend on government. The middle-class families who are shouldering the burden of paying the bill seem particularly unenthusiastic about increased spending. There are even a few who believe we could get along better if government received only 40 percent (dare I suggest less than 33 percent?) of the national income.

Problems persist particularly for the old and the young. More of the burden for solutions must be shifted to the private sector, and this must be done in such a way that *both* the individuals and the businesses benefit. Evidence has been presented here that the possibility of some very creative and productive solutions certainly exists. The private sector is much more flexible and more evaluation-oriented—the concern for the bottom line always looms large. More attention must be directed to private solutions: Data must be collected and ways to distribute such data must be developed.

Washington is a reactive town, but even reactions are frequently very slow in developing. Original, creative ideas, equally rare on Capitol Hill and in the executive branch, are met with much resistance. Congress is never so interested in the issues of evaluation and oversight as when it is criticizing a new proposal. A comparison of the list of major social expenses in the federal budget with the list of approaches provided by the private sector is instructive. Models that have been demonstrated to be effective should be of interest both to Congress and the private sector. Finding ways to encourage workable ideas needs to be brought to the top of the agenda.

As a byproduct of the demographic changes highlighted at the beginning of this chapter, the 1980s have seen the family become—for better or for worse—an issue in national politics. The federal government has a long road to travel, however, before it begins to take the perspective of the well-being of the family as a central factor in guiding policy development across a broad spectrum of issues. Sometimes intentionally, sometimes inadvertently, America's private sector has been developing programs that have a positive influence on family life. These programs include those funded by charitable giving as well as the programs listed in the Appendix.[17]

It is shocking to discover how little attention has been paid to fostering an environment in which the private sector—nonprofit as well as for-profit enterprises—could be expected to come up with an even greater number of imaginative programs to replace well-worn federal approaches. Tax and transfer policies, and the legal rights and responsibilities of firms to their workers and of parents to their children, should all be considered. This volume has made the first step. The more attention that is given to family life when making deliberations about the direction of public and private sector efforts, the more effective and satisfying the resulting programs and approaches are likely to be.

---

17. According to official statistics, total charitable giving had reached $64.9 billion by 1983. U.S. Bureau of the Census, *Statistical Abstract of the United States, 1985* (Washington, D.C.: U.S. Government Printing Office), p. 385.

APPENDIX: PROFAMILY PROGRAMS IN MAJOR CORPORATIONS

I. Health Promotion, Maintenance, Education and Care.

A. Health Promotion and Education—Physical checkups, health clinics, screening, prevention activities, exercise facilities (sometimes for use by entire family), smoking and weight programs.

B. On the Job Safety—Concern for employee's safety results in company policies and practices.

C. Blood Banks—within company programs available foster blood donation and reduce surgery costs.

II. Alcohol and Drug Abuse—Referrals, counseling, education programs both for employees and within the community. Support for treatment costs.

III. Alternate Work Arrangements

A. Policies

1. Alternate Work Schedules—Compressed or altered work day.

2. Flextime—Flexible management of working hours. Adjusting workday to personal and family needs and preferences.

3. Job Sharing/Work Sharing—Allowing full-time positions to be shared by individuals who desire only part-time employment.

4. Part-time Employment—An alternative for workers who do not wish to work full-time.

5. Apprenticeships—Enhancing employability by developing highly technical skills under expert supervision. Target populations include youth, women, college students, minorities, and older individuals.

6. Intern Programs—Work experience for young, frequently minority, individuals to facilitate a perspective of prospective employment.

7. Temporary Employment—Matching temporary company needs for work with those who do not seek permanent employment, or to those who may wish to gain experience and skill with permanent employment in mind.

B. Benefits
    1. Flexible Leave—Holiday, vacations, personal days off on a flexible schedule according to personal needs.
    2. Overtime

IV. Responsive Job Related Policies
  A. Youth
    1. Youth Employment—Providing jobs to youth (full and part-time).
    2. Youth Summer Employment—Recruiting high school students (both children of employees, and in outreach programs). Provides earnings and experience with company practices.
    3. High School Co-op Programs (Jr. Achievement)— Youth are provided with work experience while still in school. They receive both pay and high school credit.
    4. Minority Services—Responsive policies for youth, women, blacks, and other minorities in hiring, training, and company community.
    5. Scholarships—To employees' children as well as other qualified youth to ease the financial costs of education.
    6. Vocational Training Programs—Offered to employees either through onsight facilities or in cooperation with local vocational schools to obtain skills as related to job performance.
    7. Intern Programs—(See III, 6)
    8. Rehabilitation Programs—Hiring and training of individuals who may be considered poor employment risks (e.g. criminal offenders).
    9. Tuition Assistance and Reimbursement—Available to the employee and members of his family to cover the cost of books and tuition when pursuing higher education.
  B. Older Workers
    1. Retirement Program and Benefits—Pension programs and low or non-contributory health and life insurance benefits for older, non-salaried individuals.
    2. Retirement Volunteers and Workers—Bringing retired workers back into the workplace, to take advantage of their valuable experience and skills.
    3. Pre-Retirement Ed/Counseling—Special programs to ease the transition from full-time work to retirement.

C. Other Special Needs Groups

1. Equal Opportunity Employment—Beyond compliance with legal standards some companies reported particular pride in progress with both policies and individual successes in this area.

2. Military—Benefits and recognition for military service. Also responsible to veterans in hiring practices.

3. Handicapped and Disadvantaged—Employment, training and facilities for special needs individuals.

4. Employment of Handicapped/Disadvantaged.

5. Employee On the Job Training—Retraining for skills to meet changing company needs. Promotes employment stability and continuity.

V. Family Stability

A. Policies and Benefits

1. HMO Medical Policy—onsite medical staff and facilities, or cooperative arrangements with local community services to cut medical costs.

2. Medical Benefits—Coverage for medical, dental, visual, and other forms of health care at reduced or no cost to the employee.

3. Disability—Short, long term, permanent; funds for supplemental income support, retraining, etc.

4. Flexible Benefits—(III A.2, III. B.1)

5. Family Insurance Coverage—Life and accident coverage for family members.

6. Funeral Pay—Paid time off for funeral attendance.

7. Job Loss Security—Company financed unemployment insurance for unforseen job transition.

8. Life Insurance—Death benefits paid to family members.

9. Personal Leave of Absence—Time off without loss of seniority that allows the employee to take care of personal and family needs.

10. Maternity/Paternity Leave and Benefit—Time off for pregnancy and parenting responsibility. Protection for job security. Costs for medical care related to childbirth covered.

11. Paid Holidays and Vacations.

12. Profit Sharing

13. Promotion Policy/Transfer Rights—Policies which

recognize performance by offering better opportunities and higher wages.

14.   Relocation and Moving Policies—In instances where job promotion requires relocation, provisions are made for financial, emotional, and physical support of the entire family's move.

15.   Severance Pay

16.   Stock/Bond Purchase—Investment alternative offered to employees and their families.

17.   Surviving Spouse Benefit—An added benefit to life insurance which provides financial security in case of death to the widow or widower.

18.   Workers' Compensation—Financial security in case of accident while on the job.

19.   Savings—Specific programs designed to enhance financial security.

20.   Job Posting—Encouraging employment and family stability by announcing openings to employees of the company before going outside.

21.   Credit Unions—Convenient banking and savings services, sometimes in-house, available to entire family.

22.   Company Publications/Newsletters—Consumer and recreation information free classified ad space, etc.

23.   Flexible Leave—(See III B.1)

24.   Contributions—(matching or part) to employee investment programs.

B.   Services

1.   Adoption Assistance—Aid in facilitating adoption, frequently support for some of the costs of adoption.

2.   Recreational Activities—Sponsorship of athletic teams, picnics, and other special activities, which encourage physical fitness as well as family participation.

3.   Recreational Facilities—Camps, clubs, and other facilities available to employees and their families.

4.   Discounts—Services, products, tickets etc. at reduced rates to employees and families.

5.   Transportation Program—Providing van and car pools, parking facilities and other transportation conveniences to minimize the cost of travel to and from work.

6.   Child Care/Day Care—providing support and referral

services employees with child care needs. Occasionally (though rarely) providing in-house day care.

VI. Education and Community Services
    A. Education
        1. Programs
            a. Continuing Education Programs—Support for job related (and sometimes personal achievement) education.
            b. Research—Financial support for research of interest to family life (e.g. disease control, environmental concerns, and innovative techniques to better family living.
            c. Seminars, Conferences, Workshops, Ed Programs—Company sponsored programs which include a variety of interests and activities.
            d. Educational Media—Films, books, magazines produced for employees, families, and community use.
            e. Educational Facilities—In-house classrooms and instructors. Sometimes available to families in addition to employees.
            f. Employee Assistance—Counseling programs for personal, marital and other problems.
            g. Career/Life Planning—Education and counseling for occupational and other life goals.
            h. Financial Counseling—Help with taxes, personal debts, money management counseling etc.
            i. Outplacement—Aid to individuals who have been released from employment by helping with resumes, interviewing skills, and providing a clearinghouse for available jobs.
        2. Donations to Education
            a. Tuition Assistance and Reimbursement (See VI A.9)
            b. Scholarships (See VI A.5)
            c. Matching Gifts—Contributions by employees to community or education activities (including scholarship funds) matched or exceeded by company.
    B. Community Involvement
        1. Services
            a. Environmental Groups—Practices and training

concerning environmental protection including, family and community awareness and training; sometimes including community clean up and housing renovation in disadvantaged neighborhoods.

b.   Community/Civic/Organizational Participation—Providing services organizations, or encouraging employees (sometime via released time etc.) to work in community activities.

c.   Charitable Contributions—Corporate philanthropy (some as separate corporate foundations) for national and community programs providing community enrichment (bringing a symphony orchestra to perform for minority youngsters), or direct services (e.g. contributions to United Way).

d.   Social Services Leave—Position within the company is retained for those individuals who wish to work with organizations.

e.   Volunteer/Company Service Recognition—Tribute paid to those individuals who are serving the community and/or have shown outstanding performance on their jobs.

SELECTED BIBLIOGRAPHY
PART IV

Anderson, Martin. *Welfare: The Political Economy of Welfare Reform in the United States.* Stanford, Calif.: Hoover Institution Press, 1978.

Bennett, James T., and Thomas DiLorenzo. "How the Government Evades Taxes." *Policy Review* 19 (Winter 1982):71–89.

Bishop, John. "Jobs, Cash Transfers and Marital Instability." *Journal of Human Resources* 15 (Summer 1980):301–34.

————. "The Labor Supply Response to the Seattle–Denver Income Maintenance Experiment: A Reinterpretation." Paper presented at the 1981 meetings of the Western Economics Association, San Francisco, July 2–6.

Blau, Zena Smith. *Black Children/White Children.* New York: Free Press, 1981.

Brubaker, Earl R. "Demand Disclosures and Conditions on Exclusion." *Economic Journal* 94 (September 1984):536–53.

Buchanan, James M., and Dwight R. Lee. "Politics, Time and the Laffer Curve." *Journal of Political Economy* 90 (August 1982):816–19.

Danziger, Sheldon; Robert Haveman; and Robert Plotnick. "How Income Transfers Affect Work, Savings, and the Income Distribution." *Journal of Economic Literature* 19 (September 1981):975–1028.

Demsetz, Harold. "The Private Production of Public Goods." *Journal of Law and Economics* 13 (October 1970):293–306.

————. "Joint Supply and Price Discrimination." *Journal of Law and Economics* 16 (October 1973):413–15.

Duncan, Greg. *Years of Poverty, Years of Plenty*. Ann Arbor: Institute for Social Research, University of Michigan, 1984.

Economic Report of the President. Washington, D.C.: Government Printing Office, 1985.

Ellwood, David J., and Mary Jo Bane. "The Impact of AFDC on Family Structure and Living Arrangements." Washington, D.C.: U.S. Department of Health and Human Services, 1984.

Epstein, Richard A. *Takings: Private Property and the Power of Eminent Domain*. Cambridge: Harvard University Press, 1985.

Farrand, Max, ed. *Records of the Federal Convention*. Vol. 3. New Haven: Yale University Press, 1937.

Feldstein, Martin, and Lawrence Summers. "Inflation and the Taxation of Capital Income in the Corporate Section." *National Tax Journal* 32 (December 1979):445–70.

Frieden, Bernard J., and Arthur P. Solomon. *The Nation's Housing: 1975–1985*. Cambridge: Joint Center for Urban Studies of the Massachusetts Institute of Technology and Harvard University, April 1977.

Garfinkel, Irwin, and Robert Haveman. *Earnings Capacity, Poverty, and Inequality*. New York: Academic Press, 1977.

Garfinkel, Irwin, and Elizabeth Uhr. "A New Approach to Child Support." *Public Interest* 75 (Spring 1984):111–22.

General Accounting Office. "Public Assistance Benefits Vary Widely from State to State, but Generally Exceed the Poverty Line." Washington, D.C.: Government Printing Office, November 1980.

Gilder, George. *Wealth and Poverty*. New York: Basic Books, 1981.

Gottschalk, Peter, and Sheldon Danziger. "A Framework for Evaluating the Effects of Economic Growth and Transfers on Poverty." *American Economic Review* 75 (March 1985):153–61.

Green, Gordon, and Edward Welniak. *Changing Family Composition and Income Differentials*. Special Demographic Analyses CDS–80–7. Washington, D.C.: Government Printing Office, 1982.

Groeneveld, Lyle P.; Nancy Brandon Tuma; and Michael T. Hannan. "The Effects of Negative Income Tax Programs on Marital Dissolution." *Journal of Human Resources* 15 (Fall 1980):654–74.

Hayek, Friedrich A. "The Use of Knowledge in Society." *American Economic Review* 35 (September 1945):519–30.

———. *The Constitution of Liberty*. Chicago: University of Chicago Press, 1960.

———. *Law, Legislation and Liberty*. 3 vols. Chicago: University of Chicago Press, 1973, 1976, 1979.

———. *Law, Legislation and Liberty*. Reprint. (3 vols. in 1). London: Routledge and Kegan Paul, 1982.

Hendershott, Patric H. "Real User Costs and the Demand for Single-Family Housing." *Brookings Papers on Economic Activity* 2 (1980):401–44.

Honig, Marjorie. "AFDC Income, Recipient Rates, and Family Dissolution." *Journal of Human Resources* 9 (Summer 1974):303–22.

Jencks, Christopher. *Inequality: A Reassessment of the Effect of Family and Schooling in America.* New York: Basic Books, 1972.

Johnson, M. Bruce, ed. *Resolving the Housing Crisis: Government Policy, Decontrol, and the Public Interest.* San Francisco: Pacific Institute for Public Policy Research, 1982.

Keeley, Michael C. "The Effects of Negative Income Tax Programs on Marital Dissolution." November 1983. Unpublished.

Leibowitz, Arlene. "Home Investments in Children." *Journal of Political Economy* 82 (March/April 1974):S111–31.

Mellor, Earl F. "Public Goods and Services: Costs and Benefits, A Study of the Shaw-Cardozo Area of Washington, D.C." Washington, D.C.: Institute for Policy Studies, 1969.

Minarik, Joseph J., and Robert S. Goldfarb. "AFDC Income, Recipient Rates, and Family Dissolution: A Comment." *Journal of Human Resources* 11 (Spring 1976):243–50.

Moynihan, Daniel Patrick. *Family and Nation.* New York: Harcourt Brace Jovanovich, 1986.

Murray, Charles. *Losing Ground: American Social Policy, 1950–1980.* New York: Basic Books, 1984.

———. "Have the Poor Been 'Losing Ground'?" *Political Science Quarterly* 100 (Fall 1985):427–45.

Nozick, Robert. *Anarchy, State, and Utopia.* New York: Basic Books, 1974.

Plott, Charles. "The Application of Laboratory Experimental Methods to Public Choice." In C. Russell, ed., *Application of Social Choice Theory.* Washington, D.C.: Resources for the Future, 1980.

Posner, Richard. *The Economics of Justice.* Cambridge: Harvard University Press, 1981.

Raboy, David G., ed. *Essays in Supply Side Economics.* Washington, D.C.: Institute for Research on the Economics of Taxation, 1982.

Rawls, John. *A Theory of Justice.* Cambridge: Harvard University Press, 1971.

Robins, Philip; Richard West; and Michael Keeley. "A Structural Model of the Labor Supply Response to the Seattle–Denver Income Maintenance Experiments." Menlo Park, Calif.: SRI International, August 1980.

Rosen, Harvey S. "Housing Decisions and the U.S. Income Tax: An Econometric Analysis." *Journal of Public Economics* 11 (February 1979): 1–23.

Rosen, Harvey S., and Kenneth T. Rosen. "Federal Taxes and Homeownership: Evidence from Time Series." *Journal of Political Economy* 88 (February 1980):59–75.

Ross, Heather L., and Isabel Sawhill. *Time of Transition: The Growth of Families Headed by Women.* Washington, D.C.: Urban Institute, 1975.

Rothbard, Murray N. *For a New Liberty.* New York: Macmillan, 1973.

Sawhill, Isabel; G. Peabody; C. Jones; and S. Caldwell. *Income Transfers and Family Structures.* Washington, D.C.: Urban Institute, 1975.

Schneider, Friedrich, and Werner Pommerehne. "Free Riding and Collective Action: An Experiment in Public Microeconomics." *Quarterly Journal of Economics* 91 (November 1981):668–704.

Shmanske, Stephen. "The Relationship of Competitive Public Goods Models and Monopolistic Competition." California State University, Hayward. School of Business and Economics Faculty Working Paper No. 17, 1985.

Silverman, Gerald, and Michael Wiseman. "Family Fragmentation in the Aid to Dependent Children." Paper presented at the 1979 meetings of the Western Economics Association, Las Vegas, June 17–21.

Smith, Shirley J. "Estimating Annual Hours of Labor Force Activity." *Monthly Labor Review* 106 (February 1983):13–22.

Smith, Vernon. "Experiments With a Decentralized Mechanism for Public Good Decisions." *American Economic Review* 70 (September 1980): 584–99.

————, ed. *Research in Experimental Economics.* London: JAI Press, 1982.

Sowell, Thomas. *Markets and Minorities.* New York: Basic Books, 1981.

Thompson, Earl A. "The Perfectly Competitive Production of Collective Goods." *Review of Economics and Statistics* 50 (February 1968):1–12.

————. "The Private Production of Public Goods: A Comment." *Journal of Law and Economics* 16 (October 1973):407–12.

U.S. Bureau of the Census. *Characteristics of the Population Below the Poverty Level: 1980.* Washington, D.C.: Government Printing Office.

————. *Statistical Abstract of the United States, 1982.* Washington, D.C.: Government Printing Office.

————. *Statistical Abstract of the United States, 1985.* Washington, D.C.: Government Printing Office.

U.S. Department of Labor. *Economic Problems of Women.* Hearings before the Joint Economic Committee, 93rd Congress, 1st Session, Part 1, July 10, 11, 12. Washington, D.C.: Government Printing Office, 1973.

Von Humboldt, Wilhelm. *The Limits of State Action.* London: Cambridge University Press, 1969.

Weaver, Carolyn L. *The Crisis in Social Security: Economic and Political Origins.* Durham, N.C.: Duke University Press, 1982.

White, Lawrence H. "Competitive Money, Inside and Out." *Cato Journal* 3 (Spring 1983):281–99.

Williams, Walter E. "The Continuing Struggle for a Negative Income Tax: A Review Article." *Journal of Human Resources* 10 (Fall 1975):427–44.

———. *The State Against Blacks.* New York: McGraw-Hill, 1982.

Wolf, Douglas A. "Income in Labor Supply and Family Stability: An Empirical Analysis of Marital Dissolution." Ph.D. dissertation, University of Pennsylvania, 1977.

INDEX

ABOUT THE EDITORS

Joseph R. Peden is a lecturer in the history department of the Baruch College of the City University of New York. A graduate of the Columbia University Teachers College and Fordham University, he has conducted numerous scholarly colloquia and conferences sponsored by the Liberty Fund and the Institute for Humane Studies at George Mason University, including programs exploring the American family and education. He also has been Director of Academic Programs for the Center for Libertarian Studies. He is coauthor of a documentary history of western civilization.

Fred R. Glahe is professor of economics at the University of Colorado. He received his B.S. in aeronautical engineering and his M.S. and Ph.D. in economics from Purdue University. Professor Glahe is an Earhart Fellow Sponsor and an associate at the Cato Institute. He serves on the board of directors for The International Research Center for Energy and Economic Development and is associate editor for the *Journal of Private Enterprise* and a member of the board of advisors for the *Austrian Economic Review*. He is also president and founder of the Economic Institute for Research and Education.

Professor Glahe is the editor of *Adam Smith and the Wealth of Nations, The Collected Papers of Kenneth E. Boulding* (2 vols.), and author of studies for the U.S. Air Force in conjunction with General Motors Corporation.

Professor Glahe's articles have appeared in such professional and popular publications as *American Economist; Decision Sciences; Denver Post; Econometrica; Journal of Money, Credit, and Banking; Philippine Economic Journal;* and *Southern Economic Journal.*

ABOUT THE AUTHORS

Lawrence A. Alexander is currently professor of law at the University of San Diego. He received his B.A. from Williams College and his LL.B. from Yale University. He was previously research attorney for the California Court of Appeals in Los Angeles.

Dr. Alexander's articles have appeared in *Ethics, Journal of Libertarian Studies, Journal of Philosophy, Philosophy and Public Affairs, San Diego Law Review, Social Theory and Practice, Stanford Law Review, Southern California Law Review,* and other legal and philosophical journals.

Roger A. Arnold is associate professor of economics at the University of Nevada, Las Vegas. He received his B.S. from the University of Birmingham (England) and his M.A. and Ph.D. from Virginia Polytechnic Institute and State University. Professor Arnold has served on the faculty of Hillsdale College, the University of Oklahoma, and California State University, Northridge. He has also served two terms as director for the Center of Economic Education.

Professor Arnold's articles have appeared in the *Arizona Sun Times, Cato Journal, Journal of Libertarian Studies, Las Vegas Sun, New York Tribune, Wall Street Journal,* and the *Washington Times.*

William P. Baumgarth received his A.B. from Fordham University and his M.A. and Ph.D. from Harvard University. He is currently associate professor of political science at Fordham University. He has taught at Harvard and Wake Forest University.

Professor Baumgarth has authored chapters in books on the liberal economic order and on privacy. His articles and reviews have appeared in *International Philosophical Quarterly, Journal of Politics, The Political Science Reviewer,* and *Teaching Political Science.*

Brigitte Berger is professor of sociology at Wellesley College. She received her M.A. and Ph.D. from the New School for Social Research. She has previously taught at Long Island University, City University of New York (Brooklyn and Hunter College campuses), the University of Connecticut, and the University of Hartford.

Professor Berger's articles have appeared in *Challenge, Contemporary Sociology, Journal of the Institute for Socioeconomic Studies, The New Republic, The New York Times, Policy Review, The Public Interest,* and *Worldview* among others. She has lectured internationally and is the author of *The Homeless Mind—Modernization and Consciousness* (with Peter Berger and Hansfried Kellner), *Societies in Change, Sociology—A Biographical Approach* (with Peter Berger), and *The War Over the Family: Capturing the Middle Ground* (with Peter Berger).

Professor Berger is a member of the advisory councils of the Center for Religion and Society, Heritage Foundation, the Child and Family Protection Institute, and the Rockford Institute, and a member of the board of the National Center for Neighborhood Enterprise. She has served as assistant to the director of the George Washington Institute for Comparative Research in Stuttgart, West Germany. She has been a consultant to the American Enterprise Institute and on grants review committees for the National Science Foundation and the Department of Housing and Urban Development.

Gregory B. Christainsen is senior economist for the Pacific Research Institute and an associate professor at California State University, Hayward. He received his B.A. in philosophy and economics and his M.A. and Ph.D. in economics from the University of Wisconsin-Madison.

Dr. Christainsen's articles and reviews have appeared in *American*

Economic Review, The Annals of the American Academy of Political and Social Science, Chicago Tribune, Journal of Environmental Economics and Management, Los Angeles Herald-Examiner, Natural Resources Journal, Policy Review, Public Finance Quarterly, Quarterly Review of Economics and Business, Wall Street Journal, and many other publications. He received an Olive W. Garvey fellowship from the Mont Pelerin Society for his writing on the work of Nobel laureate F. A. Hayek.

Lowell E. Gallaway is distinguished professor of economics at Ohio University. He received his B.A. from Northwestern University and his M.A. and Ph.D. from Ohio State University. Professor Gallaway has served as staff economist for the Joint Economic Committee of the Congress of the United States. He has been a Fullbright-Hayes Senior Scholar, and has held General Electric, Ford Foundation, and Liberty Fund Fellowships. He has been associate editor of the *Journal of the American Statistical Association* and the *Review of Social Economy*. He also serves on the editorial advisory board of the *Austrian Economic Review*.

Professor Gallaway's published books and studies include *Manpower Economics, The "Natural" Rate of Unemployment,* and *Poverty in America.* Professor Gallaway has published over 100 articles in American and international economic journals. He is a regular contributor of articles to the popular media.

Henry Mark Holzer is professor of constitutional law at the Brooklyn Law School, where he also served as Associate Dean from 1984–1986. He received his B.A. and J.D. from New York University. He is Director of the Foreign Trained Lawyers Program and the Judicial Internship Clinical Program. He also serves as chairman and advisor to several other committees. Before his professorship at the Brooklyn Law School, Professor Holzer was an attorney specializing in constitutional, administrative, and appellate law. He has testified before the Senate Foreign Relations Committee and numerous Congressional Committees of Inquiry.

Professor Holzer is the author of *The Gold Clause: What it is and How to Use it Profitably, Government's Money Monopoly: Its Source and Scope and How to Fight It,* and *Sweet Land of Liberty? The Supreme Court and Individual Rights.* He has published numerous articles and professional papers in the *Banking Law Journal, Common Sense Viewpoint, Congressional Record, New York Law Journal, New York Law Review,* and *Wall Street Journal.*

Paul Horton received his A.B. from Occidental College, his J.D. from the Law Center, University of Southern California, and his LL.M. from the Yale Law School. He is presently professor of law at the University of San Diego. He worked previously as an attorney for Sonnenschein Levinson Carlin Nath & Rosenthal in Chicago. His articles have appeared in the *Northwestern University Law Review, University of Southern California Law Review,* and other publications.

John M. Johnson is professor of justice and women's studies and Associate Director of the School of Justice at Arizona State University. Professor Johnson received his B.A. from Indiana University and his Ph.D. from the University of California at San Diego. He was recently nominated as Arizona State University's Distinguished Research Professor.

Dr. Johnson has served as editor of *Symbolic Interaction* and *Sociological Observations* monograph series. His has authored books including *Bureaucratic Propaganda* (with David L. Altheide) and *Doing Field Research,* and has edited several books including *Bureaucracy and Freedom: Modern Studies in Bureaucratic Social Control* (with David L. Altheide) and *Existential Sociology* (with Jack D. Douglas). His articles have appeared in *American Behavioral Scientist, Journal of Family Issues, Social Problems, Studies in Symbolic Interaction,* and *Urban Life.*

Dr. Johnson founded Friends of the Family, Ltd., a shelter for abused and battered women and children. He also founded Middle Ground, a nonprofit corporation for public education on the prison problems and alternatives in corrections.

Jacqueline R. Kasun is professor of economics at Humboldt State University. She received her B.A. from the University of California at Berkeley and her M.S. and Ph.D. from Columbia University. Professor Kasun has served as research consultant for Standard Oil Company and the Haynes Foundation, and has taught at the University of Arizona and California State University at Fullerton.

Professor Kasun is the author of numerous articles that have appeared in such publications as *The Alternative, America, Christian*

Science Monitor, Current History, Liguorian, Policy Analysis, Policy Review, The Public Interest, Society, and *USA Today.*

Dwight R. Lee is professor of economics and holder of the Bernard B. and Eugenia A. Ramsey Chair of Private Enterprise at the University of Georgia. Professor Lee received his B.A. from San Diego State University and his Ph.D. from the University of California at San Diego. Most recently, Professor Lee was associate professor and research fellow at the Center for Study of Public Choice at George Mason University, and at the Virginia Polytechnic Institute and State University. He has also served on the faculties of the economics departments at the University of Colorado, United States International University, and San Diego State University. Professor Lee received the Brython P. Davis Fellowship at the University of California at San Diego and was second-prize winner of the N. Goto Essay Contest at the meetings of the Mont Pelerin Society in 1982.

Professor Lee is the coauthor of three economics textbooks and editor of *Taxation and the Deficit Economy: Fiscal Policy and Capital Formation in the United States.* His articles have appeared in a variety of scholarly and popular publications, including *The American Economist, Atlantic Economic Journal, Australian Economic Papers, Canadian Journal of Economics, Cato Journal, Chicago Tribune, Economic Inquiry, Finance Quarterly, The Freeman, Heritage Foundation Backgrounder, International Journal of Transport Economics, Kyklos, Journal of Contemporary Studies, Journal of Economics, Journal of Energy and Development, Journal of Environmental Economics and Management, Journal of Public Finance and Public Choice, Journal of Law and Economics, Journal of Political Economy, Land Economics, Management Science, Public Choice, Public Finance Quarterly, Quarterly Review of Economics and Business, Reason, Review of Economic Studies, St. Louis Post Dispatch, Southern Economic Journal,* and *Wall Street Journal.*

Professor Lee's articles have been published as monographs, including *The Inflationary Impact of Labor Unions; Economics, Politics and the All Volunteer Army; The Political Economy of Social Conflict; Environmental* vs. *Political Pollution;* and *Inflation and Unemployment.*

Lyla H. O'Driscoll is a marketing communications specialist with a Dallas computer manufacturer. She received her B.A. in political science and philosophy from the University of Nebraska and her Ph.D. in philosophy from the University of California, Los Angeles.

Dr. O'Driscoll has served as program officer of the New York Council for the Humanities, director of the Children's Rights Project of the Center for Libertarian Studies, and public affairs consultant to the Institute for Humane Studies. She has taught at Iowa State University; the University of California, Los Angeles; and California State University at Northridge.

Dr. O'Driscoll has published in the *Chicago Sunday Tribune, The Hartford Courant, Journal of Libertarian Studies,* and *Southern Journal of Philosophy.*

J. Craig Peery is professor of family sciences at Brigham Young University. He received his B.A. in psychology and his M.A. and Ph.D. in developmental psychology from Columbia University.

Dr. Peery is a member of the American Association for the Advancement of Science, the American Psychological Association, the Society for Research in Child Development, the National Council on Family Relations, and Sigma Xi: The Scientific Research Society. He is former president of the Utah Council of Family Relations. He has been a Congressional Science Fellow sponsored by the American Association for the Advancement of Science and the Society for Research in Child Development. He served for two years as Special Assistant to the Chairman of the Senate Committee on Labor and Human Resources. He has subsequently worked as a staff associate for the Senate Family and Human Services Subcommittee and has served on several national study panels dealing with families, children, and adolescents.

Dr. Peery is a guest consulting editor for several professional publications dealing with children, and has done consulting work for private foundations. He has published numerous articles on parent-infant relationships and child development that have appeared in *American Psychologist, Developmental Psychology, Human Development, Journal of Genetic Psychology,* and *Journal of Psychology.*

Barry W. Poulson is professor and chairman of the department of economics at the University of Colorado, Boulder. He received his B.A. from Ohio Wesleyan University and his M.A. and Ph.D. from the Ohio State University. He has been visiting professor at the University of North Carolina and Konan University in Kobe, Japan, visiting scholar at Cambridge University, and Fulbright professor at the University of Guadalajara. Professor Poulson has served as a research consultant for the U.S. Department of Energy, U.S. State Department, U.S. Department of Commerce, as well as the Ford Foundation, Rockefeller Foundation, Shell Oil Company, and other private companies.

Professor Poulson's articles have appeared in professional publications such as *Explorations in Economic History, The Freeman, Inter-American Economic Affairs, Journal of Economic History, Journal of Energy Development, Journal of Labor Research, Journal of Legal History, Journal of Libertarian Studies, Middle East Journal, Oxford Economic Papers, Review of Business and Economic Research, Rocky Mountain Social Science Journal,* and *Southern Economic Journal.* He is the author of *Economic History of the United States,* coauthor of *Capital Investment in the Middle East, Free Riders and Forced Riders in Academic Unions* (with L. Cross), and coeditor of *U.S.-Mexico Economic Relations: Current Issues and Future Prospects* (with T. Osborn). He has worked on other books and monographs.

Murray Rothbard is S.J. Hall Distinguished Professor of Economics at the University of Nevada, Las Vegas. He received his A.B., M.A., and Ph.D. in economics from Columbia University.

Professor Rothbard is the editor of *Journal of Libertarian Studies* and contributing editor to *Inquiry* magazine and *Libertarian Review.* He is also a senior fellow at the Cato Institute.

Professor Rothbard has written more than 50 articles and reviews for various academic journals and has authored or edited more than 25 books, including: *America's Great Depression; Conceived in Liberty* (4 vols.); *Education: Free and Compulsory; Man, Economy, and State: A Treatise on Economic Principles; The Mystery of Central Banking; A New History of Leviathan: Essays on the Rise of the American Corporate State; Power and Market: Government and the Economy;* and *What Has Government Done to Our Money?*

Richard K. Vedder is professor of economics at Ohio University. He received his B.A. from Northwestern University, and his M.A. and Ph.D. from the University of Illinois. He has been an Earhart Fellow and a Liberty Fund Fellow. Professor Vedder was research associate for the Illinois State Commission on Revenue, and economist for the Joint Economic Committee of the U.S. Congress (1981–1982).

Professor Vedder is author or coeditor of *The American Economy in Historical Perspective, Essays in Nineteenth Century Economic History,* and *Variations in Business and Economic History.* His articles have appeared in domestic and international publications, such as *Agricultural History, Atlantic Economic Journal, Business History Review, Canadian Journal of Economics, Economic Inquiry, Explorations in Economic History, Austrian Economic Review, Journal of Contemporary Studies, Journal of Economic History, Journal of Regional Science, Scottish Journal of Political Economy, South African Journal of Economics, Swedish Journal of Economics, Western Economic Journal,* and other publications.

Walter E. Williams is currently John M. Olin Distinguished Professor of Economics at George Mason University. He received his B.A. from California State University, Los Angeles and his M.A. and Ph.D. from the University of California, Los Angeles. He has served on the faculties of Los Angeles City College, California State University, Los Angeles, and Temple University.

Dr. Williams is probably best known for his TV documentary and book, *The State Against Blacks.* He is also the author of *America: A Minority Viewpoint.* Dr. Williams's articles and reviews have appeared in *American Economic Review, Economic Inquiry, Policy Review, Regulation, Social Science Quarterly,* and other popular and professional journals.

PACIFIC STUDIES IN PUBLIC POLICY

RESOLVING THE HOUSING CRISIS
Government Policy, Decontrol, and the Public Interest
Edited with an Introduction by M. Bruce Johnson

OFFSHORE LANDS
Oil and Gas Leasing and Conservation on the Outer Continental Shelf
By Walter J. Mead, et al.
Foreword by Stephen L. McDonald

ELECTRIC POWER
Deregulation and the Public Interest
Edited by John C. Moorhouse
Foreword by Harold Demsetz

TAXATION AND THE DEFICIT ECONOMY
Fiscal Policy and Capital Formation in the United States
Edited by Dwight R. Lee
Foreword by Michael J. Boskin

THE AMERICAN FAMILY AND THE STATE
Edited by Joseph R. Peden and Fred R. Glahe
Foreword by Robert Nisbet

FORTHCOMING

DEALING WITH DRUGS
Problems of Government Control

CRISIS AND LEVIATHAN
Critical Episodes in the Growth of American Government

THE NEW CHINA
Comparative Economic Development in Hong Kong, Taiwan, and
Mainland China

POLITICAL BUSINESS CYCLES
The Economics and Politics of Stagflation

RATIONING HEALTH CARE
Medical Licensing in the United States

HEALTH CARE IN AMERICA: PUBLIC AND PRIVATE

CRIME, POLICE, AND THE COURTS

MYTH AND REALITY IN SOCIAL WELFARE

RENT CONTROL IN SANTA MONICA

UNEMPLOYMENT AND THE STATE

*For further information on the Pacific Research Institute's program and a catalog
of publications, please contact:*

PACIFIC RESEARCH INSTITUTE FOR PUBLIC POLICY
177 Post Street
San Francisco, California 94108